B C L

HOW THE PRESS
AFFECTS FEDERAL
POLICYMAKING

HOW THE PRESS AFFECTS FEDERAL POLICYMAKING

SIX CASE STUDIES

MARTIN LINSKY, JONATHAN MOORE,

WENDY O'DONNELL, and DAVID WHITMAN

A Project of the
Institute of Politics
at the
John F. Kennedy
School of Government
Harvard University

W·W·NORTON & COMPANY

New York · London

Published simultaneously in Canada by Penguin Books Canada Ltd,
2801 John Street, Markham, Ontario L3R 1B4
Printed in the United States of America.

The text of this book is composed in Times Roman, with display type set in Times
Roman. Composition and manufacturing by The Maple-Vail Book Manufacturing
Group.
Book design by Jacques Chazaud.

First Edition

Library of Congress Cataloging-in-Publication Data
Main entry under title:

How the press affects federal policymaking.

"A project of the Harvard Institute of Politics at
the John F. Kennedy School of Government."
1. Government and the press—United States—Case
studies. I. Linsky, Martin. II. John F. Kennedy
School of Government. Institute of Politics.
PN4745.H68   1986   302.2'3'0973   86–729

ISBN 0-393-02328-1

W. W. Norton & Company, Inc., 500 Fifth Avenue, New York, N.Y. 10110
W. W. Norton & Company Ltd., 37 Great Russell Street, London WC1B 3NU

1 2 3 4 5 6 7 8 9 0

To John William Ward

Our special thanks to
the Charles H. Revson Foundation
for its generous support

CONTENTS

INTRODUCTION

This book contains six original case studies depicting differing ways in which the communications media impact upon policymaking in the federal government. On the one hand, they are the product of scholarly research, designed to produce analytical insights and pedagogical lessons about the impact of the press on the federal government. On the other, they are fascinating stories about the interplay of journalists and policymakers in Washington, replete with the contrasting motivations, common interests, tension and suspense that provide compelling reading.

Whether used as an aid to designing and teaching courses in political science, journalism, and public administration or for popular enlightenment, these six stories can best be read along with *Impact: How the Press Affects Federal Policymaking* by Martin Linsky, also published by W. W. Norton & Company. The book by Mr. Linsky is a narrative exposition and analysis of the subject drawing on a three-year coordinated research effort which included these case studies, along with a survey of five hundred senior policymakers from the last twenty years, lengthy interviews with twenty selected policymakers and sixteen journalists, and extensive input from a group of advisers with rich experience in journalism, government, and scholarship. Both volumes result from this project on "How the Press Affects Federal Policymaking," undertaken by the Institute of Politics of the John F. Kennedy School of Government and funded by the Charles H. Revson Foundation.

Back in 1981, recognizing that it was inadequate to attempt to understand political decision making in this country without understanding the role played by the media, that the press had an impact on the forming of public policy and the performance of political institutions, and that very little was known about how that impact was felt, we decided to try to learn more about the subject. We hoped we could see better the impact of the press on individual public officials, the institutions and processes of government, and policies themselves. Our work would have three principal purposes: reaching out to the general public to increase understanding about the real impact of the media on government decision mak-

ing, educating present and future public policymakers and journalism professionals about the role of the media, and assisting faculty interested in developing
curricula and teaching in this area.

The membership of the Faculty Study Group established to guide and over-
see the project included: F. Christopher Arterton, associate professor of political
science, Yale University; Hale Champion, executive dean, Kennedy School of
Government; John Chancellor, network correspondent, NBC News; Stephen Hess,
senior fellow, The Brookings Institution; Albert Hunt, national political correspondent, *The Wall Street Journal;* Mark Moore, Guggenheim professor of criminal justice policy and management, Kennedy School of Government; Gary Orren,
associate professor, Kennedy School of Government; Eileen Shanahan, senior
assistant managing editor, *Pittsburgh Post-Gazette;* James C. Thomson, Jr., curator
of the Neiman Foundation; John William Ward, president, American Council of
Learned Societies; and Lewis Wolfson, professor of communication, American
University. Richard E. Neustadt, Lucius N. Littauer professor of public administration at the Kennedy School, served as vice-chairman of the study group, and
I was its chairman. Martin Linsky, assistant director of the Institute of Politics,
was project director.

In selecting the six case studies which compose this volume, we employed
a range of variables. We sought cases in different time frames and administrations, in different executive branch departments involving both domestic and
foreign policy issues, and in Congress. We looked for stories to demonstrate
government officials reacting to and anticipating press coverage and using the
press. And we chose cases showing different kinds of impact on policymaking
procedures and on policy content, and focusing on the specific role of television.
Each of the cases develops a complex story, an individual mix of characteristics,
about significant press–policymaking interaction.

The 1969 reorganization of the Postal Department is a ''pre-Watergate''
case. It is about a deliberate and sustained strategy on the part of a government
agency explicitly using the press in making and implementing policy. It deals
importantly, with Congress, and it demonstrates both substantive and procedural
press impact on policymaking.

The resignation of Vice-President Agnew is a study of leaks, of efforts by
many interests—political, bureaucratic, and journalistic—to use the media to
serve their own ends. It shows major procedural influence, but no press impact
on policy outcome.

The decision of President Carter not to deploy the neutron bomb illustrates
the press's agenda-setting role and government activity reacting to rather than
anticipating press effects. It reveals profound long-term impact on both government policy and process. It is the only foreign policy case in this series.

The story of the relocation of seven hundred families from the Love Canal
area in New York State deals with issue complexity and is our only regulatory
and intergovernmental case. It covers anticipatory governmental action, leaks,
and use of the press in political struggles.

The Reagan administration's support of Bob Jones University to retain its

2

tax exemption, the only civil rights case in this series, also examines complex issues, a reactive stance by the government, and involves the issue-framing role of the press. It demonstrates the press's profound influence on policymaking procedure, a limited short-term effect on policy content, and the use of the press in personal struggles among policymakers.

The 1984 suspension of Social Security Disability reviews is a case about television's unique impact. It is the only study here involving domestic social policy, and it displays modest substantive and procedural influence by the media and both anticipatory and reactive behavior toward the media by the government.

David Whitman, coming to this project with a superb case-writing record at the Kennedy School, wrote the cases on postal reorganization, the neutron bomb, Bob Jones, and Social Security. Wendy O'Donnell, with a journalistic background and major administrative responsibilities for the project, wrote the Agnew case; and Martin Linsky wrote the Love Canal case. We are greatly indebted to the people directly involved in these cases, policymakers and journalists, who devoted long hours to interviewing and who shared documents with us in the interests of scholarly research and better understanding of press–government relations and effects. Identified in the cases themselves, they are not responsible for the final versions, but without their assistance the cases could not have been produced. Likewise, this book was made possible through the financial assistance and guidance of the Revson Foundation, but its contents are solely the responsibility of the authors.

Along with its responsibilities for research about electoral politics and for innovative programming to benefit political practitioners, the Institute of Politics has for a long time sponsored various activities relating to the interaction of the media and government. During the past few years it has taken the lead in developing a new Center on the Press, Politics, and Public Policy. This center will encourage more understanding by government officials about the role and value of the media, better coverage by media professionals of government and politics, better analysis of public policies affecting the media, and more knowledge of how the media influence our political processes and governmental institutions. It will pursue these goals through teaching of present and future public managers and policymakers, applied research, educational programs for print and television practitioners, and conferences and symposia for joint consideration of media–government problems.

Jonathan Moore
Director, Institute of Politics
September 1985

SELLING
THE REORGANIZATION OF
THE POST OFFICE

by David Whitman

N EAR THE BEGINNING of Charles Dickens's novel *Bleak House* there is a
famous passage in which Dickens wryly introduces the reader to the British High Court of Chancery. The novel opens on a gloomy day when there is
"Fog everywhere. Fog up the river, where it flows among green aits and mead-
ows; fog down the river, where it rolls defiled among the tiers of shipping and
the waterside pollution," and "the dense fog is densest," Dickens notes, "near
that leaden-headed old corporation Temple Bar. And hard by Temple Bar . . .
at the very heart of the fog, sits the Lord High Chancellor in his High Court of
Chancery." One might think Dickens's description of the fog permeating the
High Court relevant only for antiquated forms of government, but until a few
years ago there was a U.S. government agency that bore a striking resemblance
to Dickens's High Court of Chancery; namely, the United States Post Office. No
department of the federal government was so shackled by vested interests, by
stultifying personnel practices, by archaic regulations and equipment, by an absence
of elementary management practices; and last, but not least, nowhere was the
sauce of political patronage thicker than at the heart of the lavish office of the
Postmaster General. Lawrence F. O'Brien, who served as postmaster general in
the mid 1960s, once acknowledged that "there can be little doubt that the Postmaster General's office is the largest of its kind in all of the Federal bureaucracy.
If hoops were placed [at each end of the office], the Post Office Department's
top staff could engage in a full court basketball game."[1]

In 1969, capitalizing on a reform movement initiated by O'Brien, President
Richard Nixon and his postmaster general, Winton "Red" Blount, set out to
undo two centuries of tradition at the Post Office by removing it from the Cabinet, by cutting off all political patronage, and by turning the Post Office into a
government corporation. Their reorganization legislation called for a fundamen-

---

*Unless otherwise noted, all quotations come either from unpublished gov-
ernment documents or from interviews with the author.*

tal restructuring instead of the commonplace "reshuffling of bureaucratic boxes"[2]—*Business Week* went so far as to call it "the most comprehensive overhaul of a U.S. public institution ever considered"[3]—and it faced enormous obstacles in Congress. One newspaper summed up the situation early in 1969 by editorializing that passing the reorganization bill would require "one of the minor political miracles of the century."[4]

Not being the type to wait for divine intervention, Postmaster General Blount decided early in his tenure to mount not only a traditional lobbying effort to pass the bill, but to buttress it with a massive, sustained media campaign. That carefully calculated and innovative campaign became a subject of considerable controversy; critics from the postal unions asserted in congressional testimony that the Post Office mounted "one of the smoothest and most massive attempts at public brainwashing since the glory days of Joseph Paul Goebbels"[5] and even figures who were more sympathetic to the administration's proposal—such as Senator Gale McGee (D-Wy.), Chairman of the Senate Committee on Post Office and Civil Service—contended that Blount mounted a "well-organized drive to win public support without public understanding of [the legislation's] various ramifications."[6] The media campaign, however, in the eyes of Blount and several of his aides was not only appropriate but also played a key role in securing the unexpected passage of the legislation. As Blount summed up: "The campaign to draw media support was enormously important . . . if the public had been ho-hum, '50–50,' I don't think we would have reorganized the Post Office."

The Problems of the Post Office

To appreciate the state of disarray the Post Office had fallen into by the mid-1960s, it is necessary to have a crude understanding of the historical significance of the Post Office. Until the last fifty years, mail was overwhelmingly our dominant form of communication, particularly in outlying areas; there were no airplanes, cars, telephones, electronic communication systems, and even the railroads were not established until the turn of the century. From the founding of the republic the enormous importance of the Post Office had been recognized—the Constitution, for example, vested Congress with the power "to establish Post Offices and post roads"—and even today the Post Office touches the lives of more Americans on a daily basis than any other government agency.

Not only, however, was the Post Office's monopoly (i.e., communication) critical, the significance of that monopoly stood out among the powers wielded by the government during the eighteenth and nineteenth centuries. Social welfare programs, environmental protection, and a host of other domestic activities that we now associate with the federal government did not exist. As one study summarized, "In the nineteenth century, the domestic federal government was, for the most part, the Post Office and the POD was the major federal organization for the distribution of economic and political benefits."[7] Until World War II (when the Defense Department surpassed it), the Post Office had more employees than any other federal department, and during the century preceding the war,

40–60 percent of the federal civilian work force always worked for the Post Office.

The Post Office thus was the most likely source for political patronage and with ruthless regularity the local and national leadership of the Post Office changed wholesale as administrations came and went. Scandals over political graft were not uncommon and the position of the postmaster general was frequently filled by political hacks, who were distinguished more by their loyalty to the president than their business acumen. Most of the postmaster generals devoted little attention to running the department, typically operating instead as "ministers without a portfolio" among the Congress.

Congress itself was not indifferent to the political plum presented by the Post Office and over the years labored arduously to cultivate the Post Office's harvest. To a degree that was unrivaled in any other executive department or agency, Congress ran the Post Office. No one, for example, could fill one of the 32,000 local postmaster positions (existing in 1969) without first being confirmed by Congress. And Congress's influence was not limited to determining who would run the post offices: Congress also legislated how much postal employees would be paid and under what conditions, how much the Post Office would charge for various classes of mail, and—along with the General Services Administration, the Post Office, and four congressional committees—determined where the Post Office would build its facilities. The astonishing absence of managerial authority at the Post Office was well summed up by an oft-quoted exchange that took place in 1967 between Congressman Steed (D-Okla.), chairman of the House Appropriations postal subcommittee, and O'Brien, who was then postmaster general:

> MR. STEED: Would this be a fair summary: that at the present time, as the manager of the Post Office Department, you have no control over your workload, you have no control over the rates of revenue, you have no control over the pay rates of the employees that you employ, you have very little control over the conditions of the service of these employees, you have virtually no control, by the nature of it, of your physical facilities, and you have only a limited control, at best, over the transportation facilities that you are compelled to use—all of which adds up to a staggering amount of "no control" in terms of the duties you have to perform?
>
> MR. O'BRIEN: Mr. Chairman, I would have to generally agree with your premise . . . that is a staggering list of "no control." I don't know whether it has ever been put that succinctly to me. If it had been at an appropriate time, perhaps I wouldn't be sitting here.[8]

In part, Congress's domination of the Post Office had grown not out of selfish motives, but out of a long tradition that viewed the Post Office as a vital public service which had to be protected. But unlike the days in which the Pony Express had raced out to remote regions of the country to deliver mail to isolated citizens, the Post Office's clients by the mid-1960s came overwhelmingly from the commercial world. Only 13 percent of the mail in 1968 was personal correspondence; the remainder was business correspondence, dominated by routine transactions (checks, bills), advertising, and magazine and newspaper mailings. The Post Office was, moreover, not only primarily a service industry for business, it was also a very, very large business itself. At the time Blount took over, he oversaw 32,150 post offices and 739,000 employees (amounting to 36 percent of the federal civilian workforce and about 1 percent of the *entire* labor force). Six days a week mail carriers reached roughly fifty-one million families and five million businesses, and over the course of 1968, 79.5 billion pieces of mail were delivered.[9] The Post Office grandly labelled itself "the largest single business organization in the world, conducting the greatest system of communications ever known to man,"[10] and while that claim seems a bit exaggerated, there is no doubt that the Post Office was an industrial giant; in 1965 the Post Office employed more people than any business in the country with the exception of AT&T and General Motors, and its revenues exceeded those of companies like U.S. Steel, Texaco, IBM, and DuPont.[11]

Not surprisingly, the diffusion of management authority at the Post Office had become more critical as the Post Office blossomed into an enormous business. Two examples of how outmoded the management techniques and structures of the Post Office should suffice; when Arthur Summerfield, President Eisenhower's postmaster general, arrived at the Post Office, he found he would have to wait seventeen months for an operating statement of business (for the preceding month) and that the Post Office did not employ a single certified public accountant (although it handled cash transactions totaling $20 billion a year).[12] The situation was no better in the Congress. In 1968 Congress did not have one person on all of its staff who studied postal rates full-time. Instead, every few years a handful of congressmen listened to thousands of pages of testimony from powerful second-class, nonprofit, and third-class mailers—all of whom brought in their own accountants to demonstrate that they were paying more than the Post Office's costs of handling the mail. Compared, say, to the painstaking fact-finding process regulatory commissions undertook to set monopoly rates, postal rate making, *Reader's Digest* concluded, was "a circus sideshow."[13]

The unbusinesslike atmosphere of the Post Office, of course, was nothing novel—during the one hundred and thirty years preceding Blount's arrival the Post Office had run deficits one hundred and thirteen times—but there were two new strains that increased the gravity of the situation and were highlighted by an 80 percent increase in the Post Office operating deficit (to $1.1 billion) between 1964 and 1967. The first new factor was an enormous growth in the volume of mail following World War II. In 1940 the Post Office handled 28 billion pieces of mail; that volume rose to 50 billion in 1953, to 75 billion by 1966, and was projected to rise to 100 billion by 1977. This rapid increase might have been manageable were it not for a second factor—the increase in volume was not matched by commensurate increases in postal rates and the Post Office's budget. With the Vietnam War and Johnson's War on Poverty starting up, funding for the Post Office was a low priority. Equally important, when funds for the Post Office were cut back in the interest of economy, it was inevitably capital funds rather than operating funds that were reduced (since the former seemed more deferable). In an industry where major corporations devoted an average of 30 percent of their annual capital inventory to research, the Post Office devoted 2 to 3 percent. The result of all this was that the Post Office was hopelessly behind the times; as more and more mail came in, clerks at the Post Office were still sorting it into cases with 49 partitions (the same "pigeon-hole" box designed by Benjamin Franklin in the 1790s), after which it was placed in sacks, lifted manually, wheeled on hand trucks, and handled an average of ten more times before it reached its destination.

The problems of the Post Office Department finally peaked in October 1966 when the main Chicago post office broke down. The Chicago post office was the world's largest postal facility—thirteen stories high with sixty acres of work space—and for three weeks the facility was paralyzed with a backlog of over ten million pieces of mail. There were a number of reasons for the post office's temporary collapse—an unexpected influx of mail, problems filling the postmaster's vacant position, low employee morale and absenteeism, and a deteriorating, poorly designed physical plant—all of which seemed, to the postal reformers, to embody the department's problems and offer an ominous harbinger of things to come. The Chicago collapse subsequently proved instrumental, however, not only because it galvanized Larry O'Brien, but also because it dramatically drew public attention for the first time to the problems of the Post Office.

The Political Obstacles to Reorganization

Given the troubled state of the Post Office, it may seem surprising that attempts to reorganize the Post Office were considered an exercise in political futility. But however illogical the postal system was, it had served well the interests of three very powerful groups—postal employees, Congress, and the organized mailers—who had formed a classic "iron triangle" at the expense of the taxpayer.

The first and strongest side of this triangle was the cozy relationship between postal employees and Congress. Over the years, a symbiotic relationship, both between the postmasters and Congress, and between the unions and Congress, had cemented. The appointment of local postmasters was essentially the only patronage appointment (besides their own staff) available to a congressman,* so the futures of the postmasters were closely linked to the reelection of the congressmen who appointed them. To protect their appointments, many postmasters invested large amounts of time, pressure, and money, to ensure their congressmen got reelected, and in some districts, particularly in the south, the postmasters virtually ran the local county machines. At the time Blount took office, there were 2,164 postmaster positions that had gone unfilled since 1961[14] (because the Democrats had been unable to agree among themselves on who to appoint), and Republican congressmen, one of Blount's aides recalled, "were salivating over the prospect of filling them."

---

*Senators could select other appointees, particularly in the federal judiciary.

The postal unions were equally tied to the Congress, and in a number of respects were even more powerful than the postmasters. The Post Office Department was the most highly unionized federal agency; 88 percent of its employees (620,000 people) worked in one of twelve employee organizations, dominated by the AFL-CIO affiliates, the National Association of Letter Carriers (190,000 members), and the United Federation of Postal Clerks (145,000 members). Of all the government unions, the NALC and UFPC were the two most powerful, and their authority on the Hill and ability to descend on Congress with thousands of workers was nothing short of legendary. Unlike the leaders of most unions, the leaders of the NALC and UFPC spent their days wining and dining Congress and were essentially highly skilled lobbyists. In 1966, 1967, and 1968, the UFPC, for example, had higher lobbying expenditures than any other lobby[15] (a mantle which passed to the NALC in 1969). Their lobbying expenditures (annually in the $150,000–$300,000 range) were buttressed by campaign contributions made by members that mounted into the millions, and generally the unions enjoyed remarkable success,* getting the Congress to legislate pay increases eighteen times between 1945 and 1969. What made the postal unions so powerful, however, was not only their financial muscle and numbers, but their politically fortuitous distribution. As Red Blount summarized:

> Postal employees were the only people in the United States that went to every household in every congressional district every day. They had done so over a long period of time and they had great relations with their people; they got Christmas presents and those sort of things. The congressmen were deathly afraid of the postal employee walking around saying "Congressman X is not helping us and you ought to support this young guy." So it led to a natural alliance; the congressman appointed the postmaster and rural carriers, they formed his basic reelection committee, and he made sure to keep the postal employees happy.

The third partner in the triangle were the organized mailers, consisting of representative associations (the National Newspaper Association, the Direct Mail Advertising Association, the Magazine Publishers Association, the American Business Press, the National Association of Manufacturers, and so on) as well as the major mailers themselves, companies like *Time, Newsweek, LIFE,* Sears, General Mills, and McGraw-Hill. The formidable power of these companies had been manifested in continuous pressure to keep postal rates low for second-class, third-class, and "controlled circulation" mail (primarily trade publications). When these rates did not cover the Post Office's cost of handling the mail—which was often the case—Congress typically raised money to cover the shortfall by either raising first-class rates or borrowing taxpayer money for "public service" expen-

---

*The postal unions had succeeded in getting frequent increases in postal salaries and at procuring benefits for themselves and other government employees. There were, however, serious morale problems, relating chiefly to the incentive structure at the Post Office. There was no merit system and few opportunities for advancement; 85% of all postal employees were in the 5 lowest grades and 80% finished their careers in the same grade level at which they began.[16]

ditures from the Treasury. Once again there was an alluring symbiosis between the two parties; the mailers got some of their costs subsidized, in return for which Congress found powerful companies and media organs dependent on their good-will.

The silent partner in all of this, and the one, of course, most likely to get reamed, was the U.S. taxpayer. But barring an emergency, such as the short-lived breakdown of the Chicago post office, it was difficult to stir up public wrath or concern over the Post Office. So long as the mail went through, most citizens were content with the service, and they were far more preoccupied with issues like the Vietnam War.

The first sign of a crack in the triangle of interests constricting the Post Office occurred in 1967. In April, following the Chicago breakdown, Postmaster General O'Brien warned that the POD "was in a race with catastrophe" and embraced the idea of turning the Post Office into a nonprofit government corporation in an address to a stunned audience from the Magazine Publishers Association. (Under O'Brien's proposal—the outlines of which President Johnson had approved in advance—the Post Office would be removed from the Cabinet, supervised by a board of directors appointed by the President and run by a professional executive appointed by the board, able to issue bonds to provide for capital funds, and would have clearer rate setting authority). Following O'Brien's speech, President Johnson appointed Frederick Kappel, Chairman of AT&T, to head a commission to review the status of the Post Office and make recommendations for its future. The "Kappel Commission," as it came to be called, was composed of some of the nation's most prestigious business leaders,* and following a massive staff effort, released a report in June 1968 calling for the Post Office to be converted to a government corporation, roughly along the lines O'Brien had previously suggested.

Both O'Brien's speech and the Kappel Commission met with widespread editorial support, but, perhaps more important, the Kappel Commission also marked the beginning of a shift of sympathies among the organized mailers. There are several theories about why the mailers began to support the government corporation concept, but most of them boiled down to the argument that they perceived a long-term gain from it. In the short term it appeared that rates would rise more precipitously under corporate managers than under Congress, but in the long run entrusting additional authority and freedom to postal managers seemed to be the only way to assure that the Post Office would modernize and avoid the kind of collapse of mail service that occurred in Chicago.

It appeared, however, that the modest momentum for reform generated by O'Brien and the Kappel Commission was in danger of being lost during the waning days of the Johnson administration. In April 1968 O'Brien resigned as

---

*Among the commission's 10 members were the president or chairman of General Electric, Campbell Soup, and Bank of America. The dean of Harvard Business School and George Meany, president of the AFL-CIO, were also members. Meany dissented from the report's recommendation that the Post Office be converted to a government corporation.

postmaster general (to work for Robert Kennedy's campaign) and was succeeded by one of Johnson's chief troubleshooters from the White House, Marvin Watson. Watson did not share O'Brien's enthusiasm for the postal corporation concept and made no effort to push it in Congress. Several days before Nixon entered office, both L.B.J. and Watson endorsed the corporation approach, but their swansong stamp of approval did not carry much weight.

Richard Nixon, however, made it clear soon after entering office that he would not drop the ball on postal reform, living up to his campaign promise to establish a "new system" so the POD could be "run like a first-class business."[17] One of Nixon's first policy decisions, announced early in February 1969, was to abolish political patronage at the Post Office. That decision, which had the full support of Nixon's new PMG, Red Blount, stunned and enraged Republican congressmen, particularly those on the House Committee on Post Office and Civil Service (HPOC). As one of Blount's senior aides recalled: "The first time we went up to the Hill the reaction from the Republicans was nothing short of vitriolic. They had been out of power for eight years and they weren't excited about a few hundred Assistant Secretary appointments; they wanted the thousands of appointments that could come only from the Post Office." At a meeting in late February, Bryce Harlow, the White House assistant for congressional liaison, asked Nixon to defer implementing the patronage cutoff but Nixon was insistent. Blount recalled:

> Bryce argued that we could be better off and keep Congress happier if we got a few of our people in before we cut off the patronage. I argued that if we wanted to get postal reform, we would have to forego the patronage because we were facing a Congress that was ⅔ Democrats. If we had taken a year to make those appointments, the Democrats would never have taken us seriously on reform; we had to keep ourselves pure because there is no way to get a little pregnant. The President agreed and said, "Let's be realistic Red, we won't get postal reform unless we control the Congress [in 1970 or 1972], but as long as you want to march up to the Hill, I'll support you."

On the heels of the patronage cutoff, Blount and his advisers began preparing legislation to reorganize the Post Office, with the future of the bill increasingly in doubt. On the one hand, Blount and Nixon could count on editorial support for reform and endorsements from some mailer groups that had been brought along by the Kappel Commission. On the other hand, Nixon was the first president since Zachary Taylor to face a Congress in which the opposition party controlled both Houses, and many of the members of Nixon's own party were mad as hell at the administration for cutting off political patronage. The appearance of the Kappel report had also forced the postal unions to take a stand publicly on a postal corporation, and both the NALC and UFPC had come out adamantly against it, particularly the NALC. In a November 1968 speech, NALC president James Rademacher called for a "militant offensive" to be mounted against any legislation that would turn the POD into a government corporation, declaring dramatically, "if the choice is between [an illegal postal strike] and involuntary servitude to a soulless corporation, then we would have to [strike]."[18] Congressman Mo Udall (D-Ariz.), a HPOC member and the only representative in the House who had been an outspoken proponent of the corporation approach, gave one of the cheerier assessments of the legislation's chances when he stated in May 1969: "The postal unions are apprehensive and hold a veto over a public corporation at this time. However, there's a fair chance for the bill in 1970 or 1971."[19]

Marketing the Reorganization

Despite the obstacles facing them, Blount and his team—many of whom were senior business executives that agreed to come work for Blount for a few years—approached the task of reorganizing the Post Office with an almost missionary-like zeal. Blount, who had turned his Alabama construction business into a multimillion dollar enterprise before becoming president of the Chamber of Commerce, installed a quiet fire in his aides (that still glows today when they talk about their efforts). And Blount himself, according to all accounts, was legendary for his commitment to reforming the Post Office and a compelling but sometimes alienating stubbornness. As Dave Minton, former counsel to the Senate Post Office Committee recalled, "Blount was the most tenacious man I have ever known. I admired him a great deal—I did not like him at all—but goddamn, he just kept on coming back. He was as stubborn as an Alabama mule."

In March 1969, Blount turned over the drafting of legislation to his general counsel, David Nelson. Nelson canvassed headquarters personnel for suggestions about what to incorporate in the bill and his request soon stimulated the first serious thinking about the public relations aspects of the legislation. In an April 7 memo to Nelson, Jim Henderson, Blount's special assistant for public information, wrote:

> It should be accepted that a massive "selling" job will be required for any plan that will result in Congress relinquishing control over the bulk of postal operations. By law we are debarred from this kind of "selling" job, although of course the public pronouncements of the Postmaster General do not fall within that limitation. We can, however, try to engineer some form of separate organization designed to further improving postal service. Perhaps the U.S. Chamber of Commerce might designate this as "improved postal service year" and provide an ongoing organization to press for reform; or, failing that, a foundation might be enlisted to establish a working group for reorganization.

As Blount and his advisers evaluated the prospects for reform during April, they came rapidly to the conclusion that Henderson's recommendation for a "massive selling job" was on target. As Blount stated, "Sure, it would have been nice to get together in a back room with a few key congressmen, the unions, and mailers, and cut a deal to reorganize the Post Office. But there was absolutely no way that was going to happen. Congress owned the Post Office and they liked that old baby just the way it was. We needed the newspaper pressure

13

in the member's districts to help shake up things.'' ''We felt,'' a senior Blount aide recalled, ''that since the committee members had a vested interest in maintaining the system, the pressure to change had to come partly from members outside the committee, and that they weren't going to do anything without an awful lot of selling.''

Blount et al also accepted Henderson's second recommendation: that a separate organization—bluntly referred to in POD memos as the ''front organization''—be set up to push reform. There were three advantages to setting up such a group. The first, as Henderson indicated, was that it provided a way to circumvent restrictions on lobbying. Under 18 USC 1913, it was a criminal offense for a department to use appropriated funds directly or indirectly to pay for advertisements, telephone calls, letters, printed or written matter designed to influence a member of Congress on pending legislation, and subsequent appropriation acts had prohibited the use of appropriated funds for ''publicity or propaganda designed to support or defend [pending] legislation.''[20] Organizations outside the government, of course, could pursue all these activities. Second, a front organization also opened up a funding channel through which the organized mailers could discreetly counteract some of the financial muscle of the unions. From the viewpoint, that is, of both POD management and the mailers, it was preferable to have the mailers' money go toward supporting a ''good government'' group than an out-and-out ''big business'' lobby.

The third advantage, and the one that really made the POD's plan stand out, was Blount's and Henderson's decision to structure the lobby organization along bipartisan lines to suck in Democratic support. The notion of setting up a bipartisan ''citizens group'' to press for postal reform was by no means new—in fact, such an organization existed and had already offered its services to Blount— what was new was the POD's success in placing a prestigious Democrat and Republican at the helm of such a group. The existing citizens group, known as Citizens for a Postal Corporation (CIPCO), was headed by Walter Humann, and had a bipartisan membership, including Larry O'Brien. Humann's group had tried, without the support of the Post Office in 1968, to set up a Washington office as well as regional CIPCO chapters, that would press for editorials and media coverage favorable to reform and phone call / letter writing campaigns to congressmen. But Humann, who had been a White House fellow in 1967 and later served on the staff of the Kappel Commission, simply lacked the stature or fund-rising powers to make CIPCO a force. As Murray Comarow, executive director of the commission, stated in an October 1968 letter to Kappel, ''What we need is a sustained, well-organized and well-financed effort to bring to bear the weight of public opinion upon the Congress. . . . The opposition from the postal unions is sustained, well-organized, and well-financed. It cannot be effectively countered by a part-time Walter Humann working out of a post office box in Dallas.''[21]

Acting on advice he received from his staff and outsiders, Blount decided to phase out CIPCO, replacing it with a ''citizens commission'' headed by O'Brien and Thruston Morton. O'Brien, in addition to having once been PMG, had served as chairman of the Democratic Party, and Morton, who was a retired Senator, similarly had served as chairman of the Republican Party. Having the two party chairmen serve as heads of the lobby organization had a compelling bipartisan appeal, but getting O'Brien was the key. Despite previous statements expressing the view that reform could only be obtained with the help of a "grassroots lobby,"* O'Brien distrusted Nixon (a distrust that grew obviously following the Watergate burglary), and he agreed to serve as co-chairman on the citizens commission only after Bryce Harlow flew to New York in May 1969 to personally assure O'Brien that the administration would not use the committee to sandbag him or propose reform provisions with which he was uncomfortable. O'Brien then designated Claude Desautels as executive director of the group (christened the "Citizens Committee for Postal Reform (CCPR)"). Desautels, a veteran lobbyist, had been O'Brien's executive assistant for congressional affairs at the POD, and had also worked for O'Brien when the latter was Special Assistant for Congressional Affairs for Presidents Kennedy and Johnson. "Both O'Brien and Desautels," Paul Carlin, Blount's executive assistant for congressional liaison stated, "where well-regarded and close to everybody we weren't close to in Congress. They could do some things on the other side of the aisle that we couldn't."

To sum up, by May, Blount and his advisers had privately devised the outline of an ingeniously simple plan to market the reorganization of the Post Office. There would be a "massive selling" job, done partly by the POD (as was legally permissable) and partly by a bipartisan "citizens group" that would rely on contributions from the business community for funding. But the outlines of the plan needed to be filled in: What media would the POD and CCPR focus on, what kind of pitches would they make and to whom, how much money was needed, and so forth. To fill that void, both Blount and Henderson decided to add a full-time specialist to the staff who would concentrate on selling the reorganization proposal to the media. With the assistance of Bryce Harlow, who had worked for Procter & Gamble, Blount convinced Procter & Gamble to lend one of their young marketing specialists, William Dunlap, to the POD for free. (Dunlap had a POD office, but remanded his POD salary; he was paid by Procter & Gamble during 1969 and 1970 instead.) When Dunlap arrived in Washington late in April 1969, he was given two weeks to design a marketing plan to sell the reorganization legislation, scheduled to be announced in late May.

The Marketing Plan

In drawing up the marketing plan, Dunlap decided to "write it just the way I would at Procter & Gamble. Essentially I took a packaging goods approach that you use to market a product, and applied it to the government sector; identify

---

*In an August 1968 article in the *Washington Post*, O'Brien had written that reform "will come about only after great controversy and against the efforts of some highly skilled and powerful lobbying interests. . . . Postal reform will come about only after expressions of widespread public interest. The most effective lobby for change is the 'grassroots' lobby."[22]

your objectives, your strategy, target audiences, how you reach the target audiences, how much do you have to spend to get them, with what frequency you need to reach them, and so on.'' Unlike some marketing plans, Dunlap's was largely followed through on, and because of its explicitness and thoroughness, sections of it are reprinted here at some length. Dunlap summarized the basic objectives and strategy of the plan as follows:

> *The ultimate objective* of this marketing plan is the passage of the administration's legislative proposal for the creation of a federally owned corporation to operate the U.S. postal system. *Preliminary objectives* involve achievement of the widest possible public and Congressional understanding, acceptance and active support of the measure. . . .
>
> *The Purpose*
> Operating under the theory that Members of Congress are most responsive to (1) the expressed desires and demands of their own constituents, (2) the positions taken by major opinion makers, such as community leaders, the newspapers, magazines, television, etc., and (3) the views of special interest groups and large voting blocks, including business, labor, etc., our nationwide drive would be geared to stimulate the maximum amount of active support possible from such sources at both the local and national levels, and to utilize this favorable public reaction as a positive force that could be directed toward the Members of Congress to bring about enactment of the proposed legislation.
>
> *The Method*
> Through the extensive use of the news media, special articles, paid advertising, public speeches, informational materials, special promotions, etc., and the utilization of volunteers and facilities of interested groups and organizations, the campaign would endeavor to convince as many individuals and groups as possible—
>   1. for the need to transfer the Post Office Department to a government-owned corporation and the advantages to be gained by such a change.
>   2. of the superiority of the Administration's proposal over that of any other recommended legislation, and
>   3. to actively bring pressure upon Members of Congress, directly and indirectly, to support the Bill through such methods as the writing and sending of individual letters and wires, public statements, editorials, letters to the editor, resolutions, etc.

Dunlap summarized the congressional and public relations obstacles to reform as follows:

> *Problems:*
> • the reluctance of Congress, especially Members of the P.O. Committees and subcommittees, to relinquish the control they now have over the Post Office and the possible accompanying loss of ''support'' by the powerful postal unions.
> • the existence of other so-called postal reform legislation that can be expected to siphon off some Congressional support, confuse the issue in the public's

mind, and provide a rallying point for those who oppose our more "total" form of postal reform.
• the organized opposition of labor unions and most postal employee associations.
• the possibility of an apathetic public that does not share our discontent with the present operation of the postal service, is wary of change, or cannot be prodded into sufficient demonstrable support for our proposal.
• the legal restrictions against "lobbying activities" by employees.

To overcome these obstacles, Dunlap stressed that the POD would have to undertake both a broadly based national sales pitch and a more discrete campaign targeted on "special audiences." In the broad brush stroke category, Dunlap, assisted by public affairs staffer D. Jamison Cain, included the following:

General Activities to Achieve Broad Impact:

1. *News Stories*
A continuous flow of general news stories and feature stories would be issued to the news media—including the wire services, newspapers, magazines, radio, television, trade publications, etc.—that would explain every provision of the proposed legislation and publicize each new development in the campaign to win public approval and Congressional enactment. These would take such forms as the following:
• announcement of the introduction of the Administration's bill before Congress to be made at a news conference held by the PMG. Press kits would be distributed containing detailed information on the proposal's provisions.
• follow up stories providing explanations of how the proposed corporation would improve the postal system.
• statements of support by a wide variety of prestigious business, community and government leaders, etc.
• announcement of the formation of a citizens' committee at a specially-arranged news conference. Press kits would be distributed revealing plans for the launching of a nationwide campaign to secure approval for the Administration's bill.
• announcement in each state of the formation of a local committee supporting the total reform proposal.
• preparation of all national news releases would also be devised for release to local news media by use of local names and activities.
• specially arranged interviews would be set up between the PMG and other leading supporters, with Federal columnists . . . as well as the leading nationally syndicated columnists.

2. *Special Articles*
• articles bearing the PMG's byline would be prepared for submission to large-circulation national magazines, such as *Reader's Digest,* etc.
• cover stories and articles would be prepared for use by the Sunday supplements, such as *Parade, This Week,* etc.
• arrangements would be made for private interviews of the PMG with news magazines and large newspapers, such as *Time, Newsweek,* and the *New York Times,* etc., as well as some of the larger trade publications.
• special interviews would be held with the AP and UPI wire services.

3. *Editorials*
• Follow-up approaches would be made to those editors already known to support our proposal to write additional favorable editorials. Information and suggestions would be supplied to these sources periodically. Special attention would be paid to chain operations such as Scripps-Howard, American Business Press (Robert Saltzstein's Group), etc.
• Suggested editorials would be prepared for editorial writing services that supply weeklies and small dailies.
• Local contacts would be used to approach major dailies throughout the nation.
• Attention also would be given to those radio and television stations that present editorial viewpoints.
• Special efforts would be made to provide editorial matter designed to appeal to trade publications and house organs.

4. *Guest Appearances*
Arrangements would be made for the Postmaster General and other prestigious supporters of the Administration's proposal to make guest appearances on widely heard and viewed national and regional radio and television shows, such as *Meet the Press; Face the Nation; Monitor; Dimension; The Today Show; The Tonight Show; The Joey Bishop Show; Panorama;* Martin Agronsky's news program; and Walter Cronkite's *21st Century* program, for a possible show comparing present-day mail service vs. the corporation approach. . . .

5. *Letters to the Editor*
A campaign would be launched to flood the newspapers with letters to the editor. Responsibility for this would be distributed among the supporting organizations and local operations to avoid any appearance of a nationally directed or mass produced undertaking. "Suggested" letters would be prepared for appropriate distribution.

To complement this media "saturation campaign" at the national level, Dunlap outlined specific appeals that would be made to six target audiences. The details of how those appeals were to be made are omitted here, but the general marketing themes are reproduced below:

Specific Appeals for Special Audiences:
To successfully carry out our campaign, it is necessary to seek support from six separate and distinct segments of the population. These include (1) labor, (2) business, (3) the public, (4) Congress, (5) news media, and (6) postal employees. For maximum effectiveness, therefore, it is important that we select those elements of our proposal which are of the greatest interest to each group and to stress those provisions of the measure in our approach that will most appeal to that particular group's self-interests. For example:
Labor: The appeal to labor would be most effectively made by skirting the national organizations, which are expected to oppose the proposed measure, and concentrating on the local unions at the state and regional levels. Emphasis would be placed on the freedom that would be provided under the corporation for local wage negotiations, enabling the unions to bargain for

salary scales on the basis of area living costs and wage comparability instead of having to rely on the broad-based national wage scales determined by Congress. It would be pointed out that it does not make sense for postal workers in a region of the country where the cost of living is above the national average to the paid the same wages as those employees working in states where the living costs are considerably below the national average.

Business: The appeal to business would be based on the promise of improved service and reduced costs that would result from the more efficient operation of a self-sustaining, government-owned corporation. Additional benefits, such as the fast handling of priority mail, etc., also would be stressed.

The Public: A consumer-oriented approach would be used in appealing to the public. This would include faster and more reliable mail service, a reduction of the postal deficit that places a burden on the taxpayers, and a halt to the periodic rise in postage prices. An additional appeal might be made to the national pride that would be shared in having the world's most efficiently operated postal service.

Congress: Appeals would be made to Members of Congress on the basis of their obligation to provide the American public with a revitalized postal service, the opportunity to be recognized as a participant in the most significant and beneficial advance in our postal system since it was founded by Benjamin Franklin, and the positions taken in favor of postal reform in their national party platforms. In addition, there are the advantages of not being bothered by postal job seekers, or pressured by the unions for wage increases and other benefits, and a reduction in the heavy flow of constituent complaints regarding post office service and operations. Most important, of course, would be the argument that this is what the voters want and support of the measure would be to their advantage when campaigning for reelection.

News Media: The appeal to the news media is threefold—(1) to their responsibility as community leaders and opinion makers to support needed reform legislation, (2) to their self-interest as mail users, and (3) to the desire to provide their audience with full coverage of a meaningful news development.

Postal Employees: The appeals to the postal employees would evolve around the promise of better working conditions, increased prestige and expanded opportunities for advancement. At the same time, a special effort must be made to assure them of their retention of existing benefits and privileges.

Were the activities in Dunlap's plan, subsequently approved by Blount, overly extensive? Could, for example, the POD simply have targeted districts of members of the House Post Office Committee that were sitting on the fence on postal reorganization? Jim Henderson contended the saturation approach, at least initially, was critical:

We wanted to start off by capitalizing on the President's visibility. He came into the office with postal reform as one of his goals so we knew that he and the Postmaster General would draw a lot of publicity when he announced and sent up the bill. But after the newness, and the President's early momentum faded, we expected the President and the Cabinet would go run in a lot of other directions. The second advantage to focusing nationally was that in the beginning we weren't sure who our allies and opponents were. The media campaign helped flush that out and put you in a better position to respond to the particular idiosyncracies of congressmen later on.

Dunlap contended that the national media campaign was something that the POD could only benefit from:

We were not worried about overkill in any sense. The postal service was a fairly low interest category and we were trying to build awareness about the problems at the department, so our attitude was, the more the merrier. Creating that public awareness was going to help in two ways: first, if we got the bill through committee we wanted the other members to be favorably disposed, and second, if we got the reorganization passed, we wanted it to have some chance of success instead of coming at the public out of nowhere. Also when you draw the national news media, you hit the local guys automatically anyway. If Mo Udall saw Blount on *Meet the Press,* it was more impressive than sending a [POD] official out to talk to the postal service councils in Arizona.

May–August 1969: Working on the HPOC and Unions

The first order of business for POD officials was the unveiling of the reorganization legislation and the simultaneous kickoff of the CCPR. In early May, Blount apprised White House officials of the formation of the CCPR, the basic provisions of the legislation, and a tentative marketing plan surrounding the president's announcement of the reorganization on May 27. The announcement plan included a message for the president to the Congress, a statement by the president (read at the White House and followed by a press briefing with Blount), a 22-page press packet from the Post Office outlining the legislation, a POD headquarters briefing for staff (wired directly to three hundred top postmasters around the country via a "telecon" system), simultaneous publication of *Postal Life* (a POD publication sent to all postal employees) and *Memo to Mailers* (a Mail Users Council publication sent to 60,000 business executives) on the reorganization legislation, a CCPR release hailing the legislation, and a POD background packet for editorial writers. Herb Klein, the White House director of communications, approved the announcement plans and suggested that a series of regional editorial backgrounders be undertaken prior to the announcement so that coverage by the Washington press corps would not dominate the interpretation of events. POD officials readily agreed, and Blount and a handful of his aides gave backgrounders to the editorial boards of papers in six major cities during the week preceding the announcement.

The substance of the reorganization bill was also generally accepted by the White House. Under the legislation, the POD would undergo a total overhaul: The Postal Service would be run by a nine-man Board of Directors with seven members appointed by the president subject to Senate confirmation; those seven members would select a chief executive, who would select a chief operating officer, both of whom would also be members of the Board of Directors; recommendations on postal rates would be made by an expert panel of three commissioners, then reviewed and modified by the board of Directors, and would go into effect unless vetoed by the House and Senate within 60 days; the Postal Service would have broad borrowing authority of up to $10 billion; and wages, job classifications, and benefits would be determined through collective bargaining, with disagreements settled by a balanced "postal disputes panel" with resort to binding arbitration. Within five years it was expected that this nonprofit corporation would be self-supporting.

The editorial reaction to the legislation was enthusiastic, but the congressional reception was frosty. Speaker of the House John McCormack (D-Ma.) said that Nixon's proposal was "a subject for long-range consideration"[23] and minority leader Gerald Ford (R-Mich.), who was a strong supporter of the proposal, said that the president "will have to do a selling job on postal employees and Congress"[24] if he hoped to enact the reorganization. The reception was muted and even chillier among the senior members of the HPOC. Chairman Thaddeus Dulski (D-N.Y.) was widely acknowledged to be a weak chairman, yet he was not one to buck the unions. In January 1969, Dulski introduced his own 'reform' legislation—written largely by the legislative director of the UFPC— that retained congressional control over the Post Office, setting the stage for the dilution of support for "total reform" that POD officials had worried about.*

Dulski opened hearings on postal reform in April and was annoyed that Blount, as well as O'Brien and Kappel, refused to testify until the administration's bill (H.R. 11750) was sent up. His irritation was shared by the two senior committee Republicans, Congressman Corbett (R-Pa.) and Congressman Gross (R-Iowa), both of whom were furious over the patronage cutoff and opposed H.R. 11750. The second-ranking Democrat, Congressman Henderson (D-N.C.), also opposed the administration's bill, as did the third-ranking Democrat, Congressman Olsen (D-Mont.), a staunch union supporter who one member described "as the heavyweight who carried the ball for Dulski." The administration had to reach down to the fourth-ranking Democrat and Republican—Congressmen Udall (D-Ariz.) and Derwinski (R-Il.)—to find sponsors on the committee for the bill. It was against this background that hearings on the legislation resumed in June and July, with markup scheduled for September or October.

While lobbying of the HPOC and HPOC hearings continued, the administration expanded its marketing campaign on two fronts during June and July. The first front was the POD's assault on postal employees, and the second was the CCPR's effort to create editorial support for reorganization. The sell job mounted on employees by senior officials was, to some degree, supplemented

---

*Under Dulski's legislation, the POD remained a Cabinet-level agency but included a Postal Modernization Authority with authority to finance and manage capital improvements. Every four years, recommendations on postal rates would be made to the president by a Postal Finance Commission, with rates promulgated by the president unless otherwise vetoed by Congress. The PMG would remain a political appointee, and wages and fringe benefits would be set by Congress.

by ongoing national media coverage—during June and July, Blount appeared on *Meet the Press, Today,* two nationally disseminated radio broadcasts, and gave several dozen interviews to editorial boards, national reporters, and syndicated columnists—but the real P.R. priority during the summer was altering the attitudes of postal employees toward reorganization.* "There were 700,000 postal employees," Dunlap summarized, "and they were influential with the postal customers and people on the Hill. We wanted to get to them first because we thought they could be a force for change but we certainly didn't want them all stacked fervidly against us."

POD officials sought to soften attitudes of the employees primarily through two means; first, by getting favorable coverage in all of the publications of the employee organizations, and second, by flooding the employee conventions with speakers who would tout the virtues of postal reform. The POD efforts to get articles in employee newsletters and publications met with limited success—both the NALC and UFPC refused to run the POD-proposed articles or interview POD officials about the virtues of reorganization for the postal employee—but the administration found more success with its visits out to the union conventions. During June and July, senior POD officials delivered a whopping forty-six speeches to employee groups, focusing on the postal supervisors, but also including local NALC and rural carrier conventions. Every time an official gave a talk he was given a copy of a stock speech, a press release to issue, and asked to hold a local press conference afterwards. (A copy of the "stock speech to employees" is included in Appendix A. The gist of the speech was that employees would be better off under the reorganization, and were being subtly hoodwinked by alarmist national leaders in Washington.) "We essentially tried to act like good politicians," Henderson stated. "If two hundred and fifty people were at a meeting where the press was not guaranteed to be there, we didn't speak. But if twenty-five people were there and the presence of the press was guaranteed, off we went." The speeches to the employee associations were also cleverly concealed to skirt (barely) the lobbying provisions under which the POD operated. As the secretary for the National Association of Postal Supervisors later summed up: "It was incongruous to say the least to hear a POD speaker at the beginning of his speech state that he 'was not there to sell the postal reform bill because it would be illegal for him to do so'—and then proceed to do just that for the next forty minutes."[25]

In tandem with the speeches to employee conventions, the POD ran "educational" seminars in all fifteen regions for the postmasters and postal supervisors, the two employee groups expected to be most sympathetic to the reorganization legislation. Typically, a senior POD official was sent out to a region headquarters to meet with local postmasters in the morning and supervisors in the afternoon. The regional presentations are well summarized in a plan

---

* A confidential recap of a senior POD staff meeting on June 10 actually ranked the priority to be given to public relation activities. Reaching the unions / employee's ranked first, encouraging editorials in committee districts second, with a variety of subsidiary activities also listed.

prepared by Dunlap, approved at a meeting of POD top staff on June 19. The section from the employee marketing plan pertaining to the regional presentations stated:

Each Regional Manager should be asked to set up a meeting during the week of June 13 or June 30. He should invite the top 50 or so postmasters in his region, plus the region's Customer Relations Representative. He should be advised that the subject of the Postal Service Act will be discussed, along with other matters. At the meeting, a review of the highlights of the bill will be made. A press kit will be handed out. It will contain:
1. Copy of the Bill
2. Copies of PMG's employee testimony
3. Stock speeches
4. Highlights of Postal Service Act
5. President Nixon's message to Congress
6. Charts covering Bill
7. Employee Q & A [with the Assistant PMG for Personnel]

Next, a discussion should be held about what the Postmaster can do:
1. Call together his top staff and local union leaders for a briefing
2. Speeches to interested parties in his area
3. Use bulletin boards and loudspeakers for announcements
4. Suggest that local papers write editorials
5. Ask for any additional ideas they have
6. Postmasters will be asked how editorials that have been written in the various areas can be shown to employees

So that this presentation might not be misconstrued as "lobbying" for the reorganization legislation, headquarters staff were advised to end the meeting by "conclud[ing] with discussion of other subjects [than reorganization]."

The regional presentations seem to have had a modest impact upon the postmasters; the major postmaster group (NAPUS) endorsed the legislation and worked actively for its passage, apparently on the theory that the reorganization would clarify their managerial authority. But generally, the presentations to employees produced few converts and did little to dampen the opposition of the leading unions to H.R. 11750. However, the POD, with the aid of the CCPR, did produce dramatic results in its other area of concentration that summer: editorial support.

The CCPR Gets Rolling

The first weeks of the CCPR operation in June were taken up by fundraising and setting up decision-making procedures. The full-time staff of CCPR consisted of Executive Director Desautels—who was "O'Brien's man in Washington"—and Public Affairs Director James Marshall, who previously had worked for the Republican Governors Association. But the CCPR was run not by cochairmen O'Brien and Morton or by the full-time staff; instead it was largely directed by a handful of representatives from the mailer interests, who met weekly to discuss strategy and plan the week's activities. The "regulars" in the group, who were not paid for their time, included Norm Halliday, vice president of the Magazine Publisher's Association, Robert Saltzstein, counsel for the American Business Press (an association composed of business trade publications), Carroll Newton of the Madison Avenue ad agency Batten, Barton, Durstine & Osborne, with Desautels, Marshall, and Bill Dunlap of the POD rounding out the group. There was no union or citizen representation, and the group, in operation, was dominated by Saltzstein and Dunlap. Saltzstein, a crusty veteran of the postal rate wars, also served as the CCPR's counsel and oversaw its fund raising. Working with the assistance of the Business Counsel—composed of some of the nation's most powerful business executives—Saltzstein raised a staggering $130,000 within a month, and a quarter of a million dollars before the year had ended.[26] Under O'Brien and Morton's signature, Saltzstein also succeeded in drawing thirty-three "Distinguished Americans"—twenty-four of which were officers for Fortune 500 corporations—to serve as face-card "Directors" of CCPR. (Among the directors were the president or chairman of Bechtel, Westinghouse Electric, Cabot Corporation, Allied Chemical, General Foods, Whirlpool, B. F. Goodrich, Scott Paper, DuPont, Procter & Gamble, Sears, Roebuck, Union Carbide, and Mobil Oil.) A similar request to the nation's mayors and governors brought another impressive response, with fifty-eight mayors and fourteen governors signing up as directors within a month.

Once it had money and an impressive group of backers in tow, the CCPR moved quickly to draw national media attention, with O'Brien and Morton testifying before the HPOC on July 10 and speaking to the National Press Club afterwards. The appearance of the two ex-party chairmen drew editorial praise (for demonstrating that support for reorganization was "above politics") but the testimony was largely a one-shot deal. More consequential in drumming up media support were CCPR mailings that took place in late June. In a June 10 memo to Desautels (see Appendix B for a copy) Marshall laid out a preliminary plan for mobilizing public support for reorganization that included ads in the leading newspapers, a "press wingding" at the National Press Club, enlisting the aid of cartoonist Charles Schulz and his "Peanuts" characters, direct mail solicitation, a promotional film, billboard ads, a CCPR newsletter, a nationwide slogan contest, and bumper stickers. These efforts were to be "meshed with the usual efforts to gain publicity through press releases and personal contact with newsmen." By June 20, O'Brien and Saltzstein had approved most of Marshall's recommendations, and within a few days the CCPR began placing its first newspaper ads in papers like the *New York Times* and *Washington Post*. At the same time, press releases sent out May 24, May 27, and June 6 (that announced the formation of the bipartisan commission and its fundraising drive) continued to receive press play.

The CCPR efforts to build editorial support were supplemented by six editorial backgrounders given by Blount and other POD officials to papers outside Washington during June and July, and the POD's mailing of its own "press kits" to virtually all of the nation's newspapers. Blount, Henderson, Dunlap, and the POD Public Information staff threw themselves into selling H.R. 11750 with their typical zest and lack of inhibition—there are numerous references in POD memoranda, for example, to the production of "canned editorials" and "stock speeches"—and both the POD and CCPR efforts seem to have been appreciated by the nation's editors. In fact, excepting two small-town newspapers,[27] a number of editorial page editors enjoyed being spoon fed information, and, as the following selections indicate, encouraged the POD and CCPR to undertake more "selling":

> *Denver Post:* The Administration must undertake an education program to allay fears while selling the merits of the postal reform program. The program is worth a full-scale effort by the White House.
>
> *Boston Herald Traveler:* The best way for the ordinary citizen to insure that his letters in the future will be delivered promptly to their destination is to write a letter now [to their congressman] in support of reorganization of the [POD]. . . . To offset the redoubtable lobby of the postal employees, a bipartisan group called [CCPR] has been created to lobby Congress for enactment of the reorganization measure . . . but it is already clear to some observers in Washington that no amount of prestigious endorsements will suffice unless they are backed by overwhelming public support.
>
> *Milwaukee Journal:* A nationwide citizens committee . . . has been formed and is raising funds to promote the idea of mail service supplied by a self-supporting, nonpolitical government corporation. This is precisely the kind of campaign that is needed. Unless public opinion is stirred, the traditionalists in Congress will block basic changes.
>
> *Alabama (Montgomery) Journal:* [Blount] had best forget about running the [POD] and devote all of his energies to a monumental selling job. . . .He must draw the political issue in terms that the public will understand. . . . Blount had best take to the road, speaking to any and everyone who will listen to him, stating simply: "If you want better postal service, get onto your Congressman."[28]

Although POD and CCPR officials were encouraged by the media's warm reception of their efforts to sell reorganization, they remained concerned about two connections being exposed: the link between the CCPR and the POD, and the link between the CCPR and big business interests. On July 3, for example, Dunlap sent Ira Kappenstein (a key O'Brien aide in New York) suggestions for O'Brien's and Morton's July 10 HPOC testimony, including the warning that two questions likely to be asked at the hearing were, "Where's the Citizen's Committee getting its money?" and "What connection does the Citizen's Committee have with the Post Office?" A Marshall to Kappenstein memo on the O'Brien/Morton testimony advised that criticism might even be fiercer, with questions like, "Is the [CCPR] a front for magazine publishers and their organizations?" and "We noticed that you ran an ad in the *New York Times* a few weeks ago soliciting public support. Was this a dodge to cover up where you are really expecting your money to come from (namely, the big boys)?"

During the summer, the issue of the POD / CCPR link was directly taken on by the POD officials, who essentially took the tack of disavowing a connection between the two organizations. The POD's position on the issue was partly justified, for the CCPR did not—as had initially been anticipated—act as a "front" for the POD. The CCPR did not follow orders given by the Post Office, nor did POD officials seek to give them. There was, moreover, almost no coordination of congressional lobbying between Desautels and Paul Carlin, Blount's executive assistant for congressional liaison. On the other hand, Dunlap was a critical participant in the secret CCPR strategy sessions, and he reviewed all of the press releases and ads that the CCPR put out, besides assisting in setting up local corporate contacts. Moreover, he reported regularly to Henderson about the CCPR's activities, and periodically to Blount. On several occasions, Blount directly assisted the CCPR (by, for example, calling up the president of the National Association of Manufacturers and asking him to support the CCPR, or by smoothing the CCPR's fundraising road with the Business Council). Rather, however, than acknowledging that the public relations strategy of the two groups was carefully coordinated, the POD publicly downplayed any connection. On May 28, at a Q and A session following his speech to the National Press Club, Blount stated that he was "very glad to see the formation of CCPR . . . and I hope that they would be very active and I would expect that they would be. Of course it is their own effort."[29] On June 3, Congressman Gross (R-Iowa) asked Blount point-blank at a HPOC hearing, "Does the Post Office in any way finance or support [CCPR] and in view of the fact that you were president of the U.S. Chamber of Commerce, to what extent does the Chamber of Commerce finance this so-called committee?" Blount replied: "Mr. Congressman, I have no idea what the Chamber of Commerce does in regard to [CCPR], but the Post Office Department has no connection with it."[30]

Much as the POD officials sought to minimize their ties to the CCPR, the CCPR tried to minimize its corporate ties. O'Brien, Desautels, and others on the committee did seek to draw more grass roots support for the Committee—as evidenced by the clip-out coupons in CCPR ads that allowed citizens to join or contribute to CCPR—but the coupons had a poor return rate, and the CCPR failed altogether to entice representation on the committee from the postal employees. CCPR officials knew that they would soon be forced to disclose where their contributions came from when they filed lobbying reports with the Clerk of the House, but they were determined not to let their corporate connections cloud O'Brien's and Morton's July 10 appearance before the HPOC. The Q's and A's given to O'Brien and Morton that morning indicate that the two chairmen were to blur the funding issue and emphasize the "citizen" component of the CCPR's title. The suggested answers, for example, state: "Our membership funds are derived from a large variety of sources and in amounts ranging from one dollar on up. They come from private individuals and companies alike—in keeping with our objective of representing a broad spectrum of Americans. . . . I hope that I've already made it clear that the Citizen's Committee is just what the name implies. We're doing our darnedest to make ourselves as broad-based an organization as we possibly can." Fortunately for the CCPR, no committee member pressed the funding issue at the hearing, although Congressman Gross (R-Iowa) asked O'Brien to detail the contributions made to CCPR for the record (which was not, of course, printed until a number of months after-wards).[31] The *New York Times* may have waxed a bit euphoric when they likened the O'Brien / Morton testimony to ''a plea from the Red Cross or United Fund, the committee's proposal is beyond all partisanship,''[32] but no other paper raised doubts at the time about whether the CCPR was a ''bipartisan citizens'' group.

Throughout the summer, in short, POD and CCPR officials skated around any disclosures that might have been embarrassing and, at the same time, their marketing campaign picked up speed like a well-primed steamroller. As early as June 16, Dunlap reported to Herb Klein's deputy at the White House that the POD had counted 194 news stories, 232 editorials, 27 op-ed pieces, and 39 cartoons on the reorganization bill. By the end of the month, Blount informed the National Newspaper Association that 88 percent of the editorials favored H.R. 11750, 9 percent were undecided, and 3 percent were opposed.[33] Even more pleasing to POD officials were signs that the media support, in combination with relentless lobbying done by Blount and other POD officials, was beginning to stir members of the HPOC. On July 7, for example, Joseph Young, author of the ''Federal Spotlight'' column for the *Washington Star,* wrote:

> The Nixon administration's postal corporation plan is making impressive gains in Congress. With nearly a month of hearings remaining, 12 members of the 26-member House Post Office and Civil Service Committee now indicate support of the bill, while the other 14 are still counted as being opposed. . . . The support that the plan is getting on Capitol Hill is surprising almost everyone. For example, in the House committee there probably weren't three or four members favorable to the plan when it first was submitted.
>
> A committee formed to drum up support for the plan—Citizens for Postal Reform, headed by former Postmaster Gen. Lawrence O'Brien and former Sen. Thruston Morton—has done an excellent job getting mass media endorsement. The flood of favorable comment in most of the nation's newspapers and magazines and on television and radio stations has resulted in solid public opinion in favor of the plan and this reaction has reached the sensitive ears of members of Congress.[34]

Young's head count seems to have exaggerated considerably the shift to the Post Office's bill, but there is no doubt that the media coverage was taking its toll. The following exchange, which took place at a HPOC hearing on July 22, illustrates the sensitivity of committee members—in this case, Congressman Tiernan (D-R.I.) who opposed H.R. 11750 but was felt to be straddling the fence—to the onslaught of media coverage. Tiernan is talking to Patrick Nilan, the legislative director of the United Federation of Postal Clerks:

> Don't you feel there has been such a buildup by the Citizens Committee for Postal Reform and all the newspaper accounts and all the statements and speeches that have been made that no matter what we do, if we do achieve what we think is a reform of Postal Service but it doesn't include the word ''corporate,'' we are going to be criticized?
>
> MR. NILAN: I would have agreed with you a month or two back and

there's no question that the administration who proposed the Postal Corporation got a great deal of mileage out of it. You could hardly pick up a newspaper anywhere in Kansas, New England, or anyplace in the country without finding editorial or newspaper support for the program. However, we have noticed . . . at the present time the pendulum has started to swing back against the Corporation and for the H.R. 4 "Postal Reform." People are now asking what's the difference between postal reform and the so-called Corporation? What's going on?

They are, for the first time, being informed on it. Our union officers are getting invitations to appear on television in their local communities, and on radio stations, question and answer panels. The press which was formerly very unfriendly to us is now seeking releases and information concerning our position opposing the Postal Corporation and H.R. 11750. We believe it is opening up, and I don't believe it has to be a Corporation and certainly these extensive hearings have exposed the Postal Corporation weaknesses to the general public and press.

MR. TIERNAN: I congratulate you for that effort, but also I think that is due to the chairman and members of the committee expending a great deal of time for a full and open discussion of this proposal. You know, it was like a tidal wave coming on us, you almost couldn't stand up to it.[35]

As the anticorporation majority on the HPOC committee began to narrow during the summer, union leaders became increasingly concerned about the POD's marketing campaign. The union leaders were expert lobbyists and had sophisticated grass roots operations, but they were not accustomed to mobilizing or combatting a nationwide media campaign. Several key union officials freely acknowledged the frustration they felt in trying to respond to the POD-inspired propaganda. Francis Filbey, president of the UFPC, for example, pointed out to HPOC members that counterpunching the POD marketing was a bit like hitting a seamless medicine ball: "Think for a moment," Filbey stated, "of the subtle psychology applied here [by the Kappel Commission and the POD]. Postal problems are being attributed to the organization form; no blame has to be placed on postal officials or employees, or even the Congress. The structure is to blame, not the people who guide it or work on it."[36] The same grudging respect was voiced by NALC President Jim Rademacher, who told the HPOC: "I know that the barrage of newspaper editorials and comments has stirred up some superficial support for the corporation among the folks back home—people who want a better postal system and who have been brainwashed into thinking that the simple creation of a corporation will, by itself, perform miracles just through the waving of some magical wands. The average people who now favor the corporation concept, of course, don't know what is in store for them. . . . [Is the CCPR a legitimate vehicle?] Absolutely, in looking back I wished we had formed a committee for postal reform."[37]

Although union officials were concerned about the media campaign, they were also confident, as the HPOC hearings drew to an end in August, that they still had a lock on the committee. Polls taken by the AP and *New York Times* in mid-August showed thirteen members opposed to H.R. 11750, eleven for it, and two undecided.[38] In an August 29 memo to President Nixon, Blount was slightly more optimistic, estimating that the HPOC was "almost equally divided," with nine members supporting H.R. 11750, eight members opposed, and nine members on the fence. But the battle lines were only just being drawn for the critical fight that was looming after the Labor Day recess: that is, which bill the HPOC would markup, H.R. 4 (Congressman Dulski's bill), or H.R. 11750 (the administration's bill). Blount summarized the pending struggle in the memo to Nixon by writing, "while it will very definitely be an uphill fight, I believe that we do have a significant chance of getting an acceptable reform bill through in this session of Congress."

Targeting the HPOC Members (September 1969)

As the HPOC hearings ended, the POD made modest adjustments to its marketing campaign on two fronts. First, the POD set up several "media events" to draw national attention to the H.R. 11750 / H.R. 4 choice. And second, the CCPR set up a grass roots letter-writing and media campaign in the congressional districts of the ten HPOC members they considered potential converts to H.R. 11750.

During August 1969 the POD's organization plan continued to receive favorable attention in the national media,* but the coverage became both more sporadic and more pessimistic about the future of H.R. 11750. Nixon had agreed to meet on September 2 with Blount, O'Brien, and Morton to discuss the postal reform bill, and, at Dunlap and Henderson's prompting, Blount wrote the president on August 29, saying, "It would be most beneficial to our efforts if you would make a brief appearance at a press conference following our [September 2] meeting with Larry O'Brien and Thruston Morton. . . . This would underscore the importance of passage of our Postal Service Bill and the fact that you are strongly behind the bill. Your appearance would generate widespread publicity at this critical point in time, and counteract some news reports that we are losing some momentum."

Blount's request was reviewed and quickly approved by Herb Klein at the White House. Klein saw the press conference not only as an opportunity to draw attention to the administration's legislation, but also as a vehicle for momentarily containing criticism of the president. He elaborated:

> The major point of the O'Brien / Nixon / Morton meeting—which took place at the San Clemente residence—was not to have the President briefed on the progress of the Citizens Committee, but rather to use the captive reporters there that had to write a story by setting up this bipartisan press conference, with the networks and major papers in attendance. It was primarily a media event, which we had O'Brien and Morton flown out for. Whenever

---

*For example, the August 24, 1969, edition of the Sunday supplement *Parade* ran a 2-page story on "Our Crippled Giant: The Post Office." The article praised Nixon's legislation and urged citizens to write their congressmen and send donations to the CCPR to build support "for a complete overhaul of the Post Office."[39]

we were at the Western White House we were always afraid that it would look like the President wasn't working. So we had two objectives; first, showing that the work continued wherever the President was, and second, shaping the news agenda with something factual, instead of leaving the reporters who had been flown out here to their own devices. We knew they had to produce a story for their editors and would rather have them cover the press conference than dig around, say, for leaks.

Following a brief morning meeting on September 2.* Nixon, O'Brien, Blount and Morton trudged out before the television cameras to stress the need for postal reform. (Photos of the occasion, which may be something of a collector's item, show Nixon and O'Brien arm-in-arm, grinning at each other.) Nixon opened the press conference stating that "I am flanked this morning by a bipartisan group which is gathered together for what I consider to be one of the top priority measures of this Administration. . . . Within the next two weeks a major decision will be made [by the HPOC] with regard to the bill which will be reported to the House. This will be the first round in a very big battle as to whether we are to continue a system which has proved that it is inefficient [and] inadequate . . . or whether we are to have a new system that will give this country what it deserves—fast, efficient postal service."[41] Much as administration officials had hoped, Nixon's comments were covered on ABC News, CBS News, and the front page of the *New York Times.* "We had all the wagons circled that day," Dunlap stated with some pride, "we hit all our target audiences plus we had this bipartisan show of unity from the current and former postmaster general. It had to help."

Much the same kind of POD inspired "media event" took place a week later during the meeting of the National Postal Forum, a group of 2,400 business and government leaders who met annually to discuss postal problems of concern to the business community. The forum's nominal topic was the merits and demerits of postal reorganization, but it soon became clear that the POD had set up the forum to provide another impressive show of support for H.R. 11750, this time from the business community. Besides O'Brien and Morton heralding the need for reform, the president of Sears, the president of the Chamber of Commerce, and the secretary of commerce all gave speeches touting the virtues of H.R. 11750. "We closed the convention," Dunlap recalled with a chuckle, "by dramatizing the difference between partial and total reform, literally having everyone stand up and chant 'H.R. 11750, H.R. 11750'!" This cheerleading effort did not sit well with Chairman Dulski (D-N.Y.) who took to the House floor on September 9 to denounce the "gigantic and well-heeled effort to jam one particular postal reform proposal down the throats of Congress and the American people . . . if the corporation approach is such a good approach, why are they pushing the panic button in this all-out lobbying effort?"[42]

---

*At the meeting with O'Brien, Blount and Morton, Nixon was shown CCPR publications and apparently given a confidential report summarizing the local lobbying operations of CCPR (see Appendix C for a copy). There was some discussion of "personal contact"[40] to be made on postal reform but the meeting was apparently more informational in nature than a strategy session.

The "Grass Roots" Lobby

The "all-out lobbying effort" Dulski referred to included not only the enormous pressure being applied directly by POD lobbyists Blount, Carlin, and Deputy Postmaster Ted Klassen, it also included a new public relations element; a grass roots media and letter-writing campaign in the districts of ten "fence-straddling" members of the HPOC. The need for local chapters of the CCPR had been broadly anticipated in Dunlap's marketing plan, but the CCPR brought in a specialist, Jerry Bruno, to set up the "grass roots" operations and flesh out the activities the local chapters would perform. Bruno, a friend of O'Brien's, was a minor political legend in his own right, having gone from a factory worker with a ninth-grade education to become an advance man for John and Robert Kennedy. Columnist Jeff Greenfield once wrote admiringly that Bruno was "built like a fire hydrant; he has the tact of a pulling guard. . . . But Jerry Bruno knows more about the way politics works in America than a dozen political science professors and a hundred pollsters. He knows how it works because he has seen it firsthand. . . . He knows not only how to turn out a crowd, but what moves them, intrigues them, attracts them."[43]

When Bruno joined the CCPR in early August, Jim Marshall, the CCPR's public affairs director, had already drafted a nine-step plan outlining the activities the "contact man" would undertake. The gist of the plan—see Appendix D for a full copy—was that Bruno would first contact the local Chamber of Commerce and several citizens groups, such as the League of Women Voters, the Kiwanis and Rotary Clubs, get them together and from them form a local Citizens' Committee for Postal Reform. Next he would trumpet the existence of this group to the local radio, television stations, daily, and weekly newspapers, with an eye toward drawing both editorial support and news coverage. The local citizens' group, working through the umbrella organizations, would then also attempt to create letter-writing and phone call campaigns to their congressmen in support of H.R. 11750. Supplementary activities included pressuring prominent local businessmen to write their congressmen and placing ads in local newspapers. The "contact man" would have to work rapidly, because the CCPR had targeted ten districts for local CCPR chapters, and Bruno had less than six weeks in which to get the local chapters operable before the HPOC markup.

In practice Bruno pursued many of the activities outlined by Marshall, but he adopted his own style for doing so. "Marshall and a few of the Republicans on the committee," Bruno stated, "wanted me to go out to the districts with press kits, a packaged plan, and I just wouldn't do that; the local groups resented your coming in like that, but if you let them take the initiative, and dropped some ideas about what they could do, then it become 'their' idea." The other distinction between what Marshall had outlined and what Bruno did, was that Bruno relied far more heavily on business support outside the chamber—particularly from Sears and General Electric*—than had been anticipated to run the local campaigns. Bruno described his mode of operation as follows:

---

*The chairman of G.E., Fred Borch, was also chairman of the Business Council, through which the CCPR had raised most of its money. Borch was a vice-chairman of the CCPR.

We were up against these tremendous grass roots organizations that the postal unions had; they could get 400 to 500 phone calls to a congressman in a day. What we had to do was generate some competing grassroots support, because the congressmen wanted to know that they weren't going to lose a lot of votes in the next election if they supported reform. Ads were fine, support from business was fine, but, from their perspective, the ads didn't amount to votes. . . . The way I worked was that I'd go into a district with a contact from the chamber, or more typically from one of the big corporations; Sears and G.E. were particularly active. At G.E. I'd work, say, with the community relations director and with Sears I'd work with the district manager, who might have four or five stores in his area and was very politically and community oriented. We would meet in their boardrooms to map out strategy on how to generate public support through newspapers and civic groups. The corporate representative would then devote full-time to this; they'd line up and speak to the civic groups, give us a list of prominent citizens and supply not only money but manpower. With my Democratic contacts, I would get housewives and other people involved. It was a pretty good coalition, and once we had that formed, we would go get a public figure, a statesman-type to become chairman of the local committee. We'd publicize that and then start phone call and letter writing campaigns to the congressmen in support of [H.R. 11750.]

Our phone calls and letter campaigns were pretty successful; in a number of districts we got hundreds of letters written to congressmen. And we had tremendous success with the newspapers; they'd publish anything we want.

A September 5, 1969, summary of Bruno's activities (see Appendix E for a copy) gives a good impression of the range of efforts undertaken through the CCPR at the local level. A typical example of how Bruno worked was the Syracuse district of Congressman Hanley (D-N.Y.). On August 25 a senior POD official flew up to Syracuse to give a speech that had been requested by G.E.'s manager for Communication and Community Relations, J. Edward Kaish, and set up by Bill Dunlap. The POD speaker touted the virtues of H.R. 11750, and in an August 27 letter to Dunlap, Kaish reported that "we got good coverage over local radio and TV stations, plus [coverage] from the afternoon *Herald-Journal,* the larger of our two daily newspapers." The coverage in the *Herald-Journal,* which "urg[ed] all residents to write Congressman James M. Hanley in support of this bipartisan effort"[44] was not altogether surprising, since the publisher of the *Herald-Journal* had also agreed to be chairman of the just-formed local CCPR. The local chapter had forty prominent members, including the mayor of Syracuse, the president of the Syracuse Federation of Women's Clubs, as well as the backing of the Chamber of Commerce, the Jr. Chamber of Commerce, and Sears. By September 5 they had generated five to six hundred letters to Hanley in support of H.R. 11750, and, at the same time, CCPR headquarters paid for two ads (at an expense of about $1,300) in the *Herald-Journal* and *Post-Standard.*

Once a local committee had been set up, Bruno would maintain phone contact with the corporate "contact man" in the district, making periodic adjustments. For example, on September 29, Bruno reported to Desautels:

From visiting and talking to supporters for postal reform in the congressional district level, I find that there is much confusion in defining postal reform. An example—Congressman Hanley from Syracuse says he is for postal reform, but doesn't describe which reform. He indicates strong support for reform within the present structure but not the corporate plan.

Hanley gets away with this in defending his position to those for reform (the corporation plan). We have not dramatized or got our message across to the people the difference between reform (the Dulski style) and total reform (the Mo Udall bill or the corporation plan). I recommend the following:

A. You get together individually from time to time newspaper reporters that are based in Washington, reporting for papers in key Congressional Districts and feed them stories citing the differences between the two. Example—Syracuse *Herald* news story that I gave you.

B. That I be supplied with favorable editorials so they could be mailed out to our key people in the congressional districts to give them ammunition for supporting our position.

Desautels concurred with Bruno's suggestions and by October 2, CCPR had put out a press release which stated that O'Brien and Morton "objected to the use of the term [total reform] at all when it doesn't refer to the setting up of a postal corporation that would totally divorce the nation's postal service from partisan congressional politics." "Only one bill now pending," the release went on to add, "the bipartisan-sponsored H.R. 11750, provides for 'reform in its truest sense.' 'All the other bills,' [O'Brien and Morton] said, 'have latched on to the name "reform," but they don't really do the job.' "[45] Despite pressure of this sort, Hanley voted not to mark-up H.R. 11750 on October 8. (He later voted with the administration.) Within a few days of Hanley's negative vote, the Syracuse *Herald-American* ran another story (under the head "Postal reform group raps Hanley's stand") that quoted Jim Marshall's dismay at Hanley's support for a "piecemeal approach"[46] to reform.

The Unions Strike Back

By mid-September the lobbying mounted by POD officials, and the POD / CCPR P.R. campaign, were beginning to show impressive results. On September 15, the *New York Times* editorialized that "The Administration's proposal to turn the postal service over to a public corporation, thought to have fallen on deaf Congressional ears, is now conceded to have a good chance of getting through the [HPOC]."[47] On September 22, House Speaker Carl Albert (D-Okla.) stated that while Nixon's other high-priority legislation did not stand much of a chance, postal reform might well be enacted before the end of the year.[48] The following day the *Washington Post* urged a vote for H.R. 11750, noting that Blount had been "lobbying diligently. . . . And there has been an impressive, high-level citizen's committee-style effort brought to bear too."[49]

With evidence of a shift mounting, several postal unions finally decided to take on the POD and CCPR public relations campaign head-on. In mid-September, the *Postal Supervisor* (a publication of NAPS, the National Association of

Postal Supervisors) criticized the POD marketing effort, seeking to undercut the POD's high-minded position that it was rising "above politics" in calling for self-reorganization. Citing the flooding of employee conventions with POD speakers, the regional "education" efforts, and the chanting of "H.R. 11750" at the National Postal forum, NAPS' Secretary pointed out, "In a year when the [POD] has ordered an end to politics in the postal service, the Department itself has engaged in one of the best organized and most expensive lobbying efforts in recent history. In my ten years on the Washington scene, I have not witnessed a bigger campaign for any piece of legislation. . . . For people who are proud of their lack of past experience in politics . . . this team has shown Washington a lobbying campaign which will long be remembered."[50]

More consequential than this attack on the POD marketing effort, was the first of a series of frontal assaults mounted on the CCPR by the powerful United Federation of Postal Clerks. Pat Nilan, legislative director of the UFPC, was both annoyed and concerned by the CCPR's campaign, explaining:

> After the Chicago breakdown, there had been a lot of criticism of [POD] management, and my view was that the [CCPR] and the push for a postal corporation was a device to get [POD management] off the hot seat. Most of us, myself in particular, had been lifelong Democrats and I couldn't believe that the Administration would set this up and call it "bipartisan." The opposition, you ought to say, was "bipartisan" and the [CCPR] certainly had no identifiable union or any representation from the 750,000 workers their plan would affect. They gave us no opportunity to participate, and we, and a lot of thoughtful people, were concerned that this untried scheme which they were so gung-ho over was not in the best interest of the workers or the postal service itself.
>
> This gang was so hell bent to get off the hot seat that we felt we had to slow the momentum down to the point where Congress and the public looked at this in more detail and exposed some of the problems to public view. We weren't big media hypes and didn't mount a massive advertising campaign, but we did have our people develop local letter writing campaigns with materials explaining our view, plus we went after every "officer" of the [CCPR]. We got the mailing address for all of them [24 Governors, 68 Mayors, 6 former Cabinet members, and 53 "distinguished" Americans] and wrote them saying that they were not being fair and open-minded.

By the end of September, two governors and six mayors had written the CCPR or Nilan asking to have their names removed from the CCPR roster. On September 26, without revealing the existence of the letters, the UFPC issued a press release in which Nilan was quoted as saying that the CCPR had "hoodwinked" "scores of mayors and governors" by "fail [ing] to specify in their original letter of invitation that the committee was being created to lobby for a postal corporation as such. Many either didn't know this was a big business gimmick to support the corporation or thought they were endorsing the kind of postal reform within the existing departmental framework."[51]

At this critical point in the HPOC deliberations, CCPR officials felt the

UFPC attack had to be immediately rebutted and on September 21 they issued their own press release (inserted in the *Congressional Record* on October 3). "We decided to match them with righteous indignation," Jim Marshall recalled with a laugh. The CCPR press release quoted Marshall as saying:

> This fallacious and irresponsible accusation against the integrity of two of the most dedicated and respected public servants in the nation will not be tolerated. . . . Nothing less than an unqualified public apology can amend this atrocious demonstration of recklessness. . . . When you sit down and think about this preposterous charge, you realize that it's actually calling many of our most distinguished public figures and vitally concerned private citizens uninformed on a matter that's been well-publicized in the papers, on TV, and on radio for well over a year.[52]

It is not clear whether the UFPC's challenge to the CCPR's legitimacy affected HPOC members—Nilan believes it helped stem the procorporation tide—but it is clear that the local lobbying operations of the UFPC and NALC did have a tremendous impact. As Jim Rademacher, president of the NALC, recalled:

> The POD launched a tremendous lobbying campaign on this, with their ultimate weapon being the offer to build post offices in the congressional districts of [HPOC] members; the record will show that they made offers to a number of congressmen who were on the fence. We had no counter to that so we had to use the power of the pen. The membership and ladies auxiliary—which is strongly organized in about 200 cities—got actively involved writing letters and campaigning against reorganization in the same way we campaigned for congressmen. We did do some media; we had various officials do local radio and television shows, but it was difficult because we couldn't just oppose something that the American people were being told was going to improve postal service. So what we did was project the horrors of what might occur from reorganization; serious cutbacks in service, higher postage rates, and chaos during the transition. We had some success, but in a number of districts it boiled down to whether the congressman was more concerned about getting the contract for the post office or keeping the votes of the letter carriers and ladies auxiliary.

Amidst this intense pressure, the HPOC finally voted its preferences on October 8. By a 13–13 vote, the committee (voting not along party lines), rejected a motion by Udall to substitute H.R. 11750 for H.R. 4, ending the POD's hopes for steamrolling the HPOC. Just how much damage the administration suffered from the vote was a subject of debate; union officials proclaimed it the death knell of the independent corporation concept, the national media and White House officials tended to view it as a serious but not necessarily irreparable setback, and POD officials insisted it was an unanticipated display of impressive support from a committee which was now within a whisker of approving postal reorganization. When asked why the administration could not muster one more vote, most POD officials and HPOC members gave a two-word answer: the unions. Blount's view was that the union opposition was important, but that more subtle, institutionalized ties were also dragging down reform. "What we were doing,"

Blount stated, "was not only taking turf away from Congress, we were also challenging the orientation of committee members who had been intimately connected with the postal service for years, and in Washington that is a very difficult thing to dislodge."

Going Toe to Toe with the Postal Unions

During October and November 1969, the administration and unions squared off over postal reform, with neither making much headway despite the public relations battering each sought to deliver to the other. During that time, the CCPR and unions adopted some new marketing tactics, and a critical element in the reorganization fight emerged that neither the Administration nor the unions seemed able to control: the postal pay bill.

The dispute over the postal pay bill reverted back to February 1969 when President Nixon proposed that postal workers get a 3 percent salary hike, a figure he subsequently raised to 4.1 percent. Union officials, who were looking for a raise in the 10–15 percent range, labelled Nixon's offer an "insult," and their annoyance was only increased when General Schedule employees received a previously mandated "comparability" raise of 9.8 percent in July, while postal employees received a 4.7 percent increase. Faced with widespread dissatisfaction, particularly among increasingly militant members in urban areas, union leaders sought and got Congressman Udall (D-Ariz.) chairman of the HPOC Subcommittee on Compensation, to sponsor a bill that compressed the time it took to reach the top postal salary grade from 21 to 8 years and simultaneously gave postal workers an 11 percent raise, 5.4 percent effective in October 1969, with the remainder effective in April 1970. That bill, H.R. 13000, passed the House overwhelmingly on October 14 (a week after the HPOC vote) despite the threat of veto from President Nixon, who alleged the bill was inflationary. In a letter to House Minority Leader Gerald Ford (R-Mich.), read during the floor debate, Nixon also argued that while salary increases and "improvements in the condition of the postal worker are long overdue . . . they should be secured through . . . the legislation establishing a government-owned postal corporation."[53]

Nixon's plan, initially suggested by Blount, to tie the postal pay raise to passage of the reorganization legislation was not a surprise, coming after the HPOC vote, but it was also not a casual tactical bluff. "Nixon," John Ehrlichman, the president's domestic policy adviser commented, "felt strongly about postal reform and he felt strongly that the pay raise issue gave him leverage. He knew that sooner or later he would have to give in to the unions and he wanted reorganization in return."* It was conceivable that the postal unions might get

---

*Nixon evidenced his commitment to postal reorganization when he sent a message to Congress on October 11, 1969, outlining his legislative priorities for the remainder of the session, one of which was postal reform. The message stated, "I am aware of the setback which postal reform sustained in the [HPOC] on October 8. That action must be reversed. I shall persist . . . to press for this urgently needed reform."[54]

Nixon's veto overridden, but the fact that the Senate pay bill differed from the House's* meant that that could not be accomplished quickly or easily—at minimum a conference would have to be held before and after the bill was vetoed— and angry union members were pressuring their leaders to come up with the raise immediately. There was, in short, something of a standoff during October and November, with the administration holding captive the pay bill, while the unions held the reorganization legislation captive.

The administration's determination to make the unions blink first was tied in once again to a deliberate media strategy, with the CCPR now carrying the weight of the public relations activity. Part of the CCPR's media / P.R. activities following the HPOC vote were merely more of what had gone before. Asked, for example, what the local CCPR chapter did differently after the HPOC vote, Jerry Bruno replied: "More letters, more calls, and more stories." But while the CCPR continued its efforts to draw attention to postal reform, it found the national media and local media near the saturation point, particularly on the heels of the apparent rejection of H.R. 11750 by the HPOC, and with the absence of any impending vote that would revive the issue.

Accordingly, as the media became less attentive to the postal reform issue, the CCPR supplemented its ongoing media activities with a heavier emphasis on direct mail, advertising, and appeals to the business trade press. There was nothing subtle about the appeal to trade publishers, which was coordinated mostly through Bob Saltzstein and the American Business Press (of which Saltzstein was counsel). For example, the following excerpt of an October 31, 1969, memo to Desautels summarizes a meeting that Jim Mulholland, Jr., the president of Hayden Publishing Company (an ABP member) held with the publishers of various Hayden publications:

[Mr. Mulholland] requested action in the following areas:
    1. Editorials in all Hayden publications.
    2. Individuals letters to Congressmen.
    3. Use of promotion lists to alert business leaders to register their interest in reform to Congress.
    4. House [publication] ads.
Mr. Mulholland told the meeting he would like to see editorials on this subject in November or December issues (mid-December publication date) of each magazine. Said he was not insisting—presenting for editors' consideration. In his discussions with Claude Desautels of Citizens Committee for Postal Reform, Mr. Mulholland had told him that he could not ask his editors to editorialize on the subject more than once or twice between now and March. Action would be appropriate, according to Mr. Desautels, when the next postal reform bills proposed come before
    (a) the House Committee,

---

*The Senate bill, sponsored by the chairman and ranking Republican on the Senate Post Office and Civil Service Committee, provided for a two-step salary increase of 7% rather than 11%. Moreover, it provided this raise for all federal employees, not just postal workers, and so, unlike H.R. 13000 was supported by the American Federation of Government Employees.

(b) the Senate Committee,
(c) before the House,
(d) before the Senate,
(e) before the Senate and House Committee when they iron out the differences between the postal bills the House and Senate approved.
One publisher noted that all articles should include the names and addresses of the congressmen to whom readers should write and that the call to action must be clear and easy to follow.

The hard sell given to editors of business trade publications was supplemented, for the first time, by heavy use of direct mail and advertisements. A November 14 memo from Dunlap to Henderson indicates that the CCPR sent a "Dear Friend" letter under O'Brien and Morton's signatures immediately following the HPOC vote to "interested people in several key Committee districts" as well as a direct mail piece from local CCPR chairmen, requesting citizens to write their congressmen in support of H.R. 11750. The POD assisted the direct mail campaign in Congress by sending over form letters to Jeb Magruder at the White House (an assistant to Klein), prioritized the HPOC congressmen the form letters were to be sent to, and then had Magruder funnel them out to local Republican and civic organizations to produce a show of "citizen support." (See Appendix F for a copy of the Dunlap memo to Magruder and the POD and CCPR letters.)

In his November 14 memo to Henderson, Dunlap also reported that a brochure entitled "Postal Reform: What Does It Mean to You?" (set up around a question-and-answer format) was sent to "8,000 newspapers / magazines and to 5,000 interested people across the country." (The brochure, like the O'Brien / Morton letter, urged the recipients to write their congressman in support of H.R. 11750.) Similarly, Dunlap reported in a December 11 memo to Henderson that a four-page CCPR brochure "Post Office in Crisis"—which explicitly criticized H.R. 4 and asked for calls, telegrams, and letters in support of H.R. 11750— had "been sent to 9,000 newspapers (including weeklies), 5,000 mail users, magazines identified with the Magazine Publishers Association and American Business Press, and some 4,000 prominent people in congressional districts." At the same time that Congress and the media were targeted with direct mail, the CCPR sent out ads prepared by Batten, Barton, Durstine & Osborne to members of the Magazine Publishers Association (which consisted of 400 magazines, including the national news magazines) and ABP. The ads (see Appendix G for an example) were especially designed to appeal to businessmen, and employed the CCPR's favorite horror story—the Chicago post office breakdown—to prey on fears that a breakdown in mail service might soon occur without "total reform."

This renewed pitch to business and the self-interest of publishers did not go unnoticed at the UFPC, which directly, and via congressional surrogates, launched another attack on the CCPR. Unlike the first round of UFPC criticism—which focused on whether the CCPR had hoodwinked mayors and governors into being CCPR backers—the UFPC criticism following the October 8 HPOC vote concentrated on illuminating the CCPR's strong ties to big business. On October 9, Congressman Olsen (D-Mont.) inserted a list of CCPR's contributors submitted to the HPOC in the *Congressional Record*. The list provided indisputable evidence of CCPR's reliance on donations from big business; of the $261,000 raised by the committee, $202,000 came in pledges of $5,000 or more (overwhelmingly from Fortune 500 corporations), $43,500 came in donations of between $1,000 and $5,000 (given by corporations and publishers), and $15,000 were contributions from individuals (dominated apparently by several large donations from the "distinguished Americans" affiliated with the CCPR). Olson insinuated on the House floor that the list demonstrated a covert plot had been hatched between the CCPR and big business, stating, "The extent of their lobbying efforts shows that they pulled out all stops. What we still do not know . . . is exactly what they told these high-powered executives to get them to climb on the national bandwagon in behalf of turning the postal system into a public corporation." He added that the CCPR's funding breakdown also demonstrated the CCPR was hardly a "citizens committee," commenting sarcastically, "my check of the list shows 77 persons gave a dollar each, one gave 50 cents [and] another 25 cents."[55]

A week later the UFPC followed up on Olson's remarks by issuing a press release which reproduced the list of CCPR donors and attacked more emphatically the alleged "citizen" representation on the CCPR. The release quoted Nilan as saying that fifty large corporations were subsidizing

> a scare campaign to undermine public confidence in the U.S. postal service. These corporate "angels" have helped the so-called Citizens Committee for Postal Reform amass assets of over $260,000. The object of this fat-cat committee is to persuade Congress and the people that a postal corporation is the one and only answer to postal reform. . . . Large corporate interests have a legitimate interest in postal reform but too many have been scared into supporting the Committee by horrendous forecasts of doom and gloom from the [CCPR] co-chairmen. . . . One has only to read newspaper editorials around the country to see how well they have succeeded in undermining public confidence in the postal service—which still somehow manages to deliver 200 million pieces of mail per day. Luckily, most Congressmen know the score and do not frighten easily.[56]

Following this stepped-up attack, CCPR officials were contacted by *Congressional Quarterly* for a story on CCPR financing, and on October 22, Dunlap notified Blount's executive assistant that "the Postal Clerks and the Letter Carriers have made a concerted effort against members of the [CCPR] and have planted stories in the press. . . . The Citizens Committee is concerned about this [and] are attempting to take the offense in this matter." Just how to take the offense presented something of a dilemma. As Bill Dunlap acknowledged, "we knew we were running the risk of being labelled as a big business front, but what was the alternative? We started with a very low public awareness, so you had to activate groups outside the postal establishment to help." "The average Joe," Jim Marshall added, "was for reorganization because it was 'reform.' And we did try to generate grass roots support through the coupons in our ads; we asked people to join CCPR or send a donation. But the response rate was poor—we couldn't have run our office for two days on the money the ads brought in—so there was no getting around the fact that we weren't a true citizens' movement.''

CCPR officials finally settled on two responses to the "fat-cat committee" accusation. The first was to complain that the criticism was unrealistic. "It just isn't possible," Marshall told *Congressional Quarterly*, "to finance a citizens' movement on the basis of $1 contributions. We have tried to stay within the bounds of the law by reporting everything, which immediately opens us to criticism on money. I think it's damn unfair that when you're staying within the spirit of the law that people rap you on this.''[57] The second response was to point out who it was that was calling the kettle black. In an October 23 speech to the annual conference of the American Business Press. Thruston Morton lashed out, for the first time, at the postal unions, stating:

> The main power, and it is a mighty power . . . against true postal reform is the power of the postal union officers. . . . The postal union leaders launched a campaign against the Citizens' Committee as part of their attack on postal reform. They have called attention to our relatively small contributions totalling $242,835.00 as of this date. What they do not publicize is that the annual dues check-off deducted by the Post Office Department from the pay of postal workers is close to an astounding $15,000,000 each year. The National Association of Letter Carriers and the United Federation of Postal Clerks between them on the lobbying reports they filed with Congress, reported receipts for the year of 1968 of $2,152,570.01 for the Letter Carriers, and $2,488,547.23 for the Clerks, or a total of $4,641,117.24 for these two unions alone! This is the kind of money which is available to fight true postal reform. Compared to those funds contributions to the Citizens' Committee are meager indeed.[58]

To ensure that Morton's comparison was driven home, it was made the subject of a CCPR press release, included in the CCPR's *The Postal Reformer* (the CCPR's monthly newsletter, sent to every congressman and numerous newspapers) and mentioned on the House floor by Congressman Cunningham (R-Nebr.). This last rejoinder by the CCPR helped spark another effort by congressional opponents of reform to throw the ball back in the CCPR's lap— Congressman Gross (R-Iowa) warned on the House floor on October 28 that members "could expect a massive, well-financed [CCPR] propaganda campaign" during the next few weeks, and he urged them to reject "the vicious propaganda campaign being waged by the so-called citizens' committee"[59]—but generally the CCPR's fingering of the unions seems to have defused the "fat-cat committee" charges, or at least reduced the level of frequency with which the UFPC and its congressional surrogates leveled them. What the CCPR did not deter was a decision by the other major union—the NALC—to throw its financial muscle behind a media campaign that would seek to beat the Post Office and CCPR at their own game.

Fighting Fire with Fire

Up until November 1969, NALC leaders, like UFPC officials, had periodically sought to counter the POD / CCPR media campaign by asserting that both organizations were churning out information to "brainwash" the public. Those charges continued to be voiced in November at hearings held by the Senate Post Office and Civil Service Committee,* and were nourished by Blount's warning—quoted in *Life*'s November 28 cover story, "The U.S. Mail Mess"—that he would "go over the head of Congress, to the American people" to push reorganization through the Congress.** But more notable than the NALC's ongoing picking at the POD / CCPR media campaign, was the institution of the NALC's own marketing program in November 1969.

The objective of the NALC media campaign was to break both the link in Congress between reform and pay, and to pressure the president into withholding a veto of the pay bill. And while NALC leaders had never mounted a nationwide media campaign, they demonstrated an impressive ability to draw media coverage in a short period of time. The NALC plan—designed chiefly by its outspoken president, Jim Rademacher—had three steps, outlined by Rademacher at a November 20 NALC press luncheon. First, the NALC would saturate the nation's newspapers and radio stations with ads and radio spots. The ads presented a letter carrier reaching out to the public with a letter stamped "S.O.S." (for "Save Our Service"), claimed a postal corporation was unnecessary, and included a coupon for readers to mail in support of H.R. 13000 to the president. On November 24 the ad appeared in 400 newspapers, including full page spreads in the *New York Times, Washington Post, Wall Street Journal, Washington Evening Star,* and *Christian Science Monitor*. The radio spots, including a fifty-second message done by comedian Jerry Lewis (used by 300 stations), similarly urged citizens to write the president in support of the postal pay raise bill.[62]

---

*On November 25, 1969, NALC President Rademacher testified:

Ever since the controversy surrounding the proposal to abolish the Post Office Department and erect a Postal Corporation in its place arose, the public and the Congress have been deluged by a tidal wave of propaganda in favor of the proposal. Committees of citizens arose in several localities—all financed heavily by corporations in the private sector—and the mimeograph machines have been smoking as they have turned out tons of pro-Corporation propaganda. We have, in short, seen one of the smoothest and most massive attempts at public brainwashing since the German glory days of Joseph Paul Goebbels. The wave of propaganda has been so skillfully—and, one is tempted to say, cynically—handled that certain dangerous fallacies disseminated by the Corporation flacks have been repeated so often, so loudly, and insistently, that a large segment of the populace has grown to accept them as gospel truth.[60]

**The Senate committee chairman, Gale McGee (D-Wy.) was annoyed by the *Life* article, particularly since *Life* enjoyed subsidized mail rates, and within a few days of the article's appearance announced at a committee hearing: "If there is any thought anywhere of the Postmaster General or of anyone serving him, of going over the heads of this committee that was elected to do this job, I know of no quicker way to kill . . . postal reform."[61] POD officials did not appear too traumatized by this threat. A December 11 memo to Henderson from Dunlap notes that through the CCPR, "Sears representatives in 30 large cities are calling their local media, bringing the *Life* article to their attention, and asking the media to do stories on the status of the postal system."

The second part of the campaign called for swamping the White House with a true display of "citizen support" for a pay raise. Some six million cards were distributed by letter carriers to their postal patrons during the final week of November with requests that they be sent to President Nixon. Essentially, the letter carriers retraced their routes, dropping off the preaddressed cards (with blanks for the names and addresses to be filled in by the sender), and asked for their patrons' support. These stamped cards were also distributed by the NALC's Ladies Auxiliary in department stores, supermarkets, and attached to the paychecks of workers in several industries. The third and final step of the plan was contingent upon Nixon vetoing H.R. 13000; if that occurred, the NALC had plans to bring 15,000 letter carriers to Washington for a march of "poor postal people" on Capitol Hill, and Rademacher had been authorized to spend up to $1 million to procure television time to respond to a presidential message explaining a veto.[63] Underlying all of this pressure were threats, from the leaders of various postal unions that, against their wishes, postal workers might slow down mail over Christmas if denied their pay raise, or conceivably, go out on strike—which had never occurred before, was illegal, and could deal a crippling blow to the nation's economy. Events quickly demonstrated that the NALC was not talking up its sleeve, when the White House was inundated with three million coupons supporting the pay bill within a week.

In part, POD officials viewed the NALC's marketing blitz as a vindication of their own efforts. As Bill Dunlap stated:

> We felt that the union attacks on the [CCPR] and the advertising campaign by the [NALC] evidenced the fact that we were having some impact on the Hill. That was the first signal—the anguished cry of a wounded predator—when they started attacking like that. We knew we were on the right track then. We felt we had won the high ground: reform is best for the country, the employees, and the mailer; the unions' themes were all self-interest, trying to help themselves. We felt we had them painted into the corner.

It was in keeping with these views that Dunlap recommended to Henderson, in a November 25 memo, that the POD and CCPR refrain from making a major rejoinder to the union ad campaign:

> I do not feel we, or the Citizens' Committee, should take a position where we aggressively oppose the pay bill. This is because of the following:
> (1) It could give the impression we are against bettering the lot of our 750,000 employees. (2) The unions could use it against us, saying that this is the type of negative approach that the employees would get if the Post Office is connected to a government corporation. (3) It is a battle we probably could not win. We have neither the people nor the financial resources to cope with the unions on this issue.
> I feel that the unions' ad can be exploited if we take the approach that it is because of the conditions the ad mentions that we submitted our reform

proposal. This line of thinking is outlined in the attached ad which the Citizens' Committee wants to run.*

Despite Dunlap's reservations, Blount seems to have felt the massive influx of mail into the White House required a rejoinder, and on December 2 Dunlap sent a memo to Blount's A.A. attaching copy for use in response to the union mailings. Dunlap noted that the POD had 300,000 letters on hand, and that they could use postal cards (estimated cost $81,250), multilith letters ($180,000), or computer letters ($250,000) to respond to the mailings. Another $60,000 would be added to these costs "if the President responds," because franking privileges could not be used.

The POD plan, however, never came to fruition because the White House unexpectedly intervened. On December 4, Rademacher received a call from White House Special Counsel Charles Colson, who had just been appointed the previous month but was already earning a reputation as an ambitious, persuasive, and sometimes ruthless acolyte. "We got your message," Colson told Rademacher. "Why don't you come over to the White House to see if we can work out some kind of compromise."

The White House Steps In

Colson's intervention, like much of what he did in the White House, was a subject of controversy. His participation in negotiations was not well received at the POD, where Blount and his aides had struggled for months to get the reorganization bill through on their own. "I think that we were going to get that extra vote in the House Committee and everybody knew it," Blount stated. "The unions knew it and they were scrambling for position . . . the 13–13 vote was the first time the Congress hadn't said yes to them, and there was a lot of pressure on the union leaders, who were up for reelection in 1970, to get the pay increase. Hell, Rademacher sucked Colson in, he made him think he was getting some real concessions."

Some observers, however, felt the POD might not secure the extra committee vote, and that Blount's brinkmanship ran the risk of fueling a nationwide postal strike, or, alternatively, creating an embarrassing political setback for the administration (if the postal pay bill was rammed through Congress over Nixon's veto). Frederick Kappel, for example, claimed that "the real basis for congressional opposition to the Administration's reform proposal was Red Blount being blunt . . . overly so in Congress. He wouldn't budge on anything, he was too rigid."[64] Colson was much of the same view, claiming, "Blount was a guy who

---

*The CCPR did run two ads in the *Washington Post* along the lines Dunlap suggested. One CCPR ad (responding to a UFPC ad that asked for congressional support for H.R. 13000 and described the "medieval" conditions of postal employment) ran under the headline "You Said a Mouthful, Mr. Filbey." The other, similar ad ran under the headline "You Didn't Go Far Enough, Mr. Rademacher."

would stand on principle while the whole government collapsed; he enjoyed alienating people and the labor unions hated him."

Whatever the correct assessment of H.R. 11750's chances was, it was clear that Blount and Rademacher had a deep-seated distrust of each other that was not facilitating the negotiations. Blount described Rademacher as "irresponsible, very radical, and very difficult" while Rademacher contended "Blount came from a region where there was no or little concern for unions and that's exactly what he practiced in Washington. He wouldn't even meet with me for months after he came into office." Colson, in contrast to Blount, had strong ties with a number of unions, had met Rademacher during the 1968 election (when Rademacher had been one of the few union leaders to support Nixon), and "felt he could break the logjam. I talked to Bryce Harlow and then Nixon," Colson recalled, "and Nixon allowed reorganization was something he really wanted to accomplish and gave me the green light to get involved."

The White House end-run of Blount began when Colson and Rademacher met December 5, 6, and 13 to iron out a new bill, drafted with substantial assistance from Mo Udall. "I realized," Rademacher stated, "that with genuine collective bargaining we could improve the work conditions for postal employees so I slowly yielded to reorganization, caring little or nothing about the bill except what it would do for labor." Several labor provisions of concern to Rademacher were written into the tentative reorganization legislation; among them the elimination of several "steps" in the postal promotion ladder and a compression of the time from 21 to 8 years that it took to reach the top level within salary grades, a 5.4 percent raise effective in January 1970, with a subsequent 5.7 percent raise "promised" for July 1970, and binding arbitration required (instead of optional) for all labor disputes that could not be resolved by a mediation board. Essentially, the tentative reorganization bill incorporated the key provisions of H.R. 13000 (on a slower schedule) and provided the unions with more favorable circumstances under which to conduct collective bargaining. "We couldn't offer new post offices and jobs, the type of offerings the administration could make," Rademacher summarized, explaining his change of heart. "I could foresee one more [HPOC] member falling by the wayside with that kind of inducement, and the media was funneling substantial amounts of money into the procorporation campaign; there were also some brutal attacks on postal workers in *Reader's Digest, Life,* and other magazines. There was every reason to believe the [POD's] media campaign was being successful and I saw the handwriting on the wall."

Unfortunately, at least for Rademacher, the other seven postal unions, led by the UFPC, saw only doodling on the wall. On December 17, the House requested a conference on the pay bill (with the Senate following the next day), and the UFPC determined that it would seek to push H.R. 13000 through unaccompanied by reorganization. There were three reasons for the unions' opposition, apparent at a December 17 meeting at NALC headquarters. First, as Rademacher acknowledged, he "made a very serious error" in not consulting the other unions before developing the Udall / White House plan, inflaming the historic rivalry between the NALC and UFPC. Exacerbating the problem was the well-known mutual dislike that UFPC President Filbey and Rademacher had for each other. ("If Rademacher said yes," Blount stated, "Filbey said no. It was that simple.") Second, there were several provisions "promised" by the White House—such as the salary compression and the second salary hike—that did not appear in the committee print of the bill, which had been hastily drafted with the assistance of POD General Counsel Nelson. Rademacher insisted that the White House stood behind the provisions and that they would be inserted during mark-up, but his assurances did not assuage the UFPC. Finally, the other unions wanted to retain their relationship with Congress and were convinced they could beat Nixon's veto. "Eisenhower tried the same thing on us in 1960," Nilan stated. "He had a Republican controlled Senate, unlike Nixon, and we still beat him, and that didn't happen often."*

With all of the unions except NALC focused on expediting the pay bill through a forthcoming House-Senate conference, the White House moved quickly to solidify Rademacher's support for the draft legislation. On December 18, Rademacher, flanked by Colson, Henry Cashen (Colson's deputy), and Ehrlichman, met with Nixon in the Oval Office to, as Colson put it, "sprinkle holy water on the deal. Nixon told him he approved of the compromise and would stand behind it." "Colson," Ehrlichman contended, "had just cultivated the hell out of Rademacher, who was very ambitious and vain, and they played him quite well." Rademacher's memory of the meeting was

> that it lasted about fifteen minutes and essentially Ehrlichman, Colson and Cashen sat by while the President and I talked. He wanted to know about my personal background, we briefly discussed the bill, and then he asked why I hadn't been able to work this out with Mr. Blount. I bluntly told him, and he uttered an expletive about why we couldn't get along, but he was soft on Blount, he wasn't going to attack his own Postmaster General. We agreed to hold the line on what we had agreed to, but acknowledged there would be amendments and members along the line that we could not control. I had a picture taken with the President holding the new bill, we shook hands and that was it. Afterwards I got the picture for my magazine—I felt the President and Colson wanted me to release this to the press—and I had my own reasons for publicizing this.

Rademacher had, as he put it, "a serious problem" on his hands which he felt required him to draw publicity to his meeting with Nixon. For over a year, Rademacher's public addresses, talk show appearances, and articles in the NALC magazine, had dripped with militant union rhetoric and unending vows of opposition to the postal corporation; indeed, of all the union leaders, Rademacher had been identified as the leader of the anticorporation crusade. "Overnight," Rademacher stated, "I had reversed my stand and I had to convince my 200,000 members that I was doing the right thing. I almost committed political suicide by making a deal with the President; there was some real unhappiness with me

---

*During his eight years in office, Eisenhower vetoed 169 bills. Only two of his vetoes were overridden.[65]

45

and if there had been an election the next day, I might have lost.'' Within hours of the Oval Office meeting, Rademacher released details of the new deal, on background, to John Cramer, a columnist for the *Washington Daily News,* who had frequently written in a complimentary fashion about Rademacher. ''In my probably egotistical attempt,'' Rademacher stated, ''to get credit for what I felt was a great victory—here was confirmation from the President that we could reach an agreement at the highest levels—I hurt myself very seriously, because the other union leaders read this and said 'uh-uh.' '' However, now that Rademacher had gone public, he was more committed to the deal with Nixon than ever, and he stuck by it in the upcoming months, publicizing it further despite the opposition of the other unions.*

Rademacher and the administration's opposition to reporting out a pay bill was potent enough that the pay bills languished without getting into conference in January and February 1970. During those months, there was a seesaw struggle to find a reorganization proposal acceptable both to the Administration and the dissident unions, with more deals and double-dealing occurring than one finds in bad soap opera. In order, the dissident unions accused the NALC of selling out; Blount privately accused Colson of mucking up his negotiation and sought to end his involvement; Colson told the president and Harlow that Blount was reneging on deals he struck with the unions; several of the big mailers, notably *Reader's Digest,* started lobbying for new provisions to the chagrin of the ABP and others; Rademacher and Dulski purportedly agreed on a compromise that Dulski and the seven unions then backed out of; and Senator McGee (D-Wy.) accused all of the union leaders of reneging on an agreement to support his pay bill. When the smoke cleared in late February, the POD had made several minor concessions, incorporating a few of the White House promises into the legislation, and Colson's role had diminished;** the standoff, however, over reorganization remained, with Dulski unable to obtain a quorum of members for markup of H.R. 4 for three out of five scheduled sessions. Moreover, the urgency of the debate escalated with President Nixon's February 2 budget message, which deferred a 5.7 percent comparability raise for postal workers from July 1970 to January 1971 on the grounds that it was inflationary. The deferral inflamed the already aggravated unions, particularly some of the urban chapters, and by the close of Feb-

---

*For example, Rademacher printed the photo of him and Nixon agreeing to the new bill in the *Postal Record,* the NALC's monthly magazine.

**Bryce Harlow served as intermediary between Colson and Blount, although Ehrlichman also kept an eye on the pay bill / reform negotiations. ''Blount,'' Ehrlichman recalled, ''thought Colson, Cashen, and the White House were selling him out and we were determined that he wasn't going to make a deal that we couldn't live with.'' Eventually, Blount and POD General Counsel Nelson eclipsed Colson in running the negotiations, stirring some tension. At one point, Blount sent Nelson over to Colson's office to tell him that he was not to deliver a speech on postal reform scheduled for the following day at the Republican Women's Club in Washington. Colson insisted on talking directly with Blount and called him (with Nelson on the line) to complain, ''General, this speech has been laid out for weeks. What am I going to talk about?'' There was a frosty pause and Blount said: ''Tell them about the ecology.''

ruary, Dulski and McGee were preparing to move the pay bill (with a July 1970 raise) separately.

During January and February, while the administration was attempting to bring the dissident unions on board, the POD and the CCPR, for the first time, adopted, with some regret, a low profile. The POD periodically still set up meetings between Blount and editorial boards around the country, but they attracted little national media attention to the ills of the Post Office, nor did they embark on any major new efforts. In a January 16, 1970, memo, for example, Dunlap recommended to Jim Holland (Henderson's successor) that the POD run another regional "educational" program that "would enable us to favorably position the compromise reform bill with the press across the country. Specifically, we would attempt to communicate the point that this bill, although it reflects compromise, is better for everyone (the employee, the mail user, and the general public) than the current system. It would give momentum to our efforts to get the reform package passed this Spring." Dunlap's recommendation was not adopted, however, because, as he put it, "the media's position was pretty well established and at this point, we didn't want to raise any hostilities."

Much the same was the case at the CCPR, which supported the compromise bill in its newsletter *(The Postal Reformer)*, sent a letter to the mayors and governors on CCPR asking for their support, and emphasized two slightly altered themes in its periodic ads—"it's about time we considered the interests of the public" (aimed at the interest groups picking at the new legislation), and "the Citizens' Committee will not accept legislation which masquerades as reform" (also aimed at the dissident unions and mailers). But the CCPR did not do any mailings to editorial writers, direct mailings, or activate new letter writing campaigns in the local CCPR chapters. It also rejected a February 18, 1970, proposal by Jim Marshall for a renewed surge of these activities, to be supplemented by forty-second television clips from O'Brien and Morton (designed so that the local newscaster could appear to be asking the questions), radio tapes, and a CCPR sponsored poll of "John. Q. Citizen." Dunlap and others turned thumbs down on the Marshall proposal for the same reasons they kept the POD's publicists chomping at the bit;* they did not want to alienate factions that seemed near being brought on board.

The struggle in the HPOC finally began coming to a head on February 25, when Congressman Dulski (D-N.Y.) called a press conference to announce that all attempts to compromise with Blount had failed, that he planned to proceed with the mark-up of H.R. 4, and that he and Senator McGee (D-Wy.) had agreed to have a conference on the pay bill. What seemed to be a dramatic setback for

---

*By January 21, 1970, the POD's P.R. specialists had already drafted a promotion plan for the transition period (during which the POD would switch over to a government corporation). The plan had three phases: first, the preparation of promotional materials, such as a new seal and letterheads, second, an elaborate and dramatic bill signing ceremony, and third, a follow-up "saturation campaign" using "all available media to place the Postal Service Authority on a high public faith and reliability plane."

Blount and his allies spurred them into a furious eleventh hour, three-pronged assault on HPOC members. First, within a few days, Rademacher, Nelson, and John Gabusi (a Udall staffer) drafted another substitute bill with enough cosmetic changes to make it have some appeal as a new proposal. Second, NALC leaders raised the prospect that Dulski's actions might provoke a strike. Rademacher, who felt Dulski had betrayed him, angrily told a group of reporters immediately after Dulski's press conference. "My people have had enough." Noting that Nixon had told him that he would veto any pay bill not linked to reform, Rademacher warned: "There is going to be a pay bill retroactive to last January or there is going to be a national strike."[66] Rademacher's threat was driven home during the first week of March by the heads of NALC chapters in Long Island, Bronx–Mahattan, and Brooklyn, N.Y., all of whom warned that their chapters would strike before April 1 without a pay raise. Finally, the POD and NALC launched an extraordinary lobbying campaign, which "veteran committee members" described to the *Washington Star* by saying that "they had never encountered such extreme pressure in all their years in Congress."[67] Rademacher and Blount walked the halls of Congress together, Rademacher offering voter and financial support, while Blount reportedly offered new post offices, political job patronage, and the promise of "token" opposition in the next election for members supporting the administration, contrasted with well-financed Republican opposition for those Democrats and Republicans who did not side with the administration. On March 12, in a stunning upset, several critical Democrats deserted Dulski and the HPOC voted 17–6 to report out the administration's bill.

Later that day, Blount held a press conference, and both the POD and CCPR issued press releases hailing the committee's action, but the HPOC vote seemed to be too little and come too late for the militant postal workers of New York City. Blount stated at the press conference that he did not anticipate strike threats from the unions that had lost the HPOC vote, encouraging them to look at the "great opportunities"[68] the legislation provided for employees. Rademacher took a similar tack, praising the legislation and immediately sending a telegram to the Manhattan–Bronx NALC Local 36, urging them to "Stay cool. House Committee has just approved a bill which will include a sizable pay raise, collective bargaining rights." Gustave Johnson, president of NALC Local 36, distributed copies of the telegram to union members at a meeting that afternoon, but when he described the legislation many members crumbled up the telegrams and yelled "Not enough! Strike! Strike!" A strike vote that day was negative, but under pressure from members who claimed improprieties in the voting, Johnson rescheduled the vote for March 17, St. Patrick's Day. Near midnight on St. Patrick's Day, NALC Local 36 voted to strike, and was immediately joined by the other major postal unions in New York City. On March 18, all mail service in New York was completely halted, and within a week the New York walkout, to the surprise of administration officials, precipitated the first national postal strike in history. The day administration officials had dreaded but dismissed as impossible had finally arrived: the day the postman didn't knock once.

Breaking the Strike

At the height of the strike, on March 21, 152,000 postal workers, a third of the total postal workforce, walked out of 671 post offices, including nine of the ten largest in the country. Mail service was virtually at a standstill. It was a crisis which affected nearly everyone, from the IRS which was losing 1 billion dollars a day in unreceived income tax checks to the elderly individual waiting for the Social Security check to pay for food and rent. Sen. McGee called it the "most serious domestic crisis in forty years." The president went on television to tell the American people that what was at issue was nothing less than "the survival of government based on law." * Court orders succeeded in putting a stop to the picketing, but not to the strike. Appeals from national union leaders went unheeded by the runaway locals.

The media were everywhere, hounding officials as they came out of meetings and speculating about what might happen next. The vaunted public relations machines at POD and CCPR, which had put reorganization on the agenda and just gotten a bill out of committee were suddenly in a reactive mode, trying to stay on top of the latest event rather than creating it. Blount and the POD information experts saw both the obligation to minimize consumer confusion and the opportunity to use the strike as another vehicle for pushing postal reform. After the first few days of the strike, Blount used press conferences and personal appearances to send the message that the blame rested with the Congress, which had the power to pass a postal pay hike and the reorganization. Reorganization would give postal workers the right to collective bargaining, so that they would not have had to strike to pressure the Congress for more money.

Finally, on March 23, Nixon declared a national emergency, going on television to say that he was sending in the National Guard (which he called a "supplemental work force" to soften the blow). In his seven minute address, he carefully emphasized both that the strike was illegal and that the workers' grievances were legitimate and open to negotiation—though the strike could have been avoided had Congress passed reorganization, enabling postal employees to turn to collective bargaining, instead of Congress for a pay raise.

Calling in the troops effectively killed the strike. Postal employees began to return almost immediately and within twenty-four hours Blount was able to hold a press conference to announce that the return to work was significant enough so that negotiations should begin.

While administration officials were exultant over their success in facing down what they labelled as a "domestic equivalent to the Cuban missile crisis," it was not clear that the cause of postal reform had been advanced. Colson recalls that there was concern at the White House that Congress would rush through a pay bill and that the union opposition to reorganization would intensify in response

---

*An extended discussion of the strike and the media strategy pursued by the administration to break the strike is contained in "Selling the Reorganization of the Post Office (sequel)."

to the administration's having called in the National Guard. However, the White House never backed away from linking pay and reorganization in their negotiations with the unions, and major media soon began to editorialize that the need for reform was demonstrated by the strike.

Finally, after several weeks of hard bargaining, a package was worked out which provided for an immediate and retroactive pay hike, with a larger hike to take effect when reorganization was signed into law. The reorganization agreed to was in all essential respects the same as the one reported by the HPOC. George Meany, who was by then speaking for the unions, hailed it as "a tremendous step forward" because postal employees had won the right to collective bargaining.

The bill passed the House overwhelmingly on June 18. On the Senate side, 8 of the 12 members of the Senate Post Office Committee were up for re-election in the fall and didn't want the blood of another postal strike on their hands. David Minton, then counsel to the committee, says that "reform was a high visibility item in the media following the strike and that had a very influential role in pushing reorganization through." The Senate passed the bill in fundamentally the same form as it had come over from the House. When the House approved the conference committee report on August 6, reorganization was on its way to the White House, where, not surprisingly, the information folks at POD had prepared an elaborate bill-signing ceremony which received enormous and favorable press coverage.

Impact of the Media

Evaluating the contribution of the media campaign to the passage of reorganization brings mixed answers. One viewpoint, held by Bruce Harlow, Paul Carlin, Congressman Derwinski (R.-Ill.) and others, is that reorganization was fundamentally attributable to the dogged insistence of Red Blount. "As I look back," Derwinski stated, "what got postal reform through was that Blount was an unusually determined, able man who just bulldogged it." A second explanation is that postal reform was secured, essentially, through the postal strike, and that despite Blount's tenacious pressure, reform would never have been enacted had the unions not agreed to support it.

The participants who embraced the "strike" or "Red Blount bulldog" theories tend, not surprisingly, to dismiss the importance of the POD's media campaign. "I think the campaign made very little difference," POD General Counsel Nelson stated. "We were asking members of Congress to change the law and I don't think anybody in their right mind would believe that it would be possible through a carefully orchestrated media campaign to put enough pressure on congressmen to persuade them to do something they didn't think was wise." Congressman Derwinski didn't view the campaign as a virtual waste of time, but he did feel its impact was minimal. "Once you have been in Congress a few years," Derwinski stated, "you are not overly impressed with commissions and you understand what they basically are—PR vehicles. The Citizen's Commission was useful because it lent a bipartisan flavor to the battle, but any congressman on the Committee who knew his business knew that the media and letter writing pressure was artificial. The one place the editorial support was helpful was on the Floor, because a lot of members didn't know much about reorganization and that helped build momentum there.''

Those officials, however, who were directly involved in running and monitoring the media campaign considered it a vital element in the reorganization fight. ''Arguing about whether the Citizen's Commission and media activities were effective,'' Bill Dunlap contended, ''is really a moot issue. People would say the campaign wasn't working because its impact couldn't be measured, and others would argue that the lobbying efforts by the POD were breaking down or that the White House involvement wasn't helpful. You could argue either way on those issues, but the key thing was that you needed them all to effect a change of this magnitude. You had to have at least those three legs under the table or it would have fallen down from the counterpressure.'' Blount himself was of a similar opinion, stating:

> There is no one key force or event that created postal reform; it was a lot of forces and events working together. I felt the campaign to draw media support was enormously important; that's the way you move the Congress, and if we had not had the media support we would have had a bad time. I don't remember specific incidents where a Congressman would cite editorial support in his home district as his reason for changing position, but you could see that their changes corresponded to periods when public support for reorganization was voiced. I don't have any question that the media played a role, particularly the regional and local press. The national press, which gave us a fair amount of publicity, kept writing that postal reform was dead. But the regional and local press were very, very supportive, so the climate was such that a Congressman from Texas or Florida or California saw more publicity favoring reform than they had ever seen before about the Post Office, and they could say ''the people back home are thinking well of this.'' If the public had been ho-hum ''50–50,'' I don't think we would have reorganized the Post Office. The campaign helped us accomplish an exciting, fundamental reform in a drab patronage-ridden part of the government.

APPENDIX A

Sample Stock Speech

POSTAL REFORM
(STOCK SPEECH TO EMPLOYEES)

June 1969

Today I would like to discuss a subject which is supposed to be very unpopular with you—that is the total reform of our postal system.

Down in Washington, the newspaper pundits and other "experts" agree that modernizing the mail service is a good idea—but it doesn't stand a chance, they say, because the employee organizations are against it.

As is too often the case, the commentators base their views of how the nation as a whole is thinking upon the views of a few persons in Washington.

And, out of these reports from Capitol Hill and other Washington offices, a myth is developed: "The postal employees are against it."

I say it is a myth because I don't believe that most postal employees have had a chance to consider President Nixon's proposal to create a U.S. Postal Service.

This is unfortunate. No one has a bigger stake in the modernization of the postal service than the men and women who are "moving the mail."

As postal employees, you know better than anyone else the weaknesses of the present system.

- You have worked in crowded, poorly lit buildings.
- You have lifted heavy, dirty mail bags because there wasn't any equipment on the dock.
- You have tried to drive inoperative postal vehicles.

Many postal employees could add to this list.

These are the frustrations—some of the handicaps we face in trying to do a job in the Post Office Department as it exists today.

These and other problems are also the source of the service complaints we are receiving from mail users. The public is asking: Why is the mail service getting poorer despite the higher and higher postal rates?

This is why the former Postmaster General, Larry O'Brien, said we are in a race with catastrophe.

Year by year, it is becoming evident that the existing postal establishment can't meet tomorrow's needs.

And, a creaky, deficit-ridden business is not a good employer.

Frankly, I think postal employees will like what they see in total postal reform, if they take a hard look at it.

For the great majority of the postal workers, a well-managed postal enterprise will let them bargain for more pay.

Instead of the Congress fixing wage rates for the entire country, you would have the

53

right to bargain collectively for wages and fringe benefits in line with those paid by non-Federal employers in your area.

And, this makes sense—both for the mail users and the postal employee. Today, in our large metropolitan areas—where a large share of the mail originates—the Post Office is a poor employer. In New York City, for example, sanitation workers are now receiving $10,000 a year while postal clerks are starting at $6,000. In most of our larger cities, bus drivers are receiving substantially higher salaries than clerks responsible for accurately dispatching mail and following postal regulations.

Employees are asking if postal reform will bring job cutbacks; if new machinery would eliminate many of today's positions.

First of all, the legislation specifically provides that all postal employees automatically transfer to the new U.S. Postal Service on the day it begins operating.

We also want to remember that the mail service is an expanding—not a declining—industry. Each year, the total volume of mail climbs by two-to-three billion pieces. In the past two decades, the number of letters, magazines, and parcels delivered by postal employees has doubled.

Despite the antiquated conditions under which many of us work, we are in a growth industry. Increased economic activity in our nation means more and more letters, statements, and other records which must be sent through the mails. We are also serving an increasingly educated population—one in which families, universities, and businesses are receiving more and more reports, specialized publications, and other types of communications which can best be served through the mails.

The continued growth in mail volume forecasts a job for every postal worker.

But, this shouldn't be the issue in 1969.

Three decades ago—during the great depression when one fourth of the men couldn't find steady work—having a job—almost any kind of work—was an important goal.

Today, when we can't find enough qualified workers, the issue should be that of upgrading and improving postal workers' *real wages*.

And, I think the way we are going to move from an era when the great majority of postal workers are stuck in the same grade through their entire career, is through total postal reform.

A U.S. Postal Service—freed from the shackles under which we now try to deliver the mail—could introduce new mail-handling technologies and equipment which would create many new and better jobs for today's postal workers.

In some of our newer offices, you have seen how mechanization can provide higher pay. Those operating letter-sorting machines command a higher grade than the average clerk. Those responsible for the maintenance of this sophisticated equipment are also earning substantially higher wages than those now earned by the typical postal worker. The two technicians for an optical character reader, for example, are level 10 employees.

Another area of concern among our 750,000 employees involves a change from a traditional Government department to a management-type enterprise. Many of these questions are answered, I think, by the experience of the Tennessee Valley Authority.

It is widely acknowledged that TVA employees have done well, and the proposed U.S. Postal Service would be organized a lot like TVA.

And, the labor–management record of this big public authority is second to none. Through collective bargaining it has worked out agreements with unions representing employees operating this huge electric power network. The Authority has also hammered out contracts with the building trades which have brought peace to crafts which have a long history of jurisdictional conflict.

The proposed postal reform legislation would transfer all postal workers into a new postal career service with full retention of their Civil Service retirement benefits enjoyed under existing law.

In addition, any present postal employee would be eligible, at his option, to transfer to any other position in the Government which is open and for which he is qualified. It is planned that the new Postal Service would work with the Civil Service Commission in placing those wishing to transfer.

While the existing law banning strikes by Federal workers would continue, the Postal Service Act makes appropriate provisions for binding arbitration in the event of a labor–management dispute which could not be settled by other means.

In general, labor relations would be subject to the Labor–Management Relations Act of 1947. Negotiating impasses that are not settled by procedures agreed to in collective bargaining contracts would come before an impartial "postal disputes panel." This panel could apply any of a broad array of settlement techniques, including fact-finding, mediation, recommendations on any or all issues, or referral to a separate and impartial board of arbitration that would be established on a "this dispute only" basis.

These and other provisions of the Postal Reform Act of 1969 represent a sharp departure from the past. I can understand why you will want to carefully consider this proposal to create a new type of postal organization.

The need for postal reform should also be considered in terms of our own experience in the existing Department.

On the job you may see poor management, have to use improper or badly operating equipment, or work in dismal buildings.

These problems are not the fault of any one individual. They can't be blamed on the Congress or the Postmaster General or on you. The handicaps under which you work are the product of a system where authority is given to few and responsibility is placed on many.

You are also handicapped by a system where the top boss, the Postmaster General, usually doesn't stay more than two years. In the past, many of the Postmasters General have barely had time to learn how the mail is delivered before they are headed for another post.

Leadership at the local level has also been weakened in many cities as political factions try to agree on the selection of the postmaster—your boss.

These were some of the problems a Presidential Commission on Postal Organization identified in a year-long study of the postal system. The need for total postal reform was documented by this commission.

The Postal Service Act of 1969 could lift the dead hand of partisan politics from what could be one of America's most progressive industries.

President Nixon has removed all political considerations in the appointment of postmasters and rural letter carriers. Unlike the past, these positions will now be open to the most qualified persons.

Many other opportunities for advancement would be open in a postal service which had the resources and the management to develop new techniques for handling mail.

A revitalized postal service would also share more fully in the growth of the dynamic American economy. It could participate in the development of new means of communications, as well as in the growth of the print media.

A professionally managed U.S. Postal Service would offer more than a "good place to work." It could represent an opportunity to participate in the growth and prosperity of the American economy.

APPENDIX B

TO: Claude J. Desautels, Executive Director
FROM: James J. Marshall, Public Affairs Director
RE: Thoughts about the Public Affairs Campaign
DATE: June 10, 1969

A detailed plan and timetable for public affairs activities in conjunction with the postal reorganization bill is now being drafted. This plan and time schedule is being prepared with the expectation that favorable Congressional action cannot be expected immediately. Nevertheless, it is intended to have a plan which as quickly as possible will bring public expression of support and approval for a postal reorganization proposal and gain favorable publicity.

Some "off-the-top-of-the-head" ideas which might be used in our public affairs effort are described below. Some of these ideas can be used, others will have to be refined and others discarded.

1) *Influential Citizens.* It is obvious that the first step must be to obtain the support of prominent and influential citizens who will serve on the board of directors and as sponsors. This is already underway.

2) *Display of Support.* Depending on the financial situation it might be well to run three-quarter or full-page ads on behalf of the Citizens' Committee in select newspapers. This should be done only *after* the Committee has compiled an impressive board of directors and sponsors list. The objective of such ads would be:

a) To win public support for the postal reorganization effort.

b) To solicit funds and to indicate that it is truly a citizens committee.

c) To indicate the degree of support that the reorganization plan has among the influential citizens and organizations in this country.

The newspapers should include *The New York Times, The Wall Street Journal,* and *The Washington Post,* also *The Washington Evening Star* if funds would permit.

3) *National Forum.* It is imperative that a press wingding be held in Washington with the principals involved in order to draw attraction to the bipartisan and citizens' aspect of this effort.

4) *Identification.* Enlist the aid of one of the country's outstanding cartoonists who would allow us to use his popular characters in pushing the effort to win approval of the reorganization plan. The famous Peanuts characters created by Charles Schulz are my first choice. The use of Snoopy and Charlie Brown and the other Peanuts characters would capture the imagination of the American public. It would give us a tremendous boost. There are any number of publicity spin-offs that can be used if we have a well-known lovable, animated cartoon character in our corner.

5) *Direct Mail Appeal.* Letters soliciting support and financial assistance should be sent to as many organizations and prominent people as possible under the signature of Mr. O'Brien and Senator Morton. Enclosed with the letter should be favorable reprints of

editorials supporting reform along with a reprint of a favorable article from one of the country's newspapers.

6) *Promotional Film.* To the extent that finances permit, we should develop a short promotional film which might be used by local television stations and could be shown before Kiwanis, Rotary, service clubs, political organizations, labor unions, etc. The film would explain the need for Postal Reform including an appeal, possibly from President Nixon, Mr. O'Brien, Mr. Kappel, and other appropriate people. If budgeting allowed, it might be well to lead into this film through the animated use of cartoon characters, particularly the Peanuts strip. However, such a film, because of the availability of material, can be put together at a very low and reasonable cost figure.

7) *Billboards.* An attempt should be made to obtain donated billboard space from companies and firms that have an interest in postal reorganization. Once again, it might be well to put the message across in cartoon style, particularly if the Peanuts characters were available to do this.

8) *Newsletter.* To be issued on a regular basis to the news media, Congressmen, influential citizens and any others interested in postal reform.

9) *Slogan.* A snappy slogan must be thought up. Maybe turn this into a nationwide contest with the hope of getting some national publicity.

10) *Bumper Stickers.* Sometimes of dubious value. However, it might be attempted. A catchy slogan would certainly help.

11) *Unclaimed Goods.* The Citizens' Committee might put up the funds to purchase a good deal of the parcels that would be auctioned off by the Washington Post Office as "unclaimed." In turn the goods would be turned over to the poor in the city. It would be bound to get a good deal of publicity.

These are just some "quick thoughts" about promotional activities. These would be meshed with the usual efforts to gain publicity through press releases and personal contact with newsmen.

APPENDIX C

Progress Report for President Nixon

CONFIDENTIAL
PROGRESS REPORT
CITIZENS COMMITTEE FOR POSTAL REFORM

August 30th 1969

FORMATION:—The Citizens Committee for Postal Reform was established on May 26th by former Postmaster General Lawrence F. O'Brien and former Senator Thruston B. Morton. It was created to win public and Congressional support for legislation that would remove the debt-ridden Post Office Department from the President's Cabinet and replace it by an efficient, cost-conscious Post Corporation managed by a team of experienced professionals.

Four days later, on May 28th, Mr. O'Brien and Senator Morton announced that the Committee would wholeheartedly support President Nixon's postal reform legislation (H.R. 11750) because it represented the best possible solution for remedying the massive postal dilemma confronting the nation.

DIRECTORS—The Committee has obtained the backing of influential citizens from both political parties. To date there are more than 160 directors. These include 22 Governors, 65 Mayors and scores of distinguished Americans from education, banking, business, industry, and other walks of life, including five former Cabinet officers.

FUND RAISING—to finance the Citizens Committee, funds were initially raised from the Business Council. Contributions from one dollar to $5,000 have been received and close to $200,000 has been raised to date.

CONGRESSIONAL TESTIMONY—on July 10th Mr. O'Brien and Senator Morton testified on behalf of H.R. 11750 before the House Post Office and Civil Service Committee. Later that day they spoke at a luncheon at the National Press Club.

HEADQUARTERS—a permanent office was established at 1725 Eye Street, N.W., Washington, on July 1st. It is staffed by Claude J. Desautels, executive director, and James J. Marshall, public affairs director.

ADVERTISING—on June 26th and 28th a half-page ad was run in the *New York Times* asking for support for the Citizens Committee and HR 11750. The ad was prepared by Batten, Barton, Durstine and Osborn Inc. of New York City, which has agreed to serve as the volunteer agency for the Citizen Committee. B.B.D. & O. has also prepared a three-quarter page ad which is being sent this week by the Citizens Committee to the publishers of 160 daily newspapers in the top 100 markets in the country requesting that the ad be run as a public service. B.B.D. & O. is also preparing ad material for use in magazines.

NEWS MEDIA—a continuing effort is being made to obtain news stories and editorial commentary favorable to HR 11750. Press releases and informational material, including a comprehensive press kit, have been and will continue to be sent to the press. A special effort has been made to supply material to the daily and weekly newspapers, as well as the television stations in the districts served by the 26 House Post Office Committee members.

Special material, including brochures, have been prepared and distributed for use by local Citizens Committees in dealing with members of the local press. Distribution of a regularly scheduled newsletter—*The Postal Reformer*—will start this month.

ORGANIZATIONAL SUPPORT—The Citizens Committee has been working with other organizations interested in passage of H.R. 11750, including General Electric Co., J.C. Penney Co., Bank of America, American Retail Federation, Procter & Gamble, Household Finance Corp., Sears, Roebuck, Ford Motor Co., AT & T., Magazine Publishers Association, Westinghouse, 3M, Union Carbide Co., Republic Steel and the National Association of Manufacturers (NAM) among others.

The Chamber of Commerce has been especially active in the publications area, turning out special informational and progress reports on postal reform legislation and exhorting their members to write to their Congressmen on behalf of H.R. 11750. A half-hour film on the need for postal reform is being prepared by the Chamber.

Many organizations which have not taken an official position on the question of HR 11750, nevertheless, have sent out material to their membership. The information—and sometimes the material—has been supplied by the Citizens Committee. Favorable stories on the need for HR 11750 have appeared in the publications of many organizations, with the emphasis being to write to their Congressmen in support of the bill. An example of this co-operation was the sending out by the NAM in its Aug. 11th tearsheet to more than 5,000 weekly newspapers favorable editorials and cartoons in support of HR 11750.

REGIONAL COMMITTEES—Citizens organizations are being set up in the key areas where a Congressman is a member of the House Post Office Committee. Fieldman Jerry Bruno is working with interested firms (General Electric, Sears, J.C. Penney) and organizations (particularly the Chamber of Commerce) in setting up these Citizen groups.

Albany / Schenectady (Button)—committee setup headed by Robert Dirks, community relations director of General Electric. Letter-writing and publicity campaign are underway, hour long talk program has been done, and a meeting is scheduled with Rep. Button on September 5th.

Syracuse (Hanley)—Committee is set up, headed by Stephen Rogers, publisher of the *Herald & Post Standard,* who is also in charge of the letter-writing campaign. Meeting is scheduled with Hanley after Labor Day.

Pittsburgh (Corbett)—Committee is set up, headed by Melner Roberts of Sykes Advertising Agency. Son-in-law of Corbett is active with Citizens Committee. Chamber of Commerce and Mail Users have already met with Rep. Corbett and the Committee plans a meeting with him when he returns from Europe. Letter-writing campaign and publicity are underway.

El Paso (White)—John McFall of El Paso Natural Gas has organized a committee. (He is a personal friend of Rep. White.) A meeting is scheduled with Rep. White after Labor Day. Jerry Bruno will be in El Paso Friday.

New Britain (Meskill)—Committee is headed by H.S. Everett, executive vice-president of the Chamber of Commerce. Letter-writing campaign and publicity are underway. The committee has scheduled a meeting with Rep. Meskill next week.

Providence (Tiernan)—Committee will be set up shortly. C of C has already met with Tiernan. Assistant Postmaster will address the C of C on Sept. 15th. Letter writing campaign is being organized by Lou Pastore.

Buffalo (Dulski)—Committee will be set up shortly. Initial work has been started.

Philadelphia (Nix)—Phil Knox, general counsel of Sears, is attempting to enlist the support of Rev. Leon Sullivan and other black leaders. A committee has not been formed.

Jersey City (Daniels)—An effort is being made to get the backing of County Chairman John Kenny, who is a key man. Bruno has a meeting scheduled with him. A local committee has not been formed.

Goldsboro (Henderson)—Initial work in setting up a committee is being undertaken by J. C. Penney man.

CONGRESSIONAL LIAISON—Mr. Desautels has personally contacted each of the 26 members of the P.O. Committee to ask their support for HR 11750. Additionally, the Citizens Committee has already met with, and expects to work closely with, representatives of other concerned organizations which are planning to initiate liaison activities on Capitol Hill. The Citizens Committee is planning to issue to every Senator and Representative a copy of a 200-page book containing reprints of nation-wide newspaper editorials demonstrating the overwhelming public support for HR 11750.

CONGRESSIONAL TIME SCHEDULE—The House P.O. Committee plans to hold executive sessions to mark up the bill immediately. The first two sessions will be devoted to reading the bill. The first test will come when a vote is taken to determine which bill is to be marked up—HR 11750 or HR 4—probably at the third session. It is planned to hold twice-weekly sessions of the full committee through September to mark up the bill. Chairman Dulski has set a target date of Sept. 25th to have the committee report out a bill.

CONGRESSIONAL OUTLOOK—It is our opinion that, as of this date, there is not a majority of the Committee in favor of HR 11750 as it was introduced. Right now, we can count on eight votes in favor—Udall, Hamilton, Purcell, Cunningham, Derwinski, Johnson, McClure, and Lukens. However, a potential majority exists if the labor–management provisions of the bill are modified—compulsory binding arbitration.

RECOMMENDATIONS—Every Republican member of the Committee should be urged to vote in favor of marking up HR 11750 as an "expression of confidence in the administration," even if these Congressmen wish to disagree and change parts of the bill in executive session.

Mr. O'Brien will contact the Committee's Democratic members on marking up.

APPENDIX D

Draft Plan for Citizens Commission "Contact Man"

A general description of a plan of action for the contact man in a Congressional district or area follows. Our objective is to obtain as much publicity and to enlist the support of as many people and organizations as possible within a short space of time in a locale. The suggested procedure detailed here is meant to be a help to the local contact man in planning a campaign. However, he must be free to use his own judgment and strategy based on his familiarity with the district.

1. The first step is to touch base with the local Chamber of Commerce officials since they are in wholehearted support of HR 11750 and make sure that we are working together.

2. Contact the officers of the League of Women Voters, Kiwanis, Rotary, the local Postmaster, and any group or organization in your area that you feel may be sympathetic to the cause of postal reform. Preferably you should get them all together at a meeting—however, all of the groups of people you want won't go, and will have to be contacted individually.

The people who attend the meeting should form the basis for the officers of the local citizens group. Make sure every organization attending has someone as an officer of the local "Citizens Committee for Postal Reform." There may be some who will balk, since it might appear that their organization is therefore backing the legislation. Explain that they are serving as an individual. As far as is humanly possible, make sure that all of the organizations are represented. The person attending might not want to serve. In this case, get him to call someone in his organization to serve. Make certain that this is done before the meeting adjourns.

The women's groups are especially important because they will do a great deal of work if they are solidly behind a campaign.

3. *Formation of the Committee*—Announcement of the formation of the local "Citizens' Committee for Postal Reform" should be made to the local news media. A list of the local press will be supplied. Make sure that all receive copies of the press release. The national Citizens' Committee will assist in the preparation of such a release. As many names as possible should be included in the press release.

4. *Personal Visits to News Media*—All of the editors of the daily newspapers and the news directors of the television and radio stations should be personally visited. This might be done in conjunction with the announcement of the formation of the local committee or it might be done afterwards. Press kits will be supplied to you by the Washington Office along with material about the whole question of postal reform. Suggested editorials will also be sent, but care must be exercised in giving these to the news media. The weekly editors will probably welcome them, while the news people on the dailies might get upset and suspicious if you offer them "canned" editorials.

a) *Newspapers*—Make sure that you contact the editorial writers as well as the news department at the papers. We want the paper to write favorable editorials, but more important is getting them to do stories—features or possibly a series—about the local effort being made to push postal reform and the whole question of postal reform.

b) *Television*—See if the news director will do an interview with someone in the community (possibly the contact man) who is favorable to postal reform. The local postmaster might be a good possibility. Attempt to interest him in the whole question of postal reform. Further, see if the station might take a favorable editorial position on this question—particularly in support of HR 11750. (Make sure that any such editorials are transcribed and that a copy gets to the local congressman.)

c) *Radio Stations*—Use the same approach as with the television news director. However, many stations now go in for talk shows or extended interviews. See if you can be the "guest" on one of the talk shows—or be interviewed. Important: If you or someone else does get on one of the talk shows, make sure that you line up a dozen or so people to make "friendly" calls into the program urging support for HR 11750.

d) *Weekly Newspapers*—A personal visit to a weekly news editor will probably guarantee a favorable story and possibly an editorial. If a member of your committee is from the circulation area covered by the weekly, play up this fact. See if they might do a feature story based around that person and his involvement in postal reform.

5. *Personal Visit to Businessmen*—Personally call on the influential people—including the religious—in the area. The primary purpose of the visit should be to get them to promise to write a letter to their Congressman in support of HR 11750. If at all possible, you might kid them into dictating the letter while you are with them. This will insure the success of your visit. Additionally, try to interest them in becoming a member of the local committee (promise that no work is involved) and see if they will contact two other people to write to the Congressman.

6. *Telephone Campaign*—If a sufficient number of women can be interested in this project, you might enlist them in a telephone campaign. The objective: (1) to get them signed up as members of the Committee, (2) To get them to write a letter to the Congressman.

7. *Local ad*—If sufficient people join the committee you may place an ad in the local dailies and possibly the weeklies. This type of ad sometimes has quite an impact.

8. *Petition*—If it appears that there might be sufficient interest in a locale, a petition might be started in which a canvas is made of homes asking the support of people on behalf of HR 11750. Large numbers of women would be needed for any such project. Further, it shouldn't be started unless their is some good evidence that it can be successful.

9. *Local Forum*—Arrangements should be made with local organizations to devote a program to postal reform. If the group is large or prestigious, it might be possible to arrange for an outside speaker through the Washington office. The Chamber of Commerce is planning a 20-minute to half-hour film on Postal Reform and arrangements can probably be made to have this shown to groups.

APPENDIX E

Report from Jerry Bruno

September 5, 1969

BUTTON—*Albany-Schenectady:* Contact man is Robert Dirks, GE, Building 43, Schenectady, and also Don Tuttle of GE. They had a meeting attended by Frank Smith, Executive Vice President of the Schenectady Chamber of Commerce two weeks ago. The meeting was attended by 60 people who were all favorable to postal reform. They started a letter writing campaign and generated between 400–500 letters. Tuttle participated in a 2-hour radio talk show on postal reform and had a good response. Don Craig, Vice-President of GE is having lunch with the Congressman on Friday (today). They have contacted the big money contributors of Button and the contributors are now making calls to the Congressman urging him to vote for postal reform. They have made contact with Governor Rockefeller, urging him to talk to Button. Jerry will know after the luncheon what happened between Craig and Button.

HANLEY—*Syracuse:* Contact man is J. Edward Kaish, GE, Electronics Park, Syracuse and the Chairman of the local Committee is Steve Rogers, publisher of the Syracuse Herald-American, the big Newhouse paper in Syracuse. A meeting two weeks ago was attended by the Chamber of Commerce of Syracuse; John Gilgallon, General Manager of the Sears store; the head of the Federation of Women's Clubs; and the Jr. Chamber of Commerce. They have generated between 500–600 letters. There are 40 on the Committee and yesterday, they got Mayor Walsh to agree to be on the Committee. The Chamber is having a meeting with Hanley today and the Citizens Committee is meeting with Hanley tomorrow. Jerry is to get the results today of a call to be made by Rogers to Hanley yesterday. On September 11, the Federation of Women's Clubs (an organization of all the civic clubs in the city) will be urged to push postal reform and start a letter writing campaign to the Congressman, etc.

NIX—*Philadelphia:* Phil Knox, Sears General Counsel, is the contact man. They have tried a number of times and numerous ways to get to Nix. Every contact, including the Chamber of Commerce, that Knox has made has said the Mayor has tremendous influence over Nix but no one has been able to talk to the Mayor. Knox suggested that Larry O'Brien talk to Mayor Tate. The President of the Philadelphia Chamber of Commerce is supposed to have a talk with Tate in the next few days. On Jerry's own, he contacted Bill Hart, GE in New York, and Hart told Jerry that Charlie Dates, a GE salesman in the Philadelphia area visited Nix and Nix told Dates he was for reform but did not specify what type of reform. Rev. Leon Sullivan, a black minister influential in the Philadelphia area, is having a film done on his life by GE. They are financing Sullivan with large sums of money to start businesses for blacks. They will contact Sullivan to try to get Nix to be for the Administration postal reform.

CORBETT—*Pittsburgh:* Milnor Roberts, President of Sykes Advertising Co., 411 - 7th Avenue, Pittsburgh is the contact man. The Congressman is still in Europe and is due back Sunday. A meeting with the Chamber of Commerce present was held on Thursday, August 21. In attendance was John McLeane, Executive Vice President for the Chamber;

63

Theodore Hleba, Mgr., Educational Affairs, Chamber of Commerce; James Lavine, Customer Service Mgr. of Kaufmann's (a department store); and Don Dunbar, Corbett's son-in-law. They had a mailing and generated between 300–400 letters. Dunbar is very active on our side and will try to influence his father-in-law, if he ever gets back. As soon as he gets back, the Chamber of Commerce is scheduled to meet with him.

WHITE—*El Paso:* John McFall, El Paso Natural Gas Co., P.O. Box 1492, El Paso is the contact and Jack Vowell, Jr., Vowell Construction Company, P.O. Box 253, El Paso is the Chairman of the Committee. They are having a meeting with the Congressman today. Jerry will receive a report when he gets there. They have had a favorable editorial and have generated a letter-writing campaign but Jerry doesn't have any figures.

MESKILL—*New Britain:* H. S. Everett, Executive Vice President, New Britain Chamber of Commerce, 24 Washington Street, New Britain is the contact man. They have generated between 300–400 letters. There are 12 members of the Committee. They have a letter in writing from Meskill stating he is definitely going to support H.R. 11750.

TIERNAN—*Providence:* Marshall is to give the report (see following paragraph). Jerry has had contact with Bill Hart (GE, New York) who told Jerry his man went to talk to the Congressman and he is definitely going to support the Dulski bill. Knox (Sears General Counsel in Philadelphia) sent one of his top men, who is from that area, in to organize it and there has been no report yet.

From Marshall: The local Chamber of Commerce had a meeting with the Congressman to discuss the matter of postal reform. One of the Assistant PMG's plans to address the Chamber at a luncheon September 15. A letter writing campaign has been started under the direction of Lou Pastore. A Citizens Committee is in the process of being formed and potential members have been invited to the September 15 luncheon.

DANIELS—*Jersey City:* Jerry talked with Bob Burkhardt, Secretary of State, who is presently on the outs with the political boss, John Kenney. Burkhardt suggested Jerry call Bill Flanagan, the Executive Director of the New Jersey Turnpike, who has influence with Kenney. Daniels is completely under the control of Kenney. Burkhardt is a friend of Flanagan's and alerted him yesterday to expect Jerry's call. Jerry will make contact today.

DULSKI—*Buffalo:* The Chamber of Commerce is riding the fence on support of the Administration bill. The paid personnel—Herb Berry, who is an assistant to Charlie Light, the Executive Vice President of the Chamber—is giving Jerry the most problems. Friendly people are Harlan Swift, President of the Erie Savings Bank, and Charlie Cox, Sears local manager. The best person is Miss Gladys Drewelow of the Worthington Corporation but she will not be active unless the head of the Worthington Corporation personally asks her. Jerry has called Bill Dunlap of the POD to make the call to her boss but as of yesterday, the call had not been made and *it is essential that this be done.* Worthington Corporation began a letter-writing campaign and has generated about 100 letters—this is not sufficient.

HENDERSON—*Goldsboro:* Jerry is waiting for a call from Penney's. So far he has received the name of Ray Patterson from them but he has called them back three times and has not received a phone number for Patterson. "Call us back tomorrow and we should have it"—this was as of yesterday. As of the report this morning (10:30 AM), he had nothing.

APPENDIX F

POD and CCPR Form Letters for HPOC Congressmen

[POD Letter and Memo to White House]

November 21, 1969

MEMORANDUM

TO: Mr. Jeb Magruder
             Special Assistant to the President
FROM: William D. Dunlap
             Office of Public Information
SUBJECT: Letters Supporting Postal Reform

Per our conversation, attached are:

a. a list of Congressmen (recorded in order of priority) that we would like to have postal reform letters sent to.

b. The message we would like them to communicate (as illustrated by two simple letters).

Please let me know if you have any questions.

We enjoyed meeting you and look forward to working with you in the future.

CONGRESSMEN	DISTRICT	HOME TOWN	WASHINGTON OFFICE ADDRESS
SCOTT, William L.	8th	Fairfax, Va.	Room 1217, Longworth Office Building
TIERNAN, Robert O.	2nd	Warwick, R.I.	Room 1706, Longworth Office Building
BUTTON, Daniel E.	29th	Albany, N.Y.	Room 1513, Longworth Office Building
HANLEY, James M.	34th	Syracuse, N.Y.	Room 109, Cannon Office Building
HENDERSON, David N.	3rd	Wallace, N.C.	Room 217, Cannon Office Building
WHITE, Richard C.	16th	El Paso, Tex.	Room 322, Cannon Office Building
CORBETT, Robert J.	18th	Pittsburgh, Pa.	Room 2467, Rayburn Office Building

- -

Dear Congressman _____ :

As a voting taxpayer and a frequent user of the mails, I am greatly concerned about the present unnecessary high cost of operating the nation's postal system. I therefore am writing to strongly urge you to support the Administration's total postal reform proposal as a means of correcting this continuing waste of our tax dollars.

It is high time the Post Office Department was placed on an efficient, business-like footing. With this nation's technological and managerial know-how, it is not only irresponsible but inexcusable to deny the application of these capabilities in a manner that will provide the American public with a more efficient and economical mail system.

The proper handling of the mails is too critical an issue to be treated like a political football. A well-run Post Office will benefit every citizen and, indeed, the entire national economy.

By voting in favor of total postal reform, you will be representing my views and the best interests of our country.

Don't let us down.

Sincerely,

_____

Dear Congressman _____ :

I don't usually write letters to my elected representatives in Washington. As a rule, I just vote on Election Day and then hope the winner will do a good job.

However, I feel very strongly about the need to correct the sorry situation in our Post Office Department. That is why I am writing to you now. I believe it is time to stop wasting our tax dollars on a postal system that everyone agrees cannot provide the service the public needs at a cost it can afford.

The system obviously must be changed, and I think the Administration's proposal for total postal reform is the way to do it. Anything less than total reform will only perpetuate the problem, not solve it.

Please vote in favor of this Bill.

Sincerely,

_____

CCPR Form Letter

(Sent by the Chairman of the Albany-Schenectady CCPR to Congressman Button's (D-N.Y.) constituents)

Dear _____ : Don't give up. The battle for *total* Postal Reform is not lost. Yet.

You may have read in the newspapers that a tie vote in the House Post Office Committee killed the chances of getting H.R. 11750, the one bill providing meaningful postal reform, to the floor of the House.

This is not true. It will take only *one additional vote* to substitute the true reform provisions of H.R. 11750 for those of H.R. 4, the substitute bill which only further complicates, rather than improves, the postal situation.

President Nixon, Postmaster-General Blount, former President Johnson and his Postmaster-General, Larry O'Brien, are but a few of the host of top political leaders and business executives who are convinced we *must* have *total* Postal Reform to head off a complete breakdown of our postal system.

Please call, write or telegraph your Congressman, Daniel E. Button, at 1513 Longworth Office Building, Washington, D.C. 20215, (202)225–4861.

Ask him to vote to make true postal reform possible by substituting the provisions of H.R. 11750 for those of H.R. 4.

His vote, alone, can do it! And, your telephone call or letter could be just the extra urge needed to bring about Total Postal Reform.

Please act now!

CCPR Advertisements

What would it cost your business to be without mail service for three weeks?

You think it couldn't happen? Think again.

In 1966, the Chicago Post Office broke down for three weeks. For 21 days, hardly any mail went out of that office.

And, since then, conditions throughout the postal system have gotten worse—not better. Former Postmaster General Lawrence O'Brien says the entire postal system of the U. S. is under the imminent threat of total breakdown.

If you don't like that prospect, do something about it.

Write, wire or phone your congressman and tell him you want him to support true Postal Reform. Tell him you want him to back HR 11750, the only bill before Congress which provides for the *total* reorganization of the postal service on a businesslike basis (along the lines of TVA). Tell him you won't be satisfied with half measures. Tell him you can't afford to run the risk of another Post Office collapse.

HR 11750. True Postal Reform. Nothing else will do the job.

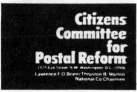

Citizens Committee for Postal Reform

1725 Eye Street N W Washington D C 20006
Lawrence F O Brien/Thruston B Morton
National Co Chairmen

The next time postal service breaks down, it's your fault.

In 1966, the Chicago Post Office ground to a halt. For three weeks, the mail was almost at a standstill.

If you want that to happen in your town, just wait.

Today's U.S. Post Office is probably the most inefficient, most antiquated big business in the United States. Unless something is done right now—by people like you—the situation is going to get worse.

Are you interested in straightening out the mess?

Right now, there's a bill before a committee of Congress called HR 11750. HR 11750 is, in brief, the recommendations of a bipartisan committee for the reorganization of the U.S. Post Office on a business like basis (along the lines of TVA). HR 11750 is designed to take the Post Office out of politics, to apply modern business methods to its operation and, in the process, to save taxpayers the $1,200,000,000 annual deficit that today's horse-and-buggy Post Office incurs.

You can help get HR 11750 out of committee and enacted into law by letting your congressman know how you feel. Tear out this column, pin it to your letterhead and mail it to your congressman today. Let your voice be heard.

If the Post Office in your city breaks down next, you can't say you haven't been warned.

Citizens Committee for Postal Reform

1725 Eye Street N W Washington D C 20006
Lawrence F O Brien/Thruston B Morton
National Co Chairmen

How would you like to have to get 268 OK's on every decision you make?

If the U.S. Post Office wants to get approval for a new Post Office facility, it has to get a majority of the 535 members of Congress to vote "yes."

That's 268 separate "yeses."

And it has to get them several times between concept and completion. On the average, it takes seven years. Seven years.

Why? Largely because Post Office appropriations have to compete for money with all sorts of requests that are politically more attractive.

So it's no wonder the Post Office tries to make do with inadequate facilities. With crowded buildings, antiquated equipment, almost unbelievable working conditions.

If you had to get 268 OK's in your business, maybe you'd give up. And maybe, like the Chicago Post Office in 1966, you'd break down, too. (Hardly a piece of mail moved for three whole weeks.)

You're in business, and you need the Post Office. You can help put it on a businesslike, efficient basis.

Write or phone your congressman today. Tell him you want to see HR 11750 passed soon. HR 11750. The *total* Postal Reform bill. The *only* true Postal Reform bill. The bill to establish a government authority and take the Post Office out of politics.

Write or phone today. Put the Post Office on a businesslike basis. Either *you* do, or nobody does.

Citizens Committee for Postal Reform
1725 Eye Street N.W. Washington D.C. 20006
Lawrence F. O'Brien / Thruston B. Morton
National Co-Chairmen

This U.S. business loses over $1,000,000,000 and 20% of its employees every year—and you pay the losses.

It's the Post Office. Your taxes must be about $1.2 billion greater to make up its annual deficits. And your postal service suffers because of the high employee turnover.

Fire the management? You can't do that with the Post Office. Its basic management decisions are made by 535 members of Congress. They control its spending for facilities, its employment costs and conditions, and the rates it can charge for services.

That was fine in 1789 when it all started, but it's time for a change—a complete change. There's a bill, HR 11750, now before Congress which provides true Postal Reform. It creates a government authority (something like TVA) to run the Post Office on a businesslike basis. President Nixon and Postmaster General Blount are behind it. So are ex-President Johnson and his Postmaster General, Lawrence O'Brien. You should be, too, unless you don't mind paying the deficits. Or wouldn't be bothered by a total breakdown of service in your city (like Chicago in 1966).

You *can* do something. Write or wire your congressman; ask him to support HR 11750, the only bill that will bring true Postal Reform. Do it today.

Citizens Committee for Postal Reform
1725 Eye Street N.W. Washington D.C. 20006
Lawrence F. O'Brien / Thruston B. Morton
National Co-Chairmen

NOTES

1. Lawrence F. O'Brien, "How the Post Office Plotted Suicide," *Washington Post*, August 18, 1968, p. B4.

2. Joel L. Fleishman, ed., *The Future of the Postal Service* (New York: Praeger, 1983), p. 44.

3. "Untangling the Mess in the Post Office," *Business Week*, March 28, 1970, p. 98.

4. "Obstacles to Post Office Reform," *Roanoke World News*, February 17, 1969, p. 6. Cited in Harold Dolenga, *An Analytical Case Study of the Policy Formation Process (Postal Reform and Reorganization)* (Ann Arbor, Mich.: University Microfilms, 1973), Northwestern University, Ph.D., Political Science, June 1973, p. 494.

5. Senate Post Office and Civil Service Committee, *Postal Modernization*, hearings, 91st. Cong., 1st sess., 1969, p. 800.

6. *Ibid.*, p. 892.

7. Charles G. Benda, "State Organizations and Policy Formation: The Reorganization of the Post Office Department," Program on Information Resources Policy, Harvard University, August 1978, Working Paper W-78-11, p. 32.

8. Quoted in President's Commission (Kappel Commission) on Postal Reorganization, *Towards Postal Excellence* (Washington, D.C.: U.S. Govt. Printing Office, June 1968), p. 34.

9. Statistics cited in "The Question of a Federal Postal Corporation," *Congressional Digest*, March 1969, p. 70.

10. *Ibid.*

11. Gerald Cullinan, *The Post Office Department* (New York: Praeger, 1968), p. xi.

12. Cited in Earl Collier, Jr., and George Bostick, "The Postal Reorganization Act: A Case Study of Regulated Industry Reform," *Virgina Law Review* 58, 1972, p. 1034.

13. James N. Miller, "The Awful Truth About the U.S. Post Office," *Reader's Digest*, November 1968.

14. Cited in *Texas Chronicle* (Houston), May 21, 1969, editorial page.

15. Cited in Frank S. Joseph, "Pressures come from many directions to set postal reform's eventual course," *National Journal*, December 13, 1969, p. 326.

16. See the Kappel Commission, *Towards Postal Excellence*, p. 16.

17. Quoted in Harold Dolenga, *An Analytical Case Study of the Policy Formation Process (Postal Reform and Reorganization)*, pp. 485,486.

18. Statement of James H. Rademacher, President, National Association of Letter Carriers, to New York City Branch 36, November 9, 1968, mimeograph text, pp. 1,12.

19. Robert B. Semple Jr., "Nixon Proposes U.S. Corporation for Mail Service," *New York Times*, May 28, 1969, pp. 1,20.

20. The prohibition was cited in a then widely circulated memorandum from the chairman of the Civil Service to all executive departments entitled "Role of the Career Official in Support of Federal Programs," January 10, 1962.

21. Quoted in Harold Dolenga, *An Analytical Case Study*, p. 397.

22. Lawrence F. O'Brien, "How the Post Office Plotted Suicide."

23. AP press release ran as "Nixon Pushes Postal Reform," *Salina Journal* (Kansas), May 27, 1969.

24. Quoted in "A Postal Corporation," *Scranton (Pa.) Journal*, May 29, 1969.

25. Donald N. Ledbetter, "The Secretary's Report," *The Postal Supervisor*, September 1969, p. 4.

26. See Charles G. Benda, "State Organizations and Policy Formation: The Reorganization of the Post Office Department," pp. 131–133.

27. See "No Solution," *Odessa American* (Tx.), June 25, 1969, p. 10–A, and "The Postmaster General writes . . . ," *Worthington Globe* (Minn.), June 3, 1969.

28. In order of citation in the text, the editorials appeared May 30, 1969; July 15, 1969; June 9, 1969; and May 29, 1969.

29. POD transcript of briefing by Postmaster General Blount to the National Press Club, May 28, 1969, pp. 19,20.

30. House Post Office and Civil Service Committee (HPOC), *Post Office Reorganization*, hearings, Part 1, 91st Cong., 1st sess., 1969, p. 182.

31. *Ibid.*, pp. 628–632.

32. "The Halt and the Blind," *New York Times*, July 11, 1969, p. 36.

33. POD Release, Remarks by Winton M. Blount at National Newspaper Association Convention, Atlantic City, N.J., June 27, 1969, p. 4.

34. Joseph Young, "Postal Corporation Plan Is Gaining in Congress," *Washington Star*, July 7, 1969.

35. HPOC, *Post Office Reorganization*, pp. 993,994.

36. *Ibid.*, p. 973.

37. *Ibid.*, pp. 747,764.

38. "Nixon Postal Corporation Plan Gaining Little Support in House," *New York Times*, August 23, 1969, p. 24.

39. Fred Blumenthal, "Our Crippled Giant," *Parade*, August 24, 1969, p. 7.

40. The O'Brien / Nixon / Blount / Morton meeting was summarized in the CCPR's first newsletter, *The Postal Reformer*, September 15, 1969, pp. 1,2.

41. White House transcript of remarks of President Nixon, San Clemente, California, September 2, 1969, p. 1.

42. *Congressional Record,* September 9, 1969, p. 24898.

43. "A Word About Jerry Bruno," in Jerry Bruno and Jeff Greenfield, *The Advance Man* (New York: William Morrow, 1971), p. 9.

44. "Postal Reform Unit Organized," *Syracuse Herald-Journal,* August 26, 1969, p. 23.

45. CCPR press release, October 2, 1969, pp. 1–3.

46. Joseph V. Ganley, "Postal Reform Groups Raps Hanley's Stand," *Syracuse Herald-American,* October 19, 1969, p. 18.

47. "Hope for the Mails," *New York Times,* September 15, 1969, p. 46.

48. Marjorie Hunter, "Albert Doubtful of House Action on Draft, Crime Bills in '69," *New York Times,* September 23, 1969, p. 20.

49. "Moving the Mail Disaster," *Washington Post,* September 23, 1969, editorial page.

50. Donald N. Ledbetter, "The Secretary's Report," *The Postal Supervisor,* September 1969, pp. 4,5.

51. Quoted in "Postal Lobby Tactics and Finances Questioned," *Congressional Quarterly,* October 24, 1969, p. 2067.

52. CCPR press release, reprinted in the *Congressional Record,* October 3, 1969, p. 28552.

53. *Congressional Record,* October 14, 1969, p. 29974.

54. Office of the White House Press Secretary, Message from the President to the Congress, October 11, 1969, p. 3.

55. *Congressional Record,* October 9, 1969, p. 29322.

56. United Federation of Postal Clerks press release, undated (released between October 16–22, 1969), pp. 1–2.

57. "Postal Lobby Tactics and Finances Questioned," *Congressional Quarterly,* October 24, 1969, p. 2067.

58. CCPR text of address by Senator Thruston Morton to the conference of the American Business Press, Chicago, Ill., October 23, 1969, pp. 6,7.

59. *Congressional Record,* October 28, 1969, p. 31915.

60. Senate Post Office and Civil Service Committee, *Postal Modernization,* hearings, 91st. Cong., 1st sess., 1969, p. 800.

61. *Ibid.,* p. 816.

62. "Letter Carriers Push Lobby Campaign for Higher Pay," *Congressional Quarterly,* December 5, 1969, p. 2510.

63. *Ibid.*

64. Quoted in Harold Dolenga, *An Analytical Case Study,* p. 527.

65. Noted in Charles Benda. "State Organizations," p. 68.

66. "Congress to Act Soon On Pay Rise Bill," *New York Times,* February 26, 1970, p. 14.

67. Joseph Young, "Heavy Pressure Is Cited in Postal Reform Battle," *Washington Star,* March 17, 1970.

68. POD Transcript of Postal Reform Legislation press conference with Postmaster General Winton M. Blount, March 12, 1970, p. 6.

THE PRESS AND THE INVESTIGATION AND RESIGNATION OF VICE PRESIDENT SPIRO T. AGNEW

by Wendy O'Donnell

O N AUGUST 5, 1973, the United States attorney for Maryland, George Beall, received a telephone call that left him an unhappy man. Jerry Landauer, an investigative reporter for the *Wall Street Journal,* was calling to say that he planned to publish a story that Vice-President Spiro Agnew was being investigated on charges of bribery, extortion, and tax fraud. In the course of the conversation Landauer recited almost verbatim portions of a letter Beall had delivered to Agnew's lawyers only five days before, informing the vice-president of the investigation.

Beall, along with several assistant U.S. attorneys, and with the knowledge of top Justice Department officials in Washington, had been conducting the investigation of Agnew for almost three months. They knew it could not stay a secret for much longer. Yet Beall was surprised when Landauer called. Perhaps he had been lulled into some sense of security during the months in which the story failed to leak; certainly he did not expect the reporter who broke the story to have the details of confidential correspondence sent to the vice-president.

How Landauer had obtained the information about the letter, Beall did not know. What the prosecutor and his colleagues did know, as soon as Landauer's call was received, was that the conduct of the investigation would be radically changed by having it made public. And while they may have known there would be a few advantages—less constraint would be needed in the wording of subpoenas, potential witnesses could be approached with less circumspection—for the most part, they believed the changes would be for the worse, would be damaging to the government's conduct of the case. From August 5, throughout the term of the investigation, Beall and his assistants feared the glare from the media's spotlight would be turned on the prosecution team and the witnesses as well as on Agnew himself. Further, it would make it impossible to run the probe as if it

---

Unless otherwise noted, all quotations come either from unpublished government documents or from interviews with the author.

were just another political corruption case. They were not wrong in their concern.

The Vice-President Becomes a Target

The Search for Corruption in Baltimore County

The investigation that ended in the downfall of Vice-President Agnew was initiated to expose corruption in Baltimore County, Maryland. It was undertaken jointly by the Maryland U.S. attorney and the Internal Revenue Service. The two agencies decided in the fall of 1972 to pursue an inquiry because rumors had been reported to both offices of officials taking bribes or kickbacks.

This type of investigation was in the best tradition of the office of the U.S. Attorney for Maryland. *The Sun* (Baltimore), at the time of the investigation, described the office's crusading history:

> The bold young idealists who work under George Beall at the United States attorney's office here are part of a tradition of tackling political corruption head-on.
>
> They have gone after senators, congressmen and top political figures with an almost revolutionary fervor and a singleness of purpose eliciting national attention. . . .
>
> Young prosecutors might be expected to be zealous in seeking strict enforcement of political corruption laws, but few federal districts in the nation have been as successful in gaining convictions under these statutes as the U.S. attorney's office in Maryland.
>
> In recent years, the office has successfully developed cases against A. Gordon Boone, a former Democratic speaker of the House of Delegates; Thomas F. Johnson, a former Eastern Shore Democratic congressman; and Daniel B. Brewster, former Democratic United States senator.[1]

When they began the investigation though, the bold young idealists did not know that their investigation would lead to the vice-president, in fact they were firmly convinced that it would and could not.

Once George Beall and Robert Browne, chief of the Intelligence Division for the I.R.S. in Maryland, decided that an investigation was needed, I.R.S. agents were sent scouring through Baltimore County looking for initial evidence of corruption. In October of 1972, they began to find such evidence relating to some architectural and engineering firms in the county. Beall then assigned two assistant U.S. attorneys to spearhead the investigation—Barnet (Barney) Skolnik and Ronald Liebman. Shortly thereafter, he added a third, Russell T. (Tim) Baker.

According to Aaron Latham who wrote a piece shortly after the vice-president's resignation on the prosecutors' thoughts and actions for *New York* magazine:

> With the help of the others, Tim Baker prepared a wave of long, complicated detailed subpoenas. They were issued on January 4, 1973, and were

returnable five days later. Twenty-six went to engineering and architectural firms. Another went to Baltimore County itself, requesting records for the years 1969, 1970 and 1971. The county reacted as if it had been invaded by a foreign power. . . .

William Fornoff, a Baltimore County administrative officer, . . . said it would take a truck to carry all the subpoenaed documents. Beall said that that was fine—they would tell the driver where to deliver his cargo when he got there. And that is what happened. The documents filled 120 filing cabinets. Robert Browne and his I.R.S. agents went to work looking for pools of cash.* They searched balance sheets as if they were the scenes of crimes. Incredibly, they had some immediate success.[2]

The success was in the form of checks, written to corporate executives, but endorsed for cash. The Baltimore team began to question officers of the companies engaged in such practices, and they began hearing that the cash was generated as kickbacks for county administrators in return for county business. The allegations specifically involved then-County Executive Dale Anderson, a Democrat, and one of his principal aides, the aforementioned William Fornoff. Anderson had succeeded Spiro Agnew as Baltimore County Executive in 1967, when Agnew had gone on to the governor's mansion.

In retrospect, Barney Skolnik says, it should not have seemed unlikely, if Anderson was taking bribes or kickbacks, that his predecessor might have too. But, unlikely or not, the prosecutors had a better reason to be uninterested in Agnew—the statute of limitations. In fact, Skolnik explains, the prosecutors originally looked on the idea that Agnew might be involved as somewhat humorous:

> There was some limited joking that . . . simply by virtue of the fact that Agnew was Anderson's predecessor, that the investigation might "lead to Agnew." The reason it was a joke . . . was because by the time we were running the investigation in early 1973, it was well over five years that Agnew had been out of [county] office. Therefore, we all knew that even if it were true that Agnew had done the same thing and even if it turned out that we developed evidence of the fact (both of which were big "ifs"), as a legal matter we couldn't prosecute because the statute of limitations had run.
>
> What we didn't, in the early causal joking, ever consciously realize as far as I can recall was that if Agnew had gotten into the habit of doing such things when he was county executive and had continued the habit in later years in other offices, it would be within the statute of limitations. That kind of chain of logic, we didn't think about.

So the investigators set about amassing evidence with regard to Anderson and Fornoff, building their case throughout the winter and early spring. Because the investigation was so large in scope, its existence was no secret in the Balti-

---

*The generation of large amounts of cash is commonly considered by law enforcement officials as a good indicator of corrupt practices. Latham notes at another point in his article "cash goes with corruption the way needles go with narcotics."[3]

more political and legal communities. And, inevitably, word spread to members of the press and into government circles in Washington.

The word eventually spread to Spiro Agnew, who in early 1973, called Attorney General Richard Kleindienst to inquire about the investigation and where it was heading. He received Kleindienst's assurances that the probe was looking at Fornoff and Anderson. Word of the call did, however, raise Tim Baker's antennae and although his colleagues were not sympathetic, Baker began to believe that Agnew might be implicated at some point down the line.

The spread of information about the investigation's existence had two immediate consequences for the prosecutors. First, they began receiving phone calls from reporters wanting to know by name who the targets of the investigation were. They were also frequently asked whether Vice-President Agnew, the most well-known political figure to come out of the county, was implicated. The prosecutors invariably told the reporters that Agnew was *not* a target and went on to deliver a brief lesson on the statute of limitations. Their direct answers to these questions would later haunt the prosecutors.

During the first week of May, the prosecutors' view of Agnew began to change dramatically. Tim Baker was having a routine conversation with the attorney for Lester Matz, one of the partners in a firm accused of kicking back fees from county contracts. A number of other individuals were already bargaining with the prosecutors and Joseph Kaplan went to the U.S. attorney's office to see what kind of deal could be struck for his client. Aaron Latham describes:

> Tim Baker happened to talk to Joseph Kaplan, who represented Lester Matz. Baker mentioned that the U.S. attorney's office was on the verge of indicting his client. Kaplan said that he had some information to trade but that he did not think the prosecutor would be interested. Baker asked what Kaplan was talking about. The lawyer said that his client could implicate a high figure in the current Republican administration. The implication, of course, was that a Republican U.S. attorney would not want to prosecute a top official in the Republican family.
>
> Joe Kaplan mentioned no names, but the young prosecutor thought immediately of Agnew. Actually, he had not stopped thinking of the vice-president, since Agnew had first professed nervousness about the case.
>
> Tim Baker got mad. The prosecutor told the lawyer that he was not only factually incorrect but immensely insulting. Baker made it clear that he wanted to hear Lester Matz's story.[4]

Baker then checked with Beall that he was willing to receive evidence on a high-level Republican, and having received Beall's assent, telephoned Kaplan. Later that week, Beall and the three assistant U.S. attorneys met with Kaplan and were told not only that Matz had paid off Agnew during his terms as county executive and governor (the latter bringing the charge within the period allowed by the statute of limitations), but that the practice had continued into the vice-presidency. At this point, the whole tenor of the investigation changed for the Baltimore team.

Investigating the Vice-President

From the start, the Baltimore team was somewhat nervous about investigating the second highest official of the U.S. government, and they were nervous for several reasons. They feared if the vice-president learned that he had become a target of the probe that he, with or without White House assistance, would try to quash the investigation. They were nervous that, if it went that far, requesting a grand jury indictment of a sitting vice-president would raise a myriad of Constitutional questions that could bog down the case. Finally, by their own statements, the prosecutors were especially nervous that somehow the investigation would be leaked to the press and that the consequences produced, unknown though they were, could be disastrous.

To avoid these potential horrors, the prosecutors took a number of unusual steps in order to keep the investigation secret. They did not tell the I.R.S. investigators working with them that Agnew had become a target. According to Tim Baker this was highly irregular: "Berney and I, in particular, had worked with [the I.R.S. agents] through other political corruption cases. We were like brothers." He stresses that the decision not to tell them did not revolve around their competence, but was a protection against leaks: "We made a decision that we would not tell the agents we had received information about Agnew . . . because we wanted to minimize the number of people who knew that Agnew's name had come up."

Additionally, the prosecutors didn't tell the other Baltimore assistant U.S. attorneys or staff members. Again, this was an unusual step. Even in sensitive political corruption cases both Beall and Baker note that it was typical to inform the other assistants and to brainstorm with them on how to proceed with the case.

On procedural matters, they were equally cautious. Baker says: "For example, we didn't send out any subpoenas that had dates on them [requesting records] from the time when Agnew was County Executive. We did this because anyone receiving the subpoena could say 'Wait a minute, this subpoena covers the period from 1962 to 1966. Spiro Agnew was County Executive in those years.' So we didn't do that, at least for a while."

Aaron Latham says that the prosecutors also concentrated on obtaining evidence from only those people who they were reasonably certain were prosecutable in connection with the payoffs. He claims that they did this, rather than casting the widest possible net for information on Agnew, because they felt individuals who were themselves under threat of prosecution would be less likely to run to the press with the story than those with no worry of court action against them.*[5]

---

*This would later become one of the issues raised by the vice-president in his charge that he was framed. Agnew contends that all of the men who tendered evidence against him were seeking to save their own skins and, therefore, their testimony was tainted.

Informing the Justice Department and the Vice-President

The next dilemma to face the Baltimore team was what and when to tell the Justice Department in Washington about the investigation. As noted earlier, Attorney General Richard Kleindienst had known of the probe's existence after he had been contacted by the vice-president, and had been told enough to give several assurances to Agnew that he was not implicated. Kleindienst, however, had resigned in April 1973 after a number of White House aides were implicated in the attempted coverup of Watergate. President Nixon had nominated Elliot Richardson as his replacement on April 30th. Richardson had impressive credentials; in addition to experience as a U.S. attorney in Massachusetts, he had served in several cabinet and subcabinet posts at the federal level. At the time of his nomination as attorney general, Richardson was serving as the Secretary of Defense. He was confirmed and assumed his new post on May 25.

Throughout May, the prosecutors had waited for the new attorney general to be put in place. Once he was installed, there was still more waiting because, without revealing to his scheduling staff why they wanted to see Richardson, they were not given high priority on his calendar. With Watergate at its height, and with Special Prosecutor Archibald Cox a constant irritant to the president, the attorney general had a great deal on his schedule. Barney Skolnik recalls of that time:

> We were really anxious to see Richardson for the obvious reason that we wanted a laying on of hands so we could proceed with [the case]. . . .
>
> I have a strong memory of what seemed like several weeks . . . of the most aggravating, agonizing kind of [discussion]: we'd be saying ''God-dammit, George, get us in there!'' and George would be saying ''He's busy.'' I think there was even some discussion with raised voices about telling the [attorney general's] secretary that the fate of the nation depended on our seeing him.

The U.S. attorney and his assistants had somewhat different concerns at the time about meeting with Richardson. In the back of the assistants' minds, according to Skolnik, was the nagging thought that Beall might not be doing all he could to get them to the attorney general because, like Nixon, Agnew, and Richardson, he was a Republican. Skolnik notes: ''There was a horrible, political aspect to it, which of course made us very uncomfortable. . . . And we were becoming increasingly uncomfortable because it was as though we were crawling further and further out on a limb. We felt very strongly that it was a legitimate place for us to be, but also as a kind of organizational matter that we ought to have the blessing of the attorney general.''

Beall explains that his reticence, if any, regarding the attorney general was not prompted by a desire to slow the investigation. Beall did encounter genuine problems getting on to Richardson's calendar. Additionally, he began to worry that once Washington had been informed, they might take the case away from the Baltimore group: ''I have to say, I did not talk to the Department of Justice [early on] because I was very fearful that we would lose control of the investigation.''

On June 12, however, Beall did get to see Richardson, although their meeting was quite brief and none of the assistant U.S. attorneys were present. Latham describes the meeting as follows:

> Beall told Richardson briefly about the Baltimore County probe; then he added a postscript about the Vice-President. Beall said that Agnew had repeatedly expressed concern about this investigation to Kleindienst, these misgivings usually being passed over the telephone, once over breakfast. Beall added, somewhat cryptically, that his office had just received its first hint that Agnew had more to worry about than unfair publicity. The U.S. attorney chose to soft-pedal the Agnew connection, presenting it in the context of rumor and gossip, Richardson did not seem unduly concerned.[6]

Although Latham's article was based on interviews with the members of the Baltimore team (including Beall) immediately after Agnew's resignation, the accountings given of this meeting vary widely from party to party. Richardson's executive assistant, J. T. Smith, who was in charge of the attorney general's schedule, does not remember it happening at all; neither does Barney Skolnik. This, however, seems to be simply an indication of the secrecy surrounding the meeting. After the passing of eleven years, even the two participants are not sure exactly what took place. George Beall does remember, though, meeting with Richardson that first time alone. What he does not remember is "soft-pedaling" the Agnew involvement. He recalls telling the attorney general as of June "we are starting to get very hard information on Agnew." He further believes that he discussed with Richardson the problems that would be generated if the press learned of the developing case: "Mr. Richardson and I, I think, talked about the problem of the press right in our very first meeting. I said to him that I thought until the information was corroborated and developed further that we ought to make sure there was no paper flowing back and forth, and that we kept to a very tight circle of people who knew of the investigation. And he agreed that we ought to keep it quiet. I don't think he told me, nor did I ask, who on his staff might be aware of our conversation, but I sure wanted to leave the impression with him that I didn't want anyone else to know about it at that point.''

At least as far as J. T. Smith was concerned, apparently Richardson honored the implication in Beall's request. Smith, by his own recollection, did not learn of the investigation until over three weeks later. At that time the U.S. attorney came with his three assistants—Skolnik, Baker, and Liebman—to lay out the case for the attorney general and to ask for his blessing to continue with it, which they received. In those intervening weeks, the Baltimore prosecutors moved forward on the case; going, as Barney Skolnik says, further and further out on the limb.

By the end of July, the investigation had progressed far enough that the attorney general, along with his staff and the Baltimore prosecutors, believed that it was time to let the vice-president know he had become a target. It was also time, Richardson thought, that the White House should at least be warned that serious charges were being leveled at Agnew. According to Aaron Latham, that decision was made at a meeting among the Baltimore and Washington Justice officials on Friday, July 27, 1973. That same day, Latham notes, Richardson telephoned to Alexander Haig to relay the warning.[7]

On August 1, a letter was delivered to Judah Best, one of the vice-president's attorneys, telling Agnew that he was under investigation for possible violations of criminal statutes relating to conspiracy, bribery and extortion, as well, possibly, as laws regarding tax evasion.[8] The news of the probe of the vice-president had failed to break all during May, June, and July. It would only take four days from the time the letter was delivered to Agnew's attorney for the media to get the story.

The Leaks

When the story that the vice-president of the United States was under investigation for suspected criminal behavior broke, there were many surprising aspects to it. The one thing that was not surprising, however, was the reporter who broke the story. *Wall Street Journal* reporter Jerry Landauer had been interested in Spiro Agnew for a long time. According to colleagues, his investigation of rumors about Agnew began while Agnew was still in the governor's mansion. Off and on in the subsequent years, Landauer had worked on amassing information and sources toward the day when he could write a story about the charges against Agnew. And the U.S. attorney's investigation of the vice-president provided just such a story.

Landauer Calls Beall

On Sunday, August 5, Landauer knew enough to begin confronting the principals. In addition to knowing that the vice-president was a target of investigation, according to statements he made to George Beall, the reporter had in fact seen the letter sent to Agnew informing him of the investigation.

Landauer called Beall at home to tell him of the pending story. The reporter told the U.S. attorney that he was preparing the run a story in the next day's newspaper saying the vice-president was under investigation. Beall, who was preparing to take his family on an outing to a local pool, says he was amazed by the specificity of Landauer's information and unhappy that the veil of secrecy around the investigation was about to be lifted. Although he probably knew it would not work, Beall says he still tried to discourage the reporter from running the story.

> I asked him how he knew about an investigation of the Vice-President of the United States and he said "It's none of your business, but I have seen a copy of a letter that you wrote to Vice-President Agnew dated August 1st in which you advised the Vice-President . . ." and then he proceeded to

quote practically verbatim from the letter. It sounded to me like he was reading me the first paragraph of the letter. And he said "Did you send such a letter?"

I replied "Mr. Landauer, I really am not in a position to talk about anything relating to any investigation of anybody, much less the Vice-President of the United States. I'm not telling you he's under investigation, and I'm not telling you he's not under investigation. I'm not telling you I sent a letter; and I'm not telling you I didn't send a letter. I'm just saying that I can't talk about people under investigation; it's just not fair, is it?" He made no response to that, but he said "I'm going to write a story and tomorrow it's going to be front page headlines. I have it on good authority." And I said, "Well, Mr. Landauer, I can't tell you what to write and not to write, but your reputation is at stake and if I were you I would not be writing any such article because I think you may run the risk of hurting your reputation as a reporter."

For a day, Beall may have believed that his strategy succeeded for the Monday morning *Wall Street Journal* carried no report of the probe. But Landauer had not backed off the story, he had simply decided to wait a day to try to get greater detail and to request a response from the vice-president.

After George Beall hung up from his talk with Landauer, he telephoned the Attorney General to tell him that the period of proceeding in secrecy had ended. Beall says:

My first call was to Elliot Richardson [at his home]. . . . I said essentially "Boss, the cat is out of the bag. The press has gotten wind of this thing we've been investigating for three months." And I think he said something to the effect of "We were fortunate to have been able to keep it quiet this long." He asked what I had told Landauer and I explained. He then said he'd rather not talk to Landauer or any reporter, but that he had to talk to the President.

On Monday, August 6, Elliot Richardson began dealing with the fact that the investigation would soon be made public. Although the *Journal* did not carry the anticipated story that morning, Richardson had little doubt that the story would soon break. He met first with George Beall to get a report on the status of the investigation. He then went to the White House to talk with President Nixon. In that conversation, Richardson provided Nixon with a broad outline of the case and informed him that the press knew about the probe. He asked for and received Nixon's agreement that the investigation should continue. The president, however, suggested that the attorney general should tell the vice-president the rough outline of the government's case; something the Baltimore prosecutors strongly opposed. Richardson, however, assented. He says:

I agreed that I should do that. Prosecutors do not normally go to a prospective defendant and tell him the nature of the case being developed against him. But, it seemed to me the situation of the Vice-President of the United States [being investigated] was enough different [to warrant telling him and] I didn't think it likely in any event it would significantly affect the case. He wasn't going to flee the country. There were going to be press stories about the case.

Late that same afternoon Richardson went to Agnew's office in the Old Executive Office Building. He says that, for his part, he summarized for the vice-president what the government's witnesses were prepared to say in court. At this point the government had several contractors, among them Lester Matz, who were willing to testify that Agnew had participated in kickback schemes. According to Richardson, as soon as he had described the government's position to Agnew, the vice-president began denouncing the U.S. attorney's office, saying that they were out to get him. Of course, the vice-president knew as well as the attorney general that the story of the investigation was about to break in the press. Jerry Landauer had not called only George Beall, he had called the vice-president's office as well.

Late Monday night, the first edition of the *Wall Street Journal* for the next day was printed. With its printing, and later into that night the printing of the *Washington Post,* the chances of keeping the story a secret any longer officially ended. That early edition of Tuesday's *Journal* carried the headline "A New Watergate? Spiro Agnew Is Target of a Criminal Inquiry; Extortion Is Alleged!". In fact, the attempts at secrecy had ended a bit earlier that evening, when the vice-president, aware from reporters' telephone calls to his office that the story was out, issued a statement confirming the existence of the probe. Agnew's statement issued at 11 P.M. on August 6, was too late to be included in the *Journal*'s story, its first edition already being published by that time, but was in time to be included in the story on the front page of the *Post* as well as to be sent nationwide on the wire services.

Richard Cohen and Jules Witcover, two *Post* reporters who wrote a book about Agnew, describe the moments leading up to the vice-president's statement. Cohen, who covered Baltimore for the *Post* was on Landauer's heels in getting the story and didn't want to be beaten by the *Journal* by even a day. As a result, he writes:

> On Monday, Agnew and his press secretary, J. Marsh Thomson, stayed behind in the Old Executive Office Building, waiting for the threatened *Wall Street Journal* story that had failed to materialize once before. But any chance that another day might pass without the investigation becoming public vanished. The *Washington Post* also had the story and, like the *Journal,* was pressing Agnew for a reply.
> "Where's the Vice President?" Thomson was asked by a *Post* reporter.
> "He's in his office," Thomson replied.
> "What's he doing there at this hour?"
> Thomson admitted Agnew was waiting for the *Journal* story to break. The *Post* gave Agnew a deadline for releasing a statement. At eleven o'clock, Thomson finally phoned it to the *Post,* the wire services, the television networks, and—lastly—the *Journal.*[9]

Even without Agnew's statement, Jerry Landauer's story in the edition of August 7, had the bulk of the information about the investigation. He wrote:

WASHINGTON—Vice President Spiro T. Agnew was formally notified by the Justice Department last week that he is a target of a far-ranging criminal investigation by the U.S. attorney's office in Baltimore. The allegations against him include bribery, extortion and tax fraud.*[10]

The *Post* and the wire services included, after similar leads, the text of Agnew's statement, which read:

I have been informed that I am under criminal investigation for possible violations of the criminal statutes. I will make no further comment until the investigation has been completed, other than to say that I am innocent of any wrongdoing, that I have confidence in the criminal justice system of the United States and that I am equally confident my innocence will be affirmed.[11]

The vice-president would only keep his vow of making no further comment for about thirty-six hours. By that time the news stories which appeared detailing the charges against him and some names of prospective witnesses, according to Agnew, forced him to change his tack. Especially exasperating to him was the fact that a number of the assertions carried in the news stories were not attributed to named individuals but to anonymous "sources." One example of the use of such sources appeared in a *Washington Post* story on August 8 (which carried a number of such attributions). It said: "The federal investigators, sources said, are seeking to tie Agnew to an alleged scheme in which prominent Republicans influenced the awarding of federal engineering and architectural contracts in return for kickbacks or political contributions from those firms."[12]

On Wednesday the vice-president changed his mind and made his first public appearance since the story broke. he called a press conference, and read the following to reporters:

Ladies and gentlemen, I have a very short statement to make following which I'll take your questions.

Because of defamatory statements that are being leaked to the news media by sources that the news reports refer to as close to the federal investigation, I cannot adhere to my original intention to remain silent following my initial statement, a few days ago, which asserted my innocence and which indicated I would have nothing further to say until the investigation was completed.

Under normal circumstances, the traditional safeguards of secrecy under such proceedings would protect the subject. But apparently this protection is not to be extended to the Vice President of the United States.

Well, I have no intention to be skewered in this fashion. And since I have no intention to be so skewered, I have called this press conference to label as false and scurrilous and malicious these rumors, these assertions and accusations that are being circulated; and to answer your questions regarding them, and any other questions that I might be able to answer concerning this general situation.[13]

---

*See Appendix A for the full text of Landauer's story.

Agnew's assertion that the leaks were intended to skewer him was the first charge in what remains an unsettled debate regarding who leaked and why. Agnew, his attorneys, and friends came to believe that somewhere in the Justice Department in Washington or Baltimore the leaks were occurring to bolster the government's case and turn public opinion against the vice-president. Some of those serving in the Justice Department at the time, however, still believe that it was the vice-president or his associates who were leaking to damage the public perception of the Justice Department.

During the August 8 press conference, Peter Lisagor of the *Chicago Daily News* asked the vice-president what motives he attributed to those who might be leaking information about the grand jury inquiry. Agnew responded:

> First of all, Mr. Lisagor, I have no knowledge of who is leaking this information. As you ladies and gentlemen know, one of the things the press does best is protect its sources so I could not comment in response to the motives of the individuals because I don't know who they are.
>
> I would say this: that the accusations that are being made, if they do come from people who are also under investigation, must be looked at as accusations that are coming from those who have found themselves in very deep trouble, and are looking to extricate themselves from this trouble and are flirting with the idea that they can obtain immunity or reduced charges, perhaps, by doing so.
>
> Now I have no tangible or definite information about the leaks. I can only respond to your questions about what I know and my position on what's been said.[14]

Later the vice-president would become less restrained about the identity of those he believed were leaking. He characterized this press conference, however, as presenting his own defense to the American people. And, at least to his own thinking, he was successful. "Moments after I ended my half-hour news conference, telegrams and telephone calls began pouring into my office. They ran overwhelmingly in my favor, as Americans across the land congratulated me upon my strong defense of my own integrity."[15]

The Leaks Continue

For a time after August 8, the investigation and the coverage it generated fell into a kind of routine, albeit an intense one. Deputy Attorney General William Ruckelshaus testifies that the offices of the Department of Justice were often filled with members of the press, noting that "once the press got wind of [the investigation] they were really hounding the whole department. You could hardly get out in the hall without being tackled by reporters. And I can remember the irony of reading a *New York Times* editorial lamenting the fact that the Justice Department was [supposedly] leaking like a sieve and looking out of my door and seeing their reporters dragging up and down the halls, looking everywhere they could to find information."

The Baltimore U.S. Attorney's office was, if anything, even worse. Before the fact of the investigation had been made public, the U.S. Attorney's office in Maryland had been a fairly open place. Reporters were able to freely wander in to the federal prosecutor's offices, talking to anyone they found available. Once the story about Agnew broke, this changed. Now reporters were crawling all over and the prosecutors began to feel as if they were under siege. As a result, George Beall installed a door blocking access from the entrance area to the working offices and placed a receptionist there. Reporters were forced to wait in the new reception room until (and if at all) a member of the staff agreed to see them.

During this period, the prosecutors were making precious few public comments. According to the *Post,* "Because of the extraordinary sensitivity of the investigation, the prosecutors in Beall's office have refused to comment about the case and last week took the extraordinary step of issuing a joint press release saying they were not the source of leaks to the press concerning the case."[16] In terms of the attorneys issuing a joint press statement declaring their own innocence in the matter of leaks, the word "extraordinary" seems an understatement.

Barney Skolnik did speak to the press once during this period, on the record and not on the substance of the case. He spoke out, in fact, on the new pressures added to the prosecutors by the publicity surrounding the case

> Skolnik . . . said there has been an increase in pressure on the prosecutors since it became known last week that they were investigating Agnew. "The public is now watching everything we do," he said. "We are very concerned that the Department of Justice and our office do this thing right, so that to the extent the public is aware now or will be at some subsequent time of how the investigation was conducted, they will see that it was handled properly."[17]

The furor over the leaks, however, was not stemmed by either the press release or Skolnik's statements, nor were the suspicions of some in Baltimore and Washington that the Justice Department had to be responsible for at least some of the leaks. Shortly after the leaked information began appearing in the press, Charles Morgan, director of the National Office of the American Civil Liberties Union (ACLU) sent a letter to Attorney General Richardson decrying the leaks and calling on the attorney general to stop them. The letter said in part:

> A review of the newspaper articles which have appeared in the past week suggests that information going well beyond [the mere fact of the investigation] . . . has in fact appeared in the press despite the fact that the investigation has not progressed to the grand jury stage.
> The release of this information raises serious questions about the due process being accorded the Vice-President and the others whose names have been mentioned. . . .
> It does seem, however, that some of the information which has appeared in the newspapers could only have come, directly or indirectly, from law enforcement officials.[18]

A story in the *Times* which detailed Morgan's letter also carried a denial by the Justice Department that they were the source of the leaks. The article quoted

Horace Webb of the department's public information staff as saying "to the best of our knowledge, none of the leaks of information have come from the department or the office of the United States Attorney George Beall." Webb also restated Elliot Richardson's policy that the department would make no comment on the investigation.

The Justice Department, however, was beginning to reach out publicly in another area, trying to limit the damage being done to their credibility by the notion that they were at the heart of the rumors and leaks. On August 19, Elliot Richardson appeared on ABC's *Issues and Answers* program. According to Richardson's associate attorney general and chief political aide, Jonathan Moore, the appearance had been scheduled earlier without the issue of leaks hanging over the attorney general's head. With both Watergate and the Agnew case at climactic points, certainly Richardson had ample justification to cancel his appearance. But, according to Moore, it was probably for just those reasons and the negative effects they were having on his department's image and morale that Richardson decided to go ahead with the interview show. A strong appearance on his part could go far in improving the public perception of the department. During the show, Richardson managed to make most of his points quite forcefully.

He was questioned that morning by Sam Donaldson, ABC's Capitol Hill correspondent, and Stephen Geer. The questions were split between Nixon's refusal to turn over the Watergate tapes to the Ervin Committee and the investigation of Agnew. From the beginning, Richardson set a tone that the department was acting both fairly and judiciously. Asked by Stephen Geer whether it was unusual for the target of the grand jury investigation to be briefed by the attorney general, Richardson responded:

No, it wasn't. The propriety of a prosecutor's giving a person who is, in some sense, under investigation, opportunity to be informed of what in general is the subject of the investigation, is not unusual.

In fact, I think in this situation it would have been unfair not to do at least that much, and I am sure that prosecutors who have had to approach similar questions would agree that a person in the vice-president's situation was entitled to have some idea of why he had received a letter from the United States Attorney.[19]

Asked whether he could describe what was discussed in meetings between Assistant Attorney General for the Criminal Division Henry Petersen and George Beall with regard to the case, Richardson explained:

No. Not only can I not tell you anything about them, but I think it is probably important to emphasize fundamental reasons why I cannot. It is, I think, fundamental to the fairness of the investigative process in any situation that there not be disclosures about it. It can be unfair to the individual as to whom allegations have been made and, of course, it can prejudice the integrity of the investigative process, itself. Those considerations underlie clearcut regulations of the Department of Justice that have been in effect, in written form, since 1965. They are basic to the ethical standards that govern the conduct of prosecutors, generally, and as a matter of fact, it is a subject of considerable distress to me that there has been as much publicity as there has been.[20]

When directly questioned on whether the leaks had come from any of Baltimore prosecutors or from any of the department staff, the attorney general said:

To the best of my knowledge, they have not. I have, of course, looked into the situation . . . and I am satisfied that neither the prosecutor not any member of his staff is responsible. If I were to find evidence that any member of the Department of Justice has been responsible for leaks, I would pursue that indication by further investigation, and if it were established that any person in the Department was actually responsible, that person would be disciplined.[21]

Punch and Counterpunch

On August 20, a new level of intensity was reached regarding the leaks when advance copies of *Time* magazine's issue dated August 27 became available. The edition carried a story titled "The Vice Presidency: Heading Towards an Indictment?" in which the magazine reported that the vice-president had met the previous week with his attorneys and, as a result, had sent a letter to George Beall saying that he would make his personal financial records available to the prosecutors and would be happy to agree to a personal interview with them. It was, however, the paragraphs which followed this news which stirred up a hornet's nest. *Time* went on to say:

Despite all the Vice President's protestations of innocence, however, *Time* has learned that in the view of Justice Department officials in Washington, the case against him is growing steadily stronger, and that an indictment appears inevitable. Besides the two Maryland contractors prepared to testify that they delivered extortion campaign contributions to Agnew (*Time*, Aug. 20), the Government has a third witness with a similar story. He is Allen I. Green, 49, president of a Maryland engineering firm, a man for many years regarded as one of Agnew's closest friends. Green reportedly has said that he gave kickbacks to Agnew about five times a year when Agnew was Governor of Maryland (1967–68) and slightly less often after he was inaugurated Vice President in 1969.

"The department has no choice," a Justice official in Washington said. "At least three witnesses have told of delivering cash payoffs to Agnew. The evidence is so strong that the case must be taken to trial." A federal grand jury in Baltimore is expected to vote an indictment next month charging Agnew with, among other things, bribery and extortion.[22]

Later the article said:

What is puzzling to some investigators is the comparatively paltry amount of money involved. Justice Department officials have declined to provide as estimate of the total amount under investigation, but one of them says: "It's less than you'd think. Agnew wasn't greedy; he was quite cheap."

Indeed, of the payments so far alleged, only a few exceeded $10,000 and many more between $2,000 and $2,500. In states where corruption thrives on a major-league scale—New Jersey or Illinois, where a secretary of state died in 1970 with $800,000 stashed in shoeboxes in his hotel room—such sums are hardly worth mentioning.

Nevertheless, Agnew has apparently realized the gravity of the Government's case against him. *Time* has learned that the Vice President has sought the help of Nixon's Watergate defense team (lawyers Fred Buzhardt, Leonard Garment and Charles Alan Wright) in preparing a constitutional defense that would prevent his having to go on trial anytime soon.[23]

[See Appendix B for the full text of *time*'s article.]

This was the clearest attribution yet for detailed information appearing in the press on the investigation, citing as it did "Justice officials in Westington." Not surprisingly it triggered a chain reaction.

On August 21, citing an advance copy of the *Time* article as the straw that broke the camel's back, the vice-president called his second press conference regarding the probe. He read to reporters from a prepared statement, declining to answer questions. In part, Agnew said:

Ladies and gentlemen, when I saw you in this room just about two weeks ago, I had no idea I'd be asking to see you again so soon.

At my last press conference I indicated that I had no expectation of another public statement on this subject in the near future. Circumstances beyond my controi, however, make it necessary for me to speak out again.

Now I know this will be a disappointment to you, but this time I will not be able to take your questions—not because I want to avoid the facts, not because I do not wish to see you fully informed—but because to do so would be to continue discussion in a public forum of what should be a secret investigation.

By such free-wheeling discussion I would be engaging in the very same tactics that I called you here to criticize. . . .

I regret to say that it has become clear that sources so frequently quoted [in news stories about the investigation]—were indeed that—persons involved in the investigatory process.

A national news magazine account headed Heading Toward an Indictment published yesterday and picked up by the wire services quotes unnamed Justice Department officials. I can only assume from this account that some Justice Department officials have decided to indict me in the press whether or not the evidence supports their position.

This is a clear and outrageous effort to influence the outcome of possible grand jury deliberations and so notwithstanding my initial decision not to comment I've had to respond publicly to the continuing charges. . . .

On Sunday the Attorney General made a nationally televised denial that any of the leaks came from his department. Mr. Richardson also indicated at that time that he would investigate any suggestion that his department has been the source of such leaks.

I have communicated with the Attorney General today and have asked that he fulfill that promise and pursue such an investigation vigorously. I hope that the national news media will also urge Mr. Richardson and the Justice Department to conduct such an investigation diligently wherever it may lead and to use all available investigatory tools to compel sworn testimony to reveal the identity of unnamed Justice Department officials and sources close to the investigation.

Now I've not called you to this meeting for the purpose of criticizing the news media. I cannot fault you for publishing information given to you by informants within the Department of Justice.

The blame must rest with those who gave this information to the press and who do so with an obvious motive of interfering with the independent investigatory processes of the grand jury.[24]

This was the first time the vice-president had publicly laid the blame for the leaks at the feet of the Justice Department. He would do so several more times, however, before the issue was rendered moot by his resignation. It must have seemed odd to some that Agnew, who in 1968 had coined the term ''nattering nabobs of negativism'' for the American news media, was absolving the press of any blame with regard to the leaks. But the situation had changed in the intervening five years, now he needed the media on his side.

The Justice Department issued a response to Agnew's charges on the same day he levelled them; in timely enough fashion that the nation's media could cover the two statements together. And in fact they did, with the *New York Times* running the texts side-by-side. In his very brief statement, Elliot Richardson said:

I fully share the Vice President's concern about unfair and inaccurate publicity. I stand by my previous statements that every reasonable step is being taken to assure that the Justice Department has not been and will not be the source of such publicity.

By observing restraint in what they report, the media themselves can help to assure fairness. I would like to point out, moreover, that we do not now have any firm basis for the assumption that the information which has appeared in the press has come from law enforcement officials.

In any case, any plausible lead implicating the Department of Justice will be pursued vigorously and appropriate disciplinary action will be taken against any department employee found to be responsible.*[25]

As Agnew noted in his statement, on the same day he issued it he also sent a letter formally protesting the leaks and calling for an investigation. He quickly, and somewhat surprisingly, received support from the White House for his request.

On August 22, President Nixon instructed Alexander Haig to relay an order to Richardson to conduct an investigation of whether any of the leaks originated with Justice Department staff people. Shortly after Haig talked to the attorney general, Nixon called a press conference at his Western White House in San Clemente. It was the first press conference in five months for the Watergate-besieged president; and while many of the questions that day revolved around Watergate, the issue of the vice-president also arose. Nixon used the opportunity

---

*See Appendix C for the full text of Agnew's statement and Richardson's reply.

of a question on his confidence in Agnew to deliver a long statement on the leaks as well. He said:

> I noted some press speculation to the effect that I have not expressed confidence in the Vice President and therefore I welcome this question, because I want to set the record straight.
>
> I had confidence in the integrity of the Vice President when I selected him as Vice President when very few knew him, as you may recall, back in 1968, knew him nationally.
>
> My confidence in his integrity has not been shaken, and in fact it has been strengthened by his courageous conduct and his ability even though he's controversial at times, as I am over the past four and a half years and so I have confidence in the integrity of the Vice President and particularly in the performance of the duties that he has had as Vice President and as a candidate for Vice President.
>
> Now obviously the question arises as to charges that have been made about activities that occurred before he became Vice President.
>
> He would consider it improper, I would consider it improper for me to comment on those charges and I shall not do so. But I will make a comment on another subject that I think needs to be commented upon and that is the outrageous leaks of information from either the grand jury or the prosecutors or the Department of Justice or all three—and incidentially I'm not going to put the responsibility on all three till I have heard from the Attorney General who at my request is making a full investigation of this at the present time.
>
> I'm not going to put the responsibility—but the leak of information with regard to charges that have been made against the Vice President and leaking them all in the press, convicting an individual, not only trying him but convicting him in the headlines and on television before he's had a chance to present his case in court is completely contrary to the American tradition. Even a Vice President has a right to some, shall I say consideration in this respect, let alone the ordinary individual.
>
> And I will say this, and the Attorney General I know has taken note of this fact, any individual in the Justice Department or in the prosecutor's office who is in the employ of the United States, who has leaked information in the case, to the press or to anybody else, will be summarily dismissed from government service.[26]

It was not the most ringing endorsement of the vice-president's integrity possible, but it was the strongest the president would make. Additionally, the Agnew camp must have been pleased with Nixon's identification of Justice Department personnel as possible leak sources, adding to the public's perception as it may have that someone on the government's team was responsible.

Bill Kovach, a reporter for the *New York Times* who covered the president's press conference, thought Nixon's list of possible sources too short. In a paragraph that seems somewhat out of the *Times'* traditional style, he wrote:

> While both Mr. Agnew and Mr. Nixon restricted their complaints to leaks of information from Federal sources, a good deal of information made pub-

lic came from other sources. So widespread has been the investigation—which began last year—and the number of people involved so large that a reservoir of information is available to the press outside the Federal system, including lawyers and friends and enemies of those under investigation.[27]

The paragraph lends some credence to the assertions by Justice officials that the leaks were coming from sources other than their department.

On August 23, the attorney general undertook a full-scale investigation of the charges that the leaks emanated from the department. That day he ordered Glen Pommerening, then the acting assistant attorney general for administration, to begin investigating any possible Justice leak sources. Richardson's aides say that while the president's "order" of the day before may have affected the timing of the start of the investigation, the attorney general had been considering such a probe prior to Haig's telephone call and Nixon's press conference.

After instructing Pommerening to begin the inquiry immediately, Richardson sent a letter to the vice-president responding to his charges of the twenty-first and informing him that an internal inquiry was being undertaken with regard to possible leaks. The first half of the letter expressed the attorney general's continuing concern with regard to the publicity and outlined the actions he'd taken. The second half, however, was possessed of a somewhat different tone, implicitly refuting Agnew's assignment of sole blame for the leaks to the Justice Department. It read:

> As I believe you are aware, no aspect of the on-going investigation referred to by United States Attorney Beall in his letter to you of August 1 has been submitted to the grand jury. Leaks of grand jury proceedings are, of course, subject to criminal sanction, but leaks at prior stages of an investigation are not. Should any of the leaks be traced to Department of Justice personnel, departmental regulations providing administrative sanctions including dismissal will apply.
>
> As you know, a considerable number of people in and out of government are aware of some details of the investigation. Its outlines are known to a number of witnesses, individuals under investigation, their lawyers, select members of my, your, and the White House staff, and certain investigative personnel of the Internal Revenue Service. For this reason, there may be no fully effective means of stopping the cynical rumors and conjectures all too evident in recent weeks. We can, however, continue to insist that those in our employ behave with extraordinary circumspection. This has been my stringent injunction upon the employees of the Department of Justice.[28]

The vice-president alleged that someone within DOJ was leaking information. Richardson turned a part of the accusation back on Agnew by pointing out that both vice-presidential and White House staffers were also aware of the investigation.

Also on August 23, ACLU director Charles Morgan sent a second letter to Richardson to keep the pressure on him about the leaks. In his letter, Morgan countered Richardson's assertion that no evidence was available indicating DOJ personnel had originated leaks by quoting articles in *Newsweek,* the *New York*

Times, the *Washington Post,* and, of course, *Time.* He further chastised the attorney general for the suggestion that the press should exercise restraint

> You implicitly recognize that you should not seek information about confidential sources from reporters and publications which rely upon them. This is refreshing in a time when concern over news sources has led the government to wiretapping, burglary, polygraphing, and the creation of the "Plumbers."
>
> However, your statement, as reported in yesterday morning's *Washington Post,* p. A–3, that "[b]y observing restraint in what they report, the media themselves can help assure fairness" shifts the burden of responsibility from you and your Department to these [sic] with whom the responsibility does not lie. The obligation of members of the press is to seek news where they can find it and to print it in order to inform the public. The responsibility to prevent such prejudicial disclosures before they reach the news media rests upon your shoulders and your shoulders alone.
>
> If there stories have come from the officials described, it is your responsibility to take appropriate action. If they have not, that responsibility demands that you publicly repudiate the stories as inaccurate.

The leaks were becoming as much of a news story as the allegations against Agnew, and on the same day the probe was initiated and Morgan's letter dispatched, United Press International carried a brief story on the leaks, attributed only to "Justice Department sources," which alleged that the White House might be the source of leaks about Agnew.

Pommerening's Investigation

Following Richardson's instructions, Glen Pommerening immediately began to structure a probe for possible leaks in Justice. In conducting his investigation, the assistant attorney general decided to use personnel from both the FBI and the Drug Enforcement Agency (DEA) as well as from regular DOJ staff.* According to Pommerening's description in a preliminary report on the investigation:

> During the initial analysis and planning phase, we identified the strategy and scope of the inquiry. An interview process was selected since it offered an objective means for collecting relevant data. However, we felt that an interview alone would not have the necessary impact to insure candid and complete information was being received. As a result we decided to supplement the interview with a sworn statement from each interviewee. The rendering of a false statement then would be a violation of 18 U.S.C. 1001 and could facilitate removal or other disciplinary action against any personnel

---

*There was, at some point, according to Jonathan Moore, a suggestion from the White House that the FBI conduct the leaks search. This was accompanied by a recommendation that lie detectors be used in the interviewing of department staffers. Moore recalls, with Richardson, rejecting both ideas. The lie detectors were refused, he says, because they would have been demoralizing, and remembers telling the White House "The reason we're not going to put the FBI in charge [of the investigation] is because they may be the source of the leaks."

who were found to be responsible for the unauthorized disclosure of information.

In order to determine the initial scope of the inquiry, senior officials of the Department of Justice, the Federal Bureau of Investigation and the U.S. Attorney's office in the District of Maryland were requested to identify people who, to their knowledge, had direct or indirect access to information on the Baltimore County investigation.

In its simplest formulation, then, Pommerening was asking anyone who knew anything about the case to identify anyone else they thought might know about it, for whatever reason, and then he planned to interview and obtain sworn statements from all those employees.

Once he had obtained a list of all the DOJ personnel who had any information about the case, he divided them into three categories: those with in-depth knowledge, some knowledge, and minimal knowledge. Teams of two, one from Pommerening's staff and the other from the FBI or DEA, conducted the interviews. It took two months before they were all complete and the final report was written.

In the first round of the investigation, Pommerening identified fifty-nine DOJ staffers who knew of the probe. Of these, only nineteen were found to have any information prior to August 6 when Jerry Landauer had his information. And of those nineteen, Pommerening found only eight had in-depth knowledge: the four Baltimore prosecutors, Elliot Richardson, Deputy Attorney General William Ruckelshaus, and two senior aides to Richardson. If Pommerening was correct and if, as Agnew charged, the leak had come from the Justice Department and not some other source, then it could not have come from a minor functionary but would have had to have been from a senior official in either Washington or Baltimore.

The questions asked by the investigatory team at each interview were fairly straightforward. There were only five questions:

1. Have you had any contact, conversation, or communication with any member of the press or other news media relative to the investigation?
2. Do you know anyone who has had contact, conversation, or communication with any member of the press or other news media relative to the investigation?
3. Have you had any contact, conversation, or communication with anyone outside the Department of Justice relative to this investigation?
4. Do you know anyone who has had contact, conversation, or communication with anyone outside the Department of Justice relative to this investigation?
5. Do you have any knowledge of any person in or out of the Department of Justice who may have been responsible for leaking to the press or other news media any information relative to this investigation?

Individuals who answered yes to any of the five questions were required to provide the details of their knowledge and all those interviewed had to sign their statements. In addition to the taking of statements, Pommerening reviewed the press coverage of the case and attempted to tabulate the leaks, correlating them to the knowledge particular staffers had at the time a leak occurred.

As Pommerening proceeded with this investigation, leaks continued about the case. major newspapers around the country often carried several stories per week relating to the vice-president and the investigation. The coverage included reports on meetings among various parties to the case, rumors regarding Agnew's possible resignation from office, and speculation on the constitutional question of whether a sitting vice-president could be indicted. On September 5, for example, the *New York Daily News* carried a story attributed only to "a source close to the investigation" which alleged that the attorney general would probably not offer an opinion on the question of the indictability of a vice-president, as might be expected, but would allow a judge to rule on the matter with no Justice Department recommendation.[29]

But one of the most surprising stories to appear did not involve a new leak, but a reported admission on the part of Attorney General Richardson. On September 5, Susanna McBee reported in the *Washington Post* that Richardson had conceded that some of the leaks in the Agnew case could have emanated from the Justice Department. "Yesterday," McBee wrote, "Richardson noted that when he ordered the internal probe two weeks ago he had no indication that the leaks had come from Justice. 'Since then I have had indications from news media themselves that some information has come from inside the Department,' he said. He added that he has talked to representatives of more than one publication and that they refuse to disclose their sources."[30] The department position remained, however, that despite the possibility of some leak sources on the inside, the major and most critical leaks in the case, including the existence of the investigation itself, had been leaked by nondepartment sources.

Although stories continued to be printed during the early days of September, major leaks seemed to become fewer. In part, this may have stemmed from the fact that the prosecutors had largely completed their investigation. Statements had been taken and documents amassed. During this time the principal activity on the prosecution side was deciding when and how the evidence would be presented to the grand jury. Additionally, Assistant Attorney General Henry Petersen had been, at Richardson's request, reviewing all the evidence the Baltimore team had assembled with an eye toward reassuring both the attorney general and the White House that the case was substantial and was not, as Agnew had alleged, a partisan effort to "get him." After reviewing the evidence and interviewing the witnesses, Petersen was convinced the case was quite strong.

Plea Bargaining

The First Round of Talks

On September 10, 1973, as the prosecutors were gearing up for the presentation of evidence about Agnew to the grand jury, the situation changed yet again. This time the attorney general received a call from the White House counsel J. Fred Buzhardt, who had been acting as a liaison among Justice, the White House, and Agnew's attorneys. Buzhardt told the attorney general that Agnew was willing to open negotiations on a plea bargain. Although the prosecutors had been hoping for such an offer, its timing came as a surprise.

However, Charles Colson, a partner in Colson and Shapiro, one of the firms representing the vice-president, explains what he believes happened in September to cause Agnew to change his approach:

> In September, Nixon called me at home and said "You're representing Agnew?" I said "yes" and he said "Well, he's got to resign. There's no other choice." At that point I was working with Agnew on an impeachment strategy to tie up the case in the House. And I had to tell the President that I was sorry, and that we were friends and I was his former assistant, but that he was interfering with my client–attorney relationship. He then gave me a message for Agnew [that the White House could no longer support him], which I relayed to Agnew and which utterly devastated him. And, at that point, Buzhardt began putting enormous pressure on, calling every day, saying "The Justice Department has shown me the evidence; Agnew's got to go." Haig also started calling. At that point the White House was running a campaign to pressure Agnew out. . . . Whether they leaked anything at that point I don't know. I can't tell you whether they were then the source of any leaks or not but, at that point, they would have had a motive just like the prosecutors.*

Colson believes the reason behind the attitude change in the White House was that, while a tainted vice-president had originally seemed to be good insurance for the president against any serious move to impeach him over Watergate, once it became clear that Agnew was likely to be indicted he became a liability, threatening to compound rather than mitigate Nixon's troubles.

On September 12, two days after he received the first phone call from Buzhardt, the attorney general along with George Beall and Henry Petersen met with the three attorneys for the vice-president—Judah Best (of Colson and Shapiro), Jay Topkis, and Martin London—to begin initial discussions on the terms of a deal. According to Jonathan Moore, the discussion focused on five major points: the count with which Agnew would be charged; his plea to the charge; the statement Agnew would make in open court; the disclosure by the Justice Department of the evidence developed against him; and whether or not Agnew would have to go to jail. On the question of Agnew's resignation, Richardson and the Justice team were adamant. There could be no negotiation; the vice-president must resign. Similarly, Agnew was adamant about not serving a jail term. He would not enter

---

*Colson disagrees with the prosecutors' assertions that having the probe made public made investigating the case more difficult by frightening potential witnesses and harming the departments' credibility. He says: "Anybody who was zealous and wanted to make the case [against Agnew] and was afraid that, for whatever reasons, it wouldn't get handled properly, that it would be covered up for political reasons, could insure that it wouldn't be, particularly in the Watergate environment, just by leaking one story. And I'm convinced that's what happened."

into any bargain that required him to go to prison. The other three points, as a result, became the principal areas of negotiation.

Throughout the next ten days, the three men from Justice met alternately with Agnew's attorneys and their own staffs, trying to hammer out a deal that would be acceptable to both sides, and critical to the Justice team, would preserve the credibility of the department when it was publicly presented.

On the charge to which Agnew would enter a plea, his lawyers offered his admission of one count of failing to pay taxes on monies he had collected, but not used, for campaign purposes in 1967. The actual plea they offered for him to enter was nolo contendere, or no contest to the charges, rather than a guilty plea. The Justice team, although undoubtedly not happy with this, agreed to the plea because the crime with which he would be charged would be a felony.

The statements the parties would submit in court, however, proved to be much stickier points in the negotiations. The prosecutors wanted to submit a statement which included full disclosure of the evidence they had amassed against Agnew, even though they would only be charging him with one crime. Their purpose in doing this was to make the evidence a part of the public record and to increase the public's understanding of the case against the vice-president and the difficult decisions the Justice Department had had to make in the course of the investigation. Agnew and his attorneys hesitated to agree to such public disclosure.

A memorandum, written by Jonathan Moore to Richardson and dated September 18, underscores just how critical department officials believed gaining the public's understanding of their position to be. Based on the premise that the negotiations with the vice-president might break down, Moore's memorandum addresses two questions: how the interests of the White House might differ from those of the Justice Department in achieving a resolution of the case, and what items were necessary to communicate to the public to win the understanding and support that the department felt was essential. In the first section relating to White House interests, Moore made one point regarding public perceptions, writing:

> It is hard to predict how things are going to break, but the point is that if Agnew plays the combination [strategy] of "resign in the national interest/counterattack to protest his innocence," the President may feel he's got to be dually responsive, depending upon what kind of a deal was actually made to get the resignation in the first place and how Agnew seems to be making out in terms of sympathy. In other words, we—together with a public sense of the integrity of the legal process—could catch some damaging backwash. If events unfold in such a way that Agnew comes out fairly early to be a real bounder, he may simply be junked. But on the other hand:
> (a) if negotiations broke down and Agnew went to the House protesting his innocence and it looked as if he might have a chance to win, the pressures would seriously increase on the President to side more with Agnew against his tormentors; or
> (b) if the deal should fail in negotiations or break down later, the White House might have to conclude it was in its interest to point out (or encour-

age others to) that Richardson and the Justice Department had, indeed, attempted to cut a sleazy deal with Agnew which was unfair to the Vice President and / or violated the very integrity of the justice process the Attorney General has himself been so vocal about.

Further, with regard to the parts of the overall situation which were necessary for the Justice Department to make the public understand, Moore identified eight items which he felt were critical for the department to address. In his memo he notes that the points overlap and would take on varying degrees of importance depending on the strategies pursued by the vice-president. The eight Moore outlined were:

1. A protracted trial of a sitting Vice President (whether in the Congress or in the Courts) would constitute the gravest danger for the Republic—in other words, his *resignation* is essential in the national interest. This point is not immediately evident or persuasive, it has to be articulated, and this can't be left for us to do by ourselves.

2. The *initiative* for a negotiation (the expression "plea-bargaining" should be avoided) came from the Vice President *and* the President (who as the Chief Executive is the one chiefly responsible for 1. above), not from the Justice Department which has a crucial role to play in the national interest but must start from its more fundamental responsibilities of insuring the integrity of the legal process. The point isn't that we shouldn't be willing to take the heat; it is that the public won't accept it if we are left to take all the heat.

3. The perception that at no time was the process of justice manipulated or diddled or compromised. This is really the *integrity* point—in the efforts to seek an effective solution to a problem of unprecedented complexity and magnitude, the Justice Department did not compromise its fundamental discipline or its Attorney General's own pledges.

4. At the same time, *fairness* to the Vice President must be perceived; the public must not get the impression that his rights were compromised or that he was harassed and destroyed by politicians worrying about their own future or that he was punished in a way disproportionate to his crime. The problem of the equitable treatment of co-defendants also comes in here.

5. The *guilt* of the Vice President must be clearly demonstrated; this is, of course, supported by our insistence of "full disclosure"—to be strengthened if it should prove to be watered down by tougher counts and a guilty plea.

6. There must be *punishment* of some kind. The Vice President and other indicted must not go scot-free, even assuming that the significance of resignation is effectively communicated as significant punishment.

7. Somewhere the *Constitutional* question of impeachment vs. indictment will have to be covered so that question is not left suspended in people's minds, so that some won't continue to wonder why Agnew was denied his special Constitutional privilege. . . . The Attorney General must in some way indicate his belief that the Constitution did not prohibit indictment and in any event had the Vice President sought such a judgment, the courts would have had the opportunity to judge the matter.

8. The *President's* own personal interests must be separated from his handling of the Agnew problem, so that he is perceived as acting with great size and statesmanship, with compassion for the Vice President, fulfilling the requirements of national, Constitutional and public interests, rather than scrambling for his own survival.

Trying To Keep the Press at Bay

As the negotiations were progressing, a new news story appeared. According to Cohen and Witcover, on September 18:

> [A] development that day jolted Washington. The *Washington Post,* under a banner headline that read "Agnew Discussing Resignation," ran a story by David S. Broder quoting a senior Republican Party leader as saying he had spent two hours trying to argue Agnew out of quitting. The source said that he was "99 ½ percent certain" that Agnew would resign, probably that week. To the nervous and even paranoid members of Agnew's staff, the story smacked of White House authorship, and could only be considered a blatant attempt to push Agnew out the door. Some pointed the finger—incorrectly—at Bryce Harlow, Agnew's friend who was also a presidential advisor. In politics-wise Washington, the story—and the clout of Broder's by-line—convinced many readers that the die had already been cast for Agnew. The impression grew the next day when the White House declined to comment on the story or even say whether the President still supported his Vice President. Washington waited for the other shoe to drop; Agnew's aides and friends seethed. Vic Gold [Agnew's former press secretary], for one, was irate. "This is calculated by the White House to keep the Agnew story alive," he said of the official "no comment" from [White House spokesman] Gerald Warren.[31]

While the story rocked the capital, Broder was, in fact, incorrect. The vice-president was not planning resignation until a bargain was struck with the prosecutors, and so the negotiations continued.

On Wednesday, September 19, the prosecution team ran into another dilemma regarding the press. They received word from the attorney general that they were to attend a meeting the next morning at a time when the grand jury was scheduled to hear testimony. If they cancelled the grand jury session, the press would be sure to know that something was happening, a tip they didn't wish to give the reporters. As a result the Baltimore team arranged with Paul Kramer, the deputy U.S. attorney, to go to the grand jury, hold them in session for an hour and then release them, instructing them not to talk about the fact that they had not heard any testimony. Kramer played his role, but even with the precautions, the *New York Times* managed to report that "crucial negotiations" had halted the investigation.[32]

Yet, while the *Times* was getting close, no one had reported that the vice-president was engaged in plea bargaining. The strategies employed by the Justice Department didn't stop the leaks as was hoped, but they did prevent the most damaging information from getting out.

In the negotiations, the major stumbling block increasingly became the details of the statements the Justice Department and the vice-president would deliver in court. Not only were Agnew's attorneys hesitant about the proposed summary of the evidence to be presented by the Justice Department, but the Justice officials found themselves battling Agnew's attorneys on what the vice-president would have to admit in his own statement. For the department, both were issues that would directly affect the way in which the public would perceive the outcome of the case. With regard to his insistence that a full summary of the evidence against the vice-president be delivered, Richardson explains

> I was very insistent upon [a full summary] because I knew that there would be people who criticized the result on the ground that Agnew was a big shot and no little guy would get away without a jail sentence in similar circumstances. That was obvious to me, and so the worst thing that could have happened would have been to be able to couple that criticism, which was inevitable, with any indication that we had withheld from public disclosure the full scope of the case against him.

Jonathan Moore acknowledges that it is somewhat unusual for the prosecution to have a say in what a defendant states in court, but notes that he felt in a case like this one it was a critical issue for the Justice Department:

> It was fascinating because our plea bargaining included giving the Vice President permission on what he would say in court. What this argument at this point came down to was not the plea, not the count, not what we were going to put in the case that was released, and not the sentencing, all of which had been pretty much agreed to. This covered what Agnew would say in his statement and it related to the degree to which he was willing to admit a knowledge on his part of the connection between payoffs and state contract awards.

Moore adds that a substantial part of the reason he advocated the Justice Department taking a strong stand on what Agnew would or would not say in court was his notion that this would be the last time the department would have any influence over what the vice-president would say publicly about the case. As a result, if they did not get him to concede a level of culpability, he would be able to turn around and deny any wrongdoing after leaving court. It seemed possible that Agnew might take the position that he had been persecuted by the Justice Department, but had resigned for the good of the nation. With his own court statement on the record admitting some awareness of the bribery scheme, any later denials Agnew might try to make would have less credibility. The battle for public perceptions, the associate attorney general believed, might well continue after the court appearance was over.

On September 22, the plea bargaining broke down over just this issue. And on that morning, the *Washington Post* ran a story under the banner headline "Agnew Lawyers Bargain on Plea." Attributed mostly to "informed sources," the story had little detail about the negotiations. As far as it went, however, it was accurate. At its most specific, the story said: "Justice officials reportedly are unwilling to make any deal that would allow Agnew to resign his office in exchange for agreement that he would not be prosecuted. Conscious of the damage done to the department's image as a result of Watergate, Justice officials apparently are insistent that Agnew plead guilty to some charge in exchange for special consideration from the government."[33]

"We've Got the Evidence"

CBS News on the twenty-second carried a story of their own about the plea bargaining. In his report, correspondent Fred Graham noted that the negotiations were being conducted "at least officially, by Attorney General Elliot Richardson himself."[34] Graham went on to say that the government's position, however, was being determined by Henry Petersen and that in the plea bargaining session with the vice-president's attorneys on September 19 "a source close to the negotiations has disclosed . . . Petersen insisted that he had evidence to win a conviction on the bribery and kickback charges and that he would insist that Agnew plead guilty at least to a reduced charge. Petersen was quoted as saying 'We've got the evidence, we've got it cold.' "[35]

Graham was quoting a source who in turn was quoting Petersen, but such distinctions are difficult to discern upon hearing, rather than reading, them. As a result, Graham's story was widely misconstrued to be quoting Petersen directly and this caused more uproar than all but the first leak in the case.

Both the *Post* and the CBS stories angered the vice-president. In his book, *Go Quietly . . . Or Else,* he wrote:

> On September 22, the *Washington Post* printed a story disclosing that my lawyers and the Justice Department had been plea bargaining for my resignation. CBS News said Henry Petersen claimed he had the evidence to convict me on bribery and kickback charges. . . .
>
> Naturally, these reports, which were picked up and repeated all across the land throughout the weekend, infuriated me. I had no doubt they were deliberately leaked by the Justice Department to wreck my credibility with the millions of Americans who still believed in me despite the calculated campaign of vilification being carried on by men in my own administration.[36]

Agnew like many others, including the majority of those commenting on Graham's story, misattributes the Petersen quotation, accusing Petersen himself of talking to the reporter. James Reston wrote an article for the *New York Times* setting forth Agnew's views that was based on, but not attributed to, an interview with the vice-president. In his story, Reston alleged:

> Mr. Agnew decided to appeal to the House to hear his case after Fred P. Graham of the Columbia Broadcasting System, on September 22, quoted Henry Petersen, Assistant Attorney General in charge of the Justice Department's Criminal Division, as saying he had refused to drop criminal charges against the Vice President because Mr. Petersen was confident that the gov-

ernment could obtain a conviction against Mr. Agnew if the case went to trial.[37]

Three days after Reston's article appeared, William Safire wrote a column for the *Times* saying:

> WASHINGTON—"We've got the evidence. We've got it cold."
> That was what Assistant Attorney General Henry Petersen told CBS reporter Fred Graham on Sept. 22 about the case against Vice President Agnew. . . .
> If the CBS report was accurate, and it has not been denied, an Assistant Attorney General has adopted the role of prosecutor, publicist, jury tamperer, and judge. . . .
> As long as Mr. Petersen remains at the Justice Department, he stands as an example to every officer of every court that it is all right to try cases in newspapers. Petersen's presence assures them that when they slip a few remarks or documents into the hands that will help put pressure on a jury to indict or convict, it will be winked at from on high.[38]

Picking up the cue in a somewhat more moderate way, *Time* magazine in early October wrote: "As to whether Petersen has been the source of some news leaks regarding the Agnew investigation, as Agnew claims, there is no doubt that he has. But Petersen has not been, by any means, the sole source of news leaks in the case."[39]

The distortion became so prevalent that correspondent Graham felt compelled to take an unusual step for a reporter. He sent a letter to the editors of the *New York Times* stating unequivocally who his source for the story was *not*. In a letter dated October 1, Graham wrote:

> The purpose of this letter is to point out that my broadcast did not quote Henry Petersen as saying anything to me, and did not imply that Mr. Petersen has discussed the Agnew case with me in any way. I am enclosing a copy of the text of my broadcast, which described a negotiations session between Justice Department attorneys and Mr. Agnew's lawyers at the Justice Department last Wednesday. Quoting "a source close to the negotiations," the broadcast stated the positions reportedly taken by Mr. Agnew's lawyers, by Attorney General Elliot Richardson, and by Mr. Petersen. It is clear from the broadcast that the quote from Mr. Petersen about the strength of his evidence was said at the meeting to Mr. Agnew's lawyers—not to me.
> Mr. Petersen has never discussed the merits of the Vice President's case with me.*[40]

As the debate was just beginning over the alleged Petersen leak, Glen Pommerening turned in his first preliminary report to the Attorney General on possible leak sources in the Justice Department. As of September 24, Pommerening had interviewed fifty-nine people who had at least heard a little about the case, and seventy-five DOJ staffers who claimed no knowledge at all. All the individ-

---

*For the full text of Graham's letter and broadcast, see Appendix D.

uals that the investigators questioned signed sworn statements that they were not the source of the leaks and did not know of anyone who was.

In his report, Pommerening also gave to Richardson a set of supplemental findings, based on an analysis of the news stories that had appeared and their possible sources. These findings said:

1. Knowledge of the Vice President's potential involvement was known to individuals outside the Department of Justice before any such evidence was developed by the Department.

2. Public disclosure of the Vice President's potential involvement in the Baltimore County investigation did not occur until the Department of Justice conveyed some information about the case to individuals outside of the Department.

3. There appears to be a high correlation between the facts transmitted by the Department of Justice to the White House and / or the Vice President and disclosures which have appeared in the press.

4. The first news story which revealed that the Vice President was under investigation has been attributed to the Vice President's staff.*

5. Analysis of information attributed to the department of Justice in several key news reports reveals, that while the information may have been damaging to the Vice President, it was generally inaccurate.

6. Professional public information officers disagree whether or not a reporter would cite a secondary source as if it were the primary source.

7. There is a Byzantine-like relationship in the Baltimore business, political and social community [contributing to the general aura of gossip and rumor].**

Pommerening's point in all these findings was that there were many other possible, and even likely, sources for the leaks outside the Department of Justice. He stressed in the concluding section of his report that his inquiry had shown a large number of people outside of DOJ who had varying degrees of knowledge about the case, noting: "Since those outside the Department received this information contemporaneously with the investigation, it is a fair assumption that the total witting population outside the Department is at least equal to, and probably exceeds, the total witting population within the Department."

Return to the Public Arena

When the plea bargaining broke down, the vice-president returned to his earlier strategy of public assaults on the prosecutors and the handling of the case.

---

*In his explanation, Pommerening notes that on August 5 when Landauer called Beall only the Baltimore U.S. attorney's office and the vice-president possessed the letter, DOJ did not even have a copy. Further, Pommerening says that "during telephone conversations on August 5 with United States Attorney Beall and Assistant United States Attorney Skolnik, Landauer identified his source for the information as a friend of his [Landauer's] in the vice-president's office. During the course of the inquiry, we have learned that Landauer has had, and continues to obtain, information concerning the vice-president which is not otherwise known to the investigative team."

**See Appendix E for full text of the Preliminary Report.

This time, however, the Justice Department would match him almost press release for press release. And the White House, with an increased stake in the case, also became involved in the battle over public perceptions.

On Tuesday, September 25, the president met with both Elliot Richardson and Spiro Agnew. And by the end of the day, the White House, as well as the attorney general and the vice-president had issued statements to the press. The first meeting the president had was with his attorney general, who informed Nixon that, in light of the break down in plea negotiations, the Justice Department intended to begin presenting evidence to the grand jury regarding the vice-president. To protect his position, Richardson also took the highly unusual step of issuing a public statement explaining how and why the department had become involved in the plea bargaining, why it had broken down and what the next step would be. His statement read:

> Recently there has been widespread and highly varied public speculation regarding both the substance and the procedure related to the investigation of the Vice President. Although it would be improper to discuss the substance of the investigation at this stage, I feel it necessary to clarify certain procedural points in order to reduce unwarranted and potentially harmful speculation.
>
> In the period of September 12 to the present, meetings and discussions have taken place between myself, Assistant Attorney General Henry E. Petersen, and U.S. Attorney for the district of Maryland, George Beall, representing the Department of Justice, and Messrs. Jay H. Topkis, Martin London and Judah Best, counsel to the Vice President. The Department of Justice agreed to participate in these meetings in response to a request by the Vice President's counsel to discuss procedural aspects of the case and options available to the Vice President. The Department did so with a view toward the possible prompt resolution of problems which might otherwise result in a Constitutional dilemma of potentially serious consequence to the nation. These discussions took place with the approval of the President's counsel and the President.
>
> The discussions have, however, failed to yield a satisfactory resolution. It has proved impossible, to this point, to reconcile the Vice President's interests, as represented by his counsel, with the Department of Justice's perception of its responsibility to assure that justice is pursued fully and fairly.
>
> On September 13, I authorized U.S. Attorney Beall to present evidence regarding the Vice President to the Federal grand jury sitting in Baltimore. It is the intention of the Department of Justice to present such evidence to the grand jury when it reconvenes on September 27.
>
> The grand jury will be used, in accordance with well-established practice, as an investigative body. This is a traditional function of a Federal grand jury, who's role, as representative of the community, is to ensure the fairness of the investigative process.

Later that day, President Nixon met with Agnew to discuss the situation. During the meeting the vice-president informed Nixon that he intended to request the House of Representatives to take over the investigation on the premise that impeachment was the only proper route for prosecuting a sitting vice-president.

After Nixon and Agnew met, the White House issued a press release on it. At best, the release gave weak support to Agnew, acknowledging that he had met with the president and his decision to try to take his case to the House, but not offering any comment on this move. The president did, finally, issue a request that the vice-president be treated fairly by the public and that they accord him the same presumption of innocence they would any other citizen.

The vice-president returned to his office, after meeting with Nixon, and began laying plans to go to Speaker of the House Carl Albert with his request. First, Agnew and his attorneys drafted a letter for the vice-president to hand-deliver to Albert. In addition to arguing that the only forum in which the vice-president constitutionally could be investigated and tried was the Congress, the letter also maintained that the leaks and rumors regarding the case had prejudiced any hearing he might get in the courts. This twofold approach would be the vice-president's strategy for the remainder of his struggle.

At 4:00 P.M. that Tuesday, Agnew took his letter to the Speaker Albert. After meeting briefly with Albert alone in the speaker's private chambers, a number of leaders from both parties were called in to the discussion, including House Majority Leader Thomas P. O'Neill, Minority Leader Gerald Ford, and Chairman of the House Judiciary Committee Peter Rodino. Their only immediate action was a decision that Albert should return to the House floor and read Agnew's letter to the members. In that way, the group thought, the letter could be made public, but it would not be Agnew's doing, instead it would be Albert's. The vice-president waited while the Speaker read the letter into the record, and then left the office. A crowd of reporters was waiting for him, and, telling them the letter spoke for itself, he gave it to the press.

According to Agnew, Albert later the same day asked Rodino if the Judiciary Committee would take over the investigation, and Rodino declined. The speaker then heard from the other side, in the form of a phone call from Elliot Richardson informing him that the Justice Department was about to begin presenting evidence to the grand jury regarding the vice-president. Albert decided he could not intervene, and on Wednesday, September 26, announced that the matter was before the courts and the House of Representatives would not interfere. Agnew had lost his battle to get his case into the congressional forum.

The next day, as Richardson had indicated to Albert, the Justice Department began to call witnesses before the grand jury. But as the grand jury was hearing testimony on September 27, a new press problem cropped up. One which, although it turned out to be quite minor, added to the prosecutors' sense that they were under siege. A crew of three newsmen for CBS were spotted on the roof of a building across from the courthouse. The news crew was shooting film of the grand jury room window. The presence of the camera crew upset the jurors sufficiently that George Beall notified the U.S. Marshall's office to pick up and detain the journalists. He then notified the FBI.

According to a memo written by the FBI's senior agent in charge in Baltimore, Beall suspected that the crew might have been trying to get film of the events inside the room, and if this were true, might be guilty of violating federal law. Beall then called CBS News in Washington, according to the memo, and they volunteered to turn over the film to the prosecutors. When the film was processed, however, it turned out that it contained neither video nor audio recordings of what went on in the grand jury room, only pictures of the building.

Almost as quickly as the Justice Department had begun calling witnesses, Agnew's attorneys filed a motion with the court asking Judge Walter Hoffman to prohibit the grand jury from hearing any evidence regarding the vice-president. The motion, submitted September 28, was based on the same two arguments that Agnew had presented to Albert—that it was unconstitutional to bring a sitting vice-president before a grand jury, and, in any case, the press leaks had unfairly biased any court's hearing of the case—but this time the vice-president's attorneys went even further in their charges that the case was prejudiced. In his affidavit supporting the motion, one of Agnew's attorneys charged:

> We have arrived at a firm conviction that personnel of the Department of Justice have engaged in a steady campaign designed to deprive the Vice President of that basic right of a free man: The right to be judged fairly.
>
> Needless to say, we reach this conclusion with the greatest reluctance. But as the weeks have gone by, the accumulation of evidence has left us with no choice.[41]

Citing a *New York Times* article that repeated the purported Petersen ''we've got it cold'' quote.

> This is, as I have said, but the latest in a flood of similarly prejudicial reports. One or two might be forgiven as the product of deplorable but perhaps inevitable inadvertence. But this case has seen leaks in such number and with such constancy as to rule out any explanation by accident. It is clear, I submit, that the Vice President is the victim of a deliberate campaign, calculated and intended to deprive him of his basic rights to due process and fair hearing.[42]

In answer to the vice-president's motion, the Justice Department issued a statement on the same day, Friday the 28th, denying Agnew's assertions about the leaks and implying that perhaps someone working for the vice-president had been responsible for the leaks. The statement read, in part:

> It is clear that there is no basis whatsoever—in fact or common sense—for the assertion that the Department of Justice has engaged ''in a steady campaign of statements to the press'' for the purpose of prejudicing grand or petit jury hearings. Such a campaign would defeat the very purpose of an investigation by the Department of Justice.
>
> The problems of publicity and speculation concerning the investigation of the Vice President date from the release to the public of the August 1st letter from U.S. Attorney Beall to the Vice President. And it is noteworthy that although the Department's investigation had been in progress for a considerable period of time prior to the release of the letter, there was, to that

point, not a single public leak of information concerning the investigation of the Vice President. . . .

To suggest further, as lawyers for the Vice President have, that the Justice Department investigation is a plot to "drive the Vice President from office" is patently ridiculous. the investigation is based on evidence which is being marshalled in as expeditious and responsible a manner as possible. The Department of Justice will continue to discharge its duties to enforce the laws of this land and will not be diverted from that duty by unsubstantiated charges.[43]

Whether they intended to be or not, however, the Justice Department was diverted from the day-to-day tasks of developing their case by the necessity of coping with the charges made against them in the arena of the press, and trying to insure that public faith in the department was not unalterably eroded. For example, a request from *Time* magazine writer Hays Gorey to see the attorney general or, failing his availability, Deputy Attorney General William Ruckelshaus, was not only forwarded to Richardson and his executive assistant for action, but was circulated among the attorney general's senior staff. In commenting on the interview request, one staff member noted: "Agnew defense is likely to leak intentionally and to accuse DOJ [of being responsible for those leaks]. It seems . . . desirable to avoid to the maximum extent possible any direct personal contact with the press by principal involved DOJ figures—at least until Agnew's lawyers take the next overt step. In general, DOJ statements should be *written, carefully drafted,* and subject for *no further comment.*"

Attack in L.A.

The next public event to occur after the exchange of charges in the press was an appearance by the vice-president at a congress of Republican women meeting in Los Angeles on Saturday, September 29. According to Cohen and Witcover, Agnew's political adviser, David Keene, recommended that the vice-president alter the speech he had prepared and capitalize on the opportunity to go on the offensive against the Justice Department.[44] The vice-president spent the night before his speech at the Palm Springs home of Frank Sinatra. En route from there to Los Angeles in the morning he apparently decided to heed Keene's advice. In his book, Agnew writes:

As I sat in the plane looking over the prepared speech that I would be delivering in less than two hours, it suddenly struck me that it just wouldn't do. Those women, and all my supporters out there, were entitled to know how I felt—what was happening. . . . I decided to cut down on the prepared speech and "wing" the thoughts I was [having] at the end.[45]

He later characterizes these "thoughts" as an "off-the-cuff attack upon the Justice Department."[46] His attack asserted:

In the past several months I have lived in purgatory. I have found myself the recipient of undefined, unclear, unattributable accusations that have surfaced in the largest and most widely circulated organs of our communications media. I want to say at this point—clearly and unequivocally—I am innocent of the charges against me.[47]

Agnew went on to charge that he had learned that the *Wall Street Journal* had obtained a copy of the August 1 letter informing him of the investigation before his own copy was delivered to his lawyers. (He offered no evidence for this assertion and no other sources support this claim.) And, as his lawyers had claimed in their affidavit for the court, Agnew said the leaks stemmed from "deliberately contrived actions" of the Justice Department.[48] Finally, as he had done in his interview with James Reston, the vice-president narrowed his attack to one man— Henry Petersen. Referring once again to the repeatedly misattributed quote about having the evidence "cold," he said:

I say this to you, that conduct of high officials in the Department of Justice, particularly the conduct of the chief of the criminal investigation division of that department, is unprofessional and malicious and outrageous, if I am to believe what has been printed in the news magazines and said on the television networks of this country, and I have had no denial that this is not the case.

Now people will say to me: "Why? You don't make sense. Why should a Republican Department of Justice and Republican prosecutors attempt to get you?" Well, I don't know all the answers, but I will say this—that individuals in the upper professional echelons of the Department of Justice have been severely stung that the President and the Attorney General found it necessary to appoint a special prosecutor, and they are trying to recoup their reputation at my expense. I'm a big trophy.

And one of those individuals has made some very severe mistakes, serious mistakes. In handling his job he considers himself a career professional, in a class by himself, but a recent examination of his record will show not only that he failed to get any of the information about the true dimensions of the Watergate matter, but that he also through ineptness and blunder prevented the successful prosecution of high crime figures because of wiretapping error.

Those are the reasons why he needs me to reinstate his reputation as a tough and courageous and hard-nosed prosecutor. Well, I'm not going to fall down and be his victim, I assure you.

. . . I want to make another thing so clear that it cannot be mistaken in the future. Because of these tactics which have been employed against me, because small and fearful men have been frightened into furnishing evidence against me—they have perjured themselves in many cases, it's my understanding—I will not resign if indicted. *I will not resign if indicted!*[49]

While the Republican women in L.A. cheered, Washington was rocked by the idea of a vice-president attacking his own administration's Justice Department in a public speech. Elliot Richardson and his staff immediately set to work on a statement defending Henry Petersen and his record in the department. Within hours of the vice-president's barrage, the attorney general had issued his counterattack, and in addition to its defense of Petersen, his statement noted that it was Richardson, not Petersen, who was running the investigation.

The president responded to Agnew's charges by calling on Richardson to provide him assurance that Petersen was not the source of any Justice Department leaks. Richardson gladly gave it.

After his speech, Agnew met privately with a group of Republican officials in California. In that meeting, according to the *New York Times,* the vice-president told the officials that he regretted not having touched on the topic of the plea bargaining in his speech, informing the officials that it was the Justice Department and not he who had initiated the sessions and that he had never seriously considered a deal. His aides then told newsmen of the private session.[50] For all the publicity, however, no repercussions were immediately felt by Agnew himself, until a member of his staff made a critical error.

On the day following Agnew's speech—Sunday, September 30—the vice-president's press secretary, J. Marsh Thomson, implied while talking to reporters that, in a speech in Chicago scheduled for October 4, the vice-president would once again attack the Justice Department. This implication was enough to convince some members of the White House staff that the vice-president had to be controlled. Describing Thomson's effect, Agnew wrote:

> [Thomson's] remark . . . was widely reported. It hit the White House like a bomb. Haig called my Chief of Staff, Art Sohmer, and told him that the President wanted no more speeches of the Los Angeles type, and that Thomson must be silenced.[51]

The vice-president followed these instructions, relieving Thomson of his duties as soon as the stories about his remark had hit the press and not delivering the advertised speech in Chicago. In fact, he began his remarks on October 4 with a statement to the press the tone of which was completely opposite to that of the L.A. speech. He said: "Tonight is not going to be an X-rated political show. It's just going to be PG. So if you have to go someplace, go. A candle is only so long before it burns out."[52]

The evening news on Monday, October 1, delivered another blow to the vice-president. That night, NBC aired a story by Carl Stern and Tom Brokaw which attributed to Justice Department officials the belief that Agnew's attorneys had been responsible for leaking the Petersen quotation. Stern reported:

> Petersen has declined to talk publicly about the case since it became known two months ago, and today he still isn't talking about it. If Petersen isn't talking, then who is? Who quoted him as saying, "We've got the evidence. We've got it cold."
>
> Officials at the Justice Department believe that word was spread by Mr. Agnew's own lawyers. It gives the Vice President ammunition for a counterattack and legal grounds to challenge the fairness of the proceedings against him. Said one official, "Publicizing the statement couldn't help us. It could only help him." Another called the Vice President's attack on Petersen a distraction, a diverting move by some very sharp lawyers.[53]

Now the speculation about the motives for the leaks was public: Agnew had said several times that he thought the Justice Department was leaking to prejudice his chances in court, force him out of office, and to try to recoup reputations that seemed to have been damaged from the initial handling of Watergate; Justice staffers now countered with their own belief that Agnew's lawyers were responsible for many of the leaks in an attempt to start a wave of sympathy for the vice-president and give him grounds on which to have the charges dismissed.

The public back-and-forth continued, as Agnew issued a statement refuting the allegations in Stern and Brokaw's story: "The Justice Department is now making the assertion that the leak of Petersen's comment came from my attorneys. This is nothing more than a pitiful attempt at a coverup. My attorneys are willing to sign an affidavit that they did not discuss anything concerning the meeting with the news media. Mr. Graham should be decent enough to confirm that his source was not my attorneys." But all that Mr. Graham was willing to confirm, as noted earlier, was that he had not talked to Henry Petersen.

On October 3, the president entered the fray once again. In a rare, informal appearance in the White House press room, the president stated his support for the manner in which the Justice Department was handling what he termed "serious" charges against his vice-president, and for Assistant Attorney General Petersen. He added the caveat, however, that resignation was a matter for Agnew alone to decide.

A Charge to the Grand Jury

Also on Wednesday the third, Judge Hoffman decided that he had better warn the grand jurors about the danger of being influenced by what the press was reporting on the case. He, therefore, wrote a supplemental charge to deliver to the jurors. Before reading it to them, however, he called Agnew's lawyers along with U.S. prosecutors Beall, Skolnik, and Liebman to his office to solicit their opinions on his text. Beall, according to a memo he later wrote for the attorney general, objected to the vice-president's counsel being present, the grand jury being "the exclusive province of judges and prosecutors and . . . not a subject for private counsel's opinions." He was overruled by Hoffman who said he found this case to be an exception.

In their meeting, Hoffman informed the prosecutors and the defense attorneys that he had already sent them a letter telling them he was inclined to grant the vice-president's request for an evidentiary hearing on the matter of leaks to the media and which camp was responsible, and that he had scheduled this hearing for October 12. (In his letter, Judge Hoffman went on to say "The burden, of course, is upon the applicant to prove that the source of the prejudicial information emanated from the Department of Justice. My own experiences with the news media are such that I recognize the news media will circulate information by frequently suggesting a source which had nothing to do with the matter.") The judge also told the prosecutors that he had granted Martin London's request that the defense attorneys be allowed to start questioning and taking depositions on the matter of leaks before the hearing on the twelfth.

Again, Beall found himself objecting but to no avail. He argued that Hoffman should not schedule a hearing on the matter of the leaks until the Justice Department had filed their brief refuting the charges filed by Agnew's attorneys (the department was preparing to do this). And, even if the hearing should be scheduled, Beall said, to allow the vice-president's attorneys to begin questioning and taking depositions on the matter before the hearing, presupposed their claims to be valid. The judge, however, cited the pressure imposed by the statute of limitations and held firm in his decision.

Hoffman then went to the grand jurors and delivered his supplemental charge. In addition to warning them that they could not base their judgments as jurors on what they read or heard outside the grand jury room, the judge went on to deliver a wholesale indictment of the role of the media in criminal proceedings. In part he said:

> Since my designation [as the District Judge for the case] and perhaps prior thereto, I have noted with great reluctance that the news media have caused many articles, statements and newscasts to be issued. While I am confident that Judge Blair, who originally charged you when you initially were convened, probably mentioned that you should hear and determine matters coming before you without regard to anything you may have heard or seen by reason of the news media, I think that you should be reminded again of same. As you know, you were sworn to secrecy as to any matters brought to your attention while sitting as grand jurors and, insofar as I am aware, you have adhered strictly to this oath of secrecy. To what extent, if any, the news media have attempted to obtain information from you, I do not know. I congratulate you for adhering to your oath of secrecy and only request that you continue to do so, even after you have completed your deliberations and have been discharged. . . .
>
> . . .[T]here must be before you some competent credible testimony establishing probable cause to render the finding of "A True Bill" [a indictment]. It would be a tragedy to the cause of the administration of justice if grand jurors returned an indictment marked "A True Bill" merely because the jurors may have heard or seen comments by the news media. . . .
>
> Since you have been permitted to go to your homes and, in general, carry on your normal business affairs except while serving as grand jurors, it would be an insult to your intelligence to inquire as to whether you have seen or heard anything concerning the party or parties under investigation. Obviously, you have. We are rapidly approaching the day when the perpetual conflict between the news media, operating as they do under Freedom of Speech and Freedom of the Press, and the judicial system, charged with protecting the rights of persons under investigation for criminal acts, must be resolved. You are not concerned with the sources of information disseminated by the news media. It is because I have learned, over a period of twenty years as a judge and an additional twenty-three years as an attorney, that the news media frequently are wholly or partially inaccurate, that I must warn you to disregard totally any comments you have seen or heard from

any source, save except what you have heard or seen in your grand jury room while in official session.

So Agnew's attorneys had won some battles with the judge. The weight of the evidence against him and the White House pressure to respond quietly, however, proved the stronger force. As noted earlier, it was a different Agnew who addressed the audience in Chicago than the one who had spoken in Los Angeles. The vice-president's passion had burned out in a mere six days. He had looked at his future and was not pleased by what he saw.

Back to the Bargaining Table

The vice-president returned to Washington on October 5 to find the court-room battles continuing. His lawyers had issued subpoenas to nine reporters for testimony on the leaks in the case. According to Cohen and Witcover the reporters included Cohen himself, Fred Graham of CBS, Nicholas Gage of *The New York Times,* Ron Sarro and Robert Walters of *The Washington Star-News,* Stephen Lesher of *Newsweek,* and the *Time* authors of the August 27 and September 3 articles.* The attorneys also planned to take depositions from Elliot Richardson, Henry Petersen, Glen Pommerening, George Beall, and Jonathan Moore. Later Barney Skolnik would be added to the list.[54]

During his absence, the Justice Department had also been active, submitting the first of their two briefs responding to the defense's motion to stop the grand jury investigation. In the first, written by Solicitor General Robert Bork, they argued that the vice-president could indeed be indicted by a grand jury. They were still at work, however, on the brief that would respond to the charge that the department had been responsible for leaks in the case.

Additionally, on October 5, Glen Pommerening submitted to Richardson his second progress report on the internal DOJ probe for leaks. The assistant attorney general explained in his report that, because the media had continued to give the story great play, his investigators had both taken new sworn statements and continued their analysis of the stories that were breaking. The second report, however, came to roughly the same conclusions as the first: all employees of the department with knowledge of the case denied either leaking information or knowing of anyone who did. Pommerening was stronger in his second report, though, in supporting the idea that a member of the vice-president's staff might be responsible, saying in the supplemental findings:

[The] inquiry has developed the following information which we have reason to believe is reliable:

a) The earlier finding that a person on the Vice President's staff was the initial and principal source of information contained in the August 7,

---

*The names of the *Time* reporters were unknown to Agnew's attorneys, since the pieces appeared without by-lines.

1973, *Wall Street Journal* story written by Jerry Landauer, has received further confirmation.

b) A person on the Vice President's staff was the initial source of the information published in several news stories that the Vice President had accepted substantial gifts of food and liquor.

c) Lester Matz, one of the principal witnesses, was himself the source of one or more news stories dealing with his testimony.

Pommerening's findings were representative of the increasing sense on the part of senior Justice Department officials that the leaking was coming principally from somewhere in the Agnew camp—either from his staff or his attorneys.

Although he had won some of his points in court, the situation was becoming more and more uncomfortable for the vice-president and on his return Friday the fifth, he met with one of his attorneys, Judah Best, and instructed him to resume negotiations on a possible plea bargain. As they had before, Agnew's attorneys used the White House as their communications link with the prosecutors—with Best calling White House counsel Fred Buzhardt who was, at the time, in Florida with the president. According to Cohen and Witcover, Buzhardt did not wish to fly back to Washington to meet Best for fear that the press would recognize him and know that something was afoot. As a result, Best grabbed a flight to Miami and met with the White House counsel in the early morning hours of October 6, in a Florida motel room to iron out the points of a possible settlement. Best then turned straight around and returned to Washington.[55]

On Sunday, October 7, the Justice team met again to discuss what they would be willing to contribute in this second round to a deal. The last negotiations had broken off on what the vice-president would be allowed to say in court. A second issue of contention now made itself felt—whether the Justice Department would go so far as to recommend that the vice-president not receive a jail sentence. The Justice team had already acceded to the notion that they would not *demand* that Agnew go to jail. The new question was whether or not they could agree to recommend to the judge that he *not* receive a sentence. Although in some respects this may seem minor, in the battle over public perception, the Justice team believed it was a different thing to have Agnew go free because the judge so ordered and to have him freed because the Justice Department requested it.

Aaron Latham, who based his *New York* article on the Baltimoreans' recollections, describes the Sunday meeting as uncomfortable for all parties. According to Latham, Richardson opened the meeting by saying that he was willing to compromise on both the sticking points—Agnew's in-court statement and a Justice recommendation of no jail. The Baltimore team had a difficult time accepting this. Latham describes:

> Barney Skolnik's was the loudest voice raised against the Attorney General's softening position. Skolnik insisted that the Vice President was "blackmailing" them and holding the country "hostage." The young prosecutor argued that no matter what Agnew said, he would have no choice but to resign if he were indicted. . . .

Henry Petersen got up, started to pace, and said heatedly: "This man is the goddamn Vice President of the United States. What do you want to do? Make him crawl on his belly?"

Skolnik shot back: "It isn't a question of making him crawl on his belly. It is a question of how what we are doing is going to be perceived."[56]

The Baltimore prosecutors even went so far, Latham says, as to consider publicly dissociating themselves from the deal, perhaps by going to the press, if Richardson became too soft.

A new point of contention rose in the discussions as a request was forwarded from Judah Best that the defense team see in advance the text of the disclosure of the evidence that the Justice Department planned to make in court. All the government attorneys were in agreement that they did not like the idea of telling Agnew ahead of time what their case would say. The group differed, however, on how far they would go in compromising on this request. Henry Petersen proposed, and had drafted, a ten page summary of the government's case. The Baltimoreans thought that Petersen gave away too much and agreed to try shortening and redrafting the document.[57] Eventually, they developed a summary that was only seven pages long.

Richardson took one action at the meeting to try to keep the Maryland prosecutors on board. He invited Barney Skolnik to join the team negotiating with the vice-president's lawyers. Cohen and Witcover describe this invitation as the "enlisting" of Skolnik, committing him to support the final deal whether he liked it or not. Skolnik, however, says that he was not co-opted by Richardson's invitation, but went into the bargaining with his eyes open, hoping his presence could influence the terms of the final bargain.

On October 8, Bork filed his second brief with Judge Hoffman answering the defense attorneys' allegations about leaks in the department. In part, Bork argued:

> Analysis of the papers submitted by counsel for the Vice President discloses that their motion is supported by neither the facts nor the law. They are engaged in an attempt to confuse the issues and to halt a legitimate investigation by the common defense tactic of trying a prosecutor.
>
> The Department of Justice is at least as concerned as counsel for the Vice President about the publicity this investigation has received. Counsel for the Vice President concede that "in all probability, such publicity is inevitable when a Vice President is the subject of a criminal investigation." . . . The Department has, nevertheless, made vigorous efforts to discover whether personnel with knowledge of the investigation have divulged facts to unauthorized persons. But since the unsupported charges made by counsel for the Vice President are serious, the Department wished to meet them head on and meet them now. For that reason, despite the lack of any basis for the charges, the Department will not object to or seek relief from the order that senior officials give their depositions under oath. Since no showing has been or can be made that any department "campaign" or conspiracy exists, however, we strongly object to the subpoenas issued by counsel for the Vice President to newsmen. We have supported the right of courts to the testi-

mony of newsmen when its relevance and importance were plain. We have never supported incursions into this sensitive area for the mere purpose of conducting fishing expeditions, and it is plain that that is all that is involved here.[58]

In the battle over public perceptions, and hence to one degree or another for the hearts and minds of the reporters covering the story, the government saw an opening it could legitimately exploit in the role of defenders of the free press against unnecessary subpoenas.

Bork then continued his argument stating that in order to prove their charges and receive a halt to the investigation counsel for the vice-president would need to do two things—show facts demonstrating there was probable reason to believe the Justice Department had engaged in a campaign of leaks, and having done that, present a valid legal theory for halting a grand jury investigation because of this breach. Both of these things, Bork claimed, Best, Topkis and London had failed to do.[59] As the counsel for the vice-president had done, Bork used copies of numerous newspaper articles to support his position.

As part of his submission, Bork delivered to Judge Hoffman the October 5 progress report Pommerening had submitted on his internal leaks investigation. Sections of the report which might have disclosed information about the government's case to the defense attorneys were, however, excised. The report itself was made public when it was submitted to the court, and not surprisingly it became news. On October 10, the *New York Times* ran a story headlined "Agnew's Office Called Possible Source of Leaks" which described Pommerening's major findings.[60]

Closing the Deal

On October 8 the Justice team was working feverishly to pull together all the aspects of the bargain they were working on with the vice-president. Liebman and Baker spent their day in Baltimore working on the full draft of the exposition of evidence to be presented in court when the deal was final.

Petersen, Beall, and Skolnik met first with Richardson to go over the deal they wished to propose to the vice-president, answering each of the terms, in one fashion or another, that Best had presented. The package as proposed included the vice-president's resignation plus a plea of nolo contendere to one count of felony tax evasion. A statement disclosing the evidence on other possible counts would be presented in court by the government and a statement would be read by Agnew conceding some level of culpability. Additionally, the government planned to make no formal recommendation as to whether Agnew should be sent to jail and they would allow the defense to see only a summary their evidence prior to the actual appearance in court. The three then went to the Olde Colony Motor Lodge in Alexandria, Virginia, where Judge Hoffman had taken a room, to meet with Agnew's attorneys and the judge.

When the Justice negotiators arrived at the motel, they found reporters and cameramen waiting for them. In fact, Judge Hoffman had called Washington to warn them that this would be the case, that the location of his motel had some-how leaked. Cohen and Witcover, describe the attorneys arrival:

> Unsettled by the television crews spread all over the place in front of the [motel] entrance, [the Justice negotiators] ordered the driver to pull down the street a bit. Suddenly, a man jumped in front of their car and flagged it down.
> "Are you looking for the judge?" he asked.
> "Who are you?" Skolnik responded.
> "I'm the manager. I'll take you up to the judge's room through the laundry room."
> They were about to accept the suggestion when Skolnik reminded them of the strategy they had [earlier] agreed on [to face the reporters and say they were seeing the judge on a procedural matter only].
> Meanwhile, Topkis, London, and Best were arriving by cab. Like the Justice men, they approached the motel as a patrol would setting out behind enemy lines in wartime. Dismissing their cab, they walked along the motel wall until they, too, spotted the camera crew. Panicked, they immediately decided to retrieve their cab and return to Washington. But the cab was nowhere to be found. Then they noticed the Justice men braving the camera's lights and somewhat sheepishly the lawyers followed the prosecutors.[61]

In the meeting between the parties, most of the items in the deal went through smoothly. They had, after all, conferred before on these same points. Two items, however, caused problems. The first was the issue of jail. Agnew's attorneys pushed for a commitment that he would not have to serve a jail sentence. Petersen, speaking for Justice, held to Richardson's position that the government preferred to leave that up to the judge. Hoffman responded that in the absence of any agreement on the matter he would withhold his decision until they were in open court. The judge did indicate, however, that he would prefer it if the Justice Department would make a recommendation, and if they were to recommend that no sentence be imposed he would probably go along with them.

The second problem occurred when Petersen gave Hoffman the seven-page summary of the evidence that the Baltimoreans had prepared. The summary had been given to the defense team earlier and they had suggested a number of changes. Topkis now argued before the judge that the department should make all of the requested changes. The issue, however, was dropped as the judge returned them to the question of the sentence.

Finally, Hoffman gave the Justice team a fright. When the issue of leaks came up, the judge indicated his anger than news reporters were present outside the motel. He went on to say that if the next day's new stories included the true purpose of the Alexandria meeting, he would assume it was the Justice attorneys who had leaked the information. Cohen and Witcover wrote the Skolnik was asked by a television reporter as he left the meeting whether plea bargaining had been taking place. He replied with a brusque "No comment."[62] The Justice team watched with trepidation for any stories the next day and were relieved to find that no one reported the bargaining.

Richardson was sufficiently concerned about the leak of the motel location to ask Jonathan Moore to prepare a memo on possible sources to reporters of that information. Moore concluded that the attorneys for the vice-president, as well as a limited number of DOJ staffers, the White House, and members of the motel staff knew of Hoffman's location, and that it was just as likely that the press had learned of the location by tracking the delivery of the proposed leaks brief to the judge from the department, as through any other source. Therefore, he noted, the reporters present at the motel remained unaware of the import of the meeting. Explaining this possibility, he wrote in his report to Richardson: "The press is extraordinarily tenacious and the reporters are being driven by their editors. They read iron filings, piece a lot of innocent and disparate pieces of information together, and do a lot of guessing. But in this case, if [the leak] happened this way, their interest was only in tracking the location of the Judge and . . . not at least at first blush because they were informed where he was and were pursuing any meeting or conference [we had scheduled].

On October 9, Richardson met with Beall, Petersen, and Skolnik in William Ruckelshaus's office at the department to review the deal as currently cast. They were later joined by Agnew's attorneys and began reviewing the agreement point-by-point. There remained the sticking points, however. Richardson tried to get the Agnew team not to insist on prior review of the department's full disclosure of their case. Topkis insisted the Justice recommend no jail sentence to the Judge.

In the afternoon, the group was joined by Judge Hoffman to finalize the terms of the deal. The attorney general tried to ascertain from the judge whether or not he would require the department to recommend no jail in order not to give Agnew a sentence. The judge insisted that unless Richardson was willing to make some kind of formal recommendation in court, that he could not commit himself in advance that the vice-president would not receive a jail term. The attorney general finally agreed to recommend in court that there be no prison term. With that out of the way, and an agreement that the vice-president's attorneys could review the exposition of the evidence just prior to his court appearance, the parties agreed that an arraignment should take place as soon as possible. Part of the reason for the haste was the pressure exerted on all the participants and part was to insure that no one backed out; yet another part, however, was to minimize the chances that the press would learn of the deal and report it before the vice-president got to court. The court date was, therefore set for the following day, October 10 at 2:00 P.M. And, virtually unprecedented in this kind of proceeding, they also agreed that the attorney general himself would present the government's case.

A hearing on the leaks issue had been scheduled for the tenth at 10:00 A.M. Out of their concern that the press would get wind of the deal, the group agreed that they would tell reporters only that the hearing was being delayed pending a proceeding at two. According to Cohen and Witcover, "they guessed correctly . . . that the press would conclude that the two o'clock session would be on the leaks issue, nothing more."[63]

The Justice team then returned to their offices to work on their part of the package while the Baltimore prosecutors return to Maryland to work through the night preparing the final exposition of the evidence—forty pages long—and of which they rushed a copy to the counsel for the vice-president at 8:00 A.M. the following day.

The Vice-President Resigns

On the evening of October 9, having been informed by his attorneys that the deal had been struck, Vice-President Agnew composed his letter of resignation to be delivered the following day to Secretary of State Henry Kissinger. Agnew then went to see President Nixon and informed him that the battle was over, he would resign his office the next day.

The system for delivering his resignation was a bit complex, since the vice-president and his attorneys wanted it delivered at the last possible minute prior to the start of the arraignment in case there were any last minute snags in the deal. They did, however, want the resignation to take effect before the court proceedings began so that Agnew did not become the first sitting vice-president in history to plead to a felony charge. As a result, it was arranged that an attorney from Best's firm, George Kaufmann, would stand outside Kissinger's office with the letter of resignation, prepared to deliver it as soon as the defense team phoned from Baltimore to say that everything was set.

The press had been allowed into the courthouse that afternoon, although they did not know the nature of the proceeding they would cover. At a few minutes before 2:00 P.M. the Justice team, led by Richardson, and Agnew's attorneys entered the courtroom. Behind them came Vice-President Agnew. When all the parties had been seated in the courtroom, Agnew authorized Best to telephone Kaufmann and have his resignation delivered. When it had been confirmed that the resignation had been accepted, the court proceedings got underway.

First Judge Hoffman had the courtroom doors locked and informed both the members of the press and spectators that they would not be permitted to leave until the session was over. He then asked Agnew a series of questions designed to insure that he understood the nature of plea bargaining and the rights he was waiving by participating in a deal. Once Hoffman was certain that Agnew understood, the judge accepted Agnew's plea of nolo contendere to one count of tax evasion. Hoffman read the terms of the plea bargain and asked if Agnew agreed to the terms. The former vice-president said that he did. Jay Topkis then announced in open court that at 2:05 that afternoon Agnew had resigned his office.

Attorney General Richardson was then given his opportunity to speak. Reading from a prepared statement, he said:

> May it please the Court, I am like every other participant in these proceedings, deeply conscious of the critical national interests which surround them. The agreement between the parties now before the Court is one which must be just and honorable, and which must be perceived to be just and honorable, not simply to the parties but above all to the American people.
> From the outset of the negotiations which have culminated in these pro-

ceedings, the Department of Justice has regarded as an integral requirement of any agreement a full disclosure of the surrounding circumstances, for only with knowledge of these circumstances can the American people fairly judge the justice of the outcome. One critical component of these circumstances is the Government's evidence. In accordance, therefore, with the agreement of counsel, I offer for the permanent record of these proceedings an exposition of the evidence accumulated by the investigation against the defendant conducted by the office of the United States Attorney for the District of Maryland as of October 10, 1973. . . .

In light of the serious wrongdoing shown by its evidence, the Government might have insisted, if permitted by the Court to do so, on pressing forward with the return of an indictment charging bribery and extortion. To have done this, however, would have been likely to inflict upon the Nation serious and permanent scars. It would have been the defendant's right to put the prosecution to its proof. [This would] have consumed not simply months but years—with potentially disastrous consequences to vital interests of the United States. Confidence in the adequacy of our fundamental institutions would itself have been put to severe trial. It is unthinkable that this Nation should have been required to endure the anguish and uncertainty of a prolonged period in which the man next in line of succession to the Presidency was fighting the charges brought against him by his own Government.

On the basis of these considerations, I am satisfied that the public interests is better served by this Court's acceptance of the defendant's plea of *nolo contendere* to a single count information charging income tax evasion.[64]

Even in his court statement, the attorney general had stressed the importance of perceptions as well as reality. He then concluded with a plea that Agnew not receive a jail term, noting first that no agreement would have been reached with Agnew had he not agreed to argue for leniency, and then saying: "Out of compassion for the man, out of respect for the office he has held, and out of appreciation for the fact that by his resignation he has spared the Nation the prolonged agony that would have attended upon his trial, I urge that the sentence imposed on the defendant by this Court not include confinement."[65]

By the time Richardson had concluded his court statement, the press already had the story that the vice-president had resigned. At 2:30 P.M., the AP ran a one-line story, reading: "WASHINGTON (AP)—Vice-President Spiro T. Agnew resigned today, his secretary said."[66] The last possible leak, insignificant though it was, had occurred in the case.

Once Richardson had completed his statement, Spiro Agnew took the floor. He told the court:

My decision to resign and enter a plea of nolo contendere rests on my firm belief that the public interest requires swift disposition of the problems which are facing me. I am advised that a full legal defense of the probable charges against me could consume several years. I am concerned that intense media interest in the case would distract public attention from important national problems—to the country's detriment.

I am aware that witnesses are prepared to testify that I and my agents received payments from consulting engineers doing business with the State of Maryland during the period I was Governor. With the exception of the admission that follows, I deny the assertions of illegal acts on my part made by the Government witnesses.

I admit that I did receive payments during the year 1967 which were not expended for political purposes and that therefore these payments were income, taxable to me in that year, and that I so knew.

I further acknowledge that contracts were awarded by state agencies in 1967 and other years to those who made such payments, and that I was aware of such awards. I am aware that government witnesses are prepared to testify that preferential treatment was accorded to the paying companies pursuant to an understanding with me when I was Governor. I stress, however, that no contracts were awarded to contractors who were not competent to perform the work and, in most instances, state contracts were awarded without any arrangement for the payment of money by contractor.

I deny that the payments in any way influenced my official actions. I am confident, moreover, that testimony presented in my behalf would make it clear that I at no time conducted my official duties as County Executive or Governor of Maryland in a manner harmful to the interests of the county or state, or my duties as Vice-President of the United States in a manner harmful to the nation; and I further assert that my acceptance of contributions was part of a long-established pattern of political fund-raising in the state. At no time have I enriched myself at the expense of my public trust.

In all the circumstances, I have concluded that protracted proceedings before the grand jury, the Congress and the courts, with the speculation and controversy inevitably surrounding them, would seriously prejudice the national interest.

These, briefly stated, Your Honor, are the reasons that I am entering a plea of nolo contendere to the charge I did receive payments in 1967 which I failed to report for the purposes of income taxation.[67]

Agnew then admitted that he received one payment in the year 1967 which he did not expend for political purposes and failed to declare on his income tax return. He denied, however, that any money received had caused him to award state contracts to those who were unqualified, and added that the acceptance of such money was a "part of a long-established pattern of political fundraising"[68] in the state of Maryland.

When Agnew had concluded, it was Judge Hoffman's turn to make a statement and then to close the proceedings, releasing the press and courtroom observers from the locked chambers. In his statement, Hoffman explained the details of the agreement between the parties to the plea, and the meaning of the nolo contendere plea itself. Hoffman went on to comment on the statements submitted by Richardson and Agnew, saying:

A detailed statement has been filed by the Department of Justice and refuted by the defendant, all of which are wholly unrelated to the charge of income tax evasion. These statements are part of the understanding between the parties and are submitted merely because of the charges and countercharges which have received so much advance publicity. . . . Since the Department of Justice, pursuant to its agreement, will be barred from prosecuting the defendant as to any criminal charge heretofore existing, the truth of these charges and countercharges can never be established by any judicial decision or action. It would have been my preference to omit these statements and end the verbal warfare as to this tragic event in history, but I am not inclined to reject the agreement for this reason alone.[69]

Judge Hoffman finally informed the parties that he would accept the agreement, including the Attorney General's request that no jail sentence be imposed on Agnew, and ended the court proceeding. Agnew was out of office, and both the charges with regard to leaks as well as the charges against the vice-president— outside of the one count of tax evasion—had been rendered moot. The attorney general, however, still had one item on his schedule in connection with the case.

On October 11, the day after their court appearance, Richardson appeared in the Great Hall of the Department of Justice to hold a press conference on the case. He was still battling for the public's opinion in relation to the justice and fairness of the case's resolution, and he made this one last attempt to explain through the vehicle of the media, what had happened. The attorney general read the reporters in the hall a short statement reiterating his hope that the American public would support what the prosecutors had done. He also urged compassion for the former vice-president, repeating the sentiments expressed in his court plea for leniency in sentencing. And finally, Richardson gave praise to the prosecutors while admitting there had been moments of dissension among their ranks.* He then allowed reporters to ask questions, and for the first time in almost four months, the attorney general did not have to worry about leaks.

Epilogue

Pommerening's Final Report

Although Spiro Agnew's resignation and the plea bargain he had struck with the Justice Department had rendered moot the Court of Appeals consideration of the leaks issue, it did not stop the questions about the leaks in the minds of the participants, nor the speculation about their source. The Justice Department continued the conduct of its internal investigation for possible departmental leaks after the October 10 resignation. The investigation even continued after the resignation on October 21, 1973, of Richardson, Moore, and William Ruckelshaus in the so-called Saturday Night Massacre at the Justice Department.

On October 26, 1973, Glen Pommerening submitted his final report to Acting Attorney General Robert Bork. Pommerening had two principal findings:

1. Based on their sworn statements, none of the 175 individuals who represent all of the Department of Justice and Internal Revenue Service participants in the Baltimore County investigation, were the source of any unauthorized dis-

---

*For the full text of the attorney general's statement, see Appendix G.

closure. [In a footnote, Pommerening wrote that it is important to note that a false statement would have been a violation of federal law.]

2. There is absolutely no empirical evidence nor credible information to substantiate the charge that the Department of Justice or any individual Department of Justice employee conducted a "campaign of leaks."

Additionally, Pommerening noted that his "continued analysis has substantiated the supplemental findings which were offered in our two earlier reports." As noted earlier, these included the fact that a member of Agnew's staff was believed to be the "initial and principal source" of the leak to Jerry Landauer as well as being the source for later news stories.

The final report differed from the first two, however, in that Pommerening made a series of recommendations to limit the likelihood of leaks in sensitive departmental cases in the future. His four recommendations were:

1. *Security within the Department of Justice should be emphasized.* Our inquiry revealed several instances of lax security in the Department. In some organizations physical and document security were woefully inadequate and were strengthened only after the allegation of leaks began, e.g., we gave assistance to the United States Attorney in Baltimore to improve the physical security of his office and of the grand jury courtroom. . . .

2. *A system for recording press contacts should be instituted within the Department of Justice.* Due to sourcing ambiguities in the press, it was frequently difficult to distinguish between news items which were the result of official Department of Justice briefings and those which might have been the result of unauthorized disclosures. While not wishing to burden the Public Information Office and the Office of the Attorney General, we feel it is necessary for the Department to maintain a more complete record of official statements and conversations with the press. This would enable the Department to immediately establish attribution for statements appearing in the news.

3. *A "limited distribution channel" should be developed within the Department of Justice which would minimize the exposure of sensitive information.* The greatest single increase in exposure within the Department occurred as a result of polygraphing potential witnesses, i.e., 36 FBI employees were exposed to varying degrees of information about the facts and / or the details of the investigation.

4. *The Standards of Conduct and Title 28 Code of Federal Regulations should be strengthened to include penalties for unauthorized disclosure of information.**

Although the development of such recommendations for reform were part of Attorney General Richardson's original mandate for Pommerening's investigation, by the time they had been submitted to Acting Attorney General Bork the department had changed so dramatically, and other events—notably the Watergate crisis—had taken center stage. They did not, therefore, receive the attention they might have a brief two weeks earlier.

---

*See Appendix H for the full text of Pommerening's Final Report.

The Leaks in Retrospect

The Baltimore prosecutors all agree, the leaks in the Agnew case turned their lives upside down. As well as the problems that naturally arose from conducting an investigation of the vice-president of the United States, the prosecutors were forced to learn to deal with the press and to cope with the ever-increasing suspicion that they were the most likely source of the leaks. The press coverage touched the lives of Elliot Richardson, William Ruckelshaus, Henry Petersen, Jonathan Moore, and J. T. Smith in much the same way, although, at their more senior level of federal service they were somewhat more accustomed to the attention than Skolnik, Baker, et al. Glen Pommerening would never have been involved in the vice-president's case if it hadn't been for the leaks. But for all it changed their lives, they are not sure at all that it changed the outcome of the case they had built.

Barney Skolnik, for example, says he does not know how the case would have gone if the press hadn't covered every move and rumor, but adds that he has no reason to believe they would have had a stronger case had there been no leaks, saying:

> The case was there to be made, and we did make it. I don't have any reason to believe that the substantive case that we would have ended up with if the press had never heard a word until we marched into the court would have been any different. It is not as though I had reason to believe there were other direct payors [of money to Agnew] who we never found, or that the peripheral corroboration that we ended up with would have been significantly different or greater if it hadn't been for the press. It sure as hell would have been easier to put the case together though. We would not have had to waste as much time and energy persuading people to come in through the basement and all that other rubbish we had to go through to get people to talk to us. . . .
>
> There is a separate question, though, which is would there have been a deal if it had all been kept a secret. And, on that, I don't know. You'd have to ask Agnew.

George Beall believes the press attention was in part responsible for keeping the pace on the case rapid, but he is also unwilling to hypothesize a change in the outcome:

> I think the press attention forced a resolution of the matter earlier than might have otherwise been the case. For example, if this were a typical criminal case, the plea bargaining would have taken place after the charges were placed: after the government completed its investigation and filed a formal statement of the charges, the process of negotiations would have begun. Of course, here the whole pre-negotiation process took place before the charges were filed. Everyone was on a faster track. Part of it was because we were dealing with the Vice President of the United States. But part was also because of the tremendous public attention that was attracted to the investigation.

Both Elliot Richardson and Tim Baker say flatly that they don't believe the coverage and the leaks affected the terms of the final deal. After denying that the outcome was changed in any way, Richardson will say that, even at the end as the bargain was being finalized, fear of leaks continued to haunt him: "the one thing the press coverage did do was to lead us to adopt measures of greater secrecy in the two meetings we had with Judge Hoffman, and the press never did catch up with those meetings."

Not surprisingly, those who participated in Agnew's defense see the effects of the press on the plea bargain in a different light. Charles Colson says that he believes the coverage "settled the outcome" of the case. Countering the Justice officials' assertion that the leaks were a deliberate strategy on the defense team's part to damage the credibility of the department and to create sympathy for their client, he argues that the options for defense were severely limited by the publicity:

> I think that without the press coverage the time pressure would have been off. The time pressure coupled with the investigation of Watergate [and the resulting pressure on the President] made it impossible.
>
> You have to separate what you later know to be the case from what you knew at the time. You may later say that you know that Agnew was accepting money illegally. But, at the time, it was not clear to Agnew's attorneys, and, unless he was a very good actor, it was not clear to Agnew that this was so. And so, if you separate the two, you may have gotten the right results, but maybe for the wrong reasons.
>
> If it had not been for the glare of publicity there would have been many more negotiations. There would have been more efforts to produce witnesses who would contradict the government's witnesses. . . .
>
> We would have done a lot of things that can be done in an investigation before there is an ultimate decision on whether to indict. But under the pressure, with Nixon in such trouble, with the whole country in a state of turmoil, and feeding out this stuff in a climate in which the mere printing of it in the *Washington Post* assumes it is fact, we were left with no options. The ultimate decision to resign was because you know in that public climate you could not judiciously resolve the situation. It's possible that four months later, without the stories it might have come to the same conclusion. But the press made it impossible to follow what would have been normal, investigative processes and normal defense maneuverings.

The middle ground in this debate is occupied by Jonathan Moore, who says that he cannot flatly assert that the media coverage and the leaks did not affect the outcome, although he is far from certain that they did, noting:

> I tend to be persuaded that there was not much of an effect on the final outcome of the case. But there is an argument that the position the Justice Department took during the plea bargaining could have been tougher on Agnew without the press. . . .
>
> Our feelings about trying to get Agnew out of office and under what conditions we could get him out may have been affected by the press because it put us on the defensive. When you are fighting for public opinion and

when you're fighting for the requirement that we began with that the public have a sense of confidence in the outcome, then the press plays an important role in what the public psychology is going to be. . . . I have already said that a public sense of confidence and trust in the outcome was one of the things we cared most about. Without the press constantly challenging our integrity we would have had a much easier time maintaining public confidence, perhaps even if we had pressed for a stronger position.

APPENDIX A

Wall Street Journal Story on Maryland U.S. Attorney's Investigation of Vice President Agnew. August 7, 1973. Page 1.

A NEW WATERGATE?

Spiro Agnew Is Target Of a Criminal Inquiry;
Extortion Is Alleged!

Bribery and Tax Fraud Also Alleged; Vice President Retains Criminal Lawyers

Nixon Is Presumably Notified

By Jerry Landauer
Staff Reporter of *The Wall Street Journal*

WASHINGTON—Vice President Spiro T. Agnew was formally notified by the Justice Department last week that he is a target of a far-ranging criminal investigation by the U.S. Attorney's office in Baltimore. The allegations against him include bribery, extortion and tax fraud.

The investigation is being carried on in strictest secrecy. On receiving the Justice Department notice, the Vice President sought a White House audience, presumably to inform President Nixon.

The Justice Department notification, sent by U.S. Attorney George Beall, was hand-delivered to Mr. Agnew. Essentially, the allegations against him stem from the award of state contracts during Mr. Agnew's tenure as Governor of Maryland in 1967 and 1968—and of federal contracts in Maryland let by the General Services Administration since Mr. Agnew became the Vice President in January 1969. The GSA is the agency in charge of constructing federal buildings.

Mr. Cox Is Notified

The subject matter of the investigation thus isn't related to the Watergate scandal. Nonetheless, the letter to Mr. Agnew was cleared at the top by Attorney General Elliot Richardson, who then notified Special Watergate Prosecutor Archibald Cox.

The fact that Mr. Agnew is under investigation doesn't necessarily mean that he'll be indicted, of course. Indeed, the prosecutors haven't yet presented to a grand jury sitting in Baltimore the evidence they've assembled.

Still, knowledgeable attorneys emphasize the significance of the notification to Mr. Agnew. "There's a natural reluctance to commit yourself in writing," one explains. "The higher the target the more persuasive the evidence must seem before a letter goes out."

Mr. Agnew's personal attorney George W. White, Jr., disclaims knowledge that his long-time friend and client is under investigation. "If that's so, I don't know anything about it," he says. Nevertheless other associates confide that the Vice President has retained

123

criminal law specialists specifically to represent him in the Baltimore proceedings.

Yesterday, Mr. Agnew's spokesmen were asked repeatedly for comment about the allegations. But they hadn't responded by the time *The Wall Street Journal* went to press last night.

A Constitutional Test

So far the Vice President hasn't been asked to testify before the grand jury. If he is called, he will in all likelihood be invited instead of subpoenaed partly in deference to his high public office. And if the case does proceed to the grand jury stage, the prosecutors will have to confront the constitutional doctrine of separation of powers—the doctrine Mr. Nixon is invoking in the Watergate case. "Frankly, this could become another test for the President if it goes that far," a former federal prosecutor says. "It may tell us whether a President or a Vice President can be indicted or whether impeachment is the only constitutional remedy."

The investigation by the U.S. Attorney's office started last January, initially probing reports of kickbacks and payoffs by contractors, consulting engineers and architects to current office-holders in Baltimore County. Baltimore County, a mushrooming bedroom community bordering the city of Baltimore, is where Mr. Agnew launched his spectacular rise to political power just a dozen or so years ago, beginning as a zoning official and moving up to county executive, a post he left to become Governor in 1967.

In recent months, that investigation has been broadened to embrace state contracts awarded during Mr. Agnew's two years as Governor, as well as the GSA contracts in Maryland since he became Vice President.

So far, the investigation hasn't led to any indictments of prominent political figures. One "information," equivalent to an indictment, was brought in June against William E. Fornoff, a key county official who served briefly under County Executive Agnew and for a longer period under Mr. Agnew's successor, incumbent Dale Anderson. Mr. Anderson, who denies any illegal acts, is also a target of the investigation.

Immunity Sought

A major development in the investigation was Mr. Fornoff's admission in court that he had acted as a conduit for cash payments from contractors to an unidentified county official starting in 1967 (after Mr. Agnew had moved to the Governor's mansion in Annapolis). Federal prosecutors let Mr. Fornoff plead guilty to one minor tax charge in exchange for testimony against other politicians and businessmen. Some of these men, in turn, have received immunity, or seek it from prosecutors, in exchange for testimony that may implicate Mr. Agnew.

One immunity-seeker is Lester Matz of Baltimore, a contributor to Agnew political campaigns and an eminently successful civil engineer who enjoys widespread contacts throughout Maryland and neighboring states.

Another is Jerome B. Wolff, whom newly elected Gov. Agnew appointed chairman of the Maryland State Roads Commission in March of 1967. Then, in early 1969, Mr. Wolff joined Mr. Agnew's vice-presidential staff as assistant for science and technology. In August 1970, he switched to part-time consultant, a role he held through December 1971.

Mr. Wolff's lawyer, Arnold Weiner, wouldn't comment. Mr. Matz's lawyer couldn't be reached.

Some Agnew friends contend the Vice President is merely a victim of circumstances in the Baltimore investigation: of overzealous assistant prosecutors who have Democratic leanings; of an indictment-minded criminal division at the Justice Department that's fearful of fresh "cover-up" charges against the background of Watergate; of a recently installed Attorney General who isn't yet in complete command; and perhaps even of associates who bandied Mr. Agnew's name about to make money for themselves.

U.S. Attorney Beall, a 36-year-old Republican appointed by President Nixon in 1970 won't confirm or deny that Mr. Agnew has become a subject of his investigation. Nor will the prosecutor comment on reports that he and his three assistants—Russell T. Baker, Jr., Ronald S. Liebman and Barnett D. Skolnik—have attended hush-hush meetings with higher-ups in Washington to discuss the Agnew case.

"What can I say?" Mr. Beall asks rhetorically. "We're operating under very severe constraints for reasons of fairness to the persons involved and for reasons of protecting cases that might emerge against prejudicial pretrial publicity attributed to the government. . . . It isn't to our advantage to answer even seemingly innocuous questions. It isn't in our interest to see any story printed."

APPENDIX B

Time Magazine article, August 27, 1973

The Vice-Presidency:
HEADING TOWARD AN INDICTMENT?

Fresh from a round of golf and good living at Frank Sinatra's spread in Palm Springs, Vice President Spiro T. Agnew returned to Washington last week to deal with the charges of corruption that have threatened his entire political future. After meeting with his attorneys for most of a day, the Vice President sent a letter to George Beall, the U.S. Attorney in Baltimore, offering to let the prosecutor examine Agnew's personal financial records for the past 6½ years "at any time you may desire." Furthermore, said Agnew, he would be happy to submit to a "personal interview" with Beall "so that I may answer any questions you have." All in all, it seemed the performance of a man anxious to prove, as Agnew has claimed, that he had "nothing to hide."

Despite all the Vice President's protestations of innocence, however, Time has learned that in the view of Justice Department officials in Washington, the case against him is growing steadily stronger, and that an indictment appears inevitable. Besides the two Maryland contractors prepared to testify that they delivered extorted campaign contributions to Agnew (Time, Aug. 20), the Government has a third witness with a similar story. He is Allen I. Green, 49, president of a Maryland engineering firm, a man for many years regarded as one of Agnew's closest friends. Green reportedly has said that he gave kickbacks to Agnew about five times a year when Agnew was Governor of Maryland (1967–68) and slightly less often after he was inaugurated Vice President in 1969.

"The department has no choice," a Justice official in Washington said. "At least three witnesses have told of delivering cash payoffs to Agnew. The evidence is so strong that the case must be taken to trial." A federal grand jury in Baltimore is expected to vote an indictment next month charging Agnew with, among other things, bribery and extortion.

Green and the Government's two other prime witnesses, Jerome Wolff and Lester Matz, both also engineering consultants and former Agnew associates, have told prosecutors that they delivered to Agnew personally cash kick-backs from their own firms and as many as a score of other state and federal contractors in Maryland. For example, Matz has claimed that on one occasion in 1971 he carried $2,500 right into the Vice President's private office in the Executive Office Building and handed it to Agnew, allegedly in return for Agnew's help in getting one of the Matz' friends a job in the General Services Administration. (That story was was promptly denied by another friend of Agnew's, Annapolis Banker J. Walter Jones, who Matz claimed was present during the transaction. "Such a thing is ridiculous," Jones said.)

Prosecutors said that many payoffs delivered to Agnew were disguised as campaign contributions and were used to finance his political races over the years. One of the traditional devices was to sell tickets to a "bull roast" or some similar political festivity, since tickets costing less than $51 need not be reported. Green, Matz and Wolff have all been contributors to Agnew campaigns at one time or another, and Agnew has freely admitted that contractors are among those who have furthered his political fortunes.

Such gifts may be open to serious conflict-of-interest questions, but nothing about them necessarily involves the crimes for which Agnew has been told he is being investigated—extortion, bribery, tax evasion (and conspiracy.) Thus the Government presumably has evidence that contractors' payments to Agnew were demanded in return for specific favors and were paid and collected in that spirit rather than as legitimate campaign funds. As for Agnew's offer to open his personal financial books, sources close to the case point out that cash payments used for campaign purposes probably would not find their way into Agnew's accounts.

What is puzzling to some investigators is the comparatively paltry amount of money involved. Justice Department officials have declined to provide an estimate of the total amount under investigation, but one of them says: "It's less than you'd think. Agnew wasn't greedy; he was quite cheap." Indeed, of the payments so far alleged, only a few exceeded $10,000, and many were between $2,000 and $2,500. In states where corruption thrives on a major-league scale—New Jersey, or Illinois, where a secretary of state died in 1970 with $800,000 stashed in shoeboxes in his hotel room—such sums are hardly worth mentioning.

Nevertheless, Agnew has apparently realized the gravity of the Government's case against him. *Time* has learned that the Vice President has sought the help of Nixon's Watergate defense team (lawyers J. Fred Buzhardt, Leonard Garment and Charles Alan Wright) in preparing a constitutional defense that would prevent his having to go on trial any time soon. The White House lawyers were specifically asked to explore the possibility that the Vice President might adopt Nixon's own argument that a President (or Vice President) cannot be criminally prosecuted until after he has been impeached, convicted and removed from office by Congress. The chances of an Agnew impeachment are not very strong at present, but the prospect of another client's demanding White House constitutional protection has hardly pleased Nixon's legal staff. "We've got enough work on our hands with Ervin and Cox," said one. "Agnew's got his own lawyers."

The Vice President was briefed on the Government's case in early August by Attorney General Elliot Richardson. In the continuing, rather paranoid hunt for secret plots or motives behind Agnew's sudden legal difficulties, his supporters have advanced the notion that Richardson may be the culprit: to wreck Agnew's presidential hopes and further his own chance for the G.O.P. nomination in 1976. Last week the chief of the Justice Department's Criminal Division, Henry E. Petersen, drove to Baltimore to inspect the evidence against Agnew collected by Beall and his three assistants, Barnet D. Skolnik, Russell T. Baker, Jr. and Ronald S. Liebman. Petersen even interrogated Engineer Matz, presumably to determine for himself the credibility of the key witness.

Too Usual. The 23-member grand jury investigating the kickback conspiracy continued to hear testimony, but it found itself temporarily without a judge when U.S. District Judge C. Stanley Blair, who served as Agnew's chief of staff during the first two years of his vice presidency, understandably asked to be relieved of the job of presiding over the inquiry. Because of various other associations with Agnew or with Maryland politics, the other judges in the district declined to take on Blair's assignment. At week's end, U.S. Appeals Court Judge Clement F. Haynsworth, Jr. selected Federal District Judge Walter E. Hoffman of Virginia, a Republican who has been on the bench for 19 years, to handle the case.

Attempting to maintain the appearance of business as usual. Agnew gamely followed a schedule last week that was all too usual for Vice Presidents: the dedication of a new dam in Littleton, Colorado (where he was welcomed by some hostile demonstrators) and a speech at the AFL-CIO Boilermakers convention in Denver. "Just as each citizen has a right to criticize those in public office," he told the union members, "so does every public official have a right to defend his actions, his honor, his integrity and his good name." Agnew was speaking of Nixon's efforts to extricate himself from Watergate, but the words clearly applied as well to his own deepening dilemma.

APPENDIX C

Transcript of Vice-President Spiro Agnew's news conference held in Washington on August 21, 1973, and published in the *New York Times,* August 22, 1973.

Ladies and gentlemen, when I saw you in this room just about two weeks ago, I had no idea I'd be asking to see you again so soon.

At my last press conference, I indicated that I had no expectation of another public statement on this subject in the near future. Circumstances beyond my control, however, make it necessary for me to speak out again.

Now I know this will be a disappointment to you, but this time I will not be able to take your questions—not because I want to avoid the facts, not because I do not wish to see you fully informed—but because to do so would be to continue discussion in a public forum of what should be a secret investigation.

By such a free-wheeling discussion I would be engaging in the very same tactics that I called you here to criticize.

On Wednesday, Aug. 1, 1973, my attorney received a letter from George Beall, United States Attorney in Maryland, advising that his office was conducting an investigation of allegations concerning possible violations by me of certain Federal criminal statutes. Properly, I made every effort to protect the traditional privacy of such an investigation.

Then on Monday, Aug. 6, 1973, I learned that some of Tuesday's newspapers would carry stories revealing that an investigation was under way and disclosing that the letter had been sent to me.

At that point I issued a statement acknowledging that I had been informed of the investigation declaring my innocence of any wrong-doing and announcing that I would make no further comments until the investigation had been completed. I had every right to expect that a similar effort to prevent publicity would be made by the Attorney General and Mr. Beall and their respective staffs in Washington and Baltimore. That, of course, was nothing more than their legal duty.

Therefore I was shocked during the course of the next 36 hours to discover that the news media were reporting numerous details concerning the investigation—detailed accusations and allegations that had to be coming from people who were actually participating in the investigation. I therefore called a press conference on Wednesday, Aug. 8, to set the record straight. Since then the leaks have continued unabated.

I regret to say that it has become clear that sources so frequently quoted—were indeed that—persons involved in the investigatory process.

A national news magazine account headed Heading Toward an Indictment published yesterday and picked up by the wire services quotes unnamed Justice Department officials. I can only assume from this account that some Justice Department officials have decided to indict me in the press whether or not the evidence supports their position.

This is a clear and outrageous effort to influence the outcome of possible grand jury deliberations and so notwithstanding my initial decision not to comment I've had to respond publicly to the continuing charges.

Any person who's been in politics and government for many years is aware of the personal and political hazards of unsubstantiated charges, rumors, innuendo and speculation. I've been subjected to these before, and I'm accustomed to fighting this kind of battle.

What I find intolerable, however, is the impact which this smear publicity may have on the rights of others, particularly private citizens who have been swept into this highly publicized investigation.

On Sunday the Attorney General made a nationally televised denial that any of the leaks came from his department. Mr. Richardson also indicated at that time that he would investigate any suggestion that his department has been the source of such leaks.

I have communicated with the Attorney General today and have asked that he fulfill that promise and pursue such an investigation vigorously. I hope that the national news media will also urge Mr. Richardson and the Justice Department to conduct such an investigation dilligently wherever it may lead and to use all available investigatory tools to compel sworn testimony to reveal the identity of unnamed Justice Department officials and sources close to the investigation.

Now I've not called you to this meeting for the purpose of criticizing the news media. I cannot fault you for publishing information given to you by informants within the Department of Justice.

The blame must rest with those who gave this information to the press and who do so with an obvious motive of interfering with the independent investigatory processes of the grand jury.

I've called this meeting to advise you of the request that I made to the Attorney General and to say again to the American people that I will fight, I will fight to prove my innocence, and that I intend to remain in the high office to which I have been twice elected.

As I said before, I have nothing to hide. I made all requested records available to the prosecutors, and I've offered to meet with them and answer any questions that they may have.

Now, according to this morning's paper, Mr. Beall said he's not sure whether he even wishes to question me. I suppose that if he only wants to hear one side of the story that's up to him. I will say only that it seems to me a very strange way to run an investigation.

Mr. Beall is quoted as saying that I have sought a meeting because it would be desirable from my standpoint.

His statement is not wholly accurate.

It's true that I'd like to meet with Mr. Beall and his staff. I would like them to hear the truth, but before I made my suggestion to Mr. Beall, my lawyers had already been notified by the Department of Justice that the way is open for the Vice President to talk to the prosecutors if he wishes.

I do wish—I hope that way remains open. It is through proper investigation of all the facts that the truth will emerge—not through trial by headline nor by hearing only one part of the story. I'm confident that the orderly processes of justice will result in my complete vindication.

Again I'm sorry that circumstances prohibit my making myself available for questions, and I understand that disappointment is likely to result, but I would ask each of you as a fair-minded individual to place himself in my position and understand the restrictions of my current stance. Thank you.

APPENDIX D

Letter from Fred Graham to the Editors of the *New York Times* and text of news story by Graham on CBS News.

CBS
Columbia Broadcasting System, Inc.
2020 M Street, N.W.
Washington, D.C. 20036

October 1, 1973

The Editors
The New York Times
229 West 43rd Street
New York, N.Y.

Sirs:

James Reston's article on September 28 quoted Vice President Agnew as saying that his confidence in the Justice Department was undermined by the fact that assistant attorney general Henry Petersen was "quoted" by me in a CBS News broadcast concerning the Agnew investigation. The thrust of Mr. Reston's story was that Mr. Agnew felt that Mr. Petersen had allowed himself to be quoted regarding the Government's evidence in the case, and that the Vice President considered this a deliberate impropriety aimed at damaging him.

Apparently the New York Times' columnist, William Safire, read the article that way, as he stated in his column today that Mr. Petersen "told" me a direct quote about his evidence in the case.

The purpose of this letter is to point out that my broadcast did not quote Henry Petersen as saying anything to me, and did not imply that Mr. Petersen has discussed the Agnew case with me in any way. I am enclosing a copy of the text of my broadcast, which described a negotiation session between Justice Department attorneys and Mr. Agnew's lawyers at the Justice Department last Wednesday. Quoting "a source close to the negotiations," the broadcast stated the positions reportedly taken by Mr. agnew's lawyers, by Attorney General Elliot Richardson, and by Mr. Petersen. It is clear from the broadcast that the quote from Mr. Petersen about the strength of his evidence was said at the meeting to Mr. Agnew's lawyers—not to me.

Mr. Petersen has never discussed the merits of the Vice President's case with me.

Very truly yours,

Fred P. Graham

GRAHAM: CBS NEWS HAS LEARNED THAT THE PLEA BARGAINING BETWEEN VICE PRES-IDENT AGNEW'S ATTORNEYS AND THE JUSTICE DEPARTMENT IS BEING CONDUCTED, AT

131

LEAST OFFICIALLY, BY ATTORNEY GENERAL ELLIOT RICHARDSON HIMSELF. BUT THE GOVERNMENT'S POSITION IS BEING SET BY ASSISTANT ATTORNEY GENERAL HENRY PETERSON, [sic] CHIEF OF THE CRIMINAL DIVISION, A VETERAN PROSECUTOR WHO HAS TAKEN A TOUGH LINE. ONE SOURCE HAS SAID THAT THE VICE PRESIDENT IS OFFERING TO RESIGN IN EXCHANGE FOR A PROMISE THAT HE WILL NOT BE PROSECUTED. BUT A SOURCE CLOSE TO THE NEGOTIATIONS HAS DISCLOSED THAT IN A PLEA-BARGAINING SESSION LAST WEDNESDAY MORNING IN THE JUSTICE DEPARTMENT, PETERSON INSISTED THAT HE HAD EVIDENCE TO WIN A CONVICTION ON THE BRIBERY AND KICKBACK CHARGES AND THAT HE WOULD INSIST THAT AGNEW PLEAD GUILTY AT LEAST TO A REDUCED CHARGE. PETERSON WAS QUOTED AS SAYING: "WE'VE GOT THE EVIDENCE, WE'VE GOT IT COLD." RICHARDSON WAS SAID TO HAVE SAT IN APPROVING SILENCE AS PETERSON HELD OUT FOR A GUILTY PLEA THAT COULD POSSIBLY INVOLVE A JAIL SENTENCE FOR AGNEW, DEPENDING UPON WHAT THE JUDGE DECIDED. CBS NEWS COULD NOT LEARN IF FURTHER MEETINGS HAD BEEN HELD SINCE WEDNESDAY OR IF EITHER SIDE HAS SINCE SHIFTED ITS POSITION. FRED GRAHAM, CBS NEWS, WASHINGTON.

APPENDIX E

Text of preliminary report on Department of Justice Internal Investigation of possible leak sources

PRELIMINARY REPORT

September 24, 1973

Inquiry Into Unauthorized Release of Information
Regarding the "Baltimore County" Investigation
Being Conducted by the United States Attorney
for the District of Maryland

PRINCIPAL FINDING

Based on our attempt to identify any Department of Justice personnel who had any possible access to the facts of the Baltimore County investigation, we developed an exposure list of 134 employees. All were interviewed and responded, in sworn statements, that they themselves were not the source of information which appeared in the news media, nor did they know of any other person who was the source.

SUPPLEMENTAL FINDINGS

Beyond our principal finding, the inquiry revealed several additional facts about the investigation and the press disclosures. They are:

1. *Knowledge of the Vice President's potential involvement was known to individuals outside the Department of Justice before any such evidence was developed by the Department.*
The Office of the United States Attorney in Baltimore did not become aware of the Vice President's substantive involvement as a potential defendant in their investigation until late May 1973. No one at the Department of Justice in Washington became aware of any potential evidence regarding the Vice President until June 12, 1973 when United States Attorney Beall briefed the Attorney General. Prior to the time that this evidence came into the possession of the Office of the United States Attorney or the Department of Justice in Washington, there were at least five separate instances where persons or groups outside the Department of Justice demonstrated an awareness of the Vice President's possible involvement in the Baltimore County investigation.

2. *Public disclosures of the Vice President's potential involvement in the Baltimore County investigation did not occur until the Department of Justice conveyed some information about the case to individuals outside of the Department.*
The United States Attorney's office in Baltimore had information about the Vice President's potential involvement for more than nine weeks before August 7 *Wall Street Journal* story. The Department of Justice in Washington had the information for approximately seven weeks before this initial press report. During the time the information was exclu-

133

sively in the possession of the Department of Justice, there were no press articles or media coverage discussing the Vice President's involvement. As soon as the information was conveyed beyond the Department of Justice, this coverage began.

3. *There appears to be a high correlation between the facts transmitted by the Department of Justice to the White House and / or the Vice President and the disclosures which have appeared in the press.*

Within the framework of their official responsibilities, both the Attorney General and Henry E. Petersen have conveyed to appropriate White House officials, on a need to know basis, some information about the investigation. The Attorney General has also conveyed some information to the Vice President as a subject of the investigation. Without knowing the full content of these briefings and conversations, it is not possible to make any casual statement other than to note the correlation. However, it is clear that there is a body of extremely sensitive (and therefore newsworthy) information which is currently in the possession of the Department of Justice. This information has not been conveyed outside the Department and it has not appeared in the press. . . .

4. *The first news story which revealed that the Vice President was under investigation has been attributed to the Vice President's staff.* *

The *Wall Street Journal* article of August 7, 1973, by Jerry Landauer referred specifically to the letter written by United States Attorney Beall to the Vice President's attorney, Judah Best. A chronology of the events related to the drafting and distribution of the letter, revealed that Landauer had the substance of the letter on August 5. At that time, the letter was available only to the U.S. Attorney's office in Baltimore and the Vice President and his lawyers. The Department of Justice in Washington did not see a copy of the letter until the August 6 meeting with United States Attorney Beall. . . . During telephone conversations on June 5 with United States Attorney Beall and Assistant United States Attorney Skolnik, Landauer identified his source for the information as a friend of his (Landauer) in the Vice President's office. During the course of the inquiry, we have learned that Landauer has had, and continues to obtain, information concerning the Vice President which is not otherwise know to the investigative team.

5. *Analysis of information attributed to the Department of Justice in several key news reports reveals, that while the information may have been damaging to the Vice President, it was generally inaccurate.*

There are at least two principal theories which might explain these inaccuracies:

a The disclosures represent the "best" information available to the source. This leads to the conclusion that the source is on the periphery of the investigation and thus does not have in depth knowledge of the facts; or

b. The disclosures have been changed purposely by the source. This could be the strategy of a source who is aware and is attempting to protect his position by doctoring the disclosures.

6. *Professional public information officers disagree whether or not a reporter would cite a secondary source as if it were the primary source.*

It is possible that there are deliberate sourcing inaccuracies in the news accounts which have attributed factual statements and direct quotations to the Justice Department and / or Justice Department officials. It appears that some reporters would not consider it a viola-

---

*This does not include the official press release by the Vice President's office on August 6 which briefly stated that the Vice President was under investigation.

tion of journalistic standards to make attributions to the Department of Justice when in fact the information came from a secondary source who had official or unofficial access to Department of Justice information.

7. *There is a Byzantine-like relationship in the Baltimore business, political and social community.*

Analysis of the principal figures in the Baltimore County investigation demonstrated the close relationship that exists among the potential defendants, the witnesses, their respective attorneys and others in Baltimore. Several defendants have the same attorney, the same individuals have had business and social ties for long periods of time, several attorneys are former Department of Justice employees and one of the Assistant United States Attorneys is a former member of the law firm representing one of the major defendants. These relationships contribute to the general aura of gossip and rumor which has been widespread in Baltimore.

CONCLUSION

Assuming the validity of the sworn statements of 134 Justice Department employees, we can conclude that they themselves were not the source of information which appeared in the news media, nor do they know of any other person who was the source.

It is essential to note that this inquiry has been limited to the Department of Justice (with a similarly limited inquiry being conducted by IRS). While we have attempted to identify all Department of Justice employees who had any access to elements of the investigation, it is possible that individuals in the Department acquired information about the investigation through informal channels which have alluded our detection.

It is also significant that the inquiry revealed a large number of persons and groups outside the Department of Justice who had varying degrees of knowledge about the investigation and the Vice President's potential involvement. Our analysis indicated that the increase of exposure was a function of the enlargement of the case. This increased exposure appears to have been geometric not only in the Department, but also outside the Department. Since those outside the Department received their information contemporaneously with the investigation, it is a fair assumption that the total witting population outside the Department is at least equal to, and probably exceeds, the total witting population within the Department.

APPENDIX F

Text of Agnew's motion to enjoin grand jury proceedings and to suppress evidence

Applicant Spiro T. Agnew, the Vice President of the United States ("applicant"), hereby moves this court, in exercise of its supervisory control over the grand jury impaneled Dec. 5, 1972 ("the grand jury"), to enter a protective order prohibiting the grand jury from conducting any investigation looking to possible indictment of applicant and from issuing any indictment, presentment or other charge or statement pertaining to applicant.

Applicant further moves this court to enjoin the Attorney General of the United States, the United States Attorney for the District of Maryland and all officials of the United States Department of Justice from presenting to the grand jury any testimony, documents or other materials looking to possible indictment of applicant and from discussing with or disclosing to any person any such testimony, documents or materials.

Applicant request for this relief is based upon the following grounds:

[1]

By letter dated Aug. 1, 1973, the United States Attorney for the District of Maryland, Hon. George Beall, notified applicant that Mr. Beall's office was conducting an investigation into alleged violations of various criminal statutes by applicant. Since Aug. 1, a constant stream of news reports, attributed to "sources close to the investigation" and the like, have indicated, first, that Mr. Beall was considering presenting evidence to the grand jury relating to applicant, and second, that the Attorney General has authorized such presentation.

The Constitution forbids that the Vice President be indicted or tried in any criminal court. In consequence, any investigation by the grand jury concerning applicant's activities will be in excess of the grand jury's jurisdiction and will constitute an abuse for which no remedy other than that specified is sufficient.

[2]

Since this matter came to public attention on Aug. 6, 1973, officials of the prosecutorial arm have engaged in a steady campaign of statements to the press which could have no purpose and effect other than to prejudice any grand or petit jury hearing evidence relating to applicant and thus to deprive applicant of all hope of a fair hearing on the merits.

In the exercise of its supervisory authority over Federal law enforcement officers, this court should bar any grand jury action relating to applicant. If the Department of Justice asserts its innocence of wrongdoing, then this court should forthwith hold a hearing at which the facts may be fully developed.

Wherefore, applicant asks this court to enter an order granting the relief requested herein, or alternatively, to direct the United States Attorney for the District of Maryland to show cause why this court should not enter such an order.

Respectfully submitted.

> PAUL, WEISS, RIFKIND,
> WHARTON & GARRISON

> By JAY H. TOPKIS, MARTIN
> LONDON and JUDAH BEST

APPENDIX G

Text of press conference by Attorney General Elliot Richardson

THE GREAT HALL
DEPARTMENT OF JUSTICE
OCTOBER 11, 1973

ATTORNEY GENERAL RICHARDSON:

Good morning, ladies and gentlemen of the press.

I wish to make it clear at the outset that it is the purpose of this press conference simply to clarify matters which may have been left somewhat less than clear with regard to proceedings by which we reached this point. My office has received numerous inquiries from you, and I have not been in a position until now to make myself available to try to answer them.

I emphatically believe that it would not serve any meritorious interests to continue to debate charges and countercharges. Our purpose should be to put the matter to rest.

There are two points I made in Court before Judge Hoffman yesterday which I would like to underscore this morning. The first relates to my strong hope that the American people understand and support what has been done. I said yesterday:

"The agreement between the parties now before the Court is one which must be just and honorable, not simply to the parties, but above all, to the American people.

"From the outset of the negotiations which have culminated in these proceedings, the Department of Justice has regarded as an integral requirement of any agreement a full disclosure of the surrounding circumstances, for only with knowledge of these circumstances can the American people fairly judge the justice of the outcome."

Second, I wish to urge consideration and compassion again for the Vice President, who has rendered a high service by resigning and relieving the nation of a prolonged and potentially disastrous period of anguish and uncertainty. I also stated in Court yesterday:

"I am firmly convinced that in all the circumstances, leniency is justified. I am keenly aware, first, of the historic magnitude of the penalties inherent in the Vice President's resignation from his high office and his acceptance of a judgement of conviction for a felony. To propose that a man who has suffered these penalties should, in addition, be incarcerated in a penal institution, however briefly, is more than I, as head of the government's prosecuting arm, can recommend or wish."

Finally, I would like to commend the government prosecutors—U.S. Attorney Beall and Assistant U.S. Attorneys Skolnik, Baker and Liebman, for their tenacious pursuit of justice and their wise counsel. Although they did not always agree with me—particularly with regard to the painful issue of sentencing—I know that they were at all times motivated by the highest regard for public interest. I would, in addition, like especially to commend Assistant Attorney General Petersen for his courageous and distinguished service in this case—the characteristics of fair and fearless prosecution of justice have been the hallmark of his more than two decades of service to the Nation.

APPENDIX H

Final Report on the Department of Justice internal investigation of possible leak sources—Summary, Principal Findings, and Recommendations

Inquiry Into Unauthorized Release of Information
Regarding the "Baltimore County" Investigation
Being Conducted by the United States Attorney
for the District of Maryland

FINAL REPORT

October 26, 1973

SUMMARY

During the inquiry we interviewed 141 Department of Justice employees who had varying degrees of exposure to the facts of and / or details of the Baltimore County investigation. Based on the continuing allegation of leaks, 20 employees were re-interviewed. . . . We not only interviewed those individuals who might have been knowledgeable of the substance of the investigation, but also those who had possible exposure to any aspect of the investigation. Using the same general criteria, the Internal Revenue Service conducted their own inquiry and interviewed 34 IRS employees.

Of the 141 Department of Justice employees interviewed, 74 had no substantive

TABLE 1

TIME OF EXPOSURE[1]

		Prior to Aug. 6	As of Oct. 10
DEGREE OF EXPOSURE[2]	In Depth	8	11
	Some Knowledge	3	13
	Minimal Knowledge	8	43
	TOTAL	19	67

[1] Aug. 6 is used as a benchmark, since on that day the Vice President's office publicly confirmed that the Vice President was under investigation. Oct. 10 is used since that was the day of the court proceeding which ended the Vice President's involvement as a potential defendant in the Baltimore County investigation.

[2] For the purposes of our analysis, we have categorized the degree of knowledge into four levels: *In depth*—a detailed awareness of all or most of the substantive facts of the investigation; *Some Knowledge*—an awareness of all or most of the facts and/or a detailed awareness of a limited aspect of the investigation; *Minimal Knowledge*—a general awareness of the facts of the investigation; *No Knowledge*—no exposure to any official investigative facts.

139

knowledge of any aspect of the investigations and 67 had varying degrees of exposure to the facts of and / or the details of the investigation. . . . This exposure occurred over the 20-week period from the time the Vice President's possible involvement was first mentioned in late May until October 10, the day of his resignation. Table 1 summarizes the Department of Justice exposure prior to the first public confirmation that the Vice President was under investigation and at the time of the Vice President's resignation.

In the course of the Department inquiry and in response to the preliminary motions which were offered by the Vice President, 21 additional Department of Justice employees had varying degrees of awareness of the Baltimore County investigation. . . .

From its inception the scope of our inquiry was limited to employees of the Department of Justice even though a number of persons outside the Department had substantial awareness of the facts and details of the Baltimore County investigation. This constraint precluded the verification and follow-up which is customary in most investigations. If allegations of unauthorized disclosure had continued, we were prepared to seek authorization to expand the scope of our inquiry to include persons outside the Department.

PRINCIPAL FINDINGS

During the course of the inquiry, 141 Department of Justice employees and 34 Internal Revenue Service employees were interviewed. All executed statements in which they swore that they themselves were not the source of information which appeared in the news media and that they did not know of any other person who was the source. As a result of the inquiry, we have concluded that:

1) Based on their sworn statement, none of the 175 individuals, who represent all of the Department of Justice and Internal Revenue Service participants in the Baltimore County investigation, were the source of any unauthorized disclosure.

2) There is absolutely no empirical evidence nor credible information to substantiate the charge that the Department of Justice or any individual Department of Justice employee conducted a "campaign of leaks."

Our continued analysis has substantiated the supplemental findings which were offered in our two earlier reports.

RECOMMENDATIONS

Based on our inquiry, we offer the following recommendations to improve the Department of Justice's response to sensitive cases in the future:

1. *Security within the Department of Justice should be emphasized.*
Our inquiry has revealed several instances of lax security in the Department. In some organizations physical and document security were woefully inadequate and were strengthened only after the allegation of leaks began, e.g., we gave assistance to the United States Attorney in Baltimore to improve the physical security of his office and of the grand jury courtroom. It is our belief that security in the Baltimore office was no worse and possibly better than the average U.S. Attorney office. Thus it is essential that all Department of Justice facilities be reviewed in light of appropriate security requirements. If we are to maintain the confidentiality required in the judicial process, the Department of Justice must develop a "security awareness" before sensitive cases develop. With the establishment of the Department Security Staff in the Office of Management and Finance, this awareness will receive the attention which has been lacking. One of the first priorities of the staff will be to develop and implement a security program for all U.S. Attorney offices so that they can meet basic security standards.

2. *A system for recording press contacts should be instituted within the Department of Justice.*

Due to sourcing ambiguities in the press, it was frequently difficult to distinguish between news items which were the result of official Department of Justice briefings and those which might have been the result of unauthorized disclosure. While not wishing to burden the Public Information Office and the Office of the Attorney General, we feel it is necessary for the Department to maintain a more complete record of official statements and conversations with the press. This would enable the Department to immediately establish attribution for statements appearing in the news.

3. *A "limited distribution channel" should be developed within the Department of Justice which would minimize the exposure of sensitive information.*

The greatest single increase in exposure within the Department occurred as a result of the polygraphing of potential witnesses, i.e., 36 FBI employees were exposed to varying degrees of information about the facts of and / or the details of the investigation. The FBI exposure list is disturbing since only one agent, the polygraph examiner, had any need for access to substantive information. Notwithstanding a strong admonition from U.S. Attorney Beall to limit the distribution of the polygraph report, a summary teletype and comprehensive memorandum concerning the polygraph examination were available to FBI employees in Philadelphia, Baltimore and Washington, D.C. In this instance, we believe that the polygraph examiner should not have been required to give any substantive information to his superiors but rather should have confirmed that he assisted the U.S. Attorney in Baltimore in conducting a sensitive case. Given the sensitivity of this case (and the potential for other such instances), the Department must develop a "limited distribution channel" for handling information which would bypass the traditional reporting procedures. While no specific instances of unauthorized disclosures were attributed to the Bureau's handling of the information, this increased exposure to the facts of the Baltimore County investigation was not an investigative necessity and was contrary to need for confidentiality. This issue is also most important in light of the proposal to establish an Office of Inspector General within the Department of Justice. The small, permanent Inspector General staff which is envisioned will use Department of Justice investigative personnel on an ad hoc basis. During the time of their assignment to the Office of Inspector General, these personnel must refrain from the reporting to their present organization so that confidentiality of the Inspector General process will be maintained.

4. *The Standards of Conduct and Title 28 Code of Federal Regulations should be strengthened to include penalties for the unauthorized disclosure of information.*

We concur with the recent review of procedures governing public statements by Department employees. (See memo to the Attorney General dated August 9, 1973, subject: *Proposed Revision of Regulations Governing Unauthorized Public Statement by Employees of the Department of Justice to Amend 28 C.F.R. 45.735–12.*) However, we feel that this alone is insufficient. At a minimum specific penalties for unauthorized disclosure should be incorporated in the appropriate sections of the C.F.R. and also in the Department of Justice Standards of Conduct. In addition, there is a continuing need to impress upon each Department employee the importance of handling sensitive information in a confidential manner. Several federal agencies have adopted a written agreement which requires confidentiality as a condition of employment. . . . Another one of the first priorities of the new Department Security Staff will be to make a thorough review of this subject and implement appropriate procedures.

NOTES

1. Theodore W. Hendricks, "The prosecutor's staff uphold bold tradition," *The Sun* (Baltimore, MD), August 12, 1973, p. 1.

2. Aaron Latham, "Closing in on Agnew: The Prosecutor's Story," *New York,* November 26, 1973, page 58.

3. *Ibid.,* p. 54.

4. *Ibid.,* p. 62.

5. *Ibid.,* p. 67.

6. *Ibid.,* p. 63.

7. *Ibid.,* p. 67.

8. See Spiro T. Agnew, *Go quietly . . . Or Else* (New York: William Morrow & Co., Inc., 1980), p. 93 for full text of Beall's letter to Best.

9. Richard M. Cohen and Jules Witcover, *A Heartbeat Away* (Viking Press: New York, 1974), pp. 152–153.

10. Jerry Landauer, "A New Watergate? Spiro Agnew is Target of Criminal Inquiry; Extortion is Alleged," *The Wall Street Journal,* August 7, 1973, p. 1.

11. Richard Cohen and Carl Bernstein, "Agnew is Target of Kickback Probe in Baltimore, Proclaims His Innocence," *The Washington Post,* August 7, 1973, p. 1.

12. Richard M. Cohen and Edward Walsh, "Agnew Investigation Mushrooms," *The Washington Post,* August 8, 1973, pp. A1, A13.

13. "Transcript of Agnew News Conference Dealing with Investigation by Grand Jury," *The New York Times,* August 9, 1973, p. 20.

14. *Ibid.*

15. Spiro T. Agnew, *Go Quietly . . . Or Else,* p. 115.

16. Edward Walsh and Richard M. Cohen, "Agnew Lawyers Study Stand on Executive Privilege," *The Washington Post,* August 12, 1973, p. B1.

17. Bill Richards, "Beall, Staff Ignore Agnew Probe Furor," *The Washington Post,* August 13, 1973, p. C2.

18. "ACLU Demands End to Agnew Inquiry Leaks," *The New York Times,* August 16, 1973, p. 27.

19. ABC News, Issues and Answers, Sunday August 19, 1973.

20. *Ibid.*

21. *Ibid.*

22. "Heading Toward an Indictment?" *Time,* August 27, 1973.

23. *Ibid.*

24. "Agnew Press Comments and Richardson Reply," *The New York Times,* August 22, 1973, p. 24.

25. *Ibid.*

26. Bill Kovach, *The New York Times,* August 23, 1973, p. 1.

27. *Ibid.*

28. Letter from Elliot L. Richardson, Attorney General to Vice-President Spiro T. Agnew, Washington, D.C., August 23, 1973.

29. Joseph Volz and William Sherman, "Richardson Faces Decision On Charges Against Agnew," *The New York Daily News,* September 5, 1973, p. 6.

30. Susanna McBee, "Leaks at Justice, Richardson Told," *Washington Post,* September 5, 1973, p. A1.

31. Cohen and Witcover, *A Heartbeat Away,* p. 239.

32. *Ibid.,* p. 240.

33. Richard M. Cohen and Lou Cannon, "Agnew Lawyers Bargain on Plea," *The Washington Post,* August 22, 1973, p. 1.

34. Fred Graham, text of story reported on CBS Evening News, August 22, 1973, taken from attachment to letter from Fred Graham to The Editors, *The New York Times,* October 1, 1973.

35. *Ibid.*

36. Spiro T. Agnew, *Go Quietly . . . ,* p. 163.

37. James Reston, "Agnew Reaches Decision: Intends to Fight, Not Quit," *The New York Times,* September 28, 1973, p. 1.

38. William Safire, "The Petersen Case," *The New York Times,* October 1, 1973, p. 35.

39. "Agnew's Nemesis at Justice," *Time,* October 8, 1973, p. 17.

40. Fred P. Graham, text of letter to the editors, *New York Times,* dated October 1, 1973.

41. Affidavit by Jay H. Topkis, United States District Court, District of Maryland, In re: Proceedings of the Grand Jury Impaneled Dec. 5, 1972: Application of Spiro T. Agnew, Vice President of the United States, Misc. No. 73, p. 1.

42. *Ibid.,* p. 2.

43. Press Release, Department of Justice, Washington, D.C., September 28, 1973.

44. Cohen and Witcover, *A Heartbeat Away,* page 264.

45. Agnew, *Go Quietly . . . Or Else,* p. 178.

46. *Ibid.*

47. *Ibid.,* p. 179.

48. Steven V. Roberts, "Agnew Declares He Will Not Quit; Attacks Inquiry," *The New York Times,* Sept. 30, 1973, p. 1.

49. Agnew, *Go Quietly . . . Or Else,* pp. 179–180.

50. James M. Naughton, "Agnew Loosed Attack After Weeks of Anger," *The New York Times,* Oct. 1, 1973, p. 1.

51. Agnew, *Go Quietly . . . Or Else,* pp. 182–183.

52. Cohen and Witcover, *A Heartbeat Away,* p. 287.

53. Carl Stern and Tom Brokaw, *NBC Nightly News,* October 1, 1973.

54. Cohen and Witcover, *A Heartbeat Away,* p. 282.

55. *Ibid.*, p. 289.

56. Latham, "Closing In On Agnew: The Prosecutors' Story," p. 72.

57. *Ibid.*

58. Robert Bork, Memorandum for the United States in Opposition to Applicant's Motion to Enjoin Grand Jury Proceedings and To Suppress Evidence, United States District Court, District of Maryland, Case Number Civil 73–965, October 8, 1972, pp. 1–2.

59. *Ibid.*

60. Anthony Ripley, "Agnew's Office Called Possible Source of Leaks," *The New York Times,* October 10, 1973, p. 16.

61. Cohen and Witcover, *A Heartbeat Away,* p. 312.

62. *Ibid.*

63. *Ibid.*, p. 325.

64. Statement of U.S. Attorney General Elliot L. Richardson, U.S. District Court for Maryland, October 10, 1973.

65. *Ibid.*

66. AP, "Bulletin Agnew 101," JC230PED, October 10, 1973.

67. Agnew, *Go Quietly . . . Or Else,* pp. 16–17.

68. *Ibid.*

69. Statement of The Honorable Judge Walter Hoffman, U.S. District Court for Maryland, October 10, 1973.

THE PRESS AND
THE NEUTRON BOMB

by David Whitman

Prelude to the Storm

A T 5:30 A.M. on June 6, 1977, Major General Joseph Bratton was awakened
by a phone call that marked the beginning of a series of extraordinary
events for him and other officials concerned with the production of the "neutron
bomb." Bratton, who was director of military applications for the Energy Research
and Development Administration (ERDA)—the successor to the Atomic Energy
Commission—was, as he put it, "responsible for all the research, development,
and production of nuclear weapons in the United States." Although Bratton was
accustomed to pressure, he was "totally taken by surprise" by the call he received
that morning from his chief aide, Major Andrews. "I thought I'd wake you,"
Andrews began, "and warn you. Have you seen today's *Washington Post?*"
"No," Bratton replied, "mine hasn't even been delivered yet." "Well, there's
a front page article," Andrews continued, "on neutron warheads being buried
in the ERDA budget. Undoubtedly, you're going to get a call from General
Starbird [the ERDA assistant administrator and Bratton's boss] on it any minute
now." Within the hour, "an extremely upset" Starbird had called. Starbird's
congressional testimony earlier that year on upcoming production in the atomic
stockpile had not been "scrubbed" (when declassified) of a reference to enhanced
radiation (ER) warheads—the so-called neutron bomb—which the *Post*'s reporter,
Walter Pincus, had picked up as the first public disclosure of the production of
neutron weapons. Neither Starbird nor Bratton thought the existence of ER technology to be classified, and as they hadn't disclosed the technical characteristics
of the weapons, Starbird "couldn't imagine," Bratton recalled, "why this had

---

*This is a heavily abridged version of the case study by David Whitman.
The abridgement was done by Martin Linsky. Unless otherwise noted, all
quotations come either from unpublished government memoranda or from
interviews with the author.*

come out as a front page story. Starbird was extremely security conscious and said the Defense Department was going to be very upset about this—which indeed they were.''

Before, however, a year had passed, Starbird's concern about a classification slip-up had been dramatically eclipsed. As Zbigniew Brzezinski, President Carter's national security adviser, later put it: ''The *Post* article touched off a political explosion that reverberated throughout the United States and Europe.''[1] In April 1978, following mass protests in several West European nations against the neutron bomb, and heated internal debate within the North Atlantic Treaty Organization (NATO), President Carter decided to defer deployment and production of neutron weapons. It was subsequently reported that Carter's controversial, and much-maligned, decision was due partly to his reluctance to embrace a bomb that the public understood to ''kill people but leave buildings intact.''[2]

That sensational and eerie impression of the neutron bomb is a paraphrase of a description of it by Walter Pincus from the first of a series of articles he wrote during the summer of 1977. Several members of Congress and most quarters of the journalism world hailed Pincus's stories as outstanding examples of investigative reporting that had brought a worrisome weapons development to the attention of the public. His critics, on the other hand (at the Defense Department and elsewhere), lamented the stories as errant sensationalism that had pried open the Pandora's box within the NATO alliance, leading to a weakening of the U.S. nuclear deterrent. But both his supporters and critics within the federal bureaucracy did appear to agree on one thing. As Harold Brown, the secretary of Defense, later summed up: ''Without the Pincus articles, they [neutron warheads] would have been deployed and nobody would have noticed.''[3]

The Origins of the Neutron Bomb: 1958–1977

The First Neutron Bomb Debate: 1955–1963

Long before Walter Pincus's stories ever appeared, the neutron bomb had provoked public controversy and received substantial press coverage. In 1955, NATO conducted a war game called ''Carte Blanche'' that was designed to illuminate the effects of a successful nuclear defense of Europe. The potential civilian toll from such a war appeared ghastly and unprecedented; if 268 atomic weapons were detonated over West German soil, 1.5 million people reportedly would be killed and another 3.5 million wounded. These startling figures gave rise to the effort to build more discriminate atomic weapons—i.e., weapons that produced less residual radiation and had a smaller blast—one of which turned out to be the neutron bomb.

In July 1959, news of research on the neutron bomb was leaked to a staff reporter on the *Washington Post* by administration officials who appeared to support the neutron bomb and oppose President Eisenhower's interest in a research-inhibiting nuclear test ban. The *Post* front page story led off:

A radically new type of atomic weapon, which could have a profound effect on the cold war and international relations is being discussed in military circles. It could make meaningless the nuclear test ban treaty that was expected to be the first step toward disarmament. The new weapon is a bomb that would produce as much man-killing radiation as a large weapon yet have the destructive blast of a small weapon and the radioactive fallout of an even smaller one. It is a bomb that would be capable of killing an enemy force without too much physical damage to an area without the fallout that would make the region uninhabitable after the attack. . . . Since the physical damage and fallout from such a weapon would be small, it would open up the possibility of fighting a war on friendly or home soil.[4]

This description of the neutron bomb was mild compared to subsequent coverage given by the *Post, U.S. News and World Report,* and other major publications. Unlike the initial *Post* story—which emphasized the tactical battlefield role of neutron weapons—subsequent coverage tended to describe neutron weapons as an apocalyptic "man-killer," a weapon that would silently decimate civilian life in populated areas while leaving property intact. In April 1960, following the appearance of an article in *Foreign Affairs* by the British physicist Freeman Dyson—who warned that the Soviets could secretly develop the neutron bomb if a test ban was implemented, leaving, in effect, the U.S. to "fight tanks with horses"[5]—the popular press again began to write about the neutron bomb. *Life* editorialized against the test ban, noting that it would let the Russians develop the neutron bomb, which could "have revolutionary applications in limited war."[6] Senator Thomas Dodd (D-Conn.), citing Dyson's article, took to the floor of the Senate to denounce the test ban negotiations and President Eisenhower for failing to inform the American public about the bomb. Dodd described the neutron bomb as a weapon that "would . . . operate as a kind of death ray. . . . If the Kremlin were to get there first . . . we [might] find ourselves confronted with a choice between annihilation or surrender."[7] On the heels of Dodd's speech, *U.S. News and World Report* devoted three pages to the neutron bomb. The article, under the headline "Most Terrible Bomb of All," led with the dire prediction: "Next—a 'death ray' bomb? . . . Once ready, it could destroy human beings by invisible streams of neutrons, leaving buildings standing."[8]

Not surprisingly, the vision of a "man-killing" bomb that left property intact stirred some moral consternation. On the one hand, the neutron bomb was defended as being more "moral" than other nuclear weapons because it was more likely to restrict injuries to combatants than other nuclear weapons. At the same time, the neutron bomb was also condemned as a ghastly capitalist invention, particularly by Soviet leaders and religious figures.

As the neutron bomb began to stir public passions and edge its way into the debate over a U.S.–Soviet nuclear test ban treaty, it started receiving attention at the highest levels of the Kennedy Administration.[9] But President John Kennedy and his Secretary of Defense Robert McNamara showed little interest in developing the weapon. McNamara felt that development of the neutron bomb might be an important gain that could result from resuming nuclear testing,[10] but he and Kennedy were committed to an "either-or" nuclear doctrine in which low yield, battlefield nuclear weapons were of little use. In 1963, when Senator Dodd agreed to sponsor a Partial Test Ban Treaty, the limited interest the administration had shown in the neutron bomb vanished, and during the next ten years research on the neutron bomb was put on the back burner.

The Slow Resurgence of the Neutron Bomb: 1973–1977

A key factor in rekindling interest in the neutron bomb was the U.S.–NATO effort to modernize the tactical nuclear force posture and stockpile beginning in the early 1970s. At the turn of the decade, military analysts projected that the Soviet Union would achieve strategic parity with the United States in a matter of years. Once the U.S. lead in strategic nuclear weapons disappeared, the possibility that the Soviet Union might resort to conventional attack in West Europe or a limited exchange of nuclear weapons increased. In response to this new possibility, Secretary of Defense James Schlesinger proposed the doctrine of "limited nuclear options" in 1974, under which the existing nuclear stockpile in Europe was to be modernized by adding more militarily efficient weapons, including, conceivably, low-yield tactical nuclear weapons that reduced collateral damage (and civilian casualities). There were a variety of ways to limit collateral damage (such as reducing yields or improving warhead accuracy) but one of the most militarily attractive options was enhanced radiation warheads which produced very little residual radiation, and thus enabled soldiers to move into an area quickly, following an attack. In addition, ER weapons were particularly well-suited to meet the Soviets' most distinct conventional advantage over NATO—an overwhelming superiority in tanks. Soviet tanks were especially resistant to blast—the predominant "kill factor" of most existing nuclear and conventional weapons in Europe—but the tank crews were susceptible to the large amounts of prompt radiation produced by nuclear weapons.

In 1976, the Office of the Secretary of Defense (OSD), Atomic Energy (AE) and the army requested that an ER capability be added modernized versions of the 8″ shell and Lance missile, two of the short-range, battlefield weapons stocked primarily in Europe. President Gerald Ford approved these requests when he signed off on the Stockpile Paper in November 1976 (authorizing the production of atomic warheads for the upcoming year). The Stockpile Paper did not even mention the ER capability on the Lance, and neither Ford nor his advisers attached any special importance to the production of ER weapons. When the weapons were reviewed by the relevant congressional committees both the Lance and the 8″ shell were approved with little fanfare.*

In view of the extraordinary controversy that subsequently enveloped the nuclear bomb, it is important to understand that most military analysts viewed the newly approved ER warheads as providing an additional military capability of modest significance in a stockpile that already contained both "worse" and

---

*ERDA (which had now "replaced" the AEC) and the Army also asked for research funding in 1977 for an ER warhead for the 155 mm shell but were turned down.

"better" weapons. Literally speaking, the neutron bomb was not a bomb at all, since it was not dropped from an airplane. And figuratively speaking, neutron warheads in no way represented a quantum jump in nuclear warfare in the vein, say, that the A-bomb or the H-bomb did. In 1974, in the existing theater nuclear stockpile in Europe, there were hundreds of weapons *already* deployed which produced far more blast and radiation than the new neutron warheads. At the same time, there were also many low-yield fission warheads that produced less blast and radiation. The neutron warheads appeared also to have no more than a modest quantitative impact on the 7,000 weapons already in the stockpile. Only 340 Lance missiles (out of approximately 1,200) were scheduled for an ER warhead; another 800 8″ shells or so would also reportedly incorporate ER. The "kill mechanism," moreover (i.e., prompt neutron / gamma radiation), did not appear particularly insidious either, since it was identical to that of other low yield nuclear weapons already deployed. (For a more detailed explanation of the existing nuclear weapons in Europe and the neutron bomb, see Appendix A.)

What *was* different about the neutron bomb was the relative balance of the effects of blast and prompt radiation. ER warheads were capable of producing a copious amount of deadly, high energy neutrons. It was therefore possible to replace the warheads on the existing Lance and 8″ shell with a lower yield ER warhead, achieving the same "kill radius" through the release of the additional neutrons, but with the possibility of less collateral damage to property. (However, since the ER warheads were planned for use in tandem with other nuclear weapons—in densely populated West Germany—they would still effect tremendous collateral damage.)

In short, the view among most military analysts was that ER weapons might result in modest, not radical reductions of collateral damage, and that the warheads represented an incremental improvement in NATO's nuclear forces and deterrent. Other parts of the modernization program, such as the building of intermediate range missiles (which could strike deep into Warsaw Pact territory), were thought to be far more controversial and potentially "destabilizing" weapon developments. For all of these reasons, the ER warheads provoked little debate within the relevant congressional committees or, more significantly, within NATO. The public, however, remained largely uninformed. Until the 1977 Starbird testimony appeared, there was virtually no mention, for example, in unclassified DOD or ERDA statements of the impending ERW production decision. In a May 1975 report to Congress on the Theater Nuclear Force (TNF) posture in Europe, Schlesinger had noted that one goal of TNF modernization would be to reduce collateral damage, and that "further reductions in collateral damage can be made by improvements in weapon systems (e.g., reduced yields, special warhead effects such as enhanced radiation, improved delivery system accuracy)"[11] but he had not mentioned plans for ER production or even explained what enhanced radiation warheads were. In June 1976, ERDA's deputy administrator, General Giller, noted in an address before the Air Force Association that the "new 8″ shell will be the first U.S. weapon specifically designed to reduce collateral damage from blast and radioactivity." (Giller's comment was reported in the Livermore Lab's

Newsline and the *ERDA News,* both in-house newsletters, but did not attract any attention in the scientific or popular media.) Giller did not indicate, moreover, whether the 8″ shell was an ER weapon or simply a low-yield fission weapon.[12] The Department of Defense (DOD) 1977 Arms Control Impact Statement on the 8″ shell similarly pointed out the increase in combat effectiveness and reduction in collateral damage the new shell would have but did not specify the ER feature.

In addition to the public's ignorance about the impending production of ER warheads, there was also a general lack of awareness about what ER technology was and what its military implications were. In the scientific and military trade press, the concept of enhanced radiation was well known and a handful of articles appeared between 1970 and 1977 advocating the development of ER warheads.[13] In the popular press, there were less than half a dozen articles produced between 1972 and 1977 that even mention ER warheads or the neutron bomb, and those that do, refer to it in passing as a potential part of the plans for TNF modernization.[14]

At the same time, however, public concern about nuclear weapons was beginning to rise in Western Europe. In 1972, Secretary of Defense Melvin Laird disclosed in an interview that the U.S. was considering deploying a new generation of smaller, cleaner tactical nuclear weapons in Western Europe. Subsequent press stories provoked a brief, inconclusive debate within the British Parliament and got modest play in the French and West German press.[15] The controversy, however, fizzled out quickly, especially once American officials stated that no decisions had been made to produce and deploy any new systems. What the "mini-nuke" controversy *did* indicate was the latent sensitivity in Western Europe to the *possibility* that the U.S. would develop and deploy short-range, low-yield weapons for detonation on European soil.

If the neutron bomb held the potential to be a particularly worrisome weapon overseas, Walter Pincus may well have been the American reporter who was best equipped to trip European alarm. In 1969, Pincus left the *Post* to head up the staff of a Senate Foreign Relations subcommittee inquiry—chaired by Senator Symington—into U.S. commitments abroad, with particular emphasis on a groundbreaking examination of the role of theater nuclear weapons. During the course of his eighteen-month stint, Pincus visited several dozen countries and routinely inquired about the placement and types of nuclear weapons present. To his astonishment, Pincus discovered that numerous American ambassadors, sometimes the ranking military officer, and, on one occasion, the leader of a foreign nation, did not know that the U.S. had tactical nuclear weapons stationed on their soil. The unclassified subcommittee report, co-authored by Pincus, stated:

> It was clear [from our trips] that many years had passed since the political implications of the placement of these weapons has been so considered. . . . In almost every one of these countries a veil of secrecy hides the presence of such weapons. Nowhere is this veil stronger than in the United States. Most people here are unaware of the fact that United States tactical nuclear warheads have been and are stationed in countries all around the world.[16]

Pincus was not only disturbed by the secrecy surrounding tactical nuclear weapons but also by the apparent mindlessness with which nuclear artillery had proliferated. ''The theory,'' Pincus explained, ''was that if you mass the short-range shells close to the border, you'd deter a surprise attack from the Russians. No President, however, was going to order the release of these weapons until the Russians attacked, so you were going to have to pick them up and run with them if attacked. These weapons were designed for use on European territory, and I didn't see why the Russians would be deterred by a weapon that didn't hit their homeland but blew the shit out of one of our Allies.''

While at the *New Republic,* in the mid '70s, Pincus followed carefully the fate of the Army's request for modernized 8″ and 155mm shells, but between 1975 and 1977, Pincus (like every other reporter in the popular press) did not know of the impending production of ER warheads and did not write about them. His interest never faded, however, and as a member of the national staff of the *Post* in 1977 he was both surprised and excited when he read Starbird's testimony. Pincus quickly put through a handful of calls to public affairs spokesmen and to weapon experts. He recalled that,

> The Army public affairs guy, whom I think I talked to, didn't know anything about the subject. I spoke with [Jerry] Schecter [the National Security Council (NSC) press spokesman] either right before or right after the story broke and he didn't know what a neutron or ER warhead was. The people I really went to were the most fervid supporters of the weapons. Most reporters don't realize that the best people to talk to are the ones that just totally disagree with you because they spend so much of their time trying to convince you that they're right.

Two of the weapons experts Pincus spoke to were Sy Schwiller, an aide on the House Armed Services Committee, who had encouraged the Army to submit requests for ER warheads, and Don Cotter, who was still the special assistant of atomic energy (OSD) at the Pentagon. Pincus summed up his initial encounters as follows:

> I spent a couple of days working on this story and spoke to about a dozen people during this time. My intention was to raise a debate about short-range nuclear weapons, because they're idiotic. However, no one I spoke to voiced anything but praise, support, and backing for this weapon. The quote that the neutron bomb ''left buildings and tanks standing'' came from Sy Schwiller. Don Cotter referred to it as ''the cookie cutter.'' The phrase that ''it kills people but leaves buildings standing'' comes from a person of the same character and feeling as Harold Agnew [Director of Los Alamos]. The depiction of this as the ''real estate'' or ''Republican bomb'' is the way that the people at Livermore, who developed the bomb, refer to it. Several of these tags didn't appear in what I wrote, but concerning the ones that did, I want to make two points. First, I did not make up these labels, and second, there were no critics at the time I wrote the story. Everyone I talked to was in favor of the weapon and proud of it. No one tried to dissuade me from writing this story; they felt the weapon was great stuff!

The Story Breaks

After the appearance of Pincus's story on June 6, 1977, the tale of Carter's decision to defer deployment of the neutron bomb—and the role that the press played in that decision—breaks down roughly into four brief periods. First, there was the initial shock of the story in June and July 1977, during which time the question of producing the neutron bomb received substantial attention in the U.S. press and U.S. Senate. Second, between August and December 1977, the controversy over the weapon shifted from the question of production to one of deployment and expanded to West Europe. During this period, U.S. officials pursued quiet diplomacy with the West Europeans and sought to develop a more aggressive public relations campaign to respond to public perceptions of the bomb. The third stage occurred between December 1977 and March 1978, when U.S. and European officials privately negotiated a deployment plan, while implementing several actions to quiet European hysteria over the bomb and counter Soviet propaganda on the weapon. Finally, at the end of March, President Carter unexpectedly rejected the deployment plan, prompting leaks from administration officials who were apparently seeking to influence the president's decision (or the coverage of the decision) when it was announced on April 7, 1978. Throughout the administration's handling of the issue, administration officials explored, but never pursued vigorously, a wide variety of avenues both to influence press coverage of the bomb and to counter public misperceptions of the weapon that the coverage reportedly had provoked.

The First Round: Ducking and Sparring with the Press

Pincus's June 6 lead revived the language of the 1960s, when neutron bombs had been described as uniquely insidious man-killers. The headline for the Monday story—"Neutron Killer Warhead Buried in ERDA Budget"—was written by headline writer Robert Williams (while Pincus was away over the weekend) and it served to portray the neutron bomb as a singularly horrific, clandestine invention. Pincus's story, which was the most important and controversial of all he wrote on the subject, read:

> The United States is about to begin production of its first nuclear battlefield weapon specifically designed to kill people through the release of neutrons rather than to destroy military installations through heat and blast.
> Funds to start building an "enhanced radiation" warhead for the 56-mile range Lance missile are buried in the Energy Research and Development Administration portion of the $10.2 billion public works appropriations bill now before Congress.
> The new warhead is the first practical use of the so-called neutron bomb theory which government scientists have been working on for many years.
> According to one nuclear weapons expert, the new warhead "cuts down on blast and heat and thus total destruction, leaving buildings and tanks standing. But the great quantities of neutrons it releases kill people."
> A heavy dose of neutrons attacks the central nervous system, according to "The Effects of Nuclear Weapons," published by the old Atomic Energy

Commission. There is "almost immediate incapacitation" with convulsions, intermittent stupor and a lack of muscle coordination. "Death is certain in a few hours to several days," according to the book.

In testimony March 17 before a House Appropriations subcommittee, Alfred D. Starbird, assistant ERDA administrator for national security, said that with the new Lance warhead, "You reduce the blast effect and get the kill radius you want through enhanced radiation."

The Lance warhead is the first in a new generation of tactical mini-nukes that have been sought by Army field commanders for many years. The leading advocates: the series of American generals who have commanded the North American Treaty Organization theater.

They have argued that the 7,000 nuclear warheads now in Europe are old, have too large a nuclear yield and thus would not be used in a war.

With lower yields and therefore less possible collateral damage to civilian populated areas, these commanders have argued, the new mini-nukes are more credible as deterrents because they just might be used on the battlefield without leading to automatic nuclear escalation.

Under the nuclear warhead production system, a President must personally give the production order. President Ford, according to informed sources, signed the order for the enhanced radiation Lance warhead.

That Lance already has regular nuclear warheads and is deployed with NATO forces in Europe.

The new Lance warhead is one of a half-dozen nuclear devices on which production is scheduled to start next year.

ERDA, as successor to the Atomic Energy Commission, finances and supervises research and production of nuclear warheads; the Defense Department pays for the delivery systems.

Thus funds for nuclear warheads is in the public works ERDA money bill that is to be taken up by the House Rules Committee today. Since the ERDA authorization has yet to pass Congress, a special rule is needed to permit voting first on its appropriation which is due to come up on the House floor June 13.

The immediate reaction to the story within the federal bureaucracy depended both on whether the affected individuals came from military or diplomatic backgrounds as well as their organizational locus. (A cast of characters and timetable of events is contained in Appendix B.) At the State Department, there were only a handful of people who had ever heard of enhanced radiation weapons, and none who had thought the weapon held any great military significance. Secretary of State Cyrus Vance and his director for politico-military (PM) affairs, Leslie Gelb, were familiar with the general concept of enhanced radiation weapons; however, the typical reaction in the State Department, as one of the desk officers, Lou Finch, recalled, was: "Is the neutron bomb a super killer that nobody has ever heard of, and have these crazy guys at the Pentagon been hiding this in their back pocket all these years?"

At the White House, immediate efforts were also made to obtain more information on ER weaponry and to limit the White House role in the issue. Only weeks before Pincus's article appeared, Carter had reaffirmed his inaugural pledge to "move this year a step toward our ultimate goal—the elimination of all nuclear weapons from this Earth." Now several White House officials, including the president himself and his press secretary, Jody Powell, were concerned that the neutron warhead represented the introduction of new technology into the American arsenal. "The President," Powell recalled, "didn't know anything about this weapon at the time, so we initially chased around to get information on it. You could tell by the way the story was played that it was going to be a stinkeroo, although no one anticipated the trouble it eventually caused." Later that afternoon, NSC spokesperson Jerrold Schecter, who worked jointly for Powell and Brzezinski, called General Bratton at ERDA to ask about the review process the Lance ER warhead had undergone. (Pincus, by this point, had already followed up his story by calling Brzezinski's and Don Cotter's offices to ask whether the Carter administration had reviewed ERDA's FY '78 weapons budget.) According to a June 6 memo, in which Bratton briefly reconstructed his conversation with Schecter, Schecter's "concern assumed primarily to involve what linkage there might be between President Carter and any approval of funding for the Lance enhanced radiation warhead production." After discussing the matter with Bratton, Schecter reported back to Powell that President Ford had signed the stockpile paper and that no specific review of ER warheads had been done by the president during the transition process. Later that afternoon, Powell told Pincus over the phone that Carter would delay the production decision, perhaps until November, but at least "until he has specifically approved the program," which Pincus duly reported the next day.

Concurrent with the president's decision to have the production decisions on ER weapons reopened, Brzezinski asked his staff to prepare a briefing for him on the weapon system, with recommendations for a public response. John Marcum, who spearheaded the review for the NSC, recalled that:

> Because of the sensitivity of the issue in Europe this wasn't a normal case of press guidance; the press guidance was almost part of the diplomatic interaction. Our basic recommendation on press guidance was that we ought to provide a more rational perspective on this as an anti-tank weapon. We felt we had to remedy the absurd impression the initial stories created; that this weapon was some weird thing that hit a building, leaving the building intact but killing the people inside.

Brzezinski seems to have passed much of the staff briefing on to the president, recalling that "I felt then, and I feel now, that the sensational press coverage was largely demagogy."

While Brzezinski and the president were being briefed and withholding a commitment to produce the warheads, the lead on dealing with the press fell, partly by default, to the Pentagon. As David Aaron, deputy director of the NSC, explained, "initially we laid off the issue to the Pentagon because it seemed to be a weapon procurement matter that the White House shouldn't get involved in." Within the Pentagon, however, there was also widespread ignorance about the subject among key civilian appointees, including the assistant secretary for public affairs, Tom Ross, who had never heard of neutron weapons. Most importantly, Secretary of Defense Harold Brown was not particularly concerned about the article. Brown had once been the director of Livermore Laboratory, where the concept of enhanced radiation had first been worked on, and he was thoroughly familiar with what ER weapons were. Brown recalled:

> I had assumed that deployment plans for the ER warheads had been going forward, although I didn't know until I read the article of how imminent the deployment plans were. My reaction to the story was just that it cast ER weapons in the worst possible light, saying that they destroyed people and saved property, neglecting to say that the "people" were the Soviet tank crews and the "property" was the houses in Germany that would fall on civilians and kill them if the property was destroyed. I didn't realize at the time though that with the publication of the article the game was, in fact, all over. I thought that since it was an incorrect characterization and there was nothing new in it, it wouldn't have a very big effect; that soon turned out to be a wrong assessment.

With Brown not seriously concerned, the task of coordinating and preparing press guidance fell primarily to Don Cotter, Brown's special assistant for atomic energy (AE), and Cotter's counterparts at ERDA. Cotter was a nuclear weapons engineer (who had been appointed by President Nixon and subsequently reappointed by Ford and Carter) and had worked for many years at the AEC's Sandia Laboratory and briefly for the CIA before becoming assistant to the secretary of Defense (Atomic Energy). As chairman of the Military Liasion Committee (MLC)—composed of two members of each service with responsibility for defining and transmitting DOD's nuclear requirements to ERDA—Cotter was one of the men most responsible for assuring the ER program was fairly represented and received adequate funding from Congress. Cotter was concerned over the disclosure of the ER capability on the Lance, and, with the assistance of ERDA personnel, drafted press guidance for ERDA, indicating that ER weaponry was not a new concept or one that was aimed at civilians, stating simply:

> Today's AP and UPI stories quoting the *Washington Post* on an enhanced radiation warhead are essentially correct. AEC and ERDA have been working on this since the early sixties. The concept is that such a weapon reduces the blast effect but its enhanced radiation (neutrons) is aimed at combatants, thus reducing collateral damage to civilian populated areas. . . . We cannot comment on production numbers or dates.

A day later, the DOD press guidance was completed, which was even terser. It stated: "The ERDA develops nuclear weapons to meet specific DOD military requirements. The details of those warhead or bomb developments are classified. It is factually correct that the ERDA is working on an improved nuclear Lance warhead . . . For security reasons we cannot identify the type of warhead being designed for specific delivery systems."
Pentagon officials gave several explanations for why they decided initially

not to counter or criticize the Pincus story. Lt. Col. Mike Burch, then one of Ross's military assistants, stated:

> A lot of time when you get in trouble in the public affairs area, the first reaction is to say nothing, particularly when you are dealing with nuclear weapons and classified issues. That happens not only for obvious reasons involving national security but also because it's very difficult to talk about nuclear weapons. Any time you deal with nuclear weapons you have what we call "the tar baby syndrome"; you touch the issue and you can't let go. There is simply no nice way to talk about nuclear weapons. You can say, "Well, they preserved the peace for forty years" but they're still the most terrible thing that man ever thought up or dreamed of.

In addition, Pentagon officials were also hoping the issue might die out. As Tom Ross recalled:

> It was evident to me early on that the way Walter wrote the story—the bomb that kills people but preserves buildings—was going to cause political problems because of Carter's identification with zero nuclear weapons (which was still fresh). It cut across the grain of what he stood for and threatened to become a lightning rod for the anti-defense faction. I didn't see how this could possibly be a winner. My feeling was that maybe Walter would get bored with the story, or others would get bored with it, and that once the passion was purged from the event the story would fade from the front page, eventually, to the point where it wasn't being covered.

Pincus and the Post *Lead the Media*

The "storm" that developed built slowly over the next several months and was largely attributable to the one-man reporting of Walter Pincus. On the day that Pincus's first story appeared, Jack Robertson, one of Senator Hatfield's aides, brought the story in to show it to Hatfield. Senator Mark Hatfield (R-Ore.) read the story, was "very "alarmed"[1] by it, and two days later introduced an amendment to strike funds for ER weapons from the appropriations bill. At the same time, other senators and several members of the House privately wrote angry letters to the Pentagon in which they asserted that DOD officials had attempted to conceal the development of neutron weapons from the Congress. At this point, ERDA and DOD officials started giving briefings on ER weapons to congressmen, congressional staff and members of the White House staff. Brigadier General Lynwood Lennon, one of the Army members of the MLC, stated that, "the crux of our approach was that we had to fight our most important fire first and that was in Congress, and then worry about explaining to our NATO allies what Pincus was saying and what he was not saying."

The making of neutron warheads into a major news story in June was essentially accomplished through the persistence of Pincus and the *Post*'s editorial board. On June 7 Pincus wrote a follow-up story containing the White House's denial of involvement. The next day the *Post* editorialized that the president should reject the neutron warhead, likening "radiation kill" to chemical warfare.

The following day Pincus reported that Senator Hatfield was seeking to bar funds for "the new neutron killer warhead" and two weeks later Pincus reported that the president and DOD were opposed to the Hatfield amendment, and were pressing instead for the Senate to approve funds for the new "killer warhead."

Pincus's stories finally began to drawn substantial attention in the national media when NBC News, where Pincus was also employed, ran a film clip on June 17 (obtained from the Armed Forces Radiology Research Institute) showing what happened to monkeys when they were irradiated with 4,600 rads of neutron radiation—the results, not surprisingly, being quite gruesome. On June 22 Pincus ran an article on the film clip,* and the next day Pincus received a call from someone "who felt the switch to neutron weapons was much broader than had previously been portrayed and that that development ought really to be questioned." Pincus's source informed him that the Lance ER was only part of a plan to shift all nuclear artillery to an enhanced radiation basis and that the budget included funds for production of an ER 8" shell and research for an ER 155 mm howitzer. Fitting an ER capacity into an 8" shell was something of a technological marvel, which was classified and which officials at the labs and DOD felt confident the Russians hadn't figured out how to do yet. Ross, at Cotter's request, accordingly told Pincus that the 8" shell was "a matter of legitimate high classification" and "there would be no comment."

On June 24 the *Post* led the paper with Pincus's story on the 8" and 155 mm howitzer. The next day the *Post* ran another front page Pincus story on Pentagon efforts to keep the development of ER warheads secret and the following day the *Post* ran a second editorial, urging Congress to support the Hatfield amendment and asserting that "the whole thing [DOD's handling of the issue] has the look of a black bag job."[2] Coming only days before the floor debate on Hatfield's amendment, the *Post* coverage helped galvanize an onslaught of press coverage in every medium.

In addition to keeping the issue alive, Pincus's articles had a definitive impact on the character of subsequent coverage. In particular, it is difficult to overstate the frequency with which neutron warheads were described in the media as "the bomb that killed people but left buildings (or property) standing." All AP and UPI stories employed the description during June and July and virtually every major newspaper in the country used it as well. (Of the sixty news articles written during June and July surveyed for this piece, fifty used some form of the description). On radio and television the reaction was similar. The nation's leading broadcasters, reporters, and talk-show hosts—Bruce Morton, John Chancellor, David Brinkley, Floyd Kalber, Walter Cronkite, Dan Rather, David Hartman, Tom Brokaw, Phil Jones, Bettina Gregory—were among the many who described neutron weapons in such terms. At the same time, the repulsive effects of radiation poisoning that Pincus had described in his first story were also widely quoted,

---

*ABC ran the clip on June 24 and NBC ran it again several weeks later on the *Today Show*.

usually in similarly clinical language. There was no discussion, however, of the fact that low-yield fission weapons also killed by radiation* or that many of the tactical nuclear weapons already deployed in Europe had both more blast and radiation than the neutron warheads.

The moral indignation that this news coverage spurred was expressed most forcibly in the op-ed columns, where writers like Mary McGrory, Jake McCarthy, Mike Royko, Claude Lewis, Gary Wills, Louise Blumenfield, Russell Baker, and Art Buchwald treated the bomb as a sign of the warped mentality of the munition makers, a kind of Twilight Zone invention that had been designed to leave place settings intact (surrounded by the skeletons of the diners). A number of other columnists, chiefly conservative ones (e.g., George Will, Peter Reich, James Kilpatrick, Patrick Buchanan, and Jeffrey Hart) took the view that killing by radiation was no more immoral than killing by blast and, that if anything, neutron weapons were more "moral" than other nuclear weapons because they limited collateral damage. There were a number of columnists who didn't treat the neutron bomb primarily as a moral issue (Carl Rowan, Herbert Scoville, William Rusher, George Will, Edward Teller, Richard Rovere, C. L. Sulzberger among them) but one rather that raised questions about how to best prevent nuclear war; i.e., was the bomb more likely to raise the "nuclear threshold" by deterring the Russians from moving into Western Europe, or was it more likely to lower the threshold by blurring the distinction between conventional and nuclear weapons, feeding the "illusion" that a nuclear weapon could be used "surgically" in a limited nuclear war. Nevertheless, even in the op-ed pieces that debated the impact of the bomb on the nuclear threshold, there was little mention of the fact that the neutron bomb was a small part of the theater nuclear arsenal (let alone the strategic one) or, that since it was a nuclear weapon, its release was always controlled by the U.S. President, not the local batallion commander.

The most balanced and knowledgeable treatment of the bomb appears to have been given, albeit a bit belatedly, on the nation's editorial pages, which split evenly over the issue and devoted substantial discussion to the effect that the bomb had on the nuclear threshold. Even the editorial coverage, however, was full of incorrect information and, on some occasions, misleading myths, prodding Congressman Christopher Dodd (D-Conn.) to comment on the House floor: "Because public opinion should be considered by Congress and the president as we try to decide whether to produce these nuclear warheads, these uninformed editorials, which do so much to shape that opinion, are particularly distressing."[4]

---

*Herbert Scoville, who strongly opposed neutron warheads, appears to have written the only piece in the popular press during June and July 1977 that noted that all low-yield fission weapons killed predominantly through radiation.[3] A July 5 edition of *All things Considered* also noted that the neutron bomb would destroy any buildings or property within a several-hundred-yard radius of ground zero.

Congress Awakens and Cotter and Pincus Go One-on-One

The media coverage of the neutron bomb helped fuel a contentious debate in the Senate, and, not surprisingly, was hailed by opponents of neutron weapons and derided by its proponents. Senator Sam Nunn (D-Ga.), who was a staunch supporter of neutron weapons, stated on the Senate floor that "what we are really saying [in this debate] is that Congress is overwhelmed with technical information on matters and that unless it [information of neutron weapons] appears on the front pages of the newspaper it does not get the attention of Congress. This is an unfortunate state of affairs . . . the misperceptions regarding this particular weapon are more widespread than those surrounding any other weapon I have seen since I have been in the Senate."[5] Opponents of the bomb, like Senator Hatfield, took the contrary view, arguing that "the only time we found out the full impact of what this kind of weapons system would do is when we read the newspapers. . . . I want to commend the news media for extending the knowledge—what little we have of it—to the citizens of this country in a relatively short time."[6]

While the press was helping ignite congressional controversy, administration officials—with the exception of Don Cotter—continued throughout June and early July to do little to respond to the press coverage. Shortly after the first Pincus story appeared, MLC members discussed how to respond to Pincus and agreed, according to Brig. General Lennon, that:

> We'd put out some information to counter these misrepresentations and have Don Cotter talk to the man—which Don wanted to do—to make sure he understood what we were doing and why. At least he'd then have a basis for understanding. We concluded on the down side that the worst that could happen is that Pincus would not change his course and that he might accuse us of trying to brainwash him. That was a rather limp concern on our part, I thought, since it's not easy to brainwash an intelligent person, and so we supported Don going ahead.

In mid-June, as Pincus continued to churn out stories on the progress of the "killer warhead" and the Hatfield amendment through the Senate Appropriations Committee, Cotter began meeting with him on a background basis. The interviews initially were reasonably cordial and constituted a kind of diplomatic minuet. Lt. Col. Hodge, Cotter's executive officer, sat in on several of the interviews, and recalled that:

> When Cotter talked with Pincus he did not get upset at him at all; their conversations were matter of fact and there was almost an adversarial friendship there. When Cotter answered a question he went into detail beyond what Pincus had asked to point out where he had gone wrong or set him back on track. But we didn't do a good job of responding to Pincus's stories because we couldn't. If Cotter told Pincus something in his story was inaccurate then the presumption became that the sentence above—which you didn't criticize—must be accurate. Moreover, if we said something was inaccurate, then you had to justify what you said. It was very difficult to

explain why some of what Pincus wrote was inaccurate without getting into classified information.

Cotter became increasingly disturbed, however, by Pincus's insistent harping on the secret "killer warheads" in the budget, and at a June 24 interview let his irritation show with Pincus's disclosure earlier that day of the ER capacity in the 8" shell. Cotter recalled:

> Pincus said we had tried to "bury" this in the ERDA budget. I told him, "Hey, read the Atomic Energy Act. It is required by law to fund ERDA to build nuclear warheads"; it was deliberately set up that way to keep it separate from DOD. Also, ERDA doesn't build anything until the President signs that stockpile paper telling them to. Pincus knew that the ER had gone through normal channels when he was writing these stories; he knew, for example, about the Sprint and the 1975 report by Schlesinger to Congress that discussed ER because I told him about it.
>
> Pincus also kept writing about "killer warheads"—Christ, what the hell else are warheads for but to kill or damage or destroy? A bow and arrow doesn't destroy buildings but no one says they're "inhumane."

Pincus defended his coverage adamantly and claimed that Cotter was reaching for straws in his effort to build a case that the ERW hadn't been advanced covertly:

> Generally, Cotter didn't bitch at all about the coverage. He loved talking about it. Cotter was one of the worst guys in the world to deal with the P.R. aspects of the neutron bomb because he thought all these things were terrific. He was livid that one day though. He went through the schtick about the [1975 Schlesinger] report, which didn't explain what ER weaponry was; all it said was that ER could reduce collateral damage and the same report said the *existing* 8" shell caused little collateral damage and was highly accurate. I had no problem at all with saying that the warheads were "buried." I didn't say they were hidden, I wrote it was buried and 99 percent of the people would not have known to have looked in ERDA's budget to find them. . . .
>
> The "killer warhead" phrase was coined by a *Post* headline writer but I did use it a number of times. We never called it a "superkiller," but it's true that all weapons are killer weapons. To be brutally honest I'd have to say that it was a slogan that helped people focus on the weapon.

Pincus was also unpersuaded by Cotter's points about the need for classification on the 8" shell:

> Cotter told me that I had breached security and that the whole reason they kept the development secret was that the Soviet Army in Europe would have a major re-equipment problem to defend itself from neutron weapons: it would set them back twenty years. This was a new rationale, which the government is great at dreaming up. Cotter essentially waved the flag and hid behind the classification issue.

Undaunted by Cotter's criticisms, Pincus, returned to the *Post* and wrote his front page story the next day under the headline "Pentagon Wanted Secrecy On

Neutron Bomb Production,'' which was followed by the "black bag" editorial, written by *Post* editorial page editor, Meg Greenfield.

Although Cotter was deeply annoyed by Pincus's coverage, he was enraged by the *Post*'s accusation that ERDA and he had pulled off a "black bag job." Cotter immediately called Ross for help and advice but found that Ross discouraged any direct response. Ross recalled that Cotter's reaction

> was rather standard, and that is that the press gets things wrong because they're malicious; the cocky *Washington Post* must have gotten the story wrong on purpose. In fact, that's rarely the case. The press get things wrong because they haven't done enough homework or gotten to the bottom of things because of classification reasons. There were the usual pressures from Cotter to talk to the *Post* and write "letters to the editor."
>
> Now Harold Brown was also a supertechnician and shared some of the annoyance with the coverage. But he'd been around the track more, he had more poise, and I didn't have to educate him on the fact that you don't win picking a fight with a reporter publicly, especially one such as Walter Pincus, who's very street smart and has very good support from Kay Graham [the *Post*'s publisher] and others. I didn't complain to Walter about his coverage; that's not my style and it doesn't work. By creating campaigns, giving heavy rebuttals, you prolong the issue rather than getting rid of it.

Cotter disregarded Ross's advice for several reasons:

> Ross, I think, regarded me as something of a wild man, running around with these plans to modernize the nuclear weapons that Jimmy Carter said we were going to get rid of. I had my own doubts about Ross's commitment to proceeding with [ER] weapons and I think he was a little annoyed that I was pressing him to do more. I didn't say "pistols at dawn" or anything when I called him, but he just seemed to prefer to brush off the responsibility, which I couldn't afford to do. I was a presidential appointee, chairman of the MLC by law, and the guy who worried about getting the Defense Department its weapons. I also had been responsible for preparing the papers for the secretary of Defense, Congress, and the president, in which the *Post* had charged we had "buried" the development of ER weapons. This was a serious, $3 billion weapon program these guys were taking cracks at, saying it was being run in a dishonorable fashion. You can't take that shit when you're the guy responsible for the program.

Apart from the Pentagon's programs (and his own reputation) being challenged, Cotter felt that:

> These stories were causing all sorts of problems for us, and promised to continue to; the Allies were nervous, the Russians were making hay out of it, and people on the Hill, like Scoop Jackson, were really pissed. I also knew that Pincus knew better because we had discussed the history previously, so it was clear there was something behind this besides just a nice juicy story. Pincus was trying to kill it, he was trying to kill the whole goddamn tac nuke program! With an article coming out every day I finally reached the end of my rope and went into talk to Charlie Seib, the *Post* ombudsman.

Unbeknownst to Cotter, Seib had already become disturbed by the *Post*'s use of the "killer warhead" phrase, and on June 24 had communicated his views to Ben Bradlee, the *Post*'s executive editor, and Howard Simons, the *Post*'s managing editor; on June 28, Seib reiterated his concern in a second memo to Bradlee and Simons that stated: "Killer' bomb has disappeared from the neutron bomb stories, but it shows up today and without the quote marks in the headline. When you stop to think about it the head comes out ridiculous; a warhead that didn't kill, that would be news."

Shortly after Seib's second memo, Cotter came into the *Post* and aired his dissatisfaction to Seib, with Pincus present. Cotter recited the history of the ER controversy, showed Seib the unclassified version of Schlesinger's 1975 report to Congress (which laid out the need for TNF modernization and mentioned ER in passing), explained why funding for neutron weapons was required by law to be in ERDA's budget, and complained about the use of the killer warhead phrase. "Pincus," Cotter recalled, "didn't say a word throughout the discussion and Seib essentially nodded and encouraged me to submit a letter." Pincus had a similar recollection of the meeting, stating:

> Cotter was really pissed about the "black bag job" editorial, but he used it to go after me. He couldn't go after me too directly because he had talked to me and he never claimed I misquoted him. Also, Seib had been my manager editor when I worked at the [Washington] *Star* [in the mid-1960s] and he wasn't going to get anything out of him. I didn't say anything; I just remember sitting in and giggling periodically.

When Cotter returned to the Pentagon he mentioned to Harold Brown and Ross that he had been over to the *Post*. "Harold," Cotter recalled, "didn't want the impression going around that we had snuck this one by, although I'm not sure he thought it was a good idea to talk to the *Post*. Ross discouraged me from writing a letter and essentially said, 'I don't think you should bring any attention to this.'" Ross's view, as Ross himself explained, was that, "Letters to the editor don't accomplish anything. They're printed on page 20 and all they do is remind people of the first story, and / or give the editors an opportunity to rebut or to cut your letter."

Cotter, who felt "the public had to be informed about what the law said," decided to go ahead and send a letter anyway. After several strongly worded drafts were toned down, Cotter sent a letter which stated that ERDA was required to fund nuclear warhead production, cited the relevant passage on ER weapons from the 1975 Schlesinger report as evidence that Congress and the public had been kept informed, and argued that neutron weapons were "accorded the required degree of classification—no more, no less" to help prevent the spread of nuclear weapon technology to U.S. adversaries. Cotter's letter—which was printed on July 20, several days after the Senate debate ended—ran under the headline, "The Neutron Bomb Was No 'Black Bag' Job," and concluded that "The *Post*'s unbalanced and, in many cases inaccurate accounts did not well serve the public or the congressional debate of the past days." As a further concession to Cotter, the *Post* also agreed at Seib's suggestion to drop the use of the phrase "killer warhead."

Although Cotter was pleased by the publication of the letter, stories containing many of the same allegations that his letter sought to rebut subsequently appeared in other papers, radio, and on TV. Expressing the frustration felt during that period, Lt. Col. Hodge summarized:

> Let's face it—we were reacting and Cotter and I discussed that a lot. We wanted to take the initiative away from the press but we couldn't seem to. It was like having a screaming contest with a guy in a radio station. You could stand outside the radio station screaming at him all day long. But he's answering you on the air.

The Rest of the Administration Responds

Apart from Don Cotter's confrontations with Pincus and the *Washington Post,* the response of the administration to the *Post* stories continued to be understated throughout June and July. The State Department remained largely uninvolved, with briefings for Congress and press guidance being handled primarily by the Pentagon and White House. As Hodding Carter, assistant secretary for public affairs, summed up: "My guidance in those days from the White House was to buck it; this was regarded as a weapon decision, which the President hadn't yet made his mind up about." At the Pentagon, Tom Ross and Harold Brown agreed that they would pursue a very low-key response in anticipation of the mid-July Senate floor vote on the Hatfield amendment, because, as Ross put it, "in public affairs you can almost never catch up with a first bad story, and Harold Brown felt that too much was being made out of this weapon both negatively and positively."

DOD began selling an "understated" case on July 1—the first day the Senate debated the neutron warheads—when Harold Brown gave John Chancellor an interview for the NBC Nightly News during which he stated that the neutron bomb was "a useful military adjunct . . . [which could] be used in military situations of interest, against tanks, for example, without doing as much damage to people and to things outside that radius."[7] In the week following Brown's interview, Ross and his staff began making information available that was designed to emphasize that the neutron bomb would destroy buildings, that it caused less blast damage to the civilian areas than the warheads it would replace, and that the bomb was a small tactical, not strategic warhead. The response was mixed. A number of columnists began to write more favorably about the weapon; at the same time, several newspapers used the information in feature stories with maps illustrating what parts of their respective cities would be uninhabitable following the detonation of a neutron warhead.[8] The information received limited play on television (except on CBS News, which ran an Ike Pappas report on July 12).

The White House also began to comment in anticipation of the Senate debate resuming in mid-July. At a June 24 press conference Powell had tried to rebut some of the prevalent criticisms of neutron weapons; his defense did not attract any press attention, however, because at the same press conference he stated that "the president has an abhorrence of nuclear weapons, period," and that the president would not make decisions on production and deployment until "early fall . . . as part of [a] regular annual review," even though he wanted Congress to authorize money for the weapon first to "keep his options open." The president's temporary support for neutron warhead funding dominated the press coverage and when the president cancelled the B-1 bomber on June 30, congressional and public pressure increased to have the president take a less ambiguous stand on the neutron bomb.

At a July 6 press conference Powell upped the timing of Carter's decision on production to "shortly after" August 15, and on July 11 Carter sent a letter drafted at the Pentagon to Senator John Stennis (D-Miss.), supporting the neutron warhead. Although the letter, stating that the weapons were "in the nation"s security interest," was quickly released to the press, Senator Stennis and other congressional supporters continued to press the White House for a more public expression of support from the president. On July 12 Carter gave a surprise news conference which was dominated by questions on the neutron bomb and the import that such weapons would have on the nuclear threshold. Carter again took the position that he had "not yet decided whether to approve the neutron bomb," and gave one of the only public, albeit indirect rebuttals of the press coverage of the bomb given by any government official during the summer of 1977, commenting, "It's not a new concept at all, not a new weapon. . . . the destruction that would result from the explosion of a neutron bomb is much less than the destruction from an equivalent weapon of other types."[9]

That evening, all three networks led the news with Carter's comments. The next day the Senate defeated the Hatfield amendment 58–38, approving instead an amendment by Senators Robert Byrd (D-W.Va.) and Howard Baker (R-Tenn.) that prohibited funds from being used to build ER weapons until the president certified to Congress they were in the national interest; following that notification Congress would have forty-five days to disapprove the weapon, but could do so only by a concurrent resolution of both houses. According to Hatfield and his chief aide, Jack Robertson, Carter's expression of support for ER warheads in the press conference only twenty-four hours before the vote, along with several other last-minute administration adjustments, was critical in swinging the vote against Hatfield.[10]

On July 14, the day after the Senate kept in funding for ER weapons, the White House released the only educational material on neutron warheads formerly provided during 1977 and the first half of 1978. The three-page release was sent to editors and news directors by the White House media liaison office, an office that had been set up by the administration to provide information to papers *outside* of Washington. The White House effort to counter the impact of the *Post* coverage outside of Washington did not, however, have much success since shortly after the Senate approved funds for the weapon, the wire services, TV, and most papers—with the exception of the *Post, New York Times,* and *Baltimore Sun*—stopped covering the issue. For Jerrold Schecter, who oversaw the development of the release, the president's position had a crucial influence on the administration's response to the press coverage:

> Part of the problem was that the president was ambivalent about the weapon. Jimmy Carter came in and said he wanted to free the world of nuclear weapons and all of a sudden he had the donkey tail pinned on him as the guy who gave us yet another new nuclear weapon; that was his basic frame of reference throughout the whole affair. . . . It was pretty hard though to go off and start giving press or policy guidance, when the man who was in charge of making policy hadn't really crystallized his own views.

The Reaction Spreads to Europe

While passions over the neutron bomb began to subside in the U.S. after the July 13 Senate debate, the debate over the bomb in Europe was just beginning to heat up. The immediate response to Pincus's stories in Europe during June was similar to what occurred in the U.S.; i.e., not much attention was devoted to the subject either by the government or the press. Pincus's story reportedly stirred some suspicions on the part of the West German chancellor, Helmut Schmidt, whose poor personal relationship with Jimmy Carter had already been established. Lou Finch, the NATO desk officer in the PM bureau, recalled,

> Sometime after the Pincus story broke, a German general, who was a close confidant of Schmidt's, told me that when Schmidt first read the story his reaction was that the White House—and not a lowly White House staffer but the president or Brzezinski—had leaked the story as part of a continuing vendetta between him and Carter. Schmidt suspected Carter was hyping the threat and trying to do so in a way that would embarrass him.

In early July, when the U.S. Senate began its debate on the Hatfield amendment, the communist media and West European press started editorializing about the subject. On July 15, two days after the Senate had approved ER funding, Carter's ambassador to the U.N., Andrew Young, told correspondents in Geneva that "were I a member of Congress I would have certainly strongly opposed and worked against the development of [the neutron] weapon. It does not make sense to spend all that money for killing folks."[1] Although Young's comments threw some kindling on the fire, the debate was not really ignited in Europe until July 17, when the German weekly *Vorwaerts* published an article by Egon Bahr under the headline "Is Mankind Going Crazy?" Bahr had a reputation for innovative, sober analysis and was a pivotal figure in the liberal wing of the SPD, the ruling party of the tenuous coalition government headed up by Schmidt. Bahr's article picked up the themes of Pincus's initial story, stating: "Reduced to a simple formula [the neutron] weapon causes no, or only slight, material damage, but 'cleanly' kills man. This is to be the final progress. Is mankind about to go crazy? . . . The neutron bomb is a symbol of the perversion of thought."[2] Bahr's view of the neutron bomb as "a symbol of mental perversion" soon became a catch phrase for the burgeoning anti-neutron bomb movement and a focus of editorial debate, particularly in West Germany. His article tended to portray the neutron bomb along the lines of a "Real Estate Bomb," and his piece, along with those of Walter Pincus, was widely quoted and set the tone for much of the European press coverage.

The influence of the U.S. media coverage in framing the debate in Europe was crucial in the view of some U.S. officials. As Harold Brown pointed out, Bahr

> . . . looked at the Pincus stories and decided that a weapon that destroyed people but left buildings standing was inhumane. Well, if the debate had been cast properly—that is, if the article had said that the people being destroyed were Soviet tank crews, and the property being saved was German homes, which otherwise would fall on civilians and kill them—then it would have been impossible for Bahr to come to the conclusion he did, without arguing that Soviet tank crews were more important than German civilians.

While the media coverage of the bomb helped frame the public debate in both the U.S. and Europe, the coverage struck home far more powerfully in Europe, since Europe was where the neutron weapons would be stored and possibly used. And, not surprisingly, European defense specialists were aghast and concerned about the way the press treated the issue. Frederick Mulley, the United Kingdom's defense minister, told the Parliament, for example, that "It is well known that the original and quite unbelievable publicity with which the neutron bomb was launched was quite indefensible."[3] West German Defense Minister Georg Leber similarly emphasized to the Bundestag (the German parliament) in September 1977 that the press had created a debate simply by giving a new name to an old concept.[4]

The response of European officials to what they considered to be troublesome press coverage appears to have been remarkably similar to that of their American counterparts. During the summer of 1977 the debate over the neutron bomb was focused chiefly in West Germany, where several SPD officials made modest efforts in July to set the record straight, particularly in the wake of the Egon Bahr article. The Defense Ministry spokesman, for example, told reporters that the bomb "is a nuclear explosive which does not represent a new category and which is not at all a miraculous situation."[5] The day after the Bahr article appeared, Schmidt himself commented on the weapon to some reporters in Bonn, stating that the term "neutron bomb" had led people to believe a new and even more terrifying weapon had been created when, in fact, the bomb was actually a battlefield weapon with a reduced blast and less heat, similar to other tactical nuclear weapons in both NATO's and the Soviet's stockpiles.[6]

The job of responding to the adverse, controversial press coverage was complicated for European officials by the advent of an enormous Soviet propaganda campaign on neutron weapons, initiated in mid-July. Beginning around July 18—the day after the Bahr article was published and several days after the U.S. Senate had approved ER funding—the Soviet Union dramatically picked up the pace of what had been a relatively modest propaganda campaign in the Soviet media. On July 19, one Soviet international front organization after another started issuing denunciations of the "diabolical" neutron bomb, while *TASS* and *Izvestia* published a continuous diet of critical articles, culminating in a broad July 30 *TASS* statement on U.S. foreign policy and the neutron bomb, the first such statement issued by *TASS* since 1974.[7] On July 27, one of the most prominent front organizations, the World Peace Council, proclaimed August 6–13 "International Week Against the Neutron Bomb," with the aim of mobilizing demonstrations and opposition both in Eastern and Western Europe. The Soviets at the same time saturated Moscow domestic and international radio service with anti-neutron bomb broadcasts. According to CIA analyses of the broadcasts, 11 percent to 13 percent of all items broadcast between July 25 and August 14— about 350 reports a week—were devoted to the neutron bomb, which was the leading news item throughout the period.[8]

Even more critical than the daily denunciations of the bomb in the Soviet media was the Soviet success in stirring concern among non-communists in Western European countries. According to a CIA analysis of the propaganda campaign, the Soviets were particularly concerned with influencing the Western European press:

> There were two types of adverse public attention for the "neutron bomb" which the Soviets hoped to generate in Western Europe and in fact, did. The first might be called "hack comment" and came from the front groups and from publications of communist parties. . . . The second type of comment, and the far more important, was that of the non-communist press situated politically in the center or on the left. . . . For the Soviets, the real success lay in the broad, adverse editorial treatment given the "neutron bomb" by this second journalistic sector.[9]

Critical media coverage in the non-communist press—inspired either by Walter Pincus's stories or Soviet propaganda—helped spur the creation of a modest anti-neutron bomb protest movement during the summer and set the stage in several countries for parliamentary debate over resolutions forbidding the deployment of ER weapons. The burgeoning debate—at least in the eyes of U.S. policymakers—forced European leaders to undo their previous passive acquiescence to neutron weapons (much as the appearance of Pincus's article had prompted President Carter to reopen decision making on the subject). In his July 18 comments, Schmidt informed reporters that "this type of new nuclear warhead naturally raises significant psychological and strategic questions that have to be clarified within our own alliance and in our relationship with the Warsaw Pact."[10]

Round II: The U.S. Ducks in Western Europe (July, August 1977)

Once the neutron bomb had become the focus of a major public debate in Europe, the Carter administration was faced again with the question of what kind of press guidance and public stance to adopt with regard to the bomb, only this time the question was posed vis-à-vis Europe rather than the Congress. At the White House, the NSC specialists on European Affairs, Jody Powell, and apparently, the president, felt that the White House should drop even the limited response to the press coverage that the president had given before the Senate debate, particularly now that the issue was receding in the U.S. Powell explained: "Even on the important issues your ability to affect coverage in Europe is limited and we had other worries on our plate then, like Bert Lance's difficulties."

At the Pentagon, the lead for preparing overseas press guidance fell to Dave McGiffert, the assistant secretary for international security affairs. McGiffert, too, felt that "no amount of catch up would stop reporters from writing about killing people and leaving buildings standing." At the prompting of Lt. Col. Burch in OSD Public Affairs (PA), the United States Information Agency (USIA)— an independent federal agency responsible for disseminating information about administration positions overseas—did send out guidance on July 22 to USIA subscribers that sought to rebut some common perceptions about neutron weapons. The guidance was intended solely for reactive purposes, however, and concluded with the direction: "Do not volunteer statements on neutron warhead. . . . Do not make any attempts to predict or anticipate the president's decision."

At the State Department, which now had the lead in preparing press guidance and educational information for consumption at the European embassies, the reticence to respond to troublesome press coverage was equally marked. The only unclassified guidance during the summer (since released) by the State Department was a July 14 message from the secretary of State to all diplomatic and consular posts, which quoted two wishywashy paragraphs (from the Arms Control Impact Statement) on the effect the Lance warhead would have on arms control negotiations. David Gompert, Les Gelb's deputy in PM, played a key role in drafting the guidance and commented:

> It was impossible to come up with a satisfactory press line in the absence of an understanding with the allies about where we were. The issue no longer was what is the weapon, the question was what are the U.S. intentions vis-à-vis the weapon? Leaks were coming out of the Pentagon and elsewhere saying, "It's our intention to deploy," which kept raising the issue of what we intended to do. You couldn't just say "the horror stories about this weapon aren't true" and leave it at that.
>
> You must also remember that the effort to establish the neutron bomb wasn't any more horrifying than other nuclear weapons failed because no one on the outside was interested. Most of the press interest was in showing that it *was* more horrible. . . . We wanted this problem to go away; we certainly weren't looking for victory—we were looking for an end to the fight.

Some senior staff at the State Department and NSC felt not only that the administration should do its best to avoid commenting on the controversy, but that the limited information already released by the Pentagon was adding fuel to the fire. Secretary of State Cyrus Vance's view was that "if it were to appear that the allies were being pressured by the United States to accept the weapon, European political opposition could become unmanageable . . . the realistic course was to consult quietly with our allies and, to the degree possible, defuse the clamor, which was being exploited by Soviet propaganda.''[11] Furthermore, a number of staff believed the arguments put forth by the Pentagon were undermining State Department efforts to privately assure the Allies that the neutron bomb didn't lower the threshold for nuclear war. One of Gelb's aides observed, for example, that "the effort at the beginning to make the neutron bomb appear less damaging and destructive than these big weapons backfired because then people started saying, 'Well, wait a minute, maybe these weapons really are useable, and you might actually set one off in Europe.' '' (Pentagon officials, however, defended their efforts; Cotter himself explained, "I'm not a political type and didn't have much sensitivity to the argument that an improved war fighting capability lowered the nuclear threshold. I saw the weapon as increasing the deterrent and putting the Soviets back to square one in designing their armor attack.'')

With concern about the neutron bomb publicity escalating, Jody Powell and Schecter informed the press on August 15 that Carter was delaying his decision on the weapon for at least another month because the President "want[ed] to consult with our allies and Congress before he makes a decision.''[12] Two days later, Vance, Brown and Brzezinski discussed the neutron bomb over lunch and reportedly decided to "conclude our consultations with the Europeans''[13] over the bomb. Later that afternoon the troika met with Carter, at which time Brzezinski was struck by the fact that "it was becoming increasingly clear that [Carter] was uncomfortable with the idea of ordering production and deployment of the ERW. The president had campaigned on the nuclear issue and his administration was focusing on arms control and nonproliferation.''[14] "We agreed,'' Brzezinski's record of the meeting stated, "that we [would] press the Europeans to show greater interest in having the bomb and therefore willingness to absorb some of the political flak or we will use European disinterest as a basis for a negative decision.''[15] Summing up the president's reservations, Brzezinski wrote in his journal that evening: "[The president] told us [that] he did not wish the world to think of him as an ogre.''[16]

Swinging and Striking Out in Europe

Quiet Diplomacy Sputters (September 1977)
    Following preliminary indications in July and August that the U.S. and the Allies were looking toward each other to make decisions on neutron weapons, the U.S. began private diplomatic negotiations in earnest over the bomb in September 1977, while, at the same time, the U.S. and NATO started pursuing a wide variety of more direct but half-hearted, unsystematic efforts to calm public apprehension over the weapon. After preliminary U.S. / NATO consultations on September 13 failed to produce a commitment from the Europeans to proceed with deployment, Schmidt personally discussed the bomb with Carter when Carter called on September 16 to discuss several other issues. Notes of their discussion indicate it went something like this:

SCHMIDT: With the public discussion of neutron weapons I don't think it would be wise to press the Europeans on the subject now. If pressured, a latent negative attitude may prevail.

CARTER: I understand, I don't want to proceed and get shot down as an international ogre. The weapon has advantages. . . .

SCHMIDT: The parliamentary debate went rather smoothly but there is a latent opposition that could be inflamed.

CARTER: What about the situation in other countries?

SCHMIDT: I'm not that well informed; the Defense Minister said there is not one [clear candidate] and several might raise problems.

CARTER: It would be good to have another country.

SCHMIDT: It would be easier if . . . your debate calmed.

CARTER: Well, tell me how? . . .

A more detailed view of the Allies' hesitancy—who had never really been asked before to *publicly* commit themselves to deployment of specific nuclear weapons—was obtained by Brzezinski during the course of a trip through Europe several weeks later. On September 27, Brzezinski discussed the issue with Britain's Prime Minister, Labour Party leader James Callaghan. Brzezinski told the Prime Minister that there was no reason to build the warheads if they would not be deployed in Europe, and that without a European commitment to deployment it would be extremely difficult to sell the weapons to Congress or the American public. Notes of the Brzezinski–Callaghan meeting indicate that both men were well aware of and quite sensitive to the obstacles introduced by the neutron bomb publicity:

> . . . Dr. Brzezinski mentioned that there is talk in Germany of linking a decision on the neutron bomb to MBFR [Mutual Balanced Force Reduction talks], and if one wanted to stall, that it would provide a means of doing so. The Prime Minister said that in his meeting with [Italian] Prime Minister Andreotti, the latter was worried about the neutron bomb issue to the extent that he did not want the subject mentioned in the briefing after the meeting. The Prime Minister [i.e., Callaghan] said he had problems with the issue as well. The Labour National Executive Committee was about to publish a pamphlet exaggerating the effects of neutron weapons. Still, the Prime Minister said he would consider the issue and give the U.S. an answer.
>
> Dr. Brzezinski said the President was concerned about the reaction to a decision; he had heard him say twice that he did not want to be seen as an "international ogre" for deploying these awful, capitalist weapons. The Prime Minister said it had been presented in the same way in Britain. He had thought of it in that light but now knew differently. Dr. Brzezinski felt the military had been somewhat stupid about the name of the weapon; now, much too late they were starting to call it a "suppressed blast" weapon. In fact, the Prime Minister noted, the destruction of people is less with the neutron weapons because they are more precise. However, public opinion lags far behind the facts and there is the need to build public understanding.

Later that same day Brzezinski met with Schmidt in Bonn to discuss neutron weapons. Schmidt opened discussion of the subject by telling Brzezinski that the label "neutron bomb" had misled people into thinking the ER warheads were outside the usual categories of nuclear weapons—an impression aggravated by the U.S. Senate debate—and, that like Callaghan, he felt neutron weapons raised formidable public relations problems which could only be surmounted in time. Notes of the conversation indicate that Schmidt stated that the

> Europeans could be convinced that ER weapons were normal if there were time for thought and study. If, however, they had them pushed down their throats, some would react. In Germany, the Chancellor continued, the parliamentary debate went rather smoothly. Yet that was deceptive: the more the government talks of ER weapons, the more opposition there is.

Schmidt's view, the notes indicate, was that a "positive decision would be hard to get quickly, but it could be done in one or two years. . . . The Chancellor did not want to say no . . . [but] there [currently] was no parliamentary majority." Schmidt also stated that he considered the question of deployment separable from the production decision.

In his reply to Schmidt, Brzezinski emphasized that production and deployment decisions would have to be linked both for the President and the Congress, but generally took a more conciliatory tone, suggesting that the president "might not be dismayed by a negative decision" and that the neutron weapon could be used as a bargaining chip in the Mutual Balanced Force Reduction (MBFR) talks, as Schmidt had mentioned. Summing up, Brzezinski stated that "the President does not want to be seen as an 'international ogre' for deploying the weapon. . . . Dr. Brzezinski suggested leaving it that he would report. Consultations would continue."

The Public–Press Mirror of the Negotiations

Not too surprisingly, these inconclusive negotiations did not lead to the output of more aggressive press guidance from U.S. officials during September. For example, on September 18 Charles Corddry reported on the front page of the *Baltimore Sun* that "government sources" said Carter was delaying ERW production while awaiting public support from the Allies, who were said to be "fearful, for domestic political reasons, of giving [ERW] much public emphasis." Corddry also reported that "administration sources" were saying that "gaining public official support would be uppermost" at the Nuclear Planning Group (NPG) meeting in mid-October. An interagency group was duly convened to prepare press guidance in response to Corddry's piece, and sent a confidential cable to the U.S. mission and NATO capitals, advising that:

> We have no comment to make beyond the general observation that modernization of [TNF] is a subject which the United States discusses with its Allies on an ongoing basis. We do not comment on which specific subjects are to be discussed at NPG meetings. The [ERW] consultations are still in process and the President has not yet reached a decision on the matter. We have no information [on] when the President may decide this question.

In Europe, NATO and the European governments themselves appear not to have been much more aggressive in educating the press and public during the fall of 1977. In Britain, Prime Minister Callaghan—who had expressed concern to Brzezinski about the need to build public understanding—did not take a position on the bomb (pending a U.S. production decision), and the Labour Party (which had a vocal antinuclear left wing and elections coming up in 1978), adopted a similar public relations approach to that of the U.S.[1] The German government—reflecting Schmidt's belief that government discussion of neutron weapons only encouraged more opposition—released only one statement on the subject during the fall.[2] Other key European governments—such as Belgium, Italy, and the Netherlands—appear not to have issued any educational material on neutron warheads formally (or otherwise) during the period.

NATO, which was thought to provide the anonymity that might allow individual nations to support ERW (i.e., under the protection of the collective NATO umbrella) was slightly more outspoken. NATO's Secretary General Joseph M. A. H. Luns commented critically about the press coverage on several occasions,[3] but Richard Shearer, head of the NPG staff, recalled Luns's efforts were to little avail:

> At least bimonthly and sometimes weekly we had delegations come to the headquarters—press delegations, foreign journalists, student delegations, visiting parliamentarians—who wanted to hear about neutron weapons. Everyone that requested an audience, either singularly or in groups, was granted one either with me, Paul Van Campen [Lun's executive assistant], or the Secretary General himself. . . . [But] no one really wanted to listen. The fact is that we were miserably outgunned; we frankly didn't know quite what to do.
>
> Now what we did do was reactive; in terms of a coordinated outreach effort I would say it was toward the nonexistent. There wasn't a lot of enthusiasm in NATO in pressing for a more vigorous public relations campaign; we were hoping the issue would die out and felt every time we threw something on the fire it just increased the conflagration.

October 1977: The Administration Begins To Regroup

As negotiations over the neutron bomb stalled in September and October, reservations began to grow within the administration, particularly outside the White House, about the low key press and public relations approach the U.S. and Alliance had adopted. At the White House, the president and Jody Powell continued not to comment on the issue during October, partly because it wasn't being covered much in the U.S. press and partly because of the lack of personal commitment from Schmidt. Brzezinski explained:

> Pincus's articles had some resonance among people who read the *Washington Post*, but in the country-at-large, the neutron bomb was certainly not a major issue. In Europe it was a major issue, and that was why getting Euro-

pean political leaders to share co-responsibility for deployment was important. We felt that asking them to share responsibility would make them more inclined to explain the nature of this weapon and stimulate them into greater efforts to justify deployment. Otherwise, it was too easy to put it on the shoulders of the Americans.

Outside the White House, however, there was a budding interest in exploring a more vigorous public education effort. At the State Department, which, as one of Gelb's aides put it—"was getting assaulted practically every day by officials from the allies' embassies bemoaning the press coverage"—Assistant Secretary for Public Affairs Hodding Carter was concerned by the lack of educational material on the subject. He commented that

> My press guidance at the time was the usual hand wrestling stuff; "This is a matter we are working on with the Allies, there is nothing for me to comment on here" and so on. The doctrine at State is, if you can put off any kind of encounter with reality until tomorrow, do it, because that gives you more room to maneuver. They're wrong to do it that way. My thesis was that if we were getting ready to do something—like push for deployment of the bomb—we really ought to be out selling like crazy in advance, so people understood why the neutron bomb made some sense. At State you couldn't sell a decision though until it had been tied in a bow and delivered, because people were always worried that something might change a bit.

The reticence at the State Department to comment reflected not only institutional tradition but the views of Secretary Vance and the assistant secretary for european affairs, George Vest, as well. During August and September, State Department officials argued that their low-key educational effort overseas might be beneficial, since it might make the Soviet propaganda effort look more transparent, which in turn would force NATO states to support deployment (or else look like they had caved into Soviet pressure).[4] By mid-October, however, Soviet propaganda had become less overt and it was clear that the Soviet media campaign had not backfired in Europe, either in private or in the press. Gelb recalled:

> It wasn't in the nature of the Carter beast to mount an educational, public relations campaign and that was a mistake. We should have done so and it would have made a difference on two counts. First, it would have helped minimize the notion that the administration was careless about security problems; it would have shown we cared and were prepared to fight for what we wanted. Second, it would have been wiser to be more political about what we were doing, to worry about building support for what we were doing, because our failure to do so allowed critics both outside and inside the administration to state our positions for us—and state them in the worst possible light.

Explaining his thinking at the time, Vance commented:

> I did think that failing to come to grips with the [anti-neutron bomb] stories could lead to major problems in getting support for production and deployment; I thought we should deal with that by explaining very clearly and

simply what the neutron bomb was and what it was intended to do. However, while I saw the press coverage as potentially posing a major problem, I also felt it was containable. The Europeans, and, I believe, Schmidt, had previously pressed us to increase our capability against Soviet armor; the ERW fulfilled that need so I felt we were working against a background of European encouragement.

The U.S. Defense Community Flails Into Action

While White House and State Department officials continued to keep a low profile, Pentagon officials and members of the defense trade press began talking and writing critically about the media coverage of the bomb during the fall. Tom Ross and Harold Brown again played a limited role in rebutting misimpressions of neutron weapons, although Brown did give several press conferences and foreign TV interviews during October in which he criticized the press, and emphasized that the bomb wouldn't lower the threshold, that it was meant to deter a massive Warsaw Pact tank attack, and that it had a less destructive effect on civilian populations and friendly forces than existing weapons. Below Brown and Ross, a number of more direct, uncoordinated efforts to rebut the press coverage emerged during the fall. Cotter's office, for example, continued to release additional technical material for use overseas. And the Army Public Affairs' office decided on its own to put out an issue of *Spotlight*—an internal publication distributed to Army troops overseas—that was devoted to countering misleading "media coverage and resultant public concern"[5] over what neutron weapons were. Concurrent with the *Spotlight* article, several trade publications published critical articles on the media coverage, largely without the prompting of Pentagon officials. In September, the conservative American Security Council devoted its monthly newsletter to "The Realities of the Neutron Bomb," and Harold Agnew, the director of Los Alamos Laboratory, wrote a primer on the technical characteristics of ER weapons (which appeared in the December issue of the *Bulletin of Atomic Scientists*) because, as he put it in an October 26 letter to Major General Bratton, "I was fed up with all the misinformation being disseminated." *Army* also ran a story in September that described the technical characteristics of the weapon,[6] and *Air Force Magazine* ran two articles in the November issue specifically devoted to criticizing the media coverage, one under the title "The Wayward Press" and the other under the head "The 'Neutron Bomb' Media Event."[7] However, in the popular press, TV, radio, and so forth, which were devoting relatively little attention to the issue, the trade stories appear to have had little, if any, impact and were almost never cited. As Lt. Col. Mike Burch, one of Ross's assistants summed up: "Some defense specialists read these articles but let's face it: we were preaching to the choir."

The Pentagon and NATO Play the Name Game

The one mildly coordinated public relations effort that the Pentagon and NATO undertook during the fall of 1977 was to find a new name for the neutron bomb. A number of key European figures, including Helmut Schmidt, Georg

Leber, and Joseph Luns, as well as W. Tapley Bennett, the U.S. ambassador to NATO, were convinced that the label "neutron bomb" had made enhanced radiation warheads seem like distinctively different atomic weapons that created a new, and even more dangerous, stage in the arms race. Eventually Luns and Bennett settled on the title "reduced blast / enhanced radiation" weapon to replace both "neutron bomb" or the simpler "enhanced radiation" weapon. The "reduced blast" tag surfaced soon after Pincus's first story appeared, and late in the summer of 1977 Bennett sent a confidential cable back to the States, requesting that the name of the ERW be changed. In the U.S., most senior staff at State, DOD, and NSC though Bennett's request was ludicrous, a view which was aptly summed up by Jim Siena's observation that "the name change was one of those classic half-assed efforts to make a problem go away by euphemism."

Among some of the political leadership, however, there was some sentiment that renaming the weapon might be helpful. Beginning in October, administration officials began to refer to "reduced blast / enhanced radiation" (RB /ER) weapons in their budget submissions, congressional testimony, etc., and Harold Brown started using the term. Unfortunately—at least for the supporters of the name change—the first reporter to publicize the new nomenclature was Walter Pincus. He had obtained a copy of the *Spotlight* article and noticed the references to "reduced blast / enhanced radiation" warheads. On December 15, the *Post* ran Pincus's story on the *Spotlight* piece and name change which led with: "The Army is stepping up its merchandising campaign in behalf of its controversial neutron weapons. For one thing, the [ERW], popularly and inaccurately (to the Pentagon's exasperation) called neutron bombs have been officially renamed." Shortly thereafter, U.S. officials began to phase out the use of the RB / ER terminology (to the point where it had effectively disappeared by mid-1978).

A similar fate befell an even more modest attempt by NATO to alter the descriptions of the neutron bomb broadcast in Europe over the Armed Forces Network (AFN). In October, the U.S. mission to NATO (headed up by Bennett) complained to AFN about the persistent description of the bomb in radio and TV broadcasts as "the weapon that killed people without destroying buildings." After consulting with the news department, the AFN commander posted a notice in mid-December which stated that the term "neutron bomb" could be used, but that the newscasters were "not to give a description of the neutron bomb as killing people and not destroying buildings" in local written material. Several civilian newscasters felt their military superiors were interfering with their prerogatives and on January 4, 1978, the *Los Angeles Times* devoted a front page story to the dispute under the headline "Military Accused of Meddling in GI News on N-Bomb."[8]

Summing up the inability of the administration to counter the efforts of the Pincus stories and other coverage overseas during the fall, NSC Deputy Director David Aaron commented:

> There was some discussion about mounting some sort of educational campaign on the issue, but we were stymied in part by the fact that there was

no real apparatus with which to do this with in Western Europe on an allied basis. NATO Public Affairs could put out some information but they weren't equipped to run a major educational effort. USIA [the United States Information Agency] was not the most capable group on this matter and was spending most of its time fighting off a reorganization. On my trips to Europe, I frequently heard pleas for help from figures like Luns and the foreign ministers—people wanted us "to do something" about public misapprehension—but no one had any suggestions for how it should be done.

Selling the Neutron Bomb Via Mock Arms Control

In November 1977 the Carter administration finally developed a proposal to sell deployment of neutron weapons that was intended to assuage European anxieties and counter Soviet propaganda. The key to the administration package was an arms control "offer" involving a deferral of the neutron bomb, in exchange for a Soviet deferral of the new SS–20 missile; the exchange idea, formulated by one of Brown's aides, was triggered by an address by Helmut Schmidt on October 28 in which he warned of the dangers of new medium-range Soviet missiles. Assuming that the Soviets would reject the exchange, U.S. officials believed the public onus for deploying new nuclear weapons would then shift to the USSR, opening the way for European deployment of neutron weapons.

Although there was some public relations appeal to the Pentagon proposal, most senior staff at State, DOD, and the NSC felt it was a ridiculous arms control offer and some feared it might actually harm things in the long run. Unlike the neutron warheads planned for the Lance and 8-inch shell, the SS–20 carried extremely powerful warheads (up to three 150 kt warheads) and could travel long distances (3,000 miles) into enemy territory. Apart from the trade constituting an apples to oranges comparison, NATO officials, particularly the Germans, were concerned that NATO lacked a modernized, long-range theater missile capability of its own and were therefore encouraging the development of missiles like the Cruise. Other officials were concerned that a SS–20 / ERW arms control offer would, as David Aaron commented, undermine "the link between ERW and the Soviet tank threat."

Despite those concerns, the Pentagon proposal ended up carrying the day, since both Harold Brown and Brzezinski strongly supported it. "Brown," Aaron recalled, "felt that we could deflect criticism of the neutron bomb by pointing out that the collateral damage and civilian toll wrought by the SS–20 was much more than that caused by the neutron bomb and that people ought to start paying more attention to the deployment of these missiles." Brzezinski was similarly impressed by the public relations potential of the deal, recalling that "it was clear to me that the European governments needed some help in making the issue more palatable politically. I thought that if we linked the ERW to the overall nuclear situation there might be some benefits."[1]

At a November 16 meeting of the Special Coordinating Committee (SCC) of the National Security Council, the ERW / SS–20 trade superceded an earlier proposal to introduce the ERW into the MBFR talks. When the meeting was over, Brown and Brzezinski, with the concurrence of Vance, agreed to recommend to the President a three step scenario for deployment of the weapon: first, following high-level consultations with the Europeans, the President would decide to produce the weapon, second, at his urging the Europeans would accept deployment, and third, the U.S. would then offer to defer deploying the weapon in exchange for the Russians doing the same with the SS–20. On November 24 Brzezinski submitted to the president a draft of a letter from him to Schmidt in which Carter would state that he was taking the Germans up on their suggestion of linking ERW to an arms control offer, that the SS–20 / ERW was one possible link, and that the arms control offer would be timed with announcements to produce and deploy ERW[2]—since it was unlikely that a weapon which had never been built would offer much arms control incentive. At the close of the month the letter was sent.

The News Leaks

On November 23, while Carter's letter was being drafted, Pincus reported in a front-page *Post* story that "sharply divided Presidential national security advisors agreed at a White House meeting last Wednesday to keep the issue of the neutron weapons out of the [MBFR] talks. The decision was a victory for proponents of the new of generation weapons, principally the Pentagon, and some [NSC] staff members. . . . The outcome of the meeting does not necessarily mean that President Carter will go ahead with production of the neutron artillery. . . . There is a consensus emerging in the national security community for a deferral in the long expected production decision."[3]

The day the *Post* story appeared, the White House sought to rebut it with Jody Powell commenting during his press briefing that the story was "based upon a leak of inaccurate and misleading information, evidently designed to influence policy."[4] Explaining his strong denial of the Pincus story, Powell commented that "every administration has people selling their preferred option to the press in an attempt to influence the president's decision. That was bad for the most part because it tended to limit the president's options by the time he got to the matter." The administration's efforts to counter Pincus's story, however, were further undermined on November 25, when a front page story by Richard Burt appeared in the *New York Times* that described the SCC meeting in some detail.[5] Burt's story, unlike Pincus's, mentioned not only the administration's disinterest in putting ERW into MBFR but also discussed in some detail the administration's proposal to trade the ERW for the SS–20. This time, no denial of the story was forthcoming from the White House.

It is not clear exactly what impact the leaks about the SCC meeting had, although they appear to have initially discouraged administration officials from talking publicly about or aggressively promoting a SS–20 / ERW deal. Late in 1977, Chancellor Schmidt wrote back to the president that he liked the idea of further consultations and an ERW arms control offer, but that he wanted to keep his options "open": in particular, Schmidt preferred an ERW trade for tanks in MBFR, instead of the SS–20 / ERW trade.[6]

While, however, the U.S. and NATO were cultivating the diplomatic ground necessary for European acceptance of an ERW / SS–20 "trade," the Soviets used the leaks as an opportunity to announce their own arms control "offer" for the neutron bomb. On December 15, the Soviet MBFR delegate said that introduction of the neutron weapon into MBFR would pose "insurmountable obstacles"[7] and a week later, Brezhnev himself proposed a "mutual renunciation of the neutron bomb." Brezhnev's proposal for a mutual renunciation of the neutron bomb had a deceptively simple appeal,* and the administration felt it had to counter Brezhnev's offer quickly. On December 29, Brzezinski told reporters that the SS–20 was "more to be alarmed about"[8] than the neutron bomb, and the following day, at a press conference in Warsaw, Poland, the president was asked by a Polish reporter about his views on Brezhnev's offer. Carter commented:

> . . . This [neutron] weapon is much less destabilizing in its effect, if it should be deployed, than, for instance, some of the advanced new Soviet weapons like the SS–20 missile, which is more destructive than any weapon held by the NATO allies and has a much greater range. So my hope is that in general we can reduce the threat of nuclear destruction in the European area. . . . We would not deploy the neutron bomb or neutron shells unless there was an agreement by our NATO allies. That is where the decision will be made.[9]

Carter's statement in Warsaw marked the height of the administration's public use of the SS–20 missile as a propaganda counter to the neutron bomb, partly because the West Germans continued to emphasize that they wanted to trade the ERW for tanks instead of the SS–20. "The SS–20 / ERW trade never caught on as an effective propaganda tool," Brzezinski acknowledged, "because the SS–20 was then too remote a system for Europeans and the notion of some equivalence never really struck home." Harold Brown was of a similar view, concluding,

> It was clear that the SS–20 was more dangerous and damaging than the neutron bomb, but the SS–20 didn't spare buildings, so it must be "okay." Bringing in the SS–20 didn't really answer that question; the bomb that "killed people and left buildings standing" was such a fine image that it really wasn't possible to do anything about it. I concluded that the battle

---

*Although U.S. officials were devoting some research to the use of ER warheads on intermediate range missiles, the ERW had primarily been developed as a short-range battlefield weapon to counter the Soviet tank threat. The Russians, however, were not concerned about a NATO tank blitzkrieg and hence didn't have much use of ER weapons. Also while it was clear the Russians could develop the technology to build neutron weapons, it appeared in 1977 that they were a number of years away from fitting the technology into an artillery shell. The Russians, in effect, were offering to "trade" a weapon they did not have (an had little use for) in exchange for the U.S. giving up a weapon it already had produced and had need of.

was essentially lost with the publics, but that if we worked very hard on the European governments, we might gradually bring them around despite the public's misapprehension of the weapons.

Despite the frustration felt by Brown and other U.S. officials, the administration did not give up its efforts to sell the neutron bomb or the neutron bomb /SS–20 "link." However, as the Russian opposition to the bomb grew especially strident during the winter of 1978, the administration turned increasingly to another option to sell the bomb: covert action.

Influencing the Western European Press, Covertly and Overtly (January–April 1978)

The U.S. decision in January 1978 to institute a covert action program in Western Europe to build support for the neutron bomb was prompted by covert and semicovert Soviet infiltration of the anti-neutron bomb movement in Europe, particularly in the Netherlands. During July and August much of the Soviet propaganda on neutron weapons had come from Soviet satellites and was broadcast over Soviet and East European media. Beginning in August, however, the Soviet campaign moved into covert and semicovert phases with the aim of building a powerful anti-neutron bomb movement in Western Europe. Shortly after the White House indicated in mid-August that the president wished to consult further with the allies, the Dutch Communist Party announced the "initiative for a broad movement of the people."[10] The "Stop the Neutron Bomb" movement, headed by the Amsterdam district leader of the Communist Party, soon joined hands with the Interchurch Peace Council (IKV)—the most powerful peace lobby in the Netherlands, drawn from the nine largest Dutch churches—to plan a series of rallies and petitions to oppose the development of the bomb. In December 1977, Romesh Chandra, the head of the Soviet front World Peace Council (WPC), visited Amsterdam to review the "Stop the Neutron Bomb's" protest plans.[11] With the aid of Chandra's advice and substantial funding from the Soviet Union, the Dutch Communist Party began planning a petition drive and a major anti-neutron rally to take place in Amsterdam in March (around the same time that the U.S. was expected to decide whether it was going to put the weapon into production) which would draw as much as possible on noncommunist support.

At the same time, the Soviets launched a private, but hard hitting campaign in diplomatic channels in Western Europe against neutron weapons. In January, Soviet and Eastern European parliamentarians and trade union leaders started sending letters to their Western counterparts in Europe and the U.S., and, even more important, Brezhnev himself directly wrote threatening letters to the head of every NATO nation about the bomb, including Carter. The English text of Brezhnev's secret letter to Carter reiterated Brezhnev's offer for a mutual repudiation of neutron weapons and gives a sense of how heated the Soviet protest was:

Dear Mr. President,

This time I am addressing you on only a single question, but one which assumes significant acuteness. . . . The seriousness of the [neutron bomb] demands that talk be candid. . . . I will say it frankly. We view attempts to belittle the threat which has arisen as a desire to confuse those in the world who now feel a rising alarm, and who are raising ever louder a voice of protest against the neutron bomb. Can it indeed be possible to believe that neutron weapons, if they are used, will be used on a limited scale, only on the battlefield and only against one or another type of forces? . . . By their nature and their destructive characteristics neutron weapons can strike not only people wearing military uniforms but also huge masses of the population. These are inhuman weapons of mass destruction; they are directed against people. Their appearance will not diminish the likelihood of nuclear conflict but enhance it. The reality is that if neutron weapons are ever used, a devastating scythe will sweep across the territories of entire countries, probably not leaving a single inch untouched. . . .

Plans connected with neutron weapons are already having a dangerous effect on the world political atmosphere and their realization would entail even greater costs. In what light would the negotiations currently underway between the USSR and the U.S. on a series of major issues for arresting the arms race appear if simultaneously the deployment of neutron weapons was forced? Not much would be left of people's trust in solving the problem of disarmament. In the success of ongoing negotiations, moreover, the negotiations themselves, at least in some cases, would face the threat of being broken off.

Brezhnev concluded with the admonishment:

It is no secret that the decision whether to start production and deployment of neutron weapons depends above all upon the U.S. government, upon you, personally, Mr. President. But this decision is of the kind that a chain of events is put into motion which in the last analysis is connected with the risk of devastation of whole countries, and the loss of millions of people. The responsibility here is exceptionally great and it is this that prompts me to address you. Since, if the choice of the United States is in favor of the neutron bomb this will put before the Soviet Union the necessity to meet the challenge. . . . We have simply no right to forego the security of our people and the security of our allies.

But it is still not too late to stop. There exists an alternative to the dangerous aggravation of the arms race and we propose it. You of course know that in my public address at the end of the last year I proposed that agreement be reached on the mutual repudiation of production of neutron weapons. I now confirm this proposal. . . .

With the receipt of the Brezhnev letters and intelligence reports about communist infiltration of the anti-neutron bomb movement coming in frequently, U.S. officials became convinced that the Russian campaign was moving into an even higher gear, exerting tremendous pressure on the NATO allies, who were simultaneously being pushed by the U.S. to publicly support deployment of the weapons. In early January a decision was made to explore a covert response to the Soviet pressure, and on January 12, 1978, Leslie Gelb, director of politico-military affairs at the State Department, sent Harold Saunders, director of the department's Intelligence and Research Bureau (INR), a memo entitled, "Proposal for Action in Response to Soviet Anti-Neutron Bomb Campaign." On January 28, after receiving the expert advice of the INR bureau, Gelb and George Vest (the assistant secretary for european affairs) sent Saunders another memo under the heading, "Covert Action to Counter International Anti-Neutron Bomb Forum," (which was the "Stop the Neutron Bomb" demonstration scheduled for Holland in mid-March). The covert action plan was approved by Brzezinski and Vance—whom Gelb remembered "had no problem with it"—as well as CIA Director Stanfield Turner. The program—which essentially involved asking U.S. sympathizers and agents in the European press corps to give more favorable press coverage to the bomb, either for free or for money if necessary—was summarized by Gelb as an effort to

> . . . get favorable newspaper articles in the Western European press. It was purely aimed at press coverage; we weren't trying to obstruct the renting of convention halls or anything like that. This campaign was chosen to supplement our overt activities, like having the embassies talk to European journalists. We thought more favorable press coverage might help show the European public that we weren't trying to upset the current nuclear balance, that the neutron bomb was a legitimate modernization move, every bit as legitimate as what the Soviets had already done in the deploying of the SS–20. We pushed the SS–20 comparison. . . . I don't know that I felt the covert action program would be decisive; I thought it would be reasonable to try to do.

Brzezinski explained, in part, why covert action was then felt to be preferable to other actions that could have been taken to influence the foreign press coverage:

> Our assumption was that the uneasiness and public outcry was *not* sufficiently strong that it would prevent the deployment decision we saw emerging in subsequent months. And, therefore, there was no feeling that one had to mount a massive public education campaign in anticipation of the decision. If, after the deployment decision had been made, it became clear that to implement it more needed to be done publicly, we would have campaigned for it with whatever intensity was necessary. In anticipation of the decision, some campaign was necessary to make sure that the notion of equivalence of certain weapons was planted in the public mind.

The details of the covert action campaign have remained classified but a sampling of British and German press coverage from the time indicates that the neutron bomb / SS–20 comparison, along with sharp criticisms of the Soviet propaganda campaign, began appearing frequently during February and March 1978. Newspapers, for example, like the *Dussledorf Rheinische Post, Die Welt, Bonn General Anzeiger, Freiburg Badische Zeitung, Rheinische Post, Sud-*

deustche Zeitung, Koblenz Rhein-Zeitung, London Times, London Daily Telegraph, and the *Economist,* began either to contrast the dangers of the SS–20 vs. the neutron bomb or ridicule the Soviet propaganda campaign against the bomb. (In the U.S., papers such as the *Christian Science Monitor, Chicago Tribune, San Diego Union, Los Angeles Times, Milwaukee Journal, Washington Star,* and *Baltimore Sun* also picked up the hue and cry.) The growing swell of anti-Soviet criticism also benefited from, and in some cases directly reflected, public statements by figures such as Hans-Dietrich Genscher, Willy Brandt, and, in particular, British Prime Minister James Callaghan.*

Although other overt activities (such as briefing foreign journalists at the European embassies) appear to have been quite limited, the SS–20 / ERW contrast was also pushed by U.S. officials privately, sometimes at the highest levels of government. For example, on February 22, President Carter met with Denmark's prime minister Anker Jorgensen and discussed, among other topics, Western European opposition to the neutron bomb. Rough notes of the discussion indicate that Carter told Jorgensen, ''the enhanced radiation warhead has been distorted by Soviet propaganda. There is no comparison between ERW—it's different—from advanced, offensive weapons like the SS–20, which is aimed against Western Europe. I've not yet ordered production or deployment; I don't want this to be disruptive, I want to strengthen NATO and not move without close and active consultation with NATO.'' Later in the meeting, Carter turned to Warren Christopher and said: ''It would be good if we could provide a comparison of the ERW and SS–20 for the Prime Minister. The ERW is small; give him something that describes the destruction caused by each weapon. . . . This is not a propaganda war but it is important to understand the difference.''

While it is not clear whether such private exchanges had any ultimate effect on Western European opinion or policy, it does appear that the combination of public statements by European leaders, along with the covert action program, had a marked effect on West European press coverage during February. For example, on March 1 the United States Information Agency, which had been closely monitoring foreign media coverage of the bomb, reported that:

> A trend in West European media toward acceptance of the neutron bomb as part of the NATO defense arsenal was intensified in the last two weeks as allied governments weighed the pros and cons of a go-ahead decision on production and deployment of the weapon. The deliberative tone of the discussion occasioned by the impending neutron decision contrasted sharply with the climate in which the proposed weapon was announced last sum-

---

*On February 21, in the British Parliament, Callaghan stated:

> The neutron bomb and its serious effects are now being used by the Soviet Union as a propaganda cover to prevent discussion of some other serious weapons being developed. I want to ensure that this is on the record. Mr. Brezhnev can help in this matter if, instead of focusing propaganda on the neutron bomb, he will enter into serious discussion at the United Nations or elsewhere on how we are to deal with some of the other weapons now being developed . . . I do not want to see the world destroyed by our terror. Nor do I want to succumb to blackmail by someone else's terror. . . . The SS–20 is a more dangerous weapon than the neutron bomb.[12]

mer. At that time, many media voices the world over reponded with apprehension and horror at the thought of a new "dirty" weapon whose killing power reportedly would exceed its physical destructive force.[13]

The growing media support for neutron warheads also seemed to create—as U.S. officials had hoped it would—more latitude for key European figures in handling the issue. In mid-February, for example, Egon Bahr—the SPD official who had helped ignite controversy in West Germany by labelling the bomb "a symbol of mental perversion" the previous summer—stated that while he still opposed deployment of the bomb, he was cognizant of the dangers of the SS–20 missiles "now threatening Europe"[14] and advocated the ERW be introduced into the MBFR talks. Schmidt himself appeared relieved by the change in coverage, commenting on March 3: "Thank God, the emotions—or the emotionalism—unleashed by this topic have receded somewhat."[15]

At the same time, however, that the passions surrounding the neutron bomb began to subside in the British and German press, new Soviet propaganda efforts and native anti-neutron bomb sentiment began peaking among leftist organizations in Western European countries such as Belgium and Holland, the only countries besides West Germany in which U.S. policymakers wished to deploy the bomb. The anti-neutron bomb demonstrations the Soviet fronts had helped coordinate came to fruition and frequent criticism of the neutron bomb cropped up at disarmament conferences during February and March. The granddaddy of the anti-neutron bomb protests—the "International Forum," which took place in Amsterdam on March 18 and 19—was particularly successful. The demonstration, led by the "Stop the Neutron Bomb" group, sold some 400,000 anti-neutron bomb window bills, stickers, and buttons, and got a stunning 1.2 million Dutch citizens to sign petitions opposing the bomb. (There are about 10 million Dutch voters altogether.) After listening to speeches by Daniel Ellsberg and others, some 50,000 demonstrators, forming a procession several miles long, marched through the streets of Amsterdam in the rain, chanting repeatedly, "Ban the Neutron Bomb!"

As the Soviet and leftist protest movement grew, U.S. and European officials became increasingly anxious in March about their ability to piece together a proposal to deploy ERW that could win European acceptance. General Alexander Haig, the NATO SACEUR, summed up U.S. and NATO concern when he commented in executive session before the Senate Armed Services committee on March 3:

> Clearly what we were faced with has been a public relations fiasco. . . .
> What no one anticipated, of course, was the sudden expose in the American press, which was immediately seized upon by the left wings in the European governments [deleted]. [Deleted] and was subsequently escalated by a highly competent and extensive Soviet propaganda campaign . . . we have insisted that we cannot make a production decision until [relevant West European nations agree to deploy ERW]. That is somewhat unusual. . . . What worries me most about this problem, however, is that the longer it is prolonged,

the more Soviet propaganda that is applied—and it is extensive at this point—
and the less chance we have of reaching a favorable decision.[16]

A Deal Comes Together

While the U.S. and USSR were conducting a battle over public opinion and
Western European press coverage of the bomb, the U.S. and its NATO allies
were secretly working out plans to produce and deploy neutron warheads. Beginning in January 1978, the lead on diplomatic negotiations shifted to NSC and
State—particularly to David Aaron and Leslie Gelb—and away from the Defense
Department, mostly since NATO military officials were already agreed that neutron weapons were desirable. "We intentionally decided," Leslie Gelb recalled,
"to switch the lead to us and NSC because the military part of the enterprise was
developing a momentum of its own which might not be supported by the political
counterparts in the European governments." At a January 23 SCC meeting, senior
officials agreed that they would include ERW in upcoming SALT consultations
and seek to get a production and deployment plan accepted by NATO in March
or April.

On January 30 an interagency SALT delegation, led by NSC Deputy Director Aaron, met with the West Germans to discuss the U.S. proposal and the
following day the same team discussed ERW with the British. Aaron found the
Germans unwilling to support deployment unless another continental nation joined
them, and found both the Germans and British to be skittish about expressing
public support for ERW deployment. Following strenuous negotiations in February and March, including one-on-one discussions between Vance and British
Foreign Secretary David Owen and U.S. presentations to the NATO permanent
representatives, a delicate compromise package emerged that met with the approval
of Schmidt, Callaghan, Bennett, Luns, Vance, Harold Brown, and Brzezinski.
The "scenario," as it was called, still included the original three steps proposed
by the U.S.—production, an arms control offer on the SS–20, and deployment
after two years if arms control failed—but was modified during the negotiations
to soften the requirement for public support of ERW deployment; support, instead,
would be voiced by NATO as a whole.

Following some furious last-minute consultations, U.S. and European officials agreed that the ERW package would be given a private dry run at a March
20 meeting of the North Atlantic Council (NAC) meeting of NATO. Assuming
no one had problems with the scenario, Joseph Luns would then issue a statement
on March 22 (following another NAC meeting), in which the alliance would
express support for the U.S. position and the following day a public announcement of NATO support would be issued. Britain, Germany, Canada, and the
U.S. would then explicitly support the statement, while the Dutch, Belgians,
Scandinavians, Norwegians, and Italians would have no comment. The scenario,
in short, was, as Leslie Gelb put it, "elaborately choreographed." "It was,"
Lynn Davis recalled, "a sort of theater, where each side, after being rehearsed,
would say just enough to satisfy the other side." "We knew we couldn't get a

unanimous alliance vote,'' one of Gelb's aides summarized, ''so we structured it to have all the appearances of a concerted alliance position.''

Not surprisingly, given the previous history of the issue, U.S. officials now included the press in their calculations for release of the scenario. Gelb recalled that ''we had it all actually scripted, the arms control emphasis, and what we were going to give to the press.'' Gelb's deputy, David Gompert, who, along with a British diplomat, drafted the NATO communique, remembered that:

> The statement was more a diplomatic document than a public relations document, but it was all public relations. The reason, after all, that it had to all be so carefully crafted was that the Dutch, Danes, and Norwegians were terrified by the public reaction they were going to get. The way to deal with that in the communique was to use it not so much to make the case for the weapon—though it clearly had to do that—as to make sure no government was clearly put in the spot. When I wrote the statement I was considering quite a bit how the press would cover it, and it was difficult to draft: we wanted to make it as clear as we possibly could that there had been a decision to go forward, but without saying that all the members of the Alliance had agreed to it.

Despite the intricate nature of the ERW scenario, U.S. officials were pleased to have finally ironed out an agreement that met their own requirements and those of the allies, and late on Friday, March 17, Vance asked Gelb and George Vest to draft a routine, information memo to the president laying out the agreement. The next day, Vance told Brown he wanted to send a joint memo and informed Gelb that he wanted Paul Warnke's (director of the Arms Control Disarmament Agency) concurrence as well with the memo. Vance also told Gelb to make the memo a decision memo, because, in Vance's words, ''though the president had checked all the right boxes on the papers sent to him, I had an uneasy feeling in my gut. I wanted to make absolutely sure, one final time, that the president was really on board.'' After Gelb obtained Warnke's concurrence, the two-page Vance–Brown memo—along with a supportive cover note from Brzezinski and drafts of the NAC communique—were sent the same day to the president, who was away vacationing at St. Simon's Island, Georgia.

The memorandum reached the president while he was out fishing, and sometime during the course of his angling—reportedly after receiving a call from Andrew Young, who opposed ERW production—the president decided to drop the ERW scenario, hook, line, and sinker. In notations in the margins of the Vance–Brown and Brzezinski memos, Carter directed Vance and Brown to ''not issue any statement re ERW'' and told Brzezinski to ''not act until consultation with me''[17] with regard to ERW production. The news of Carter's decision first reached his flabbergasted advisers when Reginald Bartholomew, a senior NSC aide, went into the White House on Sunday morning to collect any messages that might have come in from St. Simons. Bartholomew promptly called and woke up a sleepy Gelb to inform him of the news. ''You won't believe what's happened,'' Gelb remembers Bartholomew saying, ''he checked the wrong box!''

"You're joking," Gelb replied. "No, I'm not," Bartholomew said, "come on in because we've got to cancel tomorrow's meeting of the NAC."

The Roof Caves In

No one knows precisely what caused the president to abruptly cancel the ERW plan while he was out fishing that Saturday. Vance has speculated that "evidently, in [the President's] mind, all these [negotiations] had been steps in a consultative process, not a final commitment to a particular outcome. When he saw the March 18 memorandum spelling out in detail the scenario for the alliance statement of support and for the public announcement, it may have hit home that the last step was at hand, that he was essentially committed to producing and deploying a nuclear weapon that his allies—for whose security it had been developed—would not request. At that moment, I can only surmise that the President's innermost self rebelled."[1] Brzezinski has stated that "Carter felt that the European governments [particularly the FRG] were attempting to push all the political costs on him and on the United States"[2] by refusing to publicly endorse deployment unless two continental nations agreed to deployment. Still others have concluded that U.N. Ambassador Andrew Young and White House adviser Hamilton Jordan persuaded Carter to drop the neutron bomb because putting it into production would weaken the U.S. position at the upcoming U.N. Special Session on Disarmament,[3] particularly since Carter had associated himself with limiting the growth of nuclear weapons. Carter himself seconded some of Brzezinski's and Vance's speculations about his reluctance to "force" neutron weapons on the Allies,[4] commenting in his diary on March 20: "We've not gotten any firm commitment from a European nation to permit [ERW] deployment on their soil, which is the only place it would be deployed."[5]

Whatever the reason for Carter's disapproval, his unwillingness to proceed came as a complete and unpropitious surprise to Brzezinski, Vance, and Harold Brown, who thought Carter had been fully informed of the plan. On March 20, when Carter returned from St. Simons, Vice President Mondale, Hamilton Jordan, Brzezinski, Vance, and Harold Brown met with the president for an hour and a half to thrash out his doubts about the neutron bomb scenario. The meeting turned into an angry confrontation between Carter and his senior foreign policy advisers. Vance recalled:

> Brown, Brzezinski and I all told the president that he was so far out on a limb that he had to go forward. The implications of backing off, we argued, would be tremendous—U.S. credibility, the president's credibility, his standing as a leader of NATO, here and in Europe, was at stake.
>
> The president did not seem to appreciate the enormous damage to his prestige that would result from backing away from a plan that had been worked out in his name. He was angry that he was committed to ERW production and deployment and said something to the effect of: "I'll be damned if I'll produce this weapon if it's not clear that the Europeans are

going to take it and are prepared to publicly say so. We don't need it—they're the ones who need it—and so why should I go forward and take all the onus for having produced this infamous weapon, if they're not prepared to take their fair share of the opprobrium that's going to be heaped on all of us."

At the close of the meeting Carter finally agreed to consider going ahead with the neutron bomb if Schmidt and Callaghan would give explicit, public statements of support for eventual deployment of the weapon.[6]

Pressuring the President and Keeping the Press from the White House Door (March 20–March 27)

Following the cancellation of the NAC meeting, senior officials in the administration concentrated on the twin goals of reversing the decision and keeping news of it out of the press.

The approach the administration took to the media was summed up by Leslie Gelb as "if anyone asked, there was 'no final decision.' We were trying to stave off the rumors because if everything closed down on us too quickly, there would be no chance to get Carter to look at it again." And as it turned out, during the week following the president's decision to cancel the NAC scenario, the administration was surprisingly successful in shutting down media coverage of the cancellation. The only press coverage of the neutron bomb negotiations that appeared between March 20–27—by veteran Pentagon reporter Charles Corddry—echoed the position Secretary General Luns took on March 20, when he told journalists in Hamburg that he expected a decision on neutron weapons by the U.S. government in late May.[7] Several articles noted Haig's support for neutron weapons (voiced at a Pentagon press conference) but no television, radio, or newspaper, here or abroad, reported Carter's cancellation of the ERW package.

Administration officials had less success, however, in getting Carter to change his mind. On March 21, Vance and Gelb forwarded a note to the president summarizing the dismay and confusion with which the Allies had reacted to the suspension of the ERW negotiations. Gelb also called General Haig to ask him to intercede, but Haig was not too kindly disposed toward Gelb's request. As Gelb summarized:

> Haig didn't see what could be done and I assured him that it would count if he weighed in. In the end I think he sent a message to Dave Jones [chairman, Joint Chiefs of Staff] and left it to Jones to convey his views. I suspected Carter was cancelling but that wasn't something I wanted to admit, because as far as I was concerned it wasn't over yet. Sometime during the week, Brown, Zbig, and Vance would all have a chance to beard at the president and I was confident that they would get him to turn around.

The intervention of Carter's military advisers did not have much impact and Carter's own discussions with foreign leaders seem only to have strengthened his resolve to cancel the bomb. On March 22 Carter discussed his problems with the ERW plan with British Foreign Secretary David Owen and the following day met with British Prime Minister Callaghan. Neither were willing to give Carter the public commitment to deployment he was looking for and Callaghan, according to Carter, was relieved that the president was backing out.[8] On March 24, at a regularly scheduled breakfast with Brzezinski, Vance, and Brown, the president told his advisers he was thinking of sending Deputy Secretary of State Warren Christopher to Bonn to inform Schmidt of his reservations and urge him to make a public commitment to ERW deployment.

"At this point," David Aaron recalled, "the president's natural inclination—that this was neither a particularly important nor attractive weapon—reasserted itself." Harold Brown stated, "the president's personal concern about being associated with this weapon, about being depicted as an ogre, came very strongly to bear at the end." On March 26, while out at Camp David, Carter discussed the subject one more time with Brzezinski, telling him that he wanted to find a "graceful way out." "The president," Brzezinski noted in his journal, "said, in effect, that he did not wish to go through with it; that he had a queasy feeling about the whole thing; that his Administration would be stamped forever as the Administration which introduced bombs that kill people but leave buildings intact."[9] The next morning the president announced to his advisers that he had "decided against any deployment"[10] of the neutron bomb.

Taking the Press Down the Primrose Path (March 27–April 3)

The same morning that the president told his advisers that he was cancelling the neutron bomb, he directed Deputy Secretary of State Warren Christopher to fly to Europe to explain his decision to Schmidt and to find, in Brzezinski's words, "an acceptable formula for implementing his decision."[11] After going to the White House on March 27 to get oral instructions from the president, Christopher departed for Ankara and the president left for a seven-day trip to South America and Africa. Vance, who was also at the meeting with the president, returned to the State Department and asked Gelb to prepare some talking points for Christopher for his meeting with Schmidt. (Christopher had barely had any involvement in the ERW negotiations and needed to be brought up to speed.) Gelb pulled together an interagency team, which, based upon what Gelb recounted from Vance, drafted an instruction cable to Christopher, reportedly stating that "The President has reached [a] judgment not to produce the enhanced radiation weapon" but that Christopher should "tell the Chancellor that the decision is not final. We would like to hear from him."[12] Christopher remembers that the cable "was much harder than the oral and operative instructions I received directly from the president; his instruction was that he was 'inclined to cancel,' rather than 'a decision to cancel has been taken.' "

On March 31, Christopher met with Schmidt to explain the president's intentions. Schmidt, Vance recalled, "was deeply upset. He was unyielding that Germany could not be alone in accepting deployment of ERW on its soil."[13] Schmidt, who was also concerned about a domestic backlash, sent an urgent message to Washington requesting Carter to hold off announcing his decision until Foreign Minister Genscher had visited Washington to give public evidence of Schmidt's commitment to the NATO position. A previously scheduled visit of Genscher's was moved up several days and U.S. officials agreed to delay the cancellation announcement until after Genscher's April 4 visit.[14] Christopher's report of his discussions with Schmidt, along with Schmidt's cable, were sent on April 2 to the president, Vance, and Brzezinski, who were closeted together on Air Force One and were preparing to return home to Washington from Liberia. Carter, however, remained unwilling to go back on his decision to cancel, despite the continued warnings Brzezinski and Vance showered him with on the flight home on April 3.

While the president's advisers continued to meet with limited success in their efforts to change the president's mind, the administration was still having remarkable success in keeping Carter's sudden turnaround out of the news. Whereas during the first week following Carter's cancellation of the ERW scenario (March 20–27) there was no news coverage of his turnaround, during the second week (March 27–April 3) there was a fair share of news coverage, all of which, however, was misleading. On March 27, the same day Christopher had been dispatched to see Schmidt and Carter left for his trip, Richard Burt reported in the *New York Times* that "High ranking Carter Administration officials said today that the Western alliance would soon agree to a plan that would enable the United States to begin producing the controversial neutron bomb later this year."[15] Walter Pincus reported in the *Post* that anonymous sources described the cancellation of the NAC meeting as being part of "a holding pattern."[16] In Europe, the television and news reports were similar, noting that the Carter administration was "on the verge of sanctioning production," while reserving caveats at the end of articles for the "few officials [who] interpret the postponement of the talks as a sign that Mr. Carter has changed his mind and is now moving away from a decision to go ahead."[17] "This was one of those situations," a senior aide to Harold Brown commented, "when what was happening in the government was actually 180° opposite of what you would expect from reading the *New York Times*. During those two weeks after the NAC meeting was cancelled, somebody was telling reporters, particularly Richard Burt, what they wanted them to believe and print in order to put pressure on the president."

Despite missing the news that Carter was cancelling, several reporters did file critical columns on Carter's handling of the neutron bomb affair. On March 31, Rowland Evans and Robert Novak noted, for example, that "President Carter may soon announce the start of production of the neutron [bomb]. . . . Nevertheless, the agonizing indecision that has marked the administration's handling of the neutron is a signal example of superpower leadership succumbing to pedestrian politics."[18] In an April 1 news analysis, Burt stated that the neutron bomb had "left a deep scar in alliance relations, raising doubts about Mr. Carter's decisiveness." He went on to quote various anonymous officials, who described the neutron bomb affair as one that was "as badly handled as any question in recent history'' and who viewed the request for public support for deployment from the Europeans as a ''huge mistake''[19]—echoing, essentially, Burt's own, well-known views on the matter.*

On April 3 Burt finally learned from a ''non-American'' that Carter was cancelling the neutron bomb. Burt's informant had learned of Carter's plan from a senior U.S. official and had mentioned the cancellation to Burt ''in a normal, passing, encounter and more out of bewilderment and shock than out of a desire to get me to write about it. The informant didn't really seem to understand the shock waves that the disclosure would create.'' After receiving his tip, Burt confirmed the story with two NSC staff members and an ISA official at the Pentagon.

On April 4, the morning after Carter and his advisers returned from Africa, and just as Foreign Minister Genscher was arriving in Washington to talk with Carter, the *Times* led the paper with Burt's story under the headline: ''AIDES REPORT CARTER BANS NEUTRON BOMB; SOME SEEK REVERSAL.'' Burt's scoop, which became the day's leading news item, gave an accurate depiction of the previous week's events, stating:

> Administration officials said today that President Carter had decided against producing the controversial neutron bomb.
>
> The officials said that Mr. Carter had acted against the advice of most of his top foreign policy advisers in deciding recently that moving ahead with the weapon ran counter to his goal of nuclear disarmament.
>
> The decision, officials said, was made just before Mr. Carter's departure last week for Latin America and Africa and a formal announcement is expected later this week. In the announcement, Mr. Carter is expected to say that the United States will not produce the weapons and that he expects the Soviet Union to show similar restraint in the deployment of new nuclear weapons. . . .
>
> However, some top Administration officials are said to be hoping that Mr. Carter might be persuaded this week to delay outright cancellation of the weapon and simply announce a decision to defer production indefinitely. In this way, they said, Mr. Carter could leave open the possibility of deploying the neutron weapon at a later date.
>
> But the officials acknowledged that there was only a slim possibility that Mr. Carter would go back on his decision to halt the program.[21]

---

* On March 3, 1978, on *All Things Considered*, Burt commented:

> For the first time, really, this administration has gone to the Europeans and said, ''You make the decision,'' you know, concerning deployment, ''and then we'll tell you what we plan to do concerning production.'' And I think this has put the Europeans in an enormously difficult position. First of all, they've never been used to make these decisions before, but we're asking them to make this decision about an enormously controversial weapon. And I personally think that we're doing it because President Carter, a man who is opposed to nuclear weapons in his rhetoric, finds it enormously difficult himself to initiate—to make a decision on this weapon without letting the Europeans take the heat first. And in this way, I think the neutron bomb has been a badly mishandled, bungled issue.[20]

Damage Control

April 4: Deny, Deny, Deny

At senior-staff levels in the Pentagon and State Department, Burt's article was received with some bemusement as a sign that White House aides, particularly Brzezinski, were leaking the news of Carter's cancellation in order to stir a fuss and build more pressure on the president to adopt an intermediary position (such as deferral). At the White House, however, the story was not considered a laughing matter. Foreign Minister Genscher's plane was touching down for his meeting with the president, and as soon as the story appeared, congressional leaders began calling the President to ask if he was cancelling. According to a source who discussed what happened at the time with both James Schlesinger (Secretary of Energy) and Jody Powell, that morning

> . . . there was a meeting hastily convened at the White House before Genscher arrived with Brzezinski, Schlesinger, and Jody Powell. They talked about what to do about the story—Brzezinski was upset by it, coming as it did in a pressurized atmosphere—and they decided to deny it. Schlesinger and Brzezinski wanted to deny the story because they felt the furor that would be created by it would create a backlash and give them another chance to reverse the decision or at least change it somehow. Schlesinger and Brzezinski didn't so much say, "Let's try to change the president's decision"; it was more, "We haven't announced a decision yet so let's deny this."

Immediately after the White House meeting, Powell denied the story and directed State and the Pentagon to do the same—an order which was acceded to gladly, given the support for ERW at both departments. By mid-afternoon, Vance and Hodding Carter, as well as Powell had all told the press that "no decision had been made"[22] by the president to cancel the neutron bomb, and the next day Harold Brown and Klaus Boelling (Schmidt's spokesman) did the same. The president himself told majority leader Senator Byrd on April 4 that he had not made a decision and the following day told the rest of the congressional leadership the same thing. Powell's April 5 press conference was typical of the administration's criticism of the story:

Q: Did the President reach a decision?

MR. POWELL: The President has not made a final decision on the neutron bomb. Reports to the contrary simply are erroneous. Warren Christopher went to Bonn. He spoke with the German Government there. He informed them at that time that the President had not made a final decision. . . . The president's assessment . . . was delivered to the German government, and their response and what I would term the proper spirit of consultation was requested. . . .

Q: The headlines on this yesterday in the *New York Times* and the *Washington Star*—are you saying they were totally erroneous or were they only partially erroneous?

MR. POWELL: I have never seen a totally accurate headline. (Laughter)[23]

The unequivocal denial of Burt's story by administration officials was almost immediately reflected in the news coverage, which raised questions about the accuracy of Burt's story and the motives of his sources. On the April 4 midday news, CBS Pentagon correspondent Ike Pappas reported:

> Pentagon sources told CBS News the President has made no decision yet on production of the controversial neutron bomb, and the *Times* report, at this point, at least, simply is not true. The *Times* story was described as a probable leak by opponents of the bomb within the Administration, in an attempt to further influence public opinion against the bomb, and therefore perhaps sway the President to reject it. One possibility cited is that President Carter will decide to defer but not cancel production of the bomb.[24]

Anonymous administration officials continued to cast doubt on the ulterior motives of Burt's sources—the *Philadelphia Inquirer,* for example, reported in its morning edition that "well-placed sources say the [Burt] story apparently was leaked to the *New York Times* by an official who did not want the President to change his judgment [to cancel]"[25]—and by the evening of April 5, all three networks were reporting that administration officials had said a decision had not been reached.

In addition to actively seeking to discredit Burt's story, administration officials also sought to portray decisionmaking within the administration as open and soul-searching. One source was quoted in a Walter Pincus story as saying that there was a "genuine reappraisal"[26] going on in the administration, and another "senior official" was cited in the *Baltimore Sun* as saying that Carter's decision making "was not a sham reconsideration."[27] However, the most extreme expression of "the official argument," as *New York Times* reporter Hedrick Smith later put it, was "that rather than showing a tendency by Mr. Carter to vacillate on tough issues, all these fits and starts had a tactical purpose. By taking a hard line, officials say, the President sought to draw the West Germans into firmer support of the neutron warhead."[28]

April 5, 6: The Pressure Builds on the President

Although the administration enjoyed some success in establishing that the president had not decided to cancel the neutron bomb, the news that the president was seriously considering cancellation was enough to provoke tremendous outcry. The day the Burt story appeared, majority leader Senator Byrd called to ask Carter if he was cancelling and urged him not to on the grounds that it might "be seen as surrender to the Russians' massive propaganda campaign."[29] In a TV interview, minority leader Senator Baker termed cancellation "a very, very bad mistake, and another in a long line of mistakes that seriously affect the national defense of this country . . . [this] will have a very serious effect on the prospects for the ratification of any SALT treaty."[30] The following day sixty-one members of the House, who had voted against the bomb, sent Carter a letter urging him to stick to his decision to cancel and "withstand the efforts to reverse it that you will encounter in the coming days."[31]

Outside of Congress, there was strong criticism of the president's decision, particularly from leading Republicans, such as former president Gerald Ford, Ronald Reagan, and George Bush, who took turns proclaiming the significance of neutron weapons. Gerald Ford, for example, told a Republican fundraiser that, "The controversy that has erupted over the neutron bomb, coming as it does after the cancellation of the B–1 and after the reports that the Navy is being gutted by the Carter administration budget, arouses profound concern among all of us,"[32] adding that the neutron bomb was "highly essential . . . [and] the safety of Western Europe and the preservation of Western culture depend on [deploying] it."[33]

In addition to Congress and the Republicans getting into the act, the nation's leading newspapers rushed to judgment in the two days that followed the appearance of Burt's story. The tenor of the comments, with the exception of the *St. Louis-Post Dispatch* and *Newsday* (which reiterated their support for cancellation), was unsparing, despairing, and tinged with mock horror over the role of the media. Two examples should suffice:

> *Wall Street Journal:* The [Burt] report has to be described as frightening. . . . The truly scary thing, if the report proves true, is that the President has turned aside his top advisers and bought the arguments of the flaky left. There are no serious arguments against the deployment of this weapon. . . .

> *Dallas Morning News:* It would be charitable to suppose that high administration officials, through a leak to the *Times,* are hoping to marshal support for the bomb. But what if the *Times* story is essentially right and President Carter really does mean to ban the bomb as a hindrance to nuclear disarmament? It would mean that the commander in chief had taken perhaps the most naive and unsupportable position of his presidency.

Virtually every major newspaper that commented on the administration's handling of the issue urged Carter to do no less than defer neutron bomb production, using the bomb as a bargaining chip in arms control negotiations with the Russians. So complete was the editorial turnaround that even the *Washington Post* wrote that Carter seemed "to have let the choice [to cancel or proceed] be framed by others for him. [It] now seems to us he really needs to make a forthright, no-nonsense decision to proceed, with a view to negotiating the weapons out [later]."[34] Not to be outdone by the editorial page, Walter Pincus was also disappointed by and disapproved of Carter's decision. Musing over a conversation he had with Pincus at the time, Harold Brown recalled: "Pincus was appalled at what happened, although he didn't take any responsibility himself. I remember he asked, 'Gee, why didn't you trade it away?' The answer, of course, was that his articles had made sure that the president could never trade it away—he could only give it away."*

It is not clear exactly how this public maelstrom of criticism affected Carter,

---

* Pincus explained that, "By the time Carter killed the bomb—he did it so stupidly—that it had become a political issue, and I think a better decision would have been to build them and leave them in the U.S. I was just appalled at how Carter handled it; there was less problem posed by building [ERW] and sending them over, than in the damage he had done to the Alliance."

although the circumstantial evidence indicates that the president decided to seek a deferral of the neutron bomb (linked to arms control)—rather than cancellation—within a few hours of the appearance of the Burt story. Immediately after the Burt story appeared—at which point the president had considered but was apparently still rejecting the deferral scheme*—the president met with German Foreign Minister Genscher. Carter's April 4 diary entry states that, "It became obvious during the discussion between [Genscher], me, Cy, and Zbig that the Germans are playing footsie with us on the ER weapons. They want us to announce production; they will deploy them only if another European country agrees to deploy." Carter then goes on to note: "We finally decided that after two or three days I would announce that we were deferring the decision, and then the options would be predicated on European acceptance of deployment—a determination that the ER weapon is the best way to spend the money, better than ground launched cruise missiles or laser-guided antitank missiles—and predicated on the fact that the Soviets don't cooperate on MBFR, comprehensive test ban, on SALT."[36] Following the morning meeting, Vance, Brown, Brzezinski, Hamilton Jordan, and Powell met in the afternoon to draft an announcement for Carter outlining the decision, and the following afternoon Carter went over the statement with Brown, Brzezinski, and Vance.

Carter's seemingly abrupt shift from cancellation to deferral was subsequently portrayed in some quarters, including the press, as having been caused by the appearance of Burt's story. Several days after the announcement, Burt wrote, for example, that "Mr. Carter is said to have argued [on the April 3 return flight from Africa] that postponing production would only exacerbate the political problems surrounding the weapon . . . White House officials now say this congressional show of support for the weapon [provoked by the April 4 report], together with newspaper editorials backing it, bolstered the arguments of Mr. Brzezinski and others who pressed for keeping the project alive."[37] Similarly, Walter Pincus begrudingly reported on April 5 that "proponents of the weapons within the administration tried to develop a plan to get Carter to reverse his latest position [to cancel]. Disclosure by the *New York Times* of Carter's decision may have accomplished that."[38]

White House aides, however, denied that the President showed any special sensitivity to news reports or the potentially deliberate use of leaks by administration officials to influence him. David Aaron argued that Carter's "decision making in the last week wasn't swayed by press coverage, as evidenced by the *New York Times* and *Washington Post* coming out in favor of deployment at the same time he was canceling. The Burt story didn't push the president towards the middle of the road; the position of the various actors and the need to figure out something that wouldn't hang the Europeans out to dry did."

---

* Right before the meeting with Genscher, Brzezinski sent the president a memo urging Carter to defer production, link future production to Soviet arms control, and in two years be prepared to produce and deploy the weapon. Carter sent the memo back to Brzezinski with the notation: "Zbig, I must say that you never give up."[35]

Whether or not Burt's story was the determinative factor underlying the president's change of mind, Brzezinski, at least, felt the fuss stirred by the story abetted the presentation of the case for deferral. In his journal on April 5 (the day after the Burt story appeared and was denied), Brzezinski noted that he had told the president a decision to cancel would "affect the credibility of his leadership and will sow dissension within the alliance and negative congressional reactions. By the time the day was up, all of that was happening."[39] When asked point blank whether the Burt story, and the reaction to it, made the president shift his stand, Brzezinski commented, "I think there may be something to that, but you'd have to ask the president to be sure."

Packaging and Presenting the President's Decision

Carter and his advisors, in the aftermath of the furor stirred by the Burt story, were worried about the announcement of the president's decision and sought to package the deferral in a way that would minimize dissension in the Alliance, minimize criticism of Carter as weak and vacillating, and maximize the difference between Burt's "incorrect" report of cancellation and the new strategy to defer. "The president understood," David Aaron recalled, "and was forewarned that there would be a press and foreign backlash over this decision. . . . In fact, the president foresaw that this would go very hard in Germany for Schmidt and had Schmidt told that he could lay the blame off on him." To minimize dissension within the Alliance, Carter directed both Brzezinski and Powell (somewhat to their chagrin), to not mention the FRG's deployment conditions as one of his chief reasons for backing out. "In all our press backgrounders," Brzezinski recalled, "we were unable to describe fully the history of the problem or to explain how the issue came to a head. To protect Schmidt and Allied unity, Carter thus paid a high personal price."[40]

Although Carter felt he was less vulnerable to domestic criticism than Schmidt, he and his advisers were still determined to cut off any criticism they could of the president for being indecisive. On April 5, the president went over the April 7 announcement (that would be released under his name), and which had been personally drafted by his most senior advisers. "Our aim in drafting the statement," Harold Brown summarized, "was twofold. First, to keep the program going rather than cancelling it, and second to minimize the appearance that we had just executed a complete about-face." Accordingly, the statement (see Appendix C), was drafted so that is left open the possibility of eventually producing the ERW, dependent on Soviet good behavior. Carter's advisers gamely informed reporters that this "put the monkey back on the Russians' backs"[41] and demonstrated, as Brzezinski commented at the April 7 backgrounder, "that if we do go to production and deployment in the future, it will be quite clear to all political factions within the Alliance, and indeed to the entire world, that this decision to produce and deploy this weapon was only made in the presence of a failure on the part of the Soviet Union to show . . . restraint in arms programs and deployments."[42]

The strategy for the White House was twofold: first, to have Carter's decision seen as a genuine deferral, rather than a cover for cancellation, so that he could not be accused of backing away from the defense of Western Europe; and second, to have it understood that Carter had changed his position only once, and then only slightly—from yes to maybe—rather than flip-flopping twice, from going ahead to cancelling to defering. One consequence of the administration's effort to portray the president's decision as consistent and forceful was that White House aides decided again, to deny that the president had ever intended to cancel the bomb when they released his April 7 statement. At the press backgrounder that day, Brzezinski commented that he spoke "in the context of persistent rumors and reports that a decision had been made over the past several days, despite our repeated statement that it had not. And I think finally with the statement from the president, it was clear that we were accurate in our statement that it had not been made. . . . There has been only one presidential decision on this matter, and that is the one we announced today.''[43] Despite the presence of Richard Burt at the briefing (who was by now seething with rage), Jody Powell added: "You are well aware of the necessity for us making it very clear that no final decision has been made over the past several days, and that is because it had been extensively and erroneously reported that there had been a final decision. . . . I can't accept responsibility for bad reporting. I think I know how it happened. I think it happened in good faith, but it happened to be wrong."*[44]

Insofar as the issue was covered, the administration largely succeeded, much to Burt's chagrin, in discrediting his report that the president had planned to cancel. Both *Time* and *Newsweek* described Burt's report as inaccurate on the basis of information obtained either from anonymous or White House sources[45] (allegedly Powell, Hamilton Jordan, and Warren Christopher). *Time,* which labeled Burt's story a "false report,"[46] went so far as to have one "top presidential aide" observe wistfully about all the fuss over the president's decision: "I suppose it's in the nature of the presidency that we have to take responsibility for an inaccurate leak."[47] With the exception of columnists Evans and Novak, no reporter appears to have challenged the administration's denial.**

The administration also successfully secured official support for Carter's position from the NATO allies. As previously arranged, NATO Secretary General Luns read a communique after the NATO council meeting supporting the president's decision (consisting of language that was virtually identical to the President's statement). In London, Callaghan issued a statement supportive of the decision, calling upon the Soviets to restrain their arms build up, and in

---

* At the conclusion of the briefing, an angry Burt, who had never met Powell, cornered him in the hallway to express his displeasure with the White House campaign against his story. Powell ushered Burt into his office and successfully disarmed him, reportedly by explaining in a friendly tone how much trouble Burt's story had caused for the administration during the week. Burt said later he felt he had "learned something from the experience: what Jody was saying was that when you're protecting the president, all is fair in love and war."

** Evans and Novak reported that "what finally persuaded [Carter] to announce his decision last Friday to 'defer' production—instead of cancel it outright—was not [his senior] advisers but the firestorm of criticism in the *New York Times,* the *Washington Post,* and other influential papers."[48]

Bonn, the government spokesman issued a similar statement. Outside the official channels, however, all, for the administration, was chaos.

Carter's Reputation Hits the Fan

Although the administration succeeded in attaining some of its lesser objectives in the aftermath of Carter's decision—such as discrediting Burt's story and obtaining official NATO support—it failed abysmally to secure its larger objectives; i.e., portraying Carter as a decisive leader committed to military modernization, and minimizing dissent in the Alliance. With the exception of the expression of official NATO support (and a few comments from congressmen who had led the fight against the ERW), the reaction to Carter's decision was almost uniformly negative. And with the exception of some commentary by Robert Pierpoint (on CBS News and "Washington Week"), and perhaps, *Time*'s story, coverage of the neutron bomb decision gave little credence to the supposed "advantages" of Carter's approach, enumerated by Brzezinski in his backgrounder unveiling the deferral.

Immediately following the announcement of Carter's decision, proponents of increased defense in Congress hammered on the president for skimping on national defense and weakening the NATO alliance. Criticism from this sector even included observations from Democrats:

> Senator Henry Jackson (D-Wash.): "I do not think it is very logical to think the Soviets would negotiate away a weapons system [the SS–20] they have in production, for a weapon that we do not have [the] courage to produce";[49]
>
> Senator Robert Byrd (D-W. Va.): "A decision not to produce the neutron warhead would likely jeopardize Senate approval [of SALT]";[50]

with more of the same coming from other congressmen. At the same time, no official or reporter—with the exception of Charles Corddry of the *Baltimore Sun*[51]—highlighted the ironic fact that Carter's planned modernization of the artillery shells (the non-ER version of the Lance and 8 inch) would result in producing weapons more destructive than the infamous "neutron bomb."

Even more telling than the criticism from the "hawks" was the widespread perception of presidential weakness and indecisiveness coveyed by the decision. "It just seems to some of us," Senator Robert Dole (R-Kan.) commented, "that [this] follows his indecision on everything else, and it must leave some of our friends wondering what the final decision may bring, and if there will be a final decision."[52] "[This] can only worsen perceptions of U.S. unreliability," former undersecretary of State George Ball commented.[53] In Europe, the commentary was similar, particularly from the leaders of opposition parties. Franz Josef Strauss, leader of the CSU opposition in Germany, stated that Carter's decision marked the first time since World War II when the U.S. "President had heeled before the Russian Czar."[54] In Britain, the shadow defense secretary of the Tories stated that, "it now seems the Kremlin has virtually the right of veto over weapons [for] NATO."[55]

Joining the chorus of criticism was the press itself. With the exception of a handful of editorials approving the decision, article after article scored Carter for being vacillating and incompetent.* Typical of the coverage—which was stiffly criticized in the *Columbia Journalism Review***—was the headline in the *Economist:* "I'VE CHANGED MY MIND, I THINK." Although Carter was not singled out by the European media for criticism—Schmidt also came under heavy attack—the theme of presidential incompetence was much the same. Typical of the coverage was an AP dispatch from Paris which stated that Carter's actions had led European officials and the European media to "express doubts about his grasp of foreign affairs."[57] Summing up the impact of Carter's decision, Brzezinski wrote in his memoirs that the neutron bomb controversy marked one of

> . . . five major foreign policy turning points [for the Carter Administration]—each requiring either a basic shift in strategy or generating consequences of great significance to the [U.S.]. . . . The neutron bomb affair was a major setback in U.S.–European relations, particularly in our relations with West Germany. The President's credibility was damaged in Europe and at home, and personal relations between Carter and Schmidt took a further turn for the worse and never recovered.[58]

Passing the Buck

In the ferment that followed Carter's announcement, few officials stepped forward to publicly defend the president. Carter himself did not comment on the decision for almost a month, and Harold Brown—who appeared on *Face the Nation* on April 9—was the only senior administration official who defended Carter's decision in a visible, public forum in the immediate aftermath of the decision. Instead, key parts of the administration became absorbed in an internecine and international struggle over who bore responsibility for the neutron bomb "fiasco." At the State Department, a rumor swept through the EUR and PM bureaus that State was going to be blamed for what had happened. Gelb recalled that, "Ham [Jordan] and Jody [Powell] put out the story to the press that the State Department . . . in particular Les Gelb, had given the Europeans too much of their way in the negotiations. . . . Vance flatly instructed me to let it go, to let the White House dump it on us."

At the White House, there was a growing tension between the NSC and State that made for fertile ground for the "dumping" Gelb referred to. Brzezinski was becoming increasingly suspicious of Gelb and Hodding Carter's role in

---

* See, for example, William Beecher, "Behind the Neutron Indecision," *Boston Globe,* April 7, 1978, p. 2.

** Roger Morris, a former NSC aide, argued, among other points in the *Review,* that

> In a subject shrouded by bureaucratic politics, Carter's handling of the neutron bomb issue was uniformly reported, and editorially tried and sentenced, largely on unexamined assumptions taken directly from the original leak and leaker(s). . . . By surrendering initiative and interpretation to their sources, the *Times* and the *Post* from the outset became themselves central participants in the manipulative politics of the episode, their prestige increasingly invested in the thrust of the original stories.[56]

ongoing bureaucratic infighting, and on the April 3 flight home from Africa on Air Force One had asked Hodding Carter why anonymous State Department officials kept leaking critical stories about him. Carter explained that he could not keep an eye on all 7,000 employees at the State Department, to which Brzezinski coolly retorted: "I don't think reporters are getting their stories from the janitors there."[59] Later in the flight, Brzezinski mentioned to Vance, with Hodding Carter present, that cancelling the neutron bomb "would be the worst presidential decision of the first fourteen months." "To my chagrin," Brzezinski recalled, "that comment, which I made only on that occasion, appeared in the very next issue of a weekly news magazine [*Newsweek*'s cover story], thereby deepening my suspicions regarding Hodding Carter's conduct."[60]

Even more consequential than the internal squabbling within the administration was the internal feuding with Schmidt that erupted after Carter's decision was released. Schmidt's aides, and reportedly Schmidt himself, did not share Carter's reticence to refrain from blaming one another and embarked almost immediately on an unusually bitter campaign—all through anonymous sources—to discredit Carter. For example, Theo Summer, editor of *Der Zeit* and a columnist for *Newsweek*'s international edition (in addition to being a well-known confidant of Schmidt's and regular participant in the chancellor's "brain-storming" sessions in Hamburg), wrote an acerbic column for *Newsweek* in which he stated that Carter's White House

> . . . strikes observers overseas as sloppy, confused, haphazard—unexplained and probably inexplicable. . . . [Carter] has made fools not only of NATO's military leaders, but also of important political partners, and he did so precisely at a time when Schmidt, for one, has decided to forego further public bickering. The result is a dangerous erosion of confidence in the Carter Administration. It seems bent on proving to the world that it is possible to lose friends without influencing one's enemies.[61]

In Germany, similar information about the chancellor's purported views were "leaked" to the press. The widely read magazine *Der Spiegel* reported, for example, that Schmidt saw Carter as "an unfathomable amateur who tries to stamp his private morals on world politics but in reality is incapable of fulfilling his role as leader of the West."[62]

At the White House, there was some initial reluctance to engage in this sort of guerrilla warfare. "Nobody," Hodding Carter recalled, "could decide whether it was best to pee on Schmidt before he peed on you, or vice versa." Jody Powell, however, kept urging the president "to let me and others do a number on Schmidt because he was blaming it all on Carter. I wanted to point out that this great agreement Schmidt was saying we had abrogated was nothing more than an agreement not to object to us producing the warheads." The president apparently acceded to Powell's request (Powell says he would have been "disinclined to take pot shots at the government of another country without [the president's] approval"), for shortly after the April 7 announcement, numerous press and television news reports appeared citing the deployment conditions imposed by the West Germans as a stumbling block.

As relations between Schmidt and Carter reached a new low, Harold Brown flew to Bonn on April 13 to discuss the neutron bomb crisis (as well as several other matters) with Schmidt. During the course of their private conversation, Schmidt told Brown that he might have been able to give public support to the neutron bomb as early as January 1978, were it not for what he saw to be Carter's ambiguity about producing the weapon; Schmidt was particularly struck, he related to Brown, by Carter's fear (voiced in their September phone conversation) of being depicted as an "ogre." Brown, who was anxious to ease tensions, urged Schmidt to call Carter to convey the news that the Bundestag had voted to support Carter and Schmidt's position on ERW, and to assure Carter that the guerrilla warfare being waged in the press would stop. (Following a forty-minute statement to the Bundestag that morning by Schmidt, and subsequent heated debate, the Bundestag voted 240–224 to make the neutron warhead a subject for arms control talks and to defer its production and deployment.) In the early afternoon, Carter received a call from Schmidt, notes of which indicate their discussion went something like this:

> SCHMIDT: Jimmy, I have been worried by press comments alleging differences between our two countries. I want to assure you that myself and my aides will not contribute to the invention of such "leakages," which are not leaks at all but most often are just made up.
>
> CARTER: We have an uncontrolled press here, too. My confidence is in you, and if I see any stories that give me cause for concern, I'll call you directly. In the absence of a call, be sure that I have no concern.
>
> SCHMIDT: The same is true for me. Secretary Brown is here and asked me to mention that to you. We just finished talking, and he is going to meet with the press. He wanted me to tell you that he will not make any mistakes! [Laughter]
>
> CARTER: Thank you. I appreciate your support. I think we should now put the enhanced radiation weapons issue behind us for a while. . . . I look forward to the [upcoming NATO] Summit and to being in your country. I'm proud of our friendship. You've been superb. Your friendship means a great deal, more than you can know.

Schmidt and Carter's rapprochement seems to have been quite temporary. Writing in his memoirs about the phone discussion, Carter noted with some bitterness: "In spite of [his] private assurances, Helmut subsequently complained to many listeners that the United States had unilaterally aborted the plans to produce and deploy neutron weapons. The fact is that to this day no European government has been willing to agree to their deployment."[63]

Epilogue: Fallout from the Neutron Bomb

In October 1978, half a year after Carter's decision to defer production of neutron warheads was released, the White House announced that Carter had decided to authorize production of some critical components of the ERW. The announcement received little press coverage in the U.S., partly because administration spokesmen acknowledged that it would take at least a year to build a working neutron warhead, even once some of the critical components were built. In Europe, the announcement stirred a rancorous debate in the Dutch parliament, but generally received little attention, since administration officials had indicated there were no plans for European deployment.

Although attention to the neutron bomb faded dramatically following Carter's announcement, the controversy that the warheads engendered subsequently had a profound impact on intermediate range nuclear force (INF) modernization in Europe. By April 1978, internal debate over how and whether to proceed with INF modernization had been going on in NATO and in the U.S. for about half a year. The neutron bomb announcement, according to some accounts, effectively forced U.S. officials to proceed with INF.

Harold Brown emphasized that the neutron bomb controversy had a profound impact on both European planners and U.S. officials:

> The neutron bomb furor created a determination both here and in Europe to never let anything else important unravel and tended to hold the Alliance together. The catastrophic outcome of the debate shook European confidence in the U.S. determination to defend and deter war in Europe in a way that would have made it much harder for the U.S. to tell the Europeans that we really didn't need to modernize INF. Before the neutron bomb affair, it might have been possible to convince them that existing U.S. forces could balance the Soviet buildup. Afterwards, it wasn't.

In addition to spurring the decision to proceed with INF, the neutron bomb episode was widely recognized within the government to have powerfully influenced the manner in which U.S. and NATO officials presented the INF improvements. State Department aide Lou Finch commented: "We had a very well-organized, very activist public relations campaign on INF, attributed almost entirely to the failure to deal with the neutron bomb. I switched over to the Pentagon during 1979 and I would say that I had two or three reporters a day come in to talk about INF. We also had people on the outside, like Henry Kissinger, making speeches supporting the need for this." Jim Thomson of the NSC staff added: "The NSC . . . really took charge on INF; we also keep the Allies and the president continuously informed about things, and had the president check off boxes periodically so there was no doubt as to where he stood." Following this carefully choreographed consultation, NATO announced in December 1979 that it had agreed to the deployment of the modernized INF missiles.

While the INF deployments have moved to center stage in recent years, the neutron bomb has, periodically, continued to attract attention. In August of 1981, the Reagan administration announced that it was going to produce neutron warheads for the Lance and 8-inch shell but that there were no plans to deploy the weapons in Europe (except at the Allies' request). This decision sparked a flurry of protest in Europe which, unlike the 1977–78 controversy over the bomb, receded quickly. The decreased sensitivity of the bomb appears to be partially attributable to the vigorous counter public relations campaign mounted by the administration. On August 10, the day after news of Reagan's production decision was published in the *New York Times,* Secretary of Defense Caspar Weinberger defended the decision at a Pentagon press conference and in six television interviews. The following day an article by Weinberger on the same subject appeared in the *Washington Post,* and two days later Reagan emerged from his vacation at Santa Barbara to sign the budget reconciliation bill and comment on the "propaganda drive" that the Soviets had mounted over the neutron bomb.

What Difference Did the Press Make?

In assessing the impact that the press coverage of the neutron bomb and the controversy over the bomb itself had on subsequent events, Carter administration officials most often cited reawakening the dormant European antinuclear movement. "The neutron bomb had a tremendous effect in Europe," Les Gelb remarked. "With the neutron bomb debate it became clear that we were dealing with a new kind of Europe, one in which all nuclear issues had greater political significance." The European peace movement itself has generously acknowledged the benefit it derived from the neutron bomb. Promotional folders, for example, produced by the Interchurch Peace Council (IKV)—the largest and most powerful antinuclear group in The Netherlands—state, "It must be kept in mind that the year IKV launched its campaign [to rid the Netherlands of nuclear weapons], 1977, was also the year of the Neutron bomb."[1]

German professor Dr. Hans Günter Brauch has also pointed out that the dramatic quality of the press coverage was particularly instrumental in prompting Europeans to reconsider the value of nuclear weapons. "The neutron weapon," Brauch writes, "rekindled the fears and emotions of the people in many countries, becoming a symbol of the 'perversion of thought.' . . . For the first time since the public campaigns in the 1950s and 1960s against the radiation effects of atmospheric nuclear testing, public awareness of the effects of modern weapons of mass destruction became a powerful ally of the arms control community."[2] Perhaps most importantly, the neutron bomb controversy provided vital nourishment for the disarmament movement because it seemed to offer fresh testimony to the effectiveness of public protest. "I think the European peace movement felt they tasted blood with the neutron bomb," Harold Brown commented, "because it was the first time that the U.S. had been pushed away from a decision involving nuclear weapons by, in part, public activists."

As the antinuclear movement in Europe has grown, debate over nuclear weapons, not surprisingly, has also become more public. "The media coverage of the neutron bomb," Don Cotter claims, "opened up the whole box in Europe—everything has to be brought out in the open now and Europeans are antsy about any nuclear instrument." As a consequence, Cotter believes that "the media is undermining our nuclear deterrent." At a 1982 conference at The Hague, Harold Brown assessed the same phenomenon in a more positive way: "In the future, political leaders and governments will have to pay more attention in defining and articulating their nuclear policies, to reestablishing and sustaining public support and confidence. . . . . The debate will have to be carried out in public at a level comprehensible to publics and to conclusions they can afterwards support.''[3]

One dramatic measure of the change of attitude among senior policymakers toward selling nuclear weapons is that the Reagan administration has set up a cabinet-level interagency group (formalized by National Security Decision Document 77) for the sole purpose of coordinating the administration's public relations abroad, with special emphasis on obtaining more favorable media coverage and influencing younger Europeans to adopt sympathetic attitudes toward the presence of nuclear weapons and U.S. nuclear policy in Europe.[4] Reporting to that group is a special planning team which was established to develop a public relations strategy to sell the INF deployments in Europe.* Similarly, USIA, which was almost entirely uninvolved during the neutron bomb imbroglio, is actively countering Soviet propaganda over INF deployment and has, for example, paid Georgetown's Ethics and Public Policy Center roughly $200,000, reportedly to promote both the views of Europeans who support U.S. nuclear policy, and to offset the views of the European peace movement (which, according to the grant agreement, has been ''inflamed by the media'').[5]

While the neutron bomb episode forced decisionmaking about nuclear weapons out more into the open, many academic and other commentators expressed reservations about whether the public debate had really improved matters.** As Major General Key, Cotter's Deputy at OSD in 1977, argued:

> An article like Pincus's took the discussion out of the private room in which the NATO ministers met, spread it throughout the whole universe of Europe, and denied the ministers flexibility. Whereas before the appearance of the article, they felt they could sit down and rationally analyze nuclear issues, after the article appeared, they were cast in the role of responding defensively to an emotional reaction.

Even Walter Pincus was concerned about the quality of debate that followed the appearance of his articles:

> I wanted to open up a debate about the role of battlefield nuclear artillery and that got lost among the other issues; funding, who was a winner and loser, and so on.
>
> The articles did raise legitimate concern about nuclear weapons but the debate got out of hand once the Soviets picked it up. On both sides of the

---

* On a similar P.R. campaign in Canada, see Jacquie Miller, "Federal Campaign Seeks to Counter Cruise Protests," *Ottawa Citizen*, May 12, 1983, p. 1. For thoughts about P.R. strategy in Britain, see "Heseltine's Briefing to Thatcher on Cruise Timing," *Manchester Guardian*, October 31, 1983, p. 2.

** Most academics have since been quite critical of the effect of the neutron bomb controversy on subsequent debate. See, for example, Deborah Shapley, "The Media and National Security," *Daedalus*, Fall 1982, p. 204; Colin S. Gray, "NATO Strategy and the 'Neutron Bomb,' " *Policy Review*, Winter 1979, p. 24; Milton Leitenberg, "The Neutron Bomb—Enhanced Radiation Warheads," *Journal of Strategic Studies* 5:3 (September 1982), pp. 341–363; Edward Luttwak, "Tactical Advance," *New Republic*, September 16, 1983, p. 12; and Lothar Ruehl, "The Media and the Image of Defence Policy," *Adelphi Papers*, #182, 1983, p. 41.

fence now people just don't deal with the issue rationally. On the one hand, you have this enormous peace movement in Europe marching against [Reagan's] decision to build the neutron and store it here, while at the same time they show absolutely no concern about the 8-inch warheads currently in Europe—it's as if they didn't exist! They're higher yield, less useful, unsafe, they're crazy.

On the other hand, you have administration officials, who leave the 8-inch over there. Here's a weapon they've already marked as unusable, inaccurate, high collateral damage, the whole schmear; you'd think they'd remove them on their own volition and score some credit with the peace movement. Similarly, the shells currently in Europe lack new safety features that would make it impossible for terrorists to use them. Those shells, which are most vulnerable and most need the modernized safety features, will be the last to be replaced. Meanwhile, the shells stored on American military bases—are also the safe, modernized ones. That's typical of the irrationality of the whole debate.

Did the Press Kill the Bomb?

There remains, finally, the question of whether the press stopped the neutron bomb from being produced and deployed. The consensus among scholars who have commented on the subject seems to be that the media were crucial.[6] Harold Brown told columnist Phil Geyelin that, "Without the Pincus articles, they [the neutron warheads] would have been deployed and nobody would have noticed."[7] Yet if Brown is right, it is not because the press turned the U.S. public against the bomb. American public opinion polls on the bomb reveal that the *more* news American received about the neutron bomb, the *more likely* they were to support it. An August / September 1977 Roper poll found, for example, that the one quarter of the public who had "read or heard a lot" about the neutron bomb favored it 48 percent to 38 percent, while the three quarters who said they had given little or no attention to news about the neutron bomb opposed it 49 percent to 23 percent. The same correlation held true among various population groups: men, who claimed to be more conversant with the bomb, were more supportive than women; more of the college educated were both attentive and supportive than those with lower levels of education, as were those with higher incomes and executive / professional jobs. Summing up the poll data, Hodding Carter wrote in an April 3, 1978 memorandum: "Most of the public has not paid much attention to news about producing neutron bombs, but tended to oppose the idea. On the other hand, the one fourth of the public who claimed to have followed the issue closely tended to favor production."*

---

* The only published (and translated) opinion polls of European attitudes toward the neutron bomb taken during 1977 and 1978 indicate that in the Netherlands—which had the most widespread and fiercest anti-ERW movement in Europe—about half the population believed the ERW should not be produced, and one third thought its production should be stopped so long as the Soviets showed restraint. When asked about the difference between neutron weapons and other nuclear weapons, 61% said neutron weapons were no worse than other nuclear weapons and only 28% considered the ERW worse. (Seven percent said the ERW was a better weapon.)[8]

The second related fact revealed by the polls is that it was during the period when there was barely any press coverage of the neutron bomb that the American public shifted its position on the bomb to modest opposition. A *New York Times /* CBS poll taken in July 1977, right after the Senate vote on ERW, and at the height of the sensational media coverage, reported that one third of the U.S. public knew enough about the neutron bomb to form an opinion, and that third was split evenly for and against production.[9] However, polls taken at the end of August 1977—when there was virtually no media coverage—by both Roper and President Carter's private pollster Patrick Caddell, revealed, respectively, that pluralities of 46 percent and 49 percent then opposed production of the bomb.[10] In an April 1978 Harris Poll taken shortly after Carter's decision was announced, a plurality of Americans still opposed production.[11] Insofar that the public held a discernable view about production of the bomb, Carter's actions during 1977 and 1978 appear to have matched public sentiment and met with the support of a plurality of Americans. There was never widespread or bitter opposition to producing the bomb in the U.S.

The fact that the American public largely supported Carter's position raises questions about the nature of the press impact. The vocal criticism of Carter's decision that appeared in the press ran well ahead of the public's view. One way of looking at what happened is to think of the press and officials as having participated in a kind of insider's game in which they used each other to reaffirm dismay over Carter's decision making. In that view it was the way the story was reported which made the difference. David Gompert, Gelb's deputy, commented, for example, that:

> The failure to deploy the weapon resulted not only from the fact that its existence became public, but the way it became public. If somebody had printed an article that said, "The U.S., as part of a long-standing modernization program of nuclear weapons in Europe, is about to begin production of a low-yield nuclear weapon, designed to kill enemy soldiers in Russian tanks through radiation, at the same time reducing collateral damage from blast in civilian areas"—i.e., if somebody had given completely flat, accurate publicity to the program—the article would have received some attention but not had a dramatic impact.

Jody Powell also voiced concern over the message behind the message. "The neutron bomb fueled what came to be two of our biggest problems in Washington: the appearance of indecisiveness and the notion that Carter was weak on defense."

Government officials' *perceptions* of the press / public opinion nexus seem to have played a more decisive role in preventing deployment than public opinion itself. It is clear, for example, that Schmidt, Callaghan, and Carter—the latter with his fear of being depicted as an "ogre"—found the image of the bomb projected in the media to be a critical stumbling block. Some senior Carter officials, however, contend that the coverage was a necessary but not sufficient goad to stopping ERW production and deployment, and that it was the president's personal views that counted the most. Neutron warheads, they point out, are currently being produced despite public controversy, and they could have been deployed by now in Europe if the president had not backed out. As Zbigniew Brzezinski said:

> Whether the press stimulated Carter to retreat, I'm not sure but I doubt it. He was concerned about being seen as an international ogre and the way it would play in Europe, but I think that reflected as much his general feelings about nuclear weapons—he had almost quasi religious feelings on the subject—as concern with specific press stories. His uneasiness was amplified, I think, by the fact that this was early in the administration and he was being asked to assume responsibility for introducing a somewhat novel type of nuclear weapon. So while the appearance of the stories may have stopped the bomb from going through as another marginal weapon decision, they did not affect the president's deep-rooted reservations about introducing new nuclear weapons—the articles simply made him aware that here was a distinctive, novel weapon system. When Carter saw the Europeans were also very ambiguous about taking public responsibility for this particular system—an ambivalence that also predated the Pincus stories—I think that affected him as much as anything else.

In the end, there was also some praise for the coverage, particularly from journalists and educators who hailed Walter Pincus's reporting on the neutron bomb. In 1977, Pincus won the coveted George Polk award for national reporting for his stories on the bomb, and came in runner-up for the Raymond Clapper Award, given by the Standing Committee of Correspondents of the Senate Press Gallery for reporting on governmental affairs. The same year Pincus also won the National Council of Teachers of English (NCTE) George Orwell award. NCTE's newsletter reported that the prize, given for "distinguished contributions to honesty and clarity in public language," was awarded to Pincus because he was "a patient methodical journalist who knew his job and who knew the jargon of Washington, Mr. Pincus was the man responsible for bringing to public attention, and thus to a debate in the Senate, the appropriations funding for the neutron bomb. . . . His reports in the *Washington Post* called the nation's attention to this weapon designed to kill people, but to leave buildings and property intact."[12] At the same time that NCTE honored Pincus, it announced that it was giving its Doublespeak Award to the Pentagon. The Doublespeak Award, which was covered on national television, was described in the NCTE newsletter as follows:

> In 1977, the [NCTE] Committee voted that the outstanding example of misuse of public language was the attempt by the Pentagon and ERDA to slip through the appropriations for the neutron bomb by means of euphemistic jargon and by hiding the item in an obscure section of the budget request of the Energy Research and Development Administration [under] the phrase "enhanced radiation" weapon. . . . In Pentagon slang, it's called the "cookie cutter," a funny phrase which masks a horrible reality.[13]

APPENDIX A

The Neutron Bomb Compared with Other Tactical Nuclear (Fission) Weapons

The principle behind the neutron bomb is fairly simple. The existing atomic (or fission) warheads stored in Europe (and, indeed, all nuclear weapons) produce four effects: blast, heat, radioactive (residual) fallout, and a momentary burst of initial (or prompt) radiation composed chiefly of neutrons and gamma rays. About 50 percent of a fission weapon's yield typically goes into blast, 35 percent into heat, 10 percent into residual radiation, and 5 percent into prompt radiation. In thermonuclear weapons (or H bombs), where the predominant reaction was fusion instead of fission, a higher percent of the weapon's energy (and faster and more deadly neutrons) was released in prompt radiation, which could pierce tank armor more readily and kill or incapacitate exposed soldiers on the battlefield. A pure fusion explosion, for example, could reportedly release up to 80 percent of its energy in the form of fast neutrons, 20 percent of its energy in heat and blast, and result in virtually no radioactive fallout—hence, it would be a "clean" bomb. However, so far, thermonuclear fusion reactions have not been achieved except with the aid of a fission trigger—which means both that thermonuclear weapons, including the neutron bomb, are not so "clean" and that they have a tremendous blast component.

Although ER warheads release more of their energy in prompt radiation—between 30 percent and 40 percent, as opposed to 5 percent for pure fission explosions—pure fission explosions in the kiloton and subkiloton ranges also kill predominantly through prompt radiation. (The radius of deaths and injuries, that is, caused by the blast of a low yield kiloton fission weapon is exceeded by the radius of injuries and deaths caused by prompt radiation.) Not only is the neutron bomb not unique in this regard, but it, like other nuclear weapons, still releases a great deal of its energy in blast and heat (about 65 percent as compared to 85 percent in pure fission weapons). If a 1 kt ER weapon, for example, were detonated, its blast and heat would be unlike that produced by conventional weapons. Although its blast effect could be reduced somewhat by raising the height of the explosion, at the height the Army planned to detonate ER warheads, everybody, even personnel within tanks, would be killed immediately by blast within a radius of 200 meters, and out to 1 kilometer individuals would likely suffer eardrum rupture and first-degree burns on unprotected skin.

To put the addition of the neutron bomb in its appropriate context, the existing theater nuclear stockpile in Europe was composed of roughly 7,000 land-based nuclear weapons, which, according to Secretary Schlesinger, had an average yield of just under 4 kilotons (kt). (A kiloton has an explosive power equivalent to 1,000 tons of TNT. The fission bomb dropped on Hiroshima had a 10–15 kt yield, the bomb dropped on Nagasaki had a 20–25 kt yield.) Out of this immense stockpile, there were hundreds of weapons *already* deployed in Europe which produced far more blast and radiation than the neutron warheads. At the same time, there were also many low-yield fission warheads that produced less blast and radiation. (The highest reported yield for an ER warhead on one of the settings for the 8-inch shell was 2kt. Most of the settings for ER warheads were subkiloton.) Turning away from the question of yields, the neutron warheads appeared also to have no more than a modest quantitative impact on the 7,000 weapons already in the stockpile. Only 340 Lance missiles (out of approximately 1,200) were scheduled for an ER warhead; another 800 8-inch shells or so would also reportedly incorporate ER.

The neutron bomb differs from other tactical weapons in the relative balance it strikes between the effects of blast and prompt radiation. Because of the predominance of the fission reaction and several design changes that help "liberate" additional neutrons, ER warheads were capable of producing a copious amount of deadly, high energy neutrons, particularly when compared with fission weapons. Since the existing Lance and 8-inch shells used fission warheads, it was possible to replace the warheads with a lower yield ER warhead and still get the same "kill radius" through the release of the additional neutrons. The chart below indicates the radius of prompt neutron / gamma radiation projected by a 10 kt fission weapon, a 1 kt ER warhead, and a 1 kt ER fission warhead.

Radius of Initial Radiation (in yards)

Yield	Tank Crew instantly incapacitated, dead within 2 days (8000 rads)	Tank Crew temporarily incapacitated, dead within a week (3000 rads)	Vomiting, Diarrhea, Anorexia occurs within 2 hrs, 50% to 80% die within 2 months (650 rads)	Light injury (150 rads)
10 kt fission	930	1,050	1,335	1,870
1 kt ER	930	1,050	1,335	1,870
1 kt fission	515	740	875	1,310

Source: Defense Nuclear Agency (burst height is presumed to be 100 ft.).

As can be seen from the chart, a 10 kt fission warhead and a 1 kt ER warhead have the same radiation kill / casualty radius. However, the ER warhead produces only ½ to ⅓ as much blast (not shown) as the 10 kt weapon, reducing collateral damage to structures and to civilians who would be killed by the collapse of buildings. However, the degree to which ER weapons reduce "collateral damage" depends partly on whether the damage is "collateral" to property or to civilians.* As the chart also illustrates, the radiation kill / casualty radius—which presumably would reach some civilians—is much wider for a 1 kt ER weapon than for a 1 kt fission warhead. Slightly more damage, on the other hand (also not shown), would be caused to buildings by the 1 kt fission warhead than the ER warhead. The neutron bomb, in short, did not produce a radical reduction in collateral damage when compared with nuclear weapons already deployed in Western Europe.

---

* It also depends partly on the height of the burst. These comparisons are based on what the Army considers to be an optimal height.

APPENDIX B

Cast of Characters (Chief actors are flagged by capitals)

In the United States:

White House
- PRESIDENT CARTER
- ZBIGNIEW BRZEZINSKI, National Security Advisor
- DAVID AARON, Deputy National Security Advisor
- NSC Staff: Reginald Bartholemew, Robert Hunter, John Marcum, Jerrold Schecter (press aide), Jim Thomson
- JODY POWELL, Press Secretary
- JAMES SCHLESINGER, Adviser on Energy, subsequently Secretary of Energy

Department of Defense
- HAROLD BROWN, Secretary of Defense
- DONALD COTTER, Special Assistant for Atomic Energy
- Major General Gene Key, Cotter's Deputy
- Lt. Col. John Hodge, Cotter's executive officer
- Brig. Gen. Lynwood Lennon, Army representative on Military Liaison Committee
- DAVID McGIFFERT, Assistant Secretary for International Security Affairs
- Walter Slocombe, McGiffert's Principal Deputy Undersecretary, Director of SALT Task Force
- James Siena, McGiffert's Deputy Assistant Secretary for European and NATO Affairs
- Lynn Davis, McGiffert's Deputy Assistant Secretary for Policy Plans and NSC Affairs
- Henry Gaffney, staff to Lynn Davis
- THOMAS B. ROSS, Assistant Secretary for Public Affairs
- Lt. Col. Michael Burch, Ross's military assistant

Arms Control and Disarmament Agency
- PAUL WARNKE, Director

Energy Research and Development Administration
- General Alfred Starbird, Assistant Administrator
- Maj. General Joseph Bratton, Director of Military Applications

State Department
- CYRUS VANCE, Secretary of State
- Warren Christopher, Deputy Secretary of State
- GEORGE VEST, Assistant Secretary for European Affairs
- James Goodby, Vest's Deputy Assistant Secretary
- John Hawes, on Vest's European staff
- LESLIE GELB, Director of Politico-Military Affairs

- David Gompert, Gelb's Deputy
- Eric Newsome, Gelb's Special Assistant
- Lou Finch, Gelb's NATO Desk Officer
- HODDING CARTER, Assistant Secretary for Public Affairs

In Europe:

- HELMUT SCHMIDT, Chancellor of West Germany
- Georg Leber, Schmidt's Defense Minister
- Hans Dietrich Genscher, Schmidt's Foreign Minister
- EGON BAHR, a leader of liberal wing of Schmidt's party
- JAMES CALLAGHAN, Prime Minister of Britain
- David Owen, Callaghan's Foreign Secretary
- Frederick Mulley, Callaghan's Defense Minister

In NATO:

- JOSEPH LUNS, Secretary General
- Paul Van Campen, Lun's executive assistant
- Richard Shearer, head of NPG staff
- W. TAPLEY BENNETT, U.S. Ambassador to NATO
- Laurence Legere, Bennett's Deputy
- GENERAL ALEXANDER HAIG, Supreme Allied Commander for Europe

---

Timetable of Key Events During 1977–1978

1977

June 6	Walter Pincus's story, "Neutron Killer Warhead Buried in ERDA Budget," appears in *Washington Post*
June 22	Senate Appropriations Committee approves ERW production funds in a 10–10 vote.
July 6	Jody Powell says Carter will decide in mid-August on production
July 1, 13	Senate debates and approves ERW funding pending presidential decision and notification
July 17	SPD leader in West Germany, Egon Bahr, labels bomb a "symbol of mental perversion," Soviet propaganda campaign swings into full gear
Aug. 15–17	White House states that Carter will defer decision pending further consultations with Allies. Carter tells Brzezinski, Brown, and Vance he wants firmer commitments from Europeans to deploy.
Sept. 8	West German Parliament debates ERW
Sept. 13, 20	U.S. delegation, led by McGiffert, meets first with NATO NPG representatives, then with Permanent Representatives
Sept. 16	Carter and Schmidt discuss ERW over phone. Carter says he does not want to "get shot down as an international ogre."
Sept. 27	Brzezinski, in Europe, meets separately with Callaghan and Schmidt to discuss ERW
Sept. 27	U.S. House of Representatives easily passes funding for ERW

210

Oct. 11	NATO NPG in Bari, Italy
Oct. 28	Schmidt makes reference in speech in London to threat posed by the new Soviet intermediate range missiles (SS–20) in E. Europe. Urges they and ERW be part of arms control negotiations
Nov. 15	SPD convention passes resolution asking that ERW be incorporated into arms control negotiations
Nov. 16	SCC meeting at which Brzezinski, Brown, and Vance decide to offer Europeans an ERW / SS–20 arms control trade
End of Nov.	Letter from Carter to Schmidt outlines arms control initiative
Dec. 23	Brezhnev makes counter offer, proposes mutual renunciation of ERW
Dec. 30	Carter and Brzezinski, in Poland, emphasize dangers of SS–20 (vs. ERW)

1978

Jan. 5	Heated letters sent by Brezhnev to Carter and heads of NATO nations protesting ERW, Soviet propaganda campaign renews
Jan. 23	Carter sends budget to Congress, includes ERW funding for Lance and 8″ shell
Jan. 30	U.S. team, led by David Aaron, consults with West Germans and British on ERW
Feb.	U.S. covert action campaign in N. Europe begins
Feb. 24	Les Gelb, at NATO perm reps meeting in Brussels, irons out more details of ''scenario'' for ERW deployment
March 8	Dutch parliament votes against ERW deployment, major demonstration in Amsterdam
March 19	Carter, at St. Simon's Island, unexpectedly rejects ERW deployment plan and cancels upcoming NATO NAC meetings
March 20	Vance, Brzezinski, and Brown rail at Carter but fail to change his mind
March 27	Carter departs for trip to South America and Africa
March 30, 31	Warren Christopher flies to Bonn, meets first with Hans Dietrich Genscher and then Schmidt, to inform West Germans of Carter's decision
April 4	Richard Burt breaks story in *New York Times* that Carter is cancelling. Genscher arrives to talk with Carter
April 7	Carter releases statement announcing deferral of ERW production and deployment

APPENDIX C

Carter's Statement

FOR IMMEDIATE RELEASE   April 7, 1978

Office of the White House Press Secretary

THE WHITE HOUSE

PRESIDENTIAL STATEMENT
ON ENHANCED RADIATION WEAPONS

I have decided to defer production of weapons with enhanced radiation effects. The ultimate decision regarding the incorporation of enhanced radiation features into our modernized battlefield weapons will be made later, and will be influenced by the degree to which the Soviet Union shows restraint in its conventional and nuclear arms programs and force deployments affecting the security of the United States and Western Europe.

Accordingly, I have ordered the Defense Department to proceed with the modernization of the Lance missile nuclear warhead and the 8-inch weapon system, leaving open the option of installing the enhanced radiation elements.

The United States is consulting with its partners in the North Atlantic Alliance on this decision, and will continue to discuss with them appropriate arms control measures to be pursued with the Soviet Union.

We will continue to move ahead with our allies to modernize and strengthen our military capabilities, both conventional and nuclear. We are determined to do whatever is necessary to assure our collective security and the forward defense of Europe.

NOTES

Prelude to the Storm

1. Zbigniew Brzezinski, *Power and Principle* (New York: Farrar, Straus, and Giroux, 1983), p. 301.

2. *Ibid.*, p. 304.

3. Philip Geyelin, "A Bum Rap on the 'Neutron Bomb,' " *Washington Post*, September 18, 1981, op-ed page.

4. Edward Gamarekian, "New A-Bomb 'Pinpoints' Lethal Dose," *Washington Post*, July 1, 1959, p. 1.

5. Dyson's article was reprinted in the *Congressional Record*, February 21, 1963, p. 2812.

6. "The Russians Win a Round. Next Topic: Serious Inspection," *Life*, April 4, 1960, p. 33.

7. *Congressional Record*, May 12, 1960, p. 10138.

8. "Most Terrible Bomb of All—," *U.S. News and World Report*, May 30, 1960, p. 56.

9. The best discussion of the 1960s debate over the neutron bomb is Samuel T. Cohen, *The Neutron Bomb: Political, Technological, and Military Issues* (Cambridge, Mass.: Institute for Foreign Policy Analysis, November 1978), and his popular version, *The Truth About the Neutron Bomb* (New York: William Morrow, 1983). On the 1977–78 debate, see the first hand accounts of Brzezinski, *Power and Principle*, pp. 301–306; Jimmy Carter, *Keeping Faith* (Toronto: Bantam, 1982), pp. 225–229; and Cyrus Vance, *Hard Choices* (New York: Simon and Schuster, 1983), pp. 67–69, 92–98. For a more exhaustive treatment of the 1977–78 debate, particularly of the absence of an agreed-upon NATO nuclear doctrine and how the neutron bomb fed into this disagreement and alliance politics, see Sherri Wasserman, *The Neutron Bomb Controversy* (New York: Praeger, Special Studies, 1983). Also worth looking at is Cohen, *The Neutron Bomb*, pp. 35–85; Michael A. Aquino, *The Neutron Bomb* (Ann Arbor, Mich.: University Microfilms, 1980), University of California / Santa Barbara, Ph.D., Political Science, February 1980); Hans Günter Brauch, "Enhanced Radiation Weapons" (Part I—Determinants of the Weapon Acquisition Process, Part II—Public Information on ERW and Democratic Control of the Weapons Acquisition Process), Center for Science and International Security Affairs, Kennedy School of Government, Harvard University, February 15, 1978, unpublished mimeograph; Donald G. Brennan, "The Neutron Bomb Controversy," Hudson Institute, Croton-on-Hudson, April 3, 1978, paper HI-2733 / 2-P; Capt. Thomas Carl Glad, "Theater Nuclear Force Modernization as an Issue in West German Politics," M.A., National Security

Affairs, Naval Postgraduate School, Monterey, California, December 1980; and Milton Leitenberg, "Background Information on Tactical Nuclear Weapons," in *Tactical Nuclear Weapons: European Perspectives* (New York: Crane, Russak, 1978), pp. 49–64.

10. Glenn T. Seaborg, *Kennedy, Khrushchev, and the Test Ban* (Berkeley: University of California Press, 1981), p. 63.

11. Secretary of Defense James R. Schlesinger, A Report to the U.S. Congress in Compliance with PL 93-365, *The Theater Nuclear Force Posture in Europe*, May 2, 1975, p. 21. On the reaction to ERW within NATO during this period, see J. Michael Legge, *Theater Nuclear Weapons and the NATO Strategy of Flexible Response*, Rand Corporation (Santa Monica, Calif.), Paper R-2964–FF, April 1983, pp. 28–31, as well as the unabridged version of the case.

12. Text of General Giller's address, pp. 20–23.

13. See Brig. Gen. Edwin F. Black, "NATO's Unmentionable Option: Tactical Nuclear Weapons," *Washington Report* (American Security Council), December 21, 1970, reprinted in *Congressional Record*, December 30, 1970, p. 44254; Uwe Nerlich, "Some Comments on Modernization of Nuclear Stockpiles in Europe: A German View," Hudson Institute, Croton-on-Hudson, April 24, 1972, paper HI-1626–D; Colonel Rene David, "The Neutron Bomb: Myth or Reality," *Revue de Defense Nationale*, July 1972: 1160–1173 (available in English from the Army Foreign Science and Technology Center in Charlottesville, Va.); McMillian Science Associates, "Tactical Nuclear Technology in the MBFR Context," DNA Contract 001-74-0021, Sept. 3, 1974, pp. 127, 128; S.T. Cohen, "On the Stringency of Dosage Criteria for Battlefield Nuclear Operations," Rand Corporation, Paper P-5332, January 1975, p. 17; S.T. Cohen and W.R. Van Cleave, "Western European Collateral Damage from Tactical Nuclear Weapons," *Journal of the Royal United Services Institute*, Vol. 121, June 1976 p. 35; and Cecil I. Hudson, Jr. and Peter H. Haas, "New Technologies: The Prospects," in Johan Holst and Uwe Nerlich, ed., *Beyond Nuclear Deterrence* (New York: Crane Russak, 1977), p. 140.

14. The few articles that mention the ERW during these years include C. L. Sulzberger, "Solving an Ugly Dilemma," *New York Times*, November 15, 1970, p. Ell; Herbert York and Herbert Scoville, " 'New Look' in Nuclear Solutions" (Letter to the Editor), *New York Times*, February 16, 1971; William Beecher, "Over the Threshold: 'Clean' Tactical Nuclear Weapons for Europe," *Army*, July 1972; Walter Pincus, "A New Generation—Why More Nukes?" *New*

Republic, February 9, 1974; Lloyd Norman, "The Reluctant Dragon," *Army,* February 1974, p. 20; and Anthony Tucker, "U.S. Navy Irradiates and Burns Monkeys to Death," *Manchester Guardian,* May 29, 1977.

15. See Stanford Research International, Strategic Studies Center (Arlington, Va.), *An Assessment of Attitudes on Tactical Nuclear Force Modernization,* Vol. II (Main Study), DNA Contract 001–76–C–0169, December 1977, pp. 47–50.

16. Senate Foreign Relations Committee, Subcommittee on Security Agreements and Commitments Abroad, *Security Agreements and Commitments Abroad,* Committee Print, 91st Cong., 2nd sess., December 21, 1970, pp. 12, 13.

The Story Breaks

1. *Congressional Record,* July 1, 1977, p. 22018.

2. "No Neutron Warheads," *Washington Post,* June 26, 1977, p. 36.

3. Herbert Scoville, "A New Weapon to Think (and Worry) About," *New York Times,* July 12, 1977, p. 30.

4. *Congressional Record,* September 9, 1977, p. 28402.

5. *Congressional Record,* July 13, 1977, pp. 22756, 22757.

6. *Ibid,* p. 22753.

7. Transcript of NBC Nightly News, July 16, 1977.

8. See "The People Killer," *San Francisco Examiner & Chronicle,* July 3, 1977, p. 1; and "The Issue: The Neutron Bomb," *Atlanta Journal / Constitution,* August 27, 1977, p. 1–B.

9. "The President's News Conference of July 12, 1977," in *Public Papers of the President of the United States: Jimmy Carter* (Washington, D.C.: U.S. Government Printing Office, 1977), Vol. 1, p. 1231.

10. See Robert Sam Anson, "Carter Commitment Guided Neutron Bomb to Victory," *Dallas Morning News,* August 8, 1977, p. 14.

The Reaction Spreads to Europe

1. AP dispatch from Geneva, Switzerland, July 15, 1977.

2. *Foreign Broadcast Information Service (FBIS), Western Europe,* July 19, 1977, pp. J4, J5.

3. House of Commons, *The Hansard,* Vol. 944 (1977–78), February 21, 1978, p. 1200.

4. See *FBIS, Western Europe,* September 9, 1977, p. J7.

5. *FBIS, Western Europe,* July 19, 1977, p. J4.

6. *Ibid.,* pp. J2–J3.

7. "CIA Paper on Soviet propaganda (overseas)," reprinted in House Committee on Intelligence, Subcommittee on Oversight, *The CIA and the Media,* hearings, 95th Cong., 2nd sess.; 1978, p. 553.

8. *Ibid.*

9. *Ibid.,* p. 555.

10. Ellen Lentz, "West Germany Aroused Over Neutron Bomb Prospect," *New York Times,* July 24, 1977.

11. Cyrus Vance, *Hard Choices* (New York: Simon and Schuster, 1983), p. 69.

12. AP, "U.S. to Consult Allies on the Bomb," *New York Times,* August 17, 1977, p. 6. Walter Pincus reported the same news the day before in "Carter Delays Decision on Neutron Weapons," *Washington Post,* August 16, 1977.

13. Zbigniew Brzezinski, *Power and Principle* (New York: Farrar, Straus and Giroux, 1983), p. 302.

14. *Ibid.*

15. *Ibid.*

16. *Ibid.*

Swinging and Striking Out in Europe

1. See Sherri L. Wasserman, *The Neutron Bomb Controversy* (New York: Praeger, Special Studies, 1983), p. 85.

2. See *FBIS, Western Europe,* September 30, 1977, p. J4.

3. See the text of Secretary General's Address to the Annual Assembly of the Atlantic Treaty Association, Reykjavik, Iceland, August 26, 1977, p. 6.

4. Wasserman, *The Neutron Bomb Controversy,* p. 80.

5. Department of Army, Office of Chief of Public Affairs, "The Neutron Bomb," *Spotlight,* No. 77–44 (October 1977), p. 1.

6. Patrick F. Rogers, "The Neutron Bomb," *Army,* September 1977, p. 30.

7. See Claude Witze, "The Wayward Press," and Edgar Ulsamer, "The 'Neutron Bomb' Media Event," both in the November 1977 issue of *Air Force Magazine.* Witze is at pp. 20–21 and Ulsamer's article runs on pp. 66–73.

8. Murray Seeger, "Military Accused of Meddling in GI News on N-Bomb," *Los Angeles Times,* January 4, 1978, p. 8.

Selling the Neutron Bomb Via Mock Arms Control

1. Zbigniew Brzezinski, *Power and Principle* (New York: Farrar, Straus and Giroux, 1983), pp. 302, 303.

2. *Ibid.,* p. 303.

3. Walter Pincus, "Backers of Neutron Arms

Win a Round," *Washington Post,* November 23, 1977, p. 1.

4. White House transcript of Jody Powell briefing, November 23, 1977, pp. 2–6.

5. Richard Burt, "U.S. May Offer Soviets Deal Shelving Neutron Bomb," *New York Times,* November 25, 1977, p. 1.

6. Cyrus Vance, *Hard Choices* (New York: Simon and Schuster, 1983), p. 69.

7. Reuters dispatch, *New York Times,* December 16, 1977, p. 7.

8. Richard Burt, "U.S. Seeks To Counter Soviet Neutron Bomb Criticism," *New York Times,* December 31, 1977, p. 3.

9. "Transcript of the President's News Conference with U.S. and Polish Journalists," *New York Times,* December 31, 1977, p. 2.

10. J. A. Emerson Vermaat, "Moscow Fronts and the European Peace Movement," *Problems of Communism,* November / December 1982, p. 47.

11. *Ibid.*

12. House of Commons, *The Hansard,* Vol. 944 (1977–78), February 21, 1978, p. 1207.

13. United States Information Agency, "Neutron Bomb Debate," *Foreign Media Reaction,* Current Issues 5, March 1, 1978, p. 1.

14. Egon Bahr in the *Flensburger Tageblatt,* February 4, 1978, reprinted in *FBIS, Western Europe,* February 24, 1978, p. J6.

15. Quoted in Michael A. Aquino, *The Neutron Bomb* (Ann Arbor, Mich.: University Microfilms, 1980), University of California / Santa Barbara, Ph.D., Political Science, February 1980, pp. 206–207.

16. Senate Committee on Armed Services Subcommittee on Manpower and Personnel, *DOD Authorization for Appropriations for FY 1979,* hearings, Part 3, 95th Cong., 2nd sess., 1978, p. 1920.

17. Brzezinski, *Power and Principle,* p. 304.

The Roof Caves In

1. Cyrus Vance, *Hard Choices,* (New York: Simon and Schuster, 1983), p. 96.

2. Zbigniew Brzezinski, *Power and Principle,* (New York: Farrar, Straus and Giroux, 1983), p. 305.

3. Richard Burt, "Aides Report Carter Bans Neutron Bomb; Some Seek Reversal," *New York Times,* April 4, 1978, p. 4; Walter Pincus, "Neutron Arms Decision is Expected This Week," *Washington Post,* April 4, 1978, p. 4; and Rowland Evans and Robert Novak, "Behind the Neutron Indecision," *Washington Post,* April 10, 1978, p. 23.

4. Jimmy Carter, *Keeping Faith* (Toronto: Bantam Books, 1982), p. 227.

5. *Ibid.*

6. Vance, *Hard Choices,* p. 94.

7. *Foreign Broadcast Information Service (FBIS), Western Europe,* March 28, 1978, p. C1. Charles W. Corddry, "U.S. sees O.K. on Neutron Weapons by Europe allies before NATO Talks," *Baltimore Sun,* March 20, 1978, p. 6.

8. See Carter, *Keeping Faith,* p. 227.

9. Brzezinski, *Power and Principle,* p. 304.

10. *Ibid.,* p. 305.

11. *Ibid.*

12. See "Furor Over the Neutron Bomb," *Newsweek,* April 17, 1978, p. 35, and Mary McGrory, "Neutron Bomb Position Puts the Monkey on Russians' back," *Washington Star,* April 7 1978, p. 3.

13. Vance, *Hard Choices,* p. 94.

14. Richard Burt, "Neutron Bomb Controversy Strained Alliance and Caused Splits in the Administration," *New York Times,* April 9, 1978, p. 18.

15. Richard Burt, "NATO Agreement on Neutron Bomb Expected Soon," *New York Times,* March 28, 1978, p. 7.

16. Walter Pincus, "U.S. Pulls Back from NATO Neutron Weapon Discussions," *Washington Post,* March 28, 1978, p. 3.

17. See, for example, Hella Pick, "Carter to Order N-Bomb: European Allies Reluctant to Support New Weapon," *Manchester Guardian,* March 29, 1978, p. 1.

18. Rowland Evans and Robert Novak, "The Heated Debate Over the Neutron Bomb," *Washington Post,* March 31, 1978, p. 17.

19. Richard Burt, "Carter's Delay on Neutron Bomb Issue Irks Allies," *New York Times,* April 1, 1978, p. 5.

20. Transcript of discussion between James Siena, Congressman Stratton, and Richard Burt, *All Things Considered,* WETA Radio, National Public Radio Network, March 3, 1978, p. 3.

21. Richard Burt, "Aides Report Carter Bans Neutron Bomb; Some Seek Reversal," *New York Times,* April 4, 1978, p. 1.

22. Vance was shown denying the Burt report on the NBC Nightly News and the CBS Evening News on April 4. The same day, Hodding Carter was shown denying that a decision had been made on Channel 4 News in Washington, D.C.

23. White House transcript of news conference (#268) with Jody Powell, April 5, 1978, p. 2–5.

24. Transcript of WTOP Radio News, April 4, 1978, p. 1.

25. James McCartney, "Carter Aides Say Neutron Bomb Dead," *Philadelphia Inquirer,* April 5, 1978, p. 1.

26. Walter Pincus, "President Reported To Defer Neutron Weapons for Present," *Washington Post,* April 7, 1978, p. 12.

27. Henry L. Trewitt, "Carter Apparently

Acted Alone on Neutron Bomb,'' *Baltimore Sun,* April 6, 1978, p. 1.

28. Hedrick Smith, ''Carter Move May Deepen Public's Doubts,'' *New York Times,* April 8, 1978, p. 7.

29. Quoted in ''Furor Over the Neutron Bomb,'' *Newsweek,* April 17, 1978, p. 39.

30. Transcript of CBS Evening News with Walter Cronkite, April 4, 1978, pp. 2–3.

31. The letter is reprinted in the *Congressional Record,* April 6, 1978, p. 9173.

32. Transcript of CBS Morning News, April 7, 1978, p. 2.

33. Cited in S. T. Cohen, *The Neutron Bomb: Political, Technical and Military Issues* (Cambridge: Institute for Foreign Policy Analysis, Special Report, November 1978), p. 51.

34. ''The Neutron Decision,'' *Washington Post,* April 6, 1978, editorial page.

35. Brzezinski, *Power and Principle,* p. 305.

36. Carter, *Keeping Faith,* pp. 227, 228.

37. Richard Burt, ''Neutron Bomb Controversy Strained Alliance and Caused Splits in the Administration,'' *New York Times,* April 9, 1978, p. 18.

38. Walter Pincus, ''Bonn Backs Producing Neutron Arms,'' *Washington Post,* April 5, 1978, p. 6.

39. Brzezinski, *Power and Principle,* p. 306.

40. *Ibid.*

41. ''The Neutron Bomb Furor,'' *Time,* April 17, 1978, p. 14.

42. White House transcript of background briefing, April 7, 1978, p. 2.

43. *Ibid.,* pp. 2, 7.

44. *Ibid.,* p. 12.

45. ''Furor over the Neutron Bomb,'' *Newsweek,* April 17, 1978, pp. 35, 38, and ''The Neutron Bomb Furor,'' *Time,* April 17, 1978, p. 10.

46. ''The Neutron Bomb Furor,'' *Time,* April 17, 1978, p. 10.

47. *Ibid.*

48. Rowland Evans and Robert Novak, ''Behind the Neutron Decision,'' *Washington Post,* April 10, 1983, p. 23.

49. Transcript of ABC Evening News, April 7, 1978.

50. Harold Logan, ''Byrd Links Neutron Weapons, Allies,'' *Washington Post,* April 9, 1978, p. 30.

51. Charles W. Corddry, ''Carter's Neutron Alternative is Far More Destructive,'' *Baltimore Sun,* April 8, 1978, p. 1.

52. Transcript of Live-News 98, WRC Radio (Washington, D.C.), April 7, 1978, p. 1.

53. ''Furor Over the Neutron Bomb,'' *Newsweek,* April 17, 1978, p. 39.

54. Strauss discussed his comment, made several days earlier, during the debate over ERW

in the German parliament on April 13, 1978. An April 13 cable from the embassy in Bonn to Vance, Brown, and the U.S. embassies and consuls in W. Europe, cites the earlier quotation.

55. Cited in S. T. Cohen, *The Neutron Bomb,* p. 53.

56. Roger Morris, ''Eight Days in April: The Press Flattens Carter with the Neutron bomb,'' *Columbia Journalism Review,* November / December 1978, p. 30. Also see James Burnham, ''The President and the Bomb,'' *National Review,* May 12, 1978, p. 579.

57. AP dispatch from Paris, April 13, 1978.

58. Brzezinski, *Power and Principle,* pp. 193, 301.

59. Richard Burt, ''Tension Grows Between Brzezinski and State Department,'' *New York Times,* April 17, 1978.

60. Brzezinski, *Power and Principle,* p. 305.

61. Theo Summer, ''A View from Western Europe,'' *Newsweek,* April 17, 1978, p. 40.

62. Cited in AP dispatch from Paris, April 13, 1978.

63. Carter, *Keeping Faith,* pp. 228, 229.

Epilogue

1. Folder on the disarmament campaign of the Interchurch Peace Council (IKV) in the Netherlands, IKV, December 1981.

2. Hans Günter Brauch, ''Neutron Weapons—Potential Arms Control Linkages and Breakthroughs,'' *Bulletin of Peace Proposals,* vol. 9, no. 3, 1978, p. 227.

3. Brown delivered his remarks at the plenary session of the International Institute for Strategic Studies' twenty fourth annual conference at the Hague, the Netherlands, September 10, 1982. They are reprinted in Harold Brown, ''Domestic Consensus and Nuclear Deterrence,'' *Adelphi Papers,* no. 183, 1983, pp. 22, 27.

4. See Bernard Gwertzman, ''Reagan is Hopeful on Missile Accord with the Russians,'' *New York Times,* January 21, 1981, pp. 1, 7, 9; Thomas Riehle, ''Washington's Movers and Shakers,'' *National Journal,* January 29, 1983; and Judith Miller, ''U.S. Is Planning Bid to Win Over Europe's Young,'' *New York Times,* April 4, 1983, p. 1.

5. Quoted in Howard Kurtz and Pete Earley, ''Wick Adds Flair to U.S. Story,'' *Washington Post,* July 13, 1983, pp. 1, 8.

6. See Barry Rubin, ''The Media and the Neutron Warhead,'' *Washington Review,* July 1978, p. 91; Donald G. Brennan, ''The Neutron Bomb Controversy,'' Hudson Institute, Croton-on-Hudson, Paper HI–2733 / 2–P, April 3, 1978, p. 1.; and, to a lesser degree, Sherri Wasserman, *The Neutron Bomb Controversy* (New York: Praeger, Special Studies, 1983).

7. Philip Geyelin, "A Bum Rap on the 'Neutron Bomb,' " *Washington Post,* September 18, 1981, op-ed page.

8. Cited in Phillip P. Everts, "Reviving Unilaterialism," *Bulletin of Peace Proposals,* January 1980, pp. 44, 55.

9. "Public Likes Carter, Survey Finds, More for His Style Than Programs," *New York Times,* July 29, 1977, p. 1.

10. The results of both the Roper and Caddell polls are cited in the previously mentioned April 3, 1978, memo from Hodding Carter to Les Gelb, George Vest, and Joseph Nye.

11. Louis Harris, "Public Now Opposes Building of Neutron Bomb," The Harris Survey, press release, May 25, 1978, p. 1.

12. "The George Orwell Award," *Public Doublespeak Newsletter,* National Council of Teachers of English Committee on Doublespeak, Vol. IV, nos. 1–2, January / April 1978, p. 2.

13. *Ibid.*

SHRINKING THE POLICY PROCESS:
THE PRESS AND THE
1980 LOVE CANAL RELOCATION

by Martin Linsky

The History at Love Canal

THE HISTORY OF the tension, the environment, industry, and people around the site of the Love Canal began over two hundred years ago.[1] The basic geography is not hard to absorb. The Niagara River flows north, from Lake Erie to Lake Ontario. Its most dominant feature, of course, is its 186-foot plunge halfway along the course known to honeymooners around the world as Niagara Falls. Settlers in the area realized that a river moving that fast had great potential as a power-generating sources—as early as 1757 a small canal was built for a sawmill—and by the late nineteenth century, power from the river was being used to light the parks adjoining the falls.

Then in the 1890s the possibilities for future development attracted a resourceful entrepreneur by the name of William T. Love. Love had a plan: build a canal, a navigable waterway, that would divert the river away from the falls for about seven miles, falling some 280 feet before it reconnected to the old river route. That way, he reasoned, he could harness the river's power and provide free energy to industry, and to the community he planned to construct along the route of the canal, near the northernmost point. It was to be called Model City, and Love's vision was sufficiently compelling that he was accorded the privilege of addressing a joint session of the New York State Senate and Assembly, which promptly passed a law permitting him to carry on, and, not so incidentally, divert as much of the Niagara as he deemed necessary to see his project through. He began to dig, a factory and a few homes were built, and then, in the late 1890s, his fantasy withered away. The depression of those years caused his investors to pull back, and the U.S. Congress passed a law barring him from removing water from the Niagara in order to preserve the falls. Love abandoned the project, but

---

Unless otherwise indicated, all quotations come either from unpublished government documents or from interviews with the author.

left a gaping hole, nearly a mile long, ten feet deep and sixty feet wide among the fields of a quiet town known as LaSalle, situated just east of Niagara Falls.

Love's Model City never came to pass, but his vision of cheap energy was not lost. Plentiful inexpensive power is essential in the chemical business, and it was no surprise when industry began to look to the Niagara Falls area. Elon Hooker started Hooker Electrochemical Company there in 1905 in a three-room farmhouse, and by 1906 the first plant, producing caustic soda from salt brine, was already in operation. There were about seventy-five employees at that point, not a huge number but important in that small community. The company prospered, in part because it had invested in a device which was later to be central to the production of chlorine. By 1915, the company was growing rapidly and providing essential materials for the war effort. Sales reached $20 million by 1940, its stock was publicly traded, and its manufacturing facilities went national and eventually worldwide. Sales continued to rocket, climbing from $75 million in 1955 to $1.7 billion in 1978 and in the 1960s Hooker was bought by Occidental Petroleum. The Niagara Falls operation continued to be its largest, employing as many as three thousand people. Hooker's corporate headquarters remained in Niagara Falls and the company was always special in the area, even though many other corporate chemical-producing giants followed it into the region.

Hooker's growth produced, inevitably, a need to find a way to get rid of the huge amounts of chemical waste produced by its operations. The town of LaSalle had been annexed by Niagara Falls in 1927, and the canal and its surrounding fields were used by the residents of the city for swimming in the warm weather, ice skating in the winter, and all-purpose year-round fishing / outdoor recreation. The canal had been sold at public auction in 1920 and later began to be used for some municipal dumping. In 1942, the Niagara Power and Development Company gave Hooker permission to dump its wastes in the canal. The stuff was brought to the site in 55-gallon barrels which were dropped into the canal. In 1947, Niagara Power sold the canal and two adjoining seventy-foot wide strips of land to Hooker, and the dumping continued. By 1952, the old canal was nearly full. Hooker had deposited some 21,000 tons of chemical wastes on the site.

According to standards of that era, the old Love Canal was an ideal site for dumping. No one worried about such esoteric matters as toxic chemcial leaking into the water supplies. The issue was only whether the site was deep enough and well protected enough so that it would not attract an undue supply of flies and vermin. The canal's deep trough and thick clay walls seemed fine for those purposes. In retrospect, however, those who lived in the homes closest to the canal apparently knew that once Hooker started using the site, something different was going on.

A letter to the editor of the *Niagara Gazette* recounted that as early as 1943 the smell was unbearable and the white cloud that came from the site ''killed the grass and trees and burnt the paint off the backs of the houses and made the other houses all black.'' There were stories of workers who were dumping the wastes running to the nearest homes to use garden hoses to wash themselves off when some of the substances spilled on them. Children played on the site and enjoyed picking up phosphorous rocks, throwing them against the cement and watching them explode. In the hot weather, there were spontaneous fires on the site and industrial-type odors wafting through open windows of the nearby homes.

In 1953, with the site almost full and covered over with earth and clay, Love Canal came to another turning point in its tortuous history. The exact nature of the politics of the transaction is difficult to recover, but on April 28, 1953, for consideration of $1, Hooker transferred the land to the Niagara Falls Board of Education. Hooker maintains that the board was threatening to condemn the land and take the property for a new school site. Board members and staff have suggested that Hooker was dumping the site now that they had finished dumping the wastes. Hooker tried to transfer the property with a limitation in the deed that it could only be used as parkland, but the board had already developed plans for a school on the site. The deed that was finally accepted included a clause shifting to the board all "risk and liability" for use of the site from the chemical wastes buried there. The clause identified the wastes in a general way; board representatives had the year before toured the site with Hooker officials and took test borings which showed chemicals in two locations only four feet below the surface. The board proceeded with its plans, even after construction workers found what the architect described as a "pit filled with chemicals" on the site. Despite the architect's warnings that it was "poor policy" to continue with the project, the board simply resited the building some eighty-five feet north of the original location. The school was completed and opened in February 1955. The next year, with the approval of school officials, the architect ordered the contractor to relocate a kindergarten play area because it was located directly over the chemical dump.

In 1957, the next public incident over Love Canal occurred. The board's Buildings and Grounds Committee agreed to a trade of land with some homebuilders. The builders wanted part of the Love Canal site for houses, and were willing to part with parcels they owned that were desired by the board, plus pay the board $11,000. At a meeting of the board on November 7, 1957, representatives of Hooker appeared and strongly opposed the sale to the subdividers, saying that they had made it clear at the time of the original transfer that the site was unsuitable for any construction which required basements and sewer lines. In November, a divided board voted against the trade with the subdividers. During the same period, however, the city was busily constructing sewers right through the canal walls as part of the finishing and paving of a street that went over the Hooker property. Several other incursions into the canal's walls were made in the next few years. In addition, in the two years after the board accepted the deed in 1953, the board had voted to remove 17,000 cubic feet of fill for use at other sites. In 1960, the board gave the northern portion of the site to the city; and in 1961 it sold the southern portion at auction. During the 1960s and early 1970s homes were built in the area and sewer lines were laid. An expressway was constructed at the southern end of the site, necessitating the relocation of a main street and uncovering chemical wastes which Hooker agreed to cart away.

On the surface, the neighborhood was a quiet, modest family area. No one connected some apparently random but disturbing incidents to the chemicals underground.

In 1958, for example, Hooker investigated when the company was told that three or four children had been burned by debris at the property. Members of the crew building streets in the area complained of itchy skin and blisters. Black sludge was reported seeping into basement wall as early as 1959. Sump pumps had to be regularly replaced. City Hall records showed complaints from residents and reports from inspectors about hazardous conditions. The chemical odors began to be noticeable after every heavy rain. Backyards became unusable, holes opened up on the baseball diamond, trees and shrubbery that backed onto the canal site were dying. Yet it was almost by accident that in 1976 the first official public investigation began to link these events with the earlier dumping.

Earlier that year, the International Joint Commission, which monitors the water quality in the Great Lakes, had found traces of an insecticide called Mirex in fish in Lake Ontario. Mirex is an extremely toxic substance which, according to Michael Brown in his book, *Laying Waste,* had been used in the South to control ants and as a "flame retardant and placticizer" before being restricted by the FDA. While there were no studies on the effect of Mirex on humans, its devastating effects on laboratory animals were uncontroverted. In addition, it exhibited properties known to be characteristic of cancer-causing agents, and the damage caused to humans exposed to a closely related chemical, Kepone, was known and included a high incidence of sterility and liver ailments. Mirex was made in part from C–56, a highly toxic substance "capable of causing damage to every organ in the body" The New York State Department of Environmental Conservation (DEC) began trying to establish the source of the insecticide; on October 1, a story in the *Niagara Gazette* reported that a team of DEC investigators were to pay a visit to Hooker's Niagara Falls plant and to nearby chemical disposal sites, including Love Canal. At about the same time, the *Gazette* ran a letter complaining about the health problems of families near Love Canal and charging that they were connected to unaccounted-for discharges seeping into their cellars and the like.

Reporter David Pollack was assigned the story and his report, which appeared on page one on October 3, was a significant milestone on the Love Canal story. It provided what the residents needed in order to be taken seriously: public disinterested outside support for their fears that there was a connection between the illnesses in their families and the chemicals in the canal. Pollack recounted the history of Love Canal as a repository for chemical wastes, and detailed the unanswered complaints from residents during the past four year. Pollack followed up on his story by returning to the home of a Love Canal family he had spotlighted in the first piece, scooping up some of the sludge in their basement to see if it could be identified and traced. His paper was able to persuade a company called Chem-Trol Pollution Services to analyze the sample. Chem-Trol agreed to cooperate but only on the condition that its anonymity be protected; Hooker was one of the company's biggest clients. Chem-Trol's report confirmed both that the sludge contained toxic chemicals and that Hooker was their source. That information was reported in the *Gazette* on November 2. The story stimulated the first coverage in the larger Buffalo daily newspapers and seems to have spurred the DEC investigation as well. By this time the DEC regional director had already asked Hooker for a full accounting of what had been deposited in the canal and the State Department of Health for an analysis of some samples taken from the area. The newspapers pursued the story in early November, but there were no new developments for several months while DEC tried to cajole local officials and Hooker representatives into agreeing to tackle the clean-up problem. Hooker's people continued to deny responsibility, and the local officials seemed uninterested. A *Gazette* story on November 4 quoted a county health official as suggesting that individual homeowners ought to take steps to stop the discharges by, for example, cementing over the drainage holes in their basements.

DEC did not have the resources to force corrective action, but in the spring of 1977 the agency was able to direct the city to develop a clean-up plan. The city hired a consultant to devise a program, and by early May the consultant reported that conditions were serious, that more toxic chemicals were found, and that some of the drums which were filled with chemicals and buried in the canal were at or close to the surface. Local officials were still dismissing the problem, and again, Love Canal dropped out of the news for a brief period of time. But the problem would not go away and two events occurred, one in August and the other in September, which were to change the character of the Love Canal issue forever.

First, Michael Brown, a young suburban reporter for the *Gazette,* while covering a committee meeting on a related matter, heard a Love Canal resident make an eloquent plea for action. Brown returned to the office, researched the old stories, called local officials, and learned that the consulting firm had proposed a $425,000 clean-up plan. He wrote a front page story reporting all this on August 10, and the newspaper followed up ten days later with a strong editorial urging the city to move forward. The city turned down the recommendation as too expensive, but it could not turn off Michael Brown, who became the primary journalist involved with the story for over two years. His work, not only in the *Gazette,* but through articles in the *New York Times Sunday Magazine* and in the *Atlantic* in 1979 and a book in 1980,[2] helped make Love Canal into a national story. But equally important in this regard was the first visit to the site, in early September, of the U.S. Congressman who represented the area, John LaFalce. LaFalce was upset by what he saw and heard and also urged the city to act. For his efforts he was criticized by a local city councilor for "grandstanding" and stonewalled by local officials who not only rejected his suggestions, but discouraged others from cooperating. Now there was present an aggressive journalist, backed by a committed newspaper, and a responsive United States congressman, both deeply involved in rectifying what they perceived to be an injustice. Yet Hooker and local public officials continued to look the other way in the vain hope that when they turned around, the *Gazette,* LaFalce, and the residents' complaints would simply disappear. But with those forces engaged,

Love Canal was no longer a local matter, able to be resolved in a quiet friendly way between the area's political establishment and executives of Hooker. They wanted to believe that until someone proved a direct connection between Hooker, the chemicals in the canal, and the health problems of the residents, there was no need to act. Brown and LaFalce, however, were doing what good reporters and good representatives are supposed to do: to listen to legitimate complaints, find people who might be responsible for the problem or in a position to solve it, and keep the heat on them until they respond.

LaFalce would not let go of Love Canal. He arranged for another tour of the site, this time accompanied by EPA officials. In October 1977, soon after the visit, the regional EPA administrator wrote, in an internal memorandum, that based on what he had seen at Love Canal, "serious thought should be given to the purchase of some or all of the houses affected."[3] During that same month, DEC requested that EPA test the air in the basements of Love Canal homes. For the next several weeks, EPA and DEC continued to do tests of the air, water, and soil, while local officials continued to assume that the fuss would go away. In February 1978, Brown, then covering City Hall, returned to the story, pointing out that there was a "full-fledged environmental crisis" going on whether or not the local officials acknowledged it. As the results of the tests began coming in during the spring, federal and state officials became increasingly alarmed. The local authorities still declined to act, but gradually the test results, all confirming that a serious health hazard existed, became known through leaks to Michael Brown and his subsequent articles in the *Gazette*. People read that their basements were dangerous places. Brown's stories understandably increased the anxiety among Love Canal residents and spurred them to organize to seek help. The Buffalo papers were now paying more attention to the Love Canal issue.

State health and environmental authorities visited the site again, and, at the end of April, the state ordered the Niagara County Health Commission to take a series of steps to do something about the problem. The commissioner responded slowly. He tried to take care of the most visible signs of trouble by covering the exposed drums and the standing water with dirt. But he failed to take other basic remedial steps, such as putting a fence around the site and posting "No Trespassing" signs, until several more weeks had elapsed.

Slowly, but surely, New York State officials began to become more concerned—and more involved—with Love Canal. Meetings with residents were held in May, including one in which state and local officials argued on stage about the seriousness of the problem. State officials continued to express concern and Brown continued to report what they told him. He quoted a state biophysicist who said that, knowing what he knows, if he lived at Love Canal and could afford to move, he would do so.

In June, the state took blood samples from residents and asked those who lived right on the canal to fill out health questionnaires. In response to inquiries from other residents, the state agreed to test and provide questionnaires for all those who lived in the area. The public meetings between state officials and the residents increasingly assumed an air of confrontation. In the last week of June, the state began to systematically test air samples in the homes, and in early June the residents received forms from the state indicating levels of chemicals found in their houses, but providing very little information or guidance about what it all meant.

Relations between the state officials and the residents were not smooth, but at least the state appeared to be doing something. Local officials continued to run for cover. On the advice of its bond counsel, the City of Niagara Falls even withdrew from a multiparty study group trying to devise an engineering plan for the area. There were persistent rumors that the U.S. Army had contributed to the problem by disposing of materials in the canal decades before, but after conducting a brief investigation, the army declared that it had not done any dumping. Then, in mid-July, residents learned that there would be an important announcement on August 2 at a meeting held by New York Commissioner of Health Robert Whalen. The Whalen announcement was to take place in Albany, 300 miles from Love Canal, thus assuring (although it was not arranged there for that purpose) that few of the residents would be able to hear the long-awaited declarations of policy in person.

For weeks, Whalen had been studying the test results and consulting with experts from all over the country. His statement was short and to the point. Ten carcinogenic compounds had been found in vapors in homes around Love Canal. A disproportionate number of spontaneous abortions was another indication of potential toxicity. Whalen declared a public health emergency and concluded by saying that there existed ''a great and imminent peril'' to the health of the people living in and around Love Canal. He made several recommendations, among the most startling were that residents should not eat food from their gardens or use their basements. If that wasn't alarming enough, he urged that pregnant women and children under two years old living at the southern end of the area be relocated. It was a dramatic acknowledgement that Love Canal was a risky place to live.

Among those in attendance at the meeting was Lois Gibbs, who was to become a major force in the organization of Love Canal homeowners and a national spokesperson for their interests. Gibbs returned to Niagara Falls and almost immediately began to assume responsibilities as the leader of the residents' group. Meetings were held on the day of the announcement, and the following day, with the families increasingly concerned about the implications of Whalen's recommendations, and the unwillingness of the state to commit financial help for those who were relocating. The State of New York was then the first governmental entity to acknowledge the Love Canal problem, and the first to propose strong steps to deal with it. But being willing to step out in front also meant becoming the focus of all the residents' fears and frustrations. Whalen's response was forthright enough, but it did not adequately address the inevitable consequences of what he had to say. Telling people not to go into their basements, or eat from their gardens, or send their children to the local school were powerful and frightening messages. If children under two should be relocated, what about those who were two and a half or three? If pregnant women should move, what about those who wanted to conceive?

Governor Carey was not yet publicly involved, but there was tremendous pressure for him to be. He was in the middle of a reelection campaign and Love Canal had suddenly been acknowledged as a state problem. On August 4, two days after the Whalen announcement, the Love Canal Homeowners Association was officially established at a meeting at which Congressman LaFalce reported that President Carter was supporting legislation to provide some federal financial help. The governor's opponent in the Democratic primary, his own lieutenant governor, Mary Ann Krupsak, was calling for state action and wholesale relocation from the area.

On Monday, August 7, after a visit to Love Canal by Federal Disaster Assistance Administration officials, President Carter declared Love Canal an emergency. That evening, Governor Carey toured the area for the first time and announced to the crowd that the state would buy the homes bordering the canal. There was also some confusion about where the governor was drawing the line, but it was quickly sorted out and 239 families living in the so-called inner ring of homes on the canal site were to be moved.

Between August 1978, and December 1979, Love Canal residents and the state struggled toward solutions. A $9.2 million dollar state-financed construction program to secure the site by diverting the leaching and placing an eight-foot thick clay cap on the canal was bogged down for a long time over the question of an adequate safety program; residents were understandably anxious about living in the area while engineers and construction crews were disturbing the ground in and around the canal. There were studies and more studies, and fierce disagreements among federal, state, and the residents' scientists about what the studies meant and how much danger continued to exist for those who remained in their homes. There was continuing action, particularly by LaFalce at the federal level, to push for a more comprehensive federally funded relocation. The state was already committed to spending about $11.6 million on the relocation in addition to the construction. Carey continued to feel the pressure from the residents. And Love Canal stayed in the news, whether it was a temporary relocation for a few families because they had become ill from the fumes during the construction project, or a much balleyhooed visit from Jane Fonda, who added her voice to those calling for relocation.

By the end of 1979, the construction was nearly complete, but the residents who remained were dissatisfied with their lot and there was no scientific consensus on the continuing health risk for them. The Love Canal story was far from complete.

Setting the Stage for Public Policymaking

Late in 1979, senior officials at the Environmental Protection Agency decided to do something about the public perception that the government was not acting decisively about the problems of hazardous waste. From the agency's point of view, there was little legal authority to deal with incidents involving hazardous waste and too little support for the Superfund legislation, then pending in the Congress and which would, if enacted, give the government the legal tools and money to clean up the worst dumps. A Hazardous Waste Enforcement Task Force, organized and headed by Jeffrey Miller, then the acting head of the Enforcement Division at the EPA, was formed to try, as Miller recalls, "to piece together whatever authorities the government had to deal with the situations." The task force's strategy, according to Miller, was to develop lawsuits against Love Canal and other hazardous waste sites with two purposes in mind: "to affect legislation, and to try to turn the press around from criticism of the agency's handling of the hazardous waste problem, to acceptance that the agency was doing what it could but lacked all the tools it needed." One of the first products of the work of the task force was a lawsuit filed on December 20, 1979, by the Department of Justice against Hooker Chemical, the City of Niagara Falls, the Niagara County Health Department, and the Board of Education of the City of Niagara Falls. The suit asked for $124.5 million and for an end to the discharge of toxic chemicals in the area surrounding Love Canal, clean-up of the site, and relocation of the residents if necessary. It was a landmark suit, the first time that the federal government had gone after a private company which had dumped wastes into a site many years ago and no longer controlled the area. If successful, the suit would have established nationwide industry liability for the effects of abandoned toxic wastes that endangered people or the environment. It also represented a collaboration between the Justice Department's beefed-up Land and Natural Resources Division and its newly created Hazardous Waste Section and the EPA's Enforcement Division. The suit had been developed over several months by the two agencies working together and was filed by Justice on behalf of EPA.[4]

Proving that the actions of Hooker had harmed Love Canal residents was essential to establishing the company's liability. All the earlier tests had showed that the area was a toxic, and therefore dangerous, place to live. But no study had proven that health damage suffered by some of the residents could be directly traced to Hooker's wastes. Sometime in January, the lawyers handling the case at Justice decided that they needed to know more about the possible evidence of damage. Justice and EPA agreed that EPA would conduct a quick "pilot study" to see whether there was enough potential to go ahead with a full-blown rigorous scientific examination of the possible effects. The theory behind the pilot study was to look for chromosomal damage among Love Canal residents since such damage is evidence that people have been exposed to toxic chemicals. As subjects for the pilot study, they targeted people who would be most likely to show chromosomal damage because they had already exhibited some manifestations, such as cancer or children with birth defects. The study was a lawyer's "fishing expedition," according to Dr. Stephen Gage, the EPA assistant administrator for Research and Development, who said at the time that if it showed "promise" the agency would commission a full-scale project, which, if supportive, could be used in the court case.

Two other elements of the study are important to mention. First, EPA selected Dr. Dante Picciano and the firm of which he was scientific director, Biogenics of Houston, to do the study. Picciano was a somewhat controversial person in the chromosomal testing business as a result of a well-publicized fight he had with a former employer, Dow Chemical. Picciano, who had been testing Dow employees for chromosomal breakage, charged that Dow had refused to publicize his results when he found undue breakage among employees who had been exposed to certain chemicals. Second, the study lacked a control group. Picciano said at the time the EPA wanted the study done so quickly that there was no time for a control group to be tested, but Beverly Paigen, who helped him select the subjects for the study, says that the EPA used money, not time, as the excuse for not using controls.

At the time the study was commissioned, none of the senior administrators at EPA, surprisingly enough, were aware of it; the political, legislative, and public relations arms of the agency were uninvolved. Miller recalls the study being mentioned to him a couple of times during briefings on the case, but "no particular significance was attached to it" and he himself did not consider the potential impact of finding chromosomal damage among Love Canal residents.

While this potentially explosive study was unobtrusively moving forward during the spring of 1980, the attention of the Carter administration was understandably elsewhere. It was already well into an election year. The president seemed to be surviving a serious, time-consuming, and expensive intraparty challenge from Senator Edward M. Kennedy (D.-Mass.) and was relying primarily on surrogates to campaign in his behalf around the country. But the economy was not in good shape; Ronald Reagan appeared to be the likely Republican nominee and his photogenic appeal and ideological clarity were certain to cause problems. There were still American hostages in Iran and, although the president had managed to keep them off the front pages, their fate remained unresolved.

In addition, in early April there were the first inklings of the possibility of large numbers of Cubans being allowed to leave the island and seek refuge in other countries. Carter agreed on April 14 to accept 3,500 of them. Then, on April 24, the president's secret hostage rescue mission stalled, literally and figuratively, on an Iranian desert causing embarrassment, tragedy, the resignation of his secretary of State, and a lot of unexpected questions which had to be answered. On the same day, John Anderson, the moderate Republican Congressman from Illinois, further complicated Carter's reelection hopes by announcing that he was no longer a candidate for the Republican nomination for president, but would run in November as an Independent. Within a week, the trickle of Cuban refugees became a flood and by May 15, just before the Love Canal study became public, over 46,000 Cubans had arrived in the United States, needing housing, food, relocation assistance, and jobs. By the end of Love Canal week, that figure would rise to 67,000.

As the Love Canal decision came into focus over the weekend of May 16–18, the president could hardly be faulted for not making it his number one priority. On Saturday night, Miami exploded with race riots that resulted in 14 dead,

300 injured, and over $100 million in property damage. And the next day there was another eruption: Mount St. Helens. Carter declared the region a disaster area, as rescue workers began the task of cleaning up the bodies.

Finally, if there were to be an environmental crisis to solve, it was double trouble for Carter that it had to occur in New York State. Relations between the state and the federal government had been strained over Love Canal for at least two years. Governor Carey had been forced to assume the financial and administrative responsibilities for the first relocation. During that time, Carey had been trying to get the federal government to reimburse the state for its expenses, to share them, or to take over the problem. On the political front, the governor had been no friend at all. Carey was personally close to Kennedy, although he never endorsed Kennedy's candidacy. New York was critical to any Democratic presidential candidate and was one state where the presence on the ballot of John Anderson was likely to be particularly volatile. There was even talk of a Carey draft at the Democratic convention, if California's Governor Jerry Brown were to manage to win enough delegates to keep the nomination from either Kennedy or Carter. On May 9, the week before Love Canal was to become a major issue between them again, Carey announced that he was urging both Carter and Kennedy to release their delegates so that there could be an "open" Democratic convention. It was hardly an idea designed to win over the hearts and minds of Carter and his friends. Eugene Eidenberg, then deputy assistant to President Carter for intergovernmental affairs, called Carey "as serious a political problem as we had" at the time. And in the first major White House focus on the newest Love Canal problem, Jane Hansen, an aide to Jack Watson, who was secretary of the Cabinet and assistant to the president for intergovernmental affairs (and in the process of becoming chief of staff in the White House), wrote in a memo marked "Administratively Confidential" that "we're up against the politics of Governor Carey and the poor working relationship we have with him."[5]

Sometime in April, Hansen began to become involved in the Love Canal matter. No one is clear now exactly how that happened, but there had been continuing pressure from Governor Carey for federal funds and from Congressman LaFalce for federal action. In addition, Mayor Michael O'Laughlin of Niagara Falls had requested use for Love Canal residents of apartments in the area no longer needed by the Air Force for its personnel. Hansen began to put together a compendium of all the health studies of Love Canal residents, presumably to determine whether or not to recommend making those housing units available. In the course of pulling together the existing material, Hansen learned of the existence of the Justice / EPA pilot study.

Around the first of May, Dante Picciano spoke on the phone with Frode Ulvedal, head of the EPA's Health Effects Division, and gave him the preliminary results of the study. He reported that he had found chromosome aberrations in twelve of the thirty-six individuals tested. Shortly thereafter, he sent a letter, dated May 5, confirming the content of the telephone conversation. In part, the letter said:

. . . these results are believed to be significant deviations from normal, but in the absence of a control population, prudence must be exerted in the interpretation of such results.

Picciano recommended a larger study be undertaken. Miller recalls that there was a lot of activity at the EPA after the phone call from Picciano, before the report or even the letter had actually arrived. He remembers that it was assumed from the outset that the federal government would make a public release of the results:

> . . . the thought process that we went through was that if we have a piece of scientific information which indicates dangers to people living in that area, it is the responsibility of the agency to make that information known to those people. Otherwise, you may well be adding to the medical difficulties in the area, which would be irresponsible. Well, at that point, you have to ask two questions. One, is this scientifically okay or not? And second, what kind of response should the government itself make, or should it make a response?

On Thursday, May 8, Hansen met with LaFalce, who briefed her on all the activity around Love Canal since 1977. He discussed Carey's role in the matter and focused her attention on the issue of permanent relocation and the possibility of the government purchasing the homes of the residents. On Friday, Hansen was fully briefed on the Picciano study, although the report itself had not yet been received, only the May 5 letter and the phone call. Doug McMillan, who had succeeded Miller as the head of the EPA Hazardous Wastes Task Force, did the briefing. Notes from that meeting reflect agreement with Miller's assumption that the government would have to announce the results of the study. There was discussion about the timing of the announcement, and Jim Moorman, who was responsible for the lawsuit at Justice, was quoted as saying that the EPA was "leaky" and the study would not stay out of the press. There was a general consensus that the announcement of the study would affect the course of the Superfund bill through the Congress and that it should be done in coordination with LaFalce and not before the government had organized its response to the findings.

It was noted that Beverly Paigen, who had been the on-site coordinator for the study, already knew the results and so did Lois Gibbs, president of the Love Canal Homeowners Association, although in her own recounting of the events, Gibbs says that she did not know the results of the study until several days later.

That was the situation at the end of the week. Senior administrators at both Justice and the EPA were aware of the results of the Picciano study through telephone calls and a brief letter outlining them. The full report had not yet arrived. The White House was already involved, although neither Jack Watson nor the president even knew of the existence of the Picciano study, never mind the results. All involved assumed that the government would have to make public the results, both because eventually they would leak to the press and also out of a sense of responsibility to the residents of Love Canal. At that point, pressure was mounting but those officials who were talking about the problem believed that time was not yet of the essence and that the government would be able to make a reasoned and thoughtful judgment about what to do. Although some of those involved now recall thinking about the need for establishing the scientific credibility of the study, there are no clear references to that issue in notes taken at the time. There was no sense in Washington at that point that the federal government would supplant the state and local governments as the lead actor in dealing with Love Canal, although it was clear that the government would have to have some response.

On Monday evening, May 12, Hansen, along with Robert Harris and Robert Nicholas of the Council on Environmental Quality, went to Watson to brief him on the study. They told him that they were exploring the statutes to see whether the federal government had the legal authority to pay for the relocation of residents. Watson's reply was a clear directive to Hansen to pull together the pieces for the federal response: to "expedite the use of the 90 Air Force housing units, have GSA [the General Services Administration] do a survey of available housing, have HUD [the Department of Housing and Urban Development] assume responsibility for the 250-unit public project, and research the legal authority for the feds to do anything."[6]

During the next couple of days, the pace of activity began to increase. The government was trying to figure out what it could do, what it could pay for, and who or what agency would pick up the bill. Jeffrey Miller remembers that "for a week, I did nothing else but run around on this, talking to Barbara [Blum, EPA's deputy administrator], talking to Steve [Gage], talking to my people, going over to the White House, talking to people at Justice. It all runs together. Later in the week, perhaps on Thursday, May 15, it was apparent that the press knew something about the study, if not anything more than its existence." Miller recalls hearing about inquiries from the *New York Times* to the EPA press office on Thursday. And the situation there was compounded by the fact that Marlin Fitzwater, the EPA's public information officer, was on vacation. Watson and Hansen do not remember fielding any similar inquiries at the White House during that period, but by Thursday, Hansen realized that the time for decision making was beginning to shrink. She wrote a long memo to Watson stressing the need for urgent action:

> I am concerned that momentarily the press / media will have the results of health studies which reveal chromosomal abnormalities, peripheral nerve damage, and unsuccessful pregnancies among residents of Love Canal.

After commenting on the complications stemming from Carey's involvement and her own efforts to put together federal funds for relocation from several different sources, Hansen continued with her action plan:

> I think we should take the offensive *quickly* [her emphasis] in announcing the results of the studies ourselves. At that time, I recommend we also announce the following:

• The state health department and EPA are verifying the data and will determine within a week whether or not it constitutes a health hazard. (Dr. Rall of HHS is prepared to have a team of scientists start as early as this weekend.)
• The federal government is making 90 units of excess military housing available immediately as alternative housing for those who want it. We will negotiate with state and local governments on rehabilitation, payments, and maintenance costs.
• If the area is deemed uninhabitable at the end of the week, the federal government will work with the state to temporarily relocate the residents of the area while the federal and state governments pursue their lawsuits with the Hooker Chemical Company.

This announcement will provide us with some flexibility and give us at least a week to answer some important questions and determine our own course of action. . . . Carey will probably blast us for whatever we decide to do since he's still arguing that we should pay him the $10 million he used to buy up homes in Ring One. We might as well get on the offensive, express our concern by releasing the results of the study and announce some positive steps. Then we should call in the state by early next week and begin negotiating. . . .[7]

The Hansen memo had the desired effect. Watson asked for a meeting for Friday, the purpose of which, he recalled, was "to get to the bottom of the situation. There were a lot of stories, internal stories, being circulated about what was going on and how serious it was, and what the life-threatening 'quotient' was. And I wanted to understand that. I therefore had to gather in some of the technical people from the EPA and other places, who could speak directly to that, so that I could understand the degree of the risk and the nature of the risk. We were also very concerned . . . with the public's perception, not so much the public at large, but the public that was directly affected. . . . I was very concerned about wrong, rumor-filled, distorted information getting to them through the press, through other means, which would cause them to be in a state of great panic."

The meeting was scheduled for 11:00 A.M. on Friday, May 16, in Room 248 of the Old Executive Office Building. There were at least fifteen people invited, senior administrators from Justice, EPA, the Federal Emergency Management Agency (FEMA), the Council on Environmental Quality (CEQ), and the Department of Health and Human Services (HHS).

According to Watson, in conversations before the meeting Dr. Rall of HHS indicated that he could verify the results of the study with a panel of experts in about a week. There had been some interagency tension between HHS and EPA over who had the lead for the government in the environmental health area and Rall seemed eager to take responsibility for examining the EPA study's scientific validity. During the meeting, Rall noted that whatever the results of the study, it would be impossible to say with scientific certainty that there was a connection between the release of chemicals and the health problems of the residents because of the difficulty of knowing for sure what caused the chromosomal damage. This line of reasoning was frustrating to Watson, who remembers saying that "that sort of academic view of this matter was unacceptable. We had a number of people's lives potentially grievously affected or literally at stake, and we did not have the time, nor did I have the inclination, to sit around while scientists debated rather maliciously with each other about whose process was right."

Notes taken at the meeting make it clear that there was agreement that time was precious, that people in Niagara Falls knew the study had been completed, and that there was a good chance that if they did not act soon, the report would be in the press before the people who had been tested were notified of the results. The decision was made to inform the subjects immediately and to hold a press conference the next day, Saturday, to release the study and announce the response of the federal government. There was some pressure from the representatives of the Justice Department to make the public announcement on Friday, but the need first to inform the study participants was deemed to be an overriding consideration: they deserved to be informed officially what their own tests showed. Language discussed at the meeting was to find its way into the public statements: steps were being taken with an "abundance of caution," the data was "preliminary" and the government was acting "prudently" in the matter.[8] Those present at the meeting recall no debate over the general plan that was developed, no argument in favor of not releasing the results immediately. It was agreed that Wednesday would be the day for making the next decision.

After the meeting, Miller went back to his office to draft a memo for Watson with a schedule of the activities for the next twenty-four hours, including a draft of the press release and a form letter to be provided to the Love Canal residents from whom blood samples were taken. During that afternoon, it became evident that the officials' fears were realized: the study had leaked, and the *New York Times* was going to have a story about it in the Saturday paper. According to Watson and Hansen, the White House was not called by either the *Times* or the upstate papers that published the story on Saturday. The calls did come to the EPA and for the moment at least it was an EPA story, not a White House one. Watson called EPA Deputy Administrator Barbara Blum, who was in Atlanta at the time, and told her to return to Washington because she was going to hold a press conference the next day announcing the results of the study. According to the plan, each of those who had been subjects of the study would be informed individually of their results; late Friday afternoon the EPA called Lois Gibbs and asked her to notify the thirty-six families involved and arrange appointments for them between 8:00 A.M. and noon. According to Gibbs, the EPA official told her that it had to be done immediately because someone had already leaked the results of the study to the press. Gibbs and a colleague reached thirty-four of the families by 8:00 P.M.; the other two were away for the weekend. Hansen called LaFalce and reached him in his Niagara Falls office late Friday afternoon. LaFalce describes himself as being "stunned" by the news relayed by Hansen: "I had never heard about this [study] and [it] was going to be devastating when released."

LaFalce convinced them to have the press conference in his Niagara Falls office "where we could limit the number of people, where it wouldn't be wide open in an auditorium with questions from the audience. With TV cameras there it could lead to absolute chaos."

The plans for Saturday were set. While reporters for the *Times,* the *Buffalo Courier Express,* and the *Niagara Gazette* were preparing page one stories, federal officials were organizing a complex series of events that included a Washington press conference, a briefing for each of the study subjects at Lois Gibbs's Homeowners offices, a briefing for local officials followed by a press conference for local press in Congressman LaFalce's Niagara Falls office, and late morning phone calls to inform Carey and the two United States senators from New York, Daniel Patrick Moynihan and Jacob Javits.

Keeping Up With the Story

There was nothing quiet about Saturday, May 17, for those involved with Love Canal. On the front page of the *New York Times* was a story by Irvin Molotsky, attributing to "federal officials" who "asked not to be identified" the results from the Biogenics study. The story suggests strongly that the information did not come from EPA, but originated from someone who had been involved in the Friday meeting at the White House and therefore knew of the impending press conferences. Hooker spokespersons criticized the release of the study, pointed to the preliminary nature of the findings, and expressed concern that the publicity would cause panic among Love Canal residents. The article mistakenly reported that the study had only reached Washington on Thursday and that the decision to go public had been made on the day after it was received, lending further credence to the idea that this was done in haste because of the seriousness of the results. Similar front page stories appeared in both the Niagara Falls and Buffalo morning newspapers.

For Lois Gibbs, the day started before dawn. She had only a few hours' sleep, after having finally reached the last of the Biogenics subjects to schedule their meetings. As she recalls that day in her book on Love Canal:

> There was no need to set the alarm clock that Saturday morning. Reporters started calling me at 5:30 to get a story in time for the morning edition. I had hardly gotten to the office when people began to arrive—news reporters, EPA representatives, residents, doctors. Within fifteen minutes there were twenty-five people, all talking loudly. TV camera lights were turned on and off throughout the building. The EPA officials were trying to figure out how they could conduct private interviews in the midst of this circus. I ignored the craziness long enough to finish putting on my make-up and grab a cup of coffee. This was going to be a long day!
>
> As I came out of the bathroom, about eight people yelled "Lois" at the same time. No one else was doing it, so I took charge. I asked Debbie to throw the press out. Boy! Were they angry at me! I then asked the residents to wait in the kitchen and the EPA representatives to meet in my office.
>
> We found space for each of the EPA doctors to speak privately with the

families. Dr. Paigen was good enough to remain in the kitchen with the families, to answer questions about their test results. She has been so good to us. She was always around when we needed her, always willing to give herself to help us.

The EPA had set aside a half-hour for each family with one of their doctors to explain the results and answer questions. The atmosphere in the office that day was strange. The residents who were waiting were quiet. They were frightened and depressed. The newspaper reports said that eleven of the thirty-six residents tested showed broken chromosomes of a rare type. Each one who heard the news believed that they were one of the eleven. According to the news stories, the chromosome breaks meant an increased risk of miscarriages, stillborns, birth defects, cancer, or genetic damage, understandably, frightened people. Some arrived at the office crying. Others were so nervous they couldn't sit; they just paced back and forth. There wasn't much small talk.

You could feel the tension mounting. When the first families were called in to see the doctors, a cold chill ran down my back. The first family came out after their interview. The couple just stood in the doorway, not saying a word. Then they slowly walked over to Dr. Paigen and began to cry. The room became silent. The woman told Beverly that the doctors handed her and her husband a piece of paper with numbers on it, and told them that both had an abnormal number of breakages, and, as if that weren't bad enough, the breakages were of a rare type. EPA doctors couldn't tell them what that menat to their family. All the doctors would say was that the test results were only an indication of health risks in the population. No one could say what the result meant in an individual case. When the woman asked about the effects on her children, she was told that if her breakage and that of her husband were due to exposure to Love Canal chemicals, and the children were also exposed, the chances were good that the children also had chromosome breaks. There was nothing they could do as parents except move their children from Love Canal.

As the woman spoke about her children, she became even more upset. If they could have afforded to move out, she said, they would have moved a year ago! Her husband put his arm around her and took her home. As they were leaving, she looked back at the closed door where the EPA doctors were speaking with another couple and yelled "Damn you, EPA! Damn you, stupid government!"

As soon as the couple stepped out of the door, at least twenty reporters from all over the country encircled them. That poor woman. She had enough to deal with without trying to answer their questions!

While I was looking out the window, an angry yell came from upstairs. The family was shouting at an EPA official. The official went upstairs to tell them that their half hour was up. They would have to leave because other people were waiting to talk to the doctor. The family was telling him to go to hell! They were going to talk to the doctor until all their questions were answered. . . .

The tension in the office increased as people went in and out of the doctors' rooms. Most of the families were as confused when they came out as when they went in. Tempers grew shorter; people were visibly upset. Even those families with negative findings were upset, wondering whether they had been told the truth or whether their children might yet be affected. Beverly was great. She was there to try to answer the residents' questions. Debbie kept throwing out media people trying to get in. I tried to keep things running as smoothly as best I could, but it was difficult to keep from being deeply moved by my friends' tears and their shock. I kept wondering how much more those people could take! One of these days, they will go crazy, I thought.[9]

It was not much quieter for Congressman La Falce. He had done little more than provide the site for the briefing and press conference scheduled at noon in Niagara Falls. The theory was that local officials would be briefed by EPA scientists and then be available for the press. LaFalce recalls that Gibbs had done most of the work informing people that the event was to take place, but about thirty minutes before the conference began he realized that the Niagara Falls mayor had not been notified and hurriedly called him. LaFalce says he did not know until well after the press conference that the study was preliminary and without a control group. He remembers that when the conference was over the EPA officials were preparing to go back to Washington and he took them into his office:

I cornered them and I said, "No way can you come in and toss a bombshell at my constituents and tell them that they have this chromosomal damage possibilities and just walk away. You better stay here all weekend until you decide what you are going to do." . . . They were totally unprepared for this. We got the message across and they in fact did stay.

LaFalce says he talked with Carey that afternoon; Regional EPA Administrator Charles Warren had failed to reach state officials until minutes before the press conference, undoubtedly adding to Carey's frustration with Washington. LaFalce says that he and Carey discussed pushing for another declaration of emergency from the White House and for permanent relocation.

An important feature of the press conference was that despite LaFalce's warnings, the space used was big enough to accomodate some of the residents as well as the representatives of the media. Gibbs remembers that there were a hundred residents there; the *New York Times* says twenty. Which report is right is less relevant than the fact that the residents made themselves heard at the press conference, and seen on the nightly news that evening. LaFalce recalls, with begrudging respect, watching Lois Gibbs moving around the room, encouraging residents to yell questions to the officials, and doing some of that herself.

Back in Washington, Barbara Blum and Stephen Gage, the assistant administrator for research and development at the EPA, were simultaneously holding their press conference for the national press. The language of Blum's press statement was cautious, as it was supposed to be, although the press release issued by EPA was headlined, by the agency itself, "EPA finds chromosomal damage at Love Canal," thereby undermining the effort to put the study in the context of a preliminary effort which needed further review and suggesting that the EPA was interested in keeping the pressure on for the Superfund bill and in emphasizing its aggressive actions against Hooker. Whatever the intent of the government had been, the Washington press conference resulted in reports which framed the key issues which were to occupy the energies of officials at all levels of government and residents of the affected area for the next few days. On the question of relocation, Blum said that the decision would be made "probably by Wednesday" on the basis of a review of the Biogenics study. On the question of who would pay for relocation she said, "We certainly can't let money stand in the way . . . if that should prove to be necessary." She characterized the Biogenics findings as "alarming." Caution was expressed by lawyers for Hooker (who attended both press conferences) and by Gage, who noted that "The science of studying cells is not advanced enough to say definitively that there is a causal relationship between an abnormality and a disease." But the main thrust of the day's activities was clearly that something of enormous import had taken place. As LaFalce notes:

> EPA was making a big deal out of this. EPA was not saying "there is a study and we hold this study suspect." EPA was saying "We have a serious study that has created serious problems." . . . EPA handled it with such immediacy and such alarm and such a sense of urgency, that it created an aura that was impossible to cope with rationally.

LaFalce's assessment of the Saturday morning press conferences seems correct. The leak and the Saturday morning stories may have added some momentum and created a sense of urgency surrounding the issue, but the White House EPA strategy of deliberately publicizing the study results stood on its own as an expression of major concern on the part of the government. Perhaps the most significant consequence of the press conferences was that the coverage following it—unlike the Saturday morning coverage—focused more on the issue of relocation than on the Biogenics study itself. Had the study been the story, perhaps Blum's carefully worded warnings about its lack of definitiveness would not have gotten lost. In any event, there is nothing in the records of the meetings leading up to Saturday's events or in conversations with several of the participants which suggests that the federal officials involved had anticipated that they would ignite a tinderbox, both among the media and the residents of Love Canal. No one in the government seems to have suggested that publicizing the study as seriously as they did would create an irreversible demand for relocation from potentially affected Love Canal families, whose anxieties, in turn, would be fed by a national sense of outrage and compassion stoked with enormous press coverage.

The press conference in Washington made the CBS and NBC evening news, with both networks including a Niagara Falls segment showing families in distress. The Sunday *New York Times* was a Love Canal cornucopia. There were two stories on page one, one by Molotsky on the press conference in Washington which led with the relocation question, and by Josh Barbanel from Niagara Falls, which led with a family receiving the bad news from the EPA doctors and detailed the press conference hosted by LaFalce, with emphasis on the residents' demands for relocation. Barbanel quoted one resident as saying "Governor Carey doesn't want to do anything and the president is killing us." There was a sidebar on chromosomes and the connection between chromosomal damage and problems such as birth defects and cancer. Even the book section chipped in with a laudatory review of Michael Brown's book, *Laying Waste,* which, coincidentally, had just been published and included sixty pages on the history of the problems at Love Canal, laying most of the blame at the feet of Hooker Chemical.

Blum describes her role that day as being called on to "mitigate" the damage from the leak by showing that the federal government was in control and taking responsive and responsible steps. She says that the White House reaction was to "panic" and that the situation from Saturday forward was "like two people standing down in the field and being pelted with five hundred balls." What was an effort to control the flow of events did not succeed because "the situation just rolled on faster than the management of it."

That may be a view enhanced by the benefit of hindsight; while most of those who were directly involved were aware that time was of the essence, they recall feeling that they were still going to be able to make a deliberative and rational decision about relocation, that they could wait until the results of the Rall review were available midweek, and that if they decided to relocate they would be able first to put together a package of legal authority, necessary funding, and cooperation with New York State that would help ensure an orderly process.

Sometime early Saturday, Jack Watson composed a memorandum for the president. It was carefully written, with measured language seemingly designed to neither overstate nor understate the situation but clearly reflect Watson's instinct that relocation was probably just around the corner. Presumably, it was the first the president had heard of the activity around the new Love Canal crisis which had consumed so much of the time and energy of senior federal officials for the past few days. Watson began:

> I wish to apprise you of a situation which has arisen during the last few days and will no doubt gain national attention. . . .
> This week the Justice Department informed me that they had received rather alarming results of a study conducted in the course of their lawsuit against Hooker Chemical Company. While the results must be validated, health experts who have reviewed the data within the last couple of days claim that if the study is accurate, residents' health is in danger and they should leave the area as soon as possible. Justice lawyers are attempting to get Hooker to pay for temporary relocation of residents by threatening to ask the Court for a temporary injunction if they refuse to assume responsibility voluntarily. In the meantime, however, it appears that the residents face an immediate health hazard that demands speedier response than litigation.

Watson went on to discuss Friday meeting which he chaired and then continued:

. . . Justice and I did not feel that we could conceal the information until then [Wednesday, when the study could be validated]. . . .

If we are faced with such an emergency, people will have to be moved when validation is in.

The state has been characteristically uncooperative and I anticipate problems with Governor Carey in defining state and federal responsibilities. . . .

I . . . will attempt to avoid a lengthy public battle resulting in no action and growing hysteria among Love Canal residents.[10]

Watson seemed to be suggesting that the handwriting was already on the wall; he was not going to allow the Carter administration to be in the position of opposing assistance to Love Canal residents who were understandably upset about the continuing danger to their health. In retrospect, it appears that he was already paving the way for a federally-financed relocation decision.

For Dr. David Rall, Saturday was the beginning of the effort to confirm the study. Wednesday was his deadline and his plan was to assemble a team at the Biogenics office in Houston on Saturday to begin looking at the data. This was not Rall's first experience with Love Canal; as chief of the National Institute of Environmental Health Science (NIEHS), he had been head of an interagency task force which had reviewed the existing Love Canal health studies in 1979. On Friday, after the White House meeting, the EPA had called Dr. Picciano to tell him that the panel was coming to look at his work. Picciano says that he agreed to the review, but that he objected to one member of the Rall panel because there were rumors that the individual was planning to start a consulting firm. Picciano said that Rall could replace him with anyone else and also add one person from a list of five suggested by Biogenics. Chris Carter, scientific director at NIEHS, chaired the panel and apparently spent time over the weekend with Rall determining the appropriate response to Picciano's conditions. Concurrent with the NIEHS review, Doug MacMillan at the EPA continued putting together a compendium of all the health studies of Love Canal residents.

At the White House, Hansen was continuing to work on the effort to pull together the federal funds and authority that she and Watson felt were necessary should a decision to relocate be forthcoming. She had received a call from Larry Hammond at the Office of the Legal Counsel at the Justice Department on Friday saying that he needed more time to do the research on what statutes and what funds would cover relocation.

Gene Eidenberg was the White House official handling the wave of Cuban refugees flooding Florida. As of that weekend, there had been 46,000 arrivals in three weeks.[11] Eidenberg spent much of his time flying back and forth between Washington and Miami. Hansen had sent him a copy of her May 15 memo to Watson and Eidenberg was present at the Friday meeting chaired by Watson. On Saturday he was off again to Miami for the day and remembers riding out to Andrews Air Force Base with Jane Hansen briefing him on further Love Canal developments. Eidenberg had to be involved because as the chief of intergovernmental relations it would fall to him to take on the sticky negotiations with Carey. According to Eidenberg, Hansen said that the situation was "becoming unglued," and they both realized that there would be little time to work out a deal with Carey with respect to costs and responsibility before the decision had to be made.

Carey, for his part, was already frustrated by the way the federal government had handled him and the study. Sunday was the day for him to organize his response to the new Love Canal crisis. He met with his Love Canal task force at the governor's mansion in Albany to plan his strategy. The focus of attention was not on the Love Canal residents, but on the residents of the White House, as Carey believed at that point that relocation had become inevitable and the central issue was who—or which government—was going to pay the bill. Later in the day Carey and his state health commissioner, Dr. David Axelrod, spoke to the press and, in effect, opened up negotiations with the White House. He was taking a very hard line, and sending a very strong message to the Carter administration.

Carey and Axelrod criticized the study because of the lack of a control group, criticized the release of the study, and said that making the information public was "devastating psychologically" whether or not the results were later validated. Finally Carey estimated the costs of relocation as between $30 and $60 million, a far cry from the $3 to $5 million estimate Barbara Blum had given to the press the day before. Carey's figures included money he had already spent and probably estimated the costs of permanent, rather than temporary relocation. Whatever his calculations, Carey's message was received. An anonymous "high-ranking Carter administration official" characterized Carey as trying to embarrass the administration and avoid responsibility for Love Canal. Before the face-to-face negotiations even began, the *New York Times* was carrying declarations of war back and forth between the parties.

The issue of how the report became public was another sore spot. Senior Carter officials say, and their notes confirm, that they made a decision to go public hours before they knew that the results had been leaked. In fact, there was some suggestion by them that it was someone at the Friday meeting who began the chain of events resulting in the Saturday morning stories. Yet as part of their defense of their handling of the situation, they responded to Carey and others as if the Saturday press conference was scheduled because the information had already leaked and that they were trying to control the damage. The EPA's Stephen Gage was quoted in the *Times* as saying that "We would not have had a public release of information if it had not already leaked. . . . We felt it was a responsible thing to do to lay things out." From the perspective of the Carter Administration, the relocation decision and what it would entail if it was made were still open questions, so they did not want it to seem at all as if they had been responsible for creating the crisis. For instance, over the weekend Donald L. Baieder, president and chief operating officer of Hooker, wrote to Moorman declining to share in the relocation costs, agreeing to assist in a further study, and attaching a copy of his company's press release issued "after the *New York Times* carried a story which I can only conclude was inadvertently leaked to them." When Hansen prepared Eidenberg on Sunday for the beginning of the negotiations with Carey over money, she noted, "If he wants to know why we released the study before validated, tell him it was out of control because of leaks.'' Sunday was also the day for arranging another White House meeting, with essentially the same participants as before, to try to anticipate options when the results of the Rall review were in hand later in the week.

Eidenberg talked with Carey and Carey's chief aide, Robert Morgado, late at night. ''It was a very hard conversation,'' Eidenberg recalls, ''because Carey had criticized us for having made the information public, and [he] was basically saying, 'Look, you guys are the inept ones, you don't know how to handle it, you put this thing in the public domain . . . you pay for it.' '' Eidenberg remembers negotiating the conditions under which Carey would request a declaration of emergency and the White House would agree. Eventually, during conversations held in the following twenty-four hours, the deal was cut: Carey would request the declaration and they agreed that the state and the federal government would essentially share whatever costs were involved. Even as they spoke, however, the White House and EPA were still waiting for the results of the Rall review and trying to put together the money to pay the bills. Eidenberg says that it was already clear that there was a psychological emergency which had to be solved whether or not there proved to be a health one as well.

The Rall review was moving slowly. Picciano remembers receiving a call on Monday from ''Charles Carter, acting for Rall.'' Picciano says that Carter first told him that no one would be removed from the committee but that they would add one of his nominees. He then recalls another call, later in the day, informing him that none of his nominees had been selected. This call came from Carter's secretary and also carried the message that Carter and his review team were on their way to Houston to visit Biogenics. Picciano told the secretary to have Carter call when he arrived. Carter called about midnight. Picciano tried to re-open the membership issue. Carter declined to do so. There was a round of calls again on Tuesday, this time between Picciano and Blum. Finally, the review committee rejected the last nominee from Picciano and decided to make whatever review was possible without visiting the laboratory. Carter and his associates went home.

In Washington on Monday there was another White House strategy meeting, chaired by Eidenberg. At this session there was discussion of what should happen if the results of the Picciano study could not be validated and consideration was given to recommending relocation even in that case. No decision was made. The remainder of the meeting was spent on the continuing search for federal funds and authority, some updating on the results of the search for other health tests of Love Canal residents, and some awareness that EPA and HHS were not completely in accord on the question of which agency ought to have the lead role in doing health tests in this area.

But despite the continuing rational discussion of the problem at the meeting, matters were clearly getting out of White House control. White House officials, including Stuart Eizenstat, Eidenberg, and Hansen, met with LaFalce and Senator Moynihan in Moynihan's office. The two legislators expressed their anger at the way the situation was being handled, particularly at the leak of the study before the residents had been informed, and pushed the White House people on whether the study was sound and whether money was available for relocation.

Meanwhile, up at Love Canal, residents and the press spent the day at the Love Canal Residents Association offices, anxiously awaiting further word from Washington on what was going to happen. Gibbs recalls that in the early afternoon someone showed her a newspaper headline from the Buffalo *Evening News* which blared across the front page: "White House Blocked Canal Pullout." The headline fired up the residents there, and as the word spread the crowd grew from fifty to one hundred. People stopped passing cars and ignited gasoline on a lawn across the street forming the letters EPA. The police arrived. Lois Gibbs tried to locate the two EPA officials left in Niagara Falls to ask them to come to the site, hoping that "the residents would focus their anger on them." The two had stayed in the area to answer residents' questions. One was a public information officer, the other a doctor. She finally reached one of them, Frank Napal, the public information officer, and he agreed to come to the office. Napal arrived at about 4:00 P.M. Gibbs urged him to call the doctor so that there would be someone there to talk about the health issues. Napal called the physician, James Lucas, and shortly he, too, appeared at the association headquarters. Once the two officials were inside the building, Gibbs informed them that they were being held hostage. Here is her account of what happened next:

> I told them no harm would come to them, but that if they left the office, I could not be responsible for what the crowd, now numbering nearly five hundred people, would do. We had no guns, no other weapons; but for their own protection, I advised them to stay in our office. We had plenty of food, all homemade, and they could use the phone as they wished. My office was so packed with reporters and residents, no one could walk through it. I had no idea of what one did holding hostages. I thought to myself: Why didn't I watch TV more carefully!
>
> It wasn't hard to figure out that we should tell someone, never thinking the press was already telling the whole world. I decided to call the White House. I knew I would never be able to talk to the President, and I didn't want to talk to a lackey. So I put in a call to Jack Watson. . . .
>
> . . . His secretary answered. I said: "My name is Lois Gibbs, president of the LCHA, in Niagara Falls, New York. The Love Canal residents are holding two EPA officials hostage. I would like to speak to Mr. Watson about this matter." I was trying to sound calm and objective, not easy under the circumstances. The secretary in a very mechanical voice said, "Would you hold, please, Mrs. Gibbs?" She asked me to hold when I told her we were holding federal officials hostage!
>
> In a few moments, she said she would deliver my message to Watson. She went on to say that we were wrong, that we should let the EPA officials go, adding: "You people have blown Love Canal all out of proportion. I have friends who have cancer and they don't live at Love Canal and. . . ."
>
> I told her to go to hell! . . .
>
> The office was a three-ring circus. It was so hot, one could hardly move or breathe. I stood on a chair and announced that I had called the White

House. I asked every one to leave the room and I would make an announcement from the porch out front in a few minutes. The room cleared out except for a few residents who stayed while I went out front to speak to the crowd. I tried to quiet the crowd (there was no PA system). My voice isn't very loud. As people moved in toward the porch, I noticed beer bottles on the ground and many teenagers in the crowd. Beer and teenagers meant trouble.

When the crowd quieted down, I said I had notified the White House that the officials were being held hostage by the Love Canal residents. The crowd cheered. Then I said, "I don't know what Washington is going to do, but I expect a call back soon." I stressed that they should stay calm and orderly. "We have not been destructive or violent in the past. Let's not do it now. As soon as I hear something, I'll tell you." I restricted the building to no more than five people at a time and only one person from media at a time. That would ensure the safety of the hostages. The crowd was hostile: "They ain't ensuring our safety. Why should we ensure theirs?" and: "To hell with them! Let them suffer just like we have the past two years!" I had forgotten for a moment how touchy the crowd was; but they reminded me quickly enough.

I went back into the office and asked everyone to leave. I let Marie Pozniak decide who would stay. Marie knew just about everyone in the neighborhood because she dealt with them every day. She knew who could be counted on to remain level-headed in a crisis.

Back in the office, I suddenly realized what we had done. The news reporter asked me if I were worried about going to jail. I told them I wasn't doing anything wrong. I was protecting the EPA officials from the crowd. I realized that there were too many people in the room who should not be held responsible, so I asked everyone except Barbara Quimby to leave. I asked her if she would stay even if it meant she could go to jail. She said she felt safer in here than out in that crowd. She was willing to do whatever was necessary to help her children. She stood guard at the door to make sure neither residents nor the press entered without our permission and to see that the EPA officials didn't leave.

The last of the residents and the press had left. There were just four of us. Things quieted down in the rest of the building. Marie successfully ushered people out. I apologized to the hostages, telling them we were sorry they were taking the heat for the big shots in Washington sitting in plush offices.

Barbara's husband knocked on the door. She was afraid he was going to pull her out; but to her surprise, he didn't. They spoke very softly. Jim asked her if she knew what she was doing. She said she knew and that she was doing it for her children. "Please understand, Jim." He looked at her for a second. Then he told her to do what she felt she had to do, that he loved her and was proud of her. He said he would be outside the door if she needed him.

Not long after he closed the door, we heard a man's voice shouting. I couldn't make out what he was saying. I hoped Marie had posted large people at the door! At first, I couldn't tell who it was, but then my heart sank and I recognized the voice. The person hated me and the association.

He repeatedly accused us of holding secret meetings with officials. He could not be described as cool and collected; in fact he was just the opposite.

Marie told us he was outside and her "guards wouldn't let him in." He was accusing us of holding a secret meeting with EPA. She said he had gone off again and was furious. She no sooner closed the door than there was a crash. The window next to me splattered in a thousand pieces. I was as frightened as everyone else in room. I looked around to see if anyone was hurt. Jim Quimby came charging through the door to see what happened. Our hostages, sensing the crowd's mood, were becoming edgy themselves.

Out front people seemed to be milling around confused. I had no idea if someone shot at the window or threw something or what happened! One of the residents pushed through the hedge outside and poked his head into the space where the window once was. He asked if everyone was all right. He explained that the person thought we were holding a secret meeting and put his arm through the window. He said that the man cut his elbow but that he would be okay.

I asked the resident to get some strong men outside the windows and doors. I turned back to see one of the hostages helping clean up the glass. He was holding the dust pan while Barbara's husband swept the pieces into it. For some reason, that struck me funny. He looked as if he belonged with us, not as though he was being held against his will. Unfortunately, the other man was not as calm. He looked white. He sat there as if he were waiting for something horrible to happen to him.

I explained to both hostages that everything was under control. People were guarding the windows and doors to protect them. I said that to try to reassure them, especially the one who was so frightened.

The phone rang. It was Chuck Warren, from the EPA regional office in New York City. He wanted to know what was going on. I explained about the five hundred angry people out front, the broken window, and the EPA officials whom we were calling hostages to keep the crowd happy. I said that, in all truth, we were protecting them—in hopes they wouldn't arrest us. He asked me to let them go. I reminded him of the crowd and the broken window. I told him it was impossible; they would never make it off the porch before the crowd attacked them. I said that I felt a responsibility to protect people from possible harm, which was more than the government felt toward us.[12]

Warren asked to talk to Napal, who reassured him that the hostage-taking was somewhat benign. Napal said that he didn't feel "physically threatened." It was just that he couldn't leave.

The next caller was LaFalce. He was furious at Gibbs, and told her that the incident was "going to work against her." He warned her that, however innocent it began, holding people against their will with an angry crowd outside had the potential for disaster. Gibbs told LaFalce that she wanted to talk with the president. LaFalce told her that he was going to have dinner with the president that evening and would talk to him about the problems at Love Canal.

LaFalce was telling the truth, but not quite all of it. Just by coincidence he was scheduled to have dinner with Mr. Carter at the White House, but along with fifty or seventy-five other members of the House of Representatives. At any rate, that dinner date seemed to give both Gibbs and LaFalce a little breathing space. LaFalce urged her to release the hostages, and the conversation ended. Gibbs went outside, told the crowd that LaFalce was meeting with the president to discuss the residents' concerns, and that LaFalce wanted them to release the EPA officials. The crowd cheered the news of the LaFalce–Carter meeting, but clearly was opposed to the idea of letting Napal and Lucas go free. According to Miller, the FBI brought its kidnap team to the EAP and established telephone contact with Gibbs and the hostages. During the early evening, Gibbs repeatedly went outside to speak to the crowd and her colleagues brought the hostages some supper.

In Washington, Blum issued a statement in response to the news of the hostage-taking to the effect that the EPA was moving as rapidly as possible to evaluate the study and that the "well-being of the Love Canal residents is our highest priority." Meanwhile LaFalce was having his "dinner meeting" with Carter. When he went to the White House, LaFalce did not know whether he would get a chance to speak with the president so he typed a letter for Carter, urging relocation as soon as possible, calling the White House actions to that point "unresponsive," and expressing anger at what he called a "lack of federal leadership."

By a stroke of good fortune, LaFalce was seated for dinner at the same table as the president. As he recalls, "It was a round table, and there were perhaps three other members of Congress at the same table as well as some members of the administration. Assistant Secretary of the Treasury Fred Bergsten was on my right, and the president was two or three people to my left. He was terribly preoccupied, and it was difficult to engage him in conversation. . . . I did try to address Love Canal, . . . but he wanted to discuss social events. He was having a great conversation about jogging with Congressman Butler Derek of South Carolina, and when I tried to bring up Love Canal . . . it was really not appropriate. When I told him that at this very moment people of Love Canal were holding officials of the EPA hostage, he sort of laughed and said, 'I don't know what the problem is, nobody is keeping them at Love Canal. They can leave any time they want.' "

LaFalce never reported that part of the conversation to the Love Canal residents, but he did call them after dinner to let them know that he had talked with the president and that the president was going to take all their requests "under serious consideration." That gave Gibbs another excuse to go out and talk to the crowd and, more important, to the assembled television cameras and reporters, who were instrumental in keeping the story alive and keeping the heat on federal and state officials. "It was all media hoopla," LaFalce commented recently. "But the media was the victim there. They were the ones being manipulated."

At nine o'clock, the FBI called Gibbs and told her that she had seven minutes to release the EPA officials. She went outside to face the crowd, hoping to win their approval or at least acquiescence for what appeared to be the desirable option of letting them go, rather than having the FBI storm the place. She made a fiery speech, suggesting, among other things, that the hostage-taking would be like a "Sesame Street picnic" compared with what would happen next if now action was taken. Finally, three FBI agents, four U.S. marshalls, and six members of the Niagara Falls Police Department entered the building and escorted Napal and Lucas away. The crowd hooted and spat as the contingent made its way to the awaiting cars. There were no arrests, and Washington officials now downplay the impact of the event, but in retrospect it seems to have played some role in making relocation even more inevitable than it was before.

The Decision and Its Aftermath

The decision to relocate the families at Love Canal seems to have been made by Tuesday morning, even if only implicitly. Hansen and Watson remember stopping to talk between the White House and the Old Executive Office Building on Monday evening or perhaps Tuesday morning. She recalls Watson saying "something like, 'I think these people have been jerked around enough . . . we'll just have to go ahead and do it and suffer whatever the political consequences are.' "

If there was an actual decision meeting, it was the one held at nine o'clock Tuesday morning, chaired by Eidenberg. The White House had already made a special point of alerting both OMB and the Congressional liaison office that they were going to have to come up with some money to pay for relocation, although the estimate was still in the $5–$10 million range. And EPA had completed its review of all the federal, state and private studies which had ever been done on Love Canal residents. It was an impressive list: thirteen separate studies, all suggesting, but none irrevocably concluding that there was some connection between the leakage from Love Canal and the health of the residents. No one was any longer arguing for waiting until the review of the Picciano study was finished.

At the Tuesday morning meeting, the conflict between the scientists and the politicians was evident. The experts from HHS were quoted as saying that they "feel in their gut there's a problem, but that they wouldn't recommend relocation based on the science." And the surgeon general was represented as "probably" favoring relocation although he "wouldn't say there was a health emergency." This attitude did not sit well in the White House. Remember that Watson had been similarly frustrated at the first big Love Canal meeting the previous Friday, and referred to this syndrome as the "writing-a-scientific-treatise-on-the-head-of-a-pin." Eidenberg recalls the gap between the "scientific doubt within the expert scientific community . . . and the absolute certainty among the public at large and the residents of the Love Canal area." The representative from FEMA, William Wilcox, said that there was no choice but to relocate. The representative from Justice, Larry Hammond, urged that the decision not be dependent on precedent. Realizing that the scientists were in doubt, the precedent and legal authority were not clear, and the money was not yet in hand, Eidenberg stated the position that was to become the key justification for relocation. "In light of the suggestive data," he said, "prudence requires action to minimize futher exposure."[13]

He then moved the meeting on to a discussion of the "exact steps" to be taken to get ready for an announcement on the following day, Wednesday. First, of course, was the negotiation with Carey. Eidenberg was to call Morgado to discuss the request from the Governor for a declaration of emergency, but "no request would be entertained without a commitment of $5 million" from the state, representing 50 percent of the high side of the federal estimate of the costs. Eidenberg and Hansen would ask Watson to talk with James McIntyre at OMB before going to the President. FEMA was to be responsible for the actual relocation negotiations and logistics. Jeffrey Miller of the EPA was to work on a draft statement for the announcement. Justice was to provide a memo on why relocation would not set a precedent for future similar situations involving environmental risk. And FEMA was to do the same on the possibilities for temporary housing.

The temporariness—or permanence—of the relocation was apparently never addressed head-on. The federal officials seemed to assume that it would be temporary, but LaFalce and others close to the residents realized that the notion of temporary relocation did not make much sense in either practical or financial terms. The costs of long term "temporary" relocation were potentially much higher than the costs of buying the homes of the residents at their market value before the trouble started, and letting them make their futures elsewhere.

After the negotiations with Morgado and Carey were completed, Watson sent a memorandum to the president. "Since Barbara Blum made the announcement this weekend," it began, "two federal employees were taken hostage by a frustrated populace who are demanding relocation by the state and / or federal government." Watson then recommended that the President declare an emergency, noting that New York State "is willing to split the costs of whatever we do by 50 percent." Arguing that the "human element of this cannot be overlooked," Watson went on to lay out the action plan:

> The understandable concern and anxiety which has been precipitated by the release of this most recent study requires our immediate response. If you approve my recommendation to declare an emergency, a team of people whom I've appointed immediately will begin working with the state in drafting a request from the Governor to you. We would announce jointly with the state tomorrow that we both are amending our lawsuits against Hooker whom we hold ultimately accountable; that we are undertaking further, more conclusive studies; but that in the meantime we are responding prudently and immediately to the human need which is evident at Love Canal.

Tuesday's *New York Times* was full of Love Canal again. In addition to the fifth front page story in the past four days—this one on the hostage-taking—there was an editorial urging compensation for the "psychological effect" of the "premature" release of information about the study. A piece under the headline "Caution Urged on Data from Love Canal," in the science section, suggested that the link between damage to health of humans and hazardous waste was tough to make and, in any event, would not necessarily mean future danger even if the connection to existing health problems was proven. The CBS Evening News ran a long segment on the whole situation, including the hostage taking and the dispute over the makeup for the panel reviewing the Picciano study.

While the CBS story was airing, Eidenberg and Carey were deep in negotiations over the details of the request for an emergency declaration and the sharing of the costs. The federal leverage was that the state desperately wanted help; the state leverage was that Carey knew how much pressure Carter was under to act. The two crucial issues, how much each would pay and whether the federal commitment was for permanent or temporary relocation, were not resolved. The two sides finally agreed on language for Carey's telegram requesting help. Looking back on it, it seems clear that the intergovernmental tussle was going to get a lot worse before it got better. During the negotiations, Carey talked with Vice-President Mondale and members of the New York congressional delegation in an effort to force a bigger federal commitment. At least twice, Carey and Eidenberg talked on the phone, with Carey insisting that the federal government agree to buy the homes and Eidenberg arguing that federal law would not permit it. As Eidenberg later said to reporters, "The governor's problem is that he can't understand that . . . we have no legal authority to get into the real estate business." Carey did not get all he wanted in the agreement on the language of the telegram: buying the homes was not mentioned and New York State was asking for federal sharing of costs, not a full financial bailout. Yet it did contain a dig at the Administration's handling of the problem; Carey was requesting the help, it said, because of the publicized EPA report.

Word of ongoing, intense negotiations was leaking out and those involved at the White House were frantically trying to work out the agreement with Carey, respond to the press inquiries, and prepare for the press conference, all at the same time. It was decided that Blum would again be the spokesperson, supported by John Macy, Jr., administrator of FEMA. Hansen, Eidenberg, and Watson all participated in the briefing session for them, cautioning them to "get the rhetoric and hyperbole down," and to "make points about other studies, not just EPA's." There was specific discussion about the likelihood of a question on permanent relocation and the advice there was to suggest that they were conducting further studies and that there was no authorization for buying homes, "but if the situation warrants it" the federal government would respond.[14]

Wednesday, the day of the press conference, began predictably enough. On Tuesday night Carey's office told the *New York Times'* Robin Herman the details of the negotiated agreement between the state and the federal governments so that the *Times* was able to go with another front page Love Canal story preempting an announcement from the Carter administration. Headlined "Accord Is Reported on Evacuation of Last 710 Love Canal Families," Herman's story did everything the governor could have wanted. In addition to stealing the thunder from the press conference, it focused attention on the two issues which were still unresolved: whether the relocation would be permanent or temporary, and how much the feds would pay. In addition, the Herman article cast more doubt on EPA's management revealing that Dr. Robert S. Gordon, a member of the team reviewing the Picciano study, had written an "internal memorandum" critical of the study, saying its findings could be no more than "suggestive." If the Herman story were not enough of a backdrop for the press conference, the *Times* also ran two other Love Canal stories, one from Niagara Falls reporting that the Love Canal residents were holding a peaceful vigil as they awaited word from Washington, and the other reporting the results of a new study of the residents which found nerve damage in the majority of those tested.

At noon, Blum and Macy held the press conference, announcing that the president had agreed to declare a federal emergency and that the federal government would pay for temporary relocation. During the press conference, Blum put the federal share at $3–$5 million. While she tried to stress, as she later recalled, that the decision was made "not on the study, but on the panic caused in Love Canal," the coverage of the announcement stressed the studies. Carey, for his part, immediately criticized the federal response and reiterated his call for permanent relocation, purchase of homes, and a federal financial commitment to "match" the $35 million he said the state had already spent at Love Canal.

At Love Canal itself, Lois Gibbs had been trying all morning to find out what the federal government was going to say. She remembers being told by the woman handling the press for the EPA that she would have to wait until noon, just like everyone else. She finally found someone at EPA who read the press release to her just as the press conference was getting underway, and she repeated it word for word so that the Love Canal residents who had come to the Homeowners Association office during the morning could hear. When the relocation commitment was announced, pandemonium followed. Gibbs recalled in her biography that "everyone was hugging me. TV and newspaper people were congratulating us. . . . Someone brought a case of champagne. Corks were popping. . . . People were laughing, crying, hugging each other, dancing around and saying: 'We won! We won! We're out.' " Families began pacing and moving immediately to area motels, not even awaiting detailed instructions from the government.[15]

The relief in Niagara Falls and the continued determination in Albany were matched by frustration in Washington about the process of decisionmaking, and realization that things are often not as they appear to be. For Eidenberg there was the difficulty of having the White House in an election year appearing to be responsible for what he believed was essentially a problem for the state government. For Blum, there was the difficulty of being the spokesperson for what she recently termed "the worst public policy decision made during my four years with the government." And for Hansen, it was returning to her office *after* the relocation decision and finally receiving HHS assessment of the Picciano study, whose findings had prompted the relocation. The Picciano study, according to the report, provided "inadequate basis for any scientific or medical inferences from the data (even of a tentative or preliminary nature) concerning exposure to mutagenic substances because of residence in the Love Canal area."

The Aftermath of the Relocation Announcement

Given the significance of the decision to relocate and vagueness about the federal–state commitments to relocation, it was not surprising that the Love Canal issue did not move quickly off the desks of the policymakers or out of sight of the press corps.

Coverage of the EPA press conference was straightforward, perhaps even understated because the story had leaked the day before. All three networks covered the story Wednesday night, with reports on each of them from both Washington and Niagara Falls. All three noted a connection between the relocation and the Picciano study, although Dan Rather at CBS added that the HHS panel had warned that the chromosomal damage found in the study was not necessarily related to chemicals from the canal. The front page of Thursday's *New York Times* reported the relocation decision, with emphasis on the studies and on Carey's concerns. There were inside stories on Carey's position and on the reaction of Love Canal families to the decision, and an editorial headlined "More Cruelty at Love Canal," which was critical both of the EPA and of Biogenics, and called Carter's action "the only humane decision" in light of the justifiable panic of the residents.

Carey kept the public pressure on. On Thursday, May 22, he let it be known that the state had tried to get the federal government to do a comprehensive and well-designed study of the health effect on Love Canal residents in 1979. His administration estimated that it would cost more to temporarily relocate the families for a year than to buy the homes and thus offer permanent relocation. Congress held hearings at which government scientists reiterated their lack of confidence in the studies, prompting one congressman, Long Island Republican Norman Lent, to suggest that if it wasn't science that dictated the relocation it must have been politics. On Friday, Carey released his "plan," a detailed permanent relocation proposal which would have the federal government assuming $20 million of the $25 million cost. Adding to the confusion, the researchers who had done the study which had found the nerve damage began to back off their earlier statements that the findings were significant. All the while, FEMA was trying to manage the relocation while the White House was trying to continue the dialogue with Carey and stave off an increasing financial or logistical commitment.

Love Canal had touched a broad-based fear about the dangers of toxic wastes. In ten days there had been an enormous amount of national coverage; thirty-one separate articles in the *New York Times,* including eight front page stories and three editorials; and thirty-one and a half minutes on the nightly network news programs. There was only one thing left: a *60 Minutes* story. That came on Sunday, May 25. It focused more on inaction by the State of New York than on the federal role, although Harry Reasoner ended the piece by asking "Who's going to pay for all this?" That, of course, was Carey's question, too, and he managed to keep it alive as the relocation began.

The White House and EPA continued to state publicly that they had no authority to buy the homes and that they were not committed to spending more than the original $3–$5 million that was estimated, but residents of Love Canal were getting a distinctly different impression. They were led to believe by federal and state officials that the decision on permanent relocation—which really meant purchase of their homes—would depend in some way on the results of further studies or more complete review of the existing studies.

By May 26, only five days after the relocation decision, FEMA's Macy was writing to the EPA's Blum asking for assurances that no permanent federal role in the area was being contemplated and suggesting that the quicker that the EPA could make a decision on permanent relocation the better he would like it. The next day, Dr. Stephen Gage of EPA telephoned a meeting of Love Canal area leaders, regional EPA and FEMA officials, and members of the governor's task force to say that the federal government could not undertake permanent relocation whatever the outcome of further tests. The reaction was swift. The Love Canal Homeowners Association began remobilizing, Macy wrote Jack Watson suggesting that Gage's comments "essentially refuted the federal position and residents' understanding," and LaFalce, Moynihan and Javits began to grease the congressional wheels to break the state–federal deadlock. Blum wrote Watson, complaining that "The administration is not talking in one voice," suggesting that there must be an effort "to involve the residents enough to make them part of the process without having them serve an omnipresent, antagonistic role that keeps the federal agency representatives from working openly and efficiently with each other." At the end of May, there was another Love Canal meeting in the Old Executive Office Building. Watson reiterated the administration position that permanent relocation was not an option, that the temporary relocation did not hinge on the chromosome study but on the "preponderance of the evidence" and that Blum should be the single voice for federal policy on the question.

With the New York congressional delegation in gear, the Democratic convention approaching, Senator Kennedy announcing hearings on Love Canal, and Carey keeping the heat on, the permanent relocation of the residents of Love Canal had become the proverbial political football. As Hansen wrote to Watson on May 31,

> Many of the political types around the White House are beginning to involve themselves in the Love Canal situation, especially now that Sen. Kennedy has called the hearings. . . . In my opinion, the discussion reflects an overreaction to, and limited focus on, the New York press. People have got to understand that, short of declaring that the federal government will purchase people's homes, we cannot win with Carey, the state, Love Canal residents, or the New York press. The best we can do is cut our losses, both in New York and with Kennedy.
>
> On the other hand, there is substantial national press, which basically conveys that President Jimmy Carter is the one who has finally, after 2 ½ years of requests for help from all levels of government, responded to the tragic plight of these people. . . .

She predicted that until the administration caved in and agreed, Carey would ensure that the residents continued to press their case and that the New York media would continue to "dramatize their plight." She wrote that memo the day after the *New York Times* had waded in again, this time with an editorial strongly urging permanent federally financed relocation.

Contrary to Hansen's expectation, Love Canal did not remain simply a local New York state story during the summer months. In early June Carey and FEMA signed a relocation agreement and Congress began to move on both the environmental Superfund legislation and special legislation to authorize and fund the purchase of the Love Canal homes. A week later Carey announced that he was asking the federal government for a loan of $20 million to purchase the homes, and at the end of July the Carter administration finally agreed to loan New York State $15 million to buy up to 550 of the residences. Lois Gibbs made appearances on *Good Morning America* and the *Phil Donahue Show,* and Tom Hayden and Jane Fonda sponsored a California speaking tour for her. She also led and organized a demonstration at the Democratic National Convention in New York City, keeping the pressure for permanent relocation squarely on the President. Gibbs believes her appearance on *Good Morning America,* during which she continued her criticism of Carter, catalyzed the Administration into working out the final agreement on permanent relocation. Less than two weeks after her appearance, and after Congress had approved the necessary appropriations and authorizations, Carter signed the agreement with New York State at a well-publicized and well-attended meeting in Niagara Falls.

The original Picciano study and the nerve damage study continued to be reviewed by panels of scientists throughout the summer. In October, a panel authorized by the state legislature and headed by Dr. Lewis Thomas made a report on all the health studies that was widely interpreted as dismissing their findings. The Thomas report moved some of the continuing controversy into the scientific community, since at that point the immediate political stalemate had been broken. The scientific controversy was covered in *Science* magazine and lent enough credence to the criticism of the Picciano study that he sued the magazine. In December, the Congress enacted the Superfund bill and Carter, then a lame-duck president, signed it into law. By February 1981, over 400 families had been permanently relocated from Love Canal, with others still making arrangements.

With the relocation, coverage of the plight of Love Canal residents has faded but the controversy over what the evidence means still endures. In 1982, the federal government released an EPA report which concluded, after monitoring the chemicals at Love Canal for two years, that the area was habitable. The conclusion was buttressed by another federal report, this one by the Department of Health and Human Services, on the health effects. The following year, the federal government released another two-year study of health effects and concluded that "no specific relationship existed between exposure to chemical agents in the Love Canal area and increased frequency of chromosomal damage."

On the other hand, the Congressional Office of Technology Assessment released its own report, in June of 1983, which criticized the two 1982 federal reports and said that the conclusion that it was okay for people to resettle at the Love Canal had no scientific basis. In the early fall, another study, this one of animals around the Love Canal area (done under the direction of a professor at SUNY / Binghamton), indicated there were continuing problems on the site.

Finally, in September 1983, the EPA discovered chemical leaks and backed off the declaration of habitability made a year before. The EPA's answer to when it would reach a final determination was March . . . of 1985. Or maybe, they added, it would not until 1988. Hooker's parent company, Occidental Petroleum, settled some of the Love Canal lawsuits in October, and in December the EPA sued Hooker to try to recover the $45 million that had been spent to that date cleaning up the site.

Four years after President Carter declared the emergency and agreed to the temporary relocation, most of the families had moved. Local officials had tried to begin revitalizing the area. The future was not clear. But one thing was certain: no one can say for sure what the scientific evidence concludes about the damage to residents as a result of the chemicals buried at Love Canal, but anyone can add up the lives that have been altered and the dollars that have been spent since the day the results of the Justice Department's pilot study were leaked to the press.

NOTES

1. The historical background of the Love Canal crisis presented here draws primarily on two comprehensive and well-written accounts of the circumstances and events that led to it: *Laying Waste: the Poisoning of America by Toxic Chemicals,* by Michael H. Brown, New York, Pantheon Books, 1979; and *Love Canal: Science, Politics and People,* by Adeline Gordon Levine, Lexington, MA, Lexington Books, 1982. Unless otherwise noted, the pre-1980 references will be from these works.

2. "Love Canal U.S.A.," Michael H. Brown, *The New York Times Sunday Magazine,* January 21, 1979, pp. 23–24.

"Love Canal and the Poisoning of America," Michael H. Brown, *The Atlantic,* December 1979, pp. 33–47.

Laying Waste, op. cit.

3. Levine, p. 19.

4. Much of the information that follows was gathered from interviews with participants conducted by Martin Linsky for this project. Among those interviewed were: Barbara Blum, Eugene Eidenberg, Jane Hansen, Hon. John LaFalce, Jeffrey Miller, and Jack Watson. All the quotations which are not footnoted are from those interviews. Transcripts of the interviews are on file at the John F. Kennedy School of Government, Harvard University.

5. Memo from Jane Hansen to Jack Watson dated May 15, 1980.

6. Memo of May 12, 1980, Jack Watson to Jane Hansen.

7. Memo from Jane Hansen to Jack Watson dated May 15, 1980.

8. Notes taken at meeting of May 16, 1980, with Hansen, Watson, and Jeffrey Miller.

9. Lois Marie Gibbs, *Love Canal: My Story,* Albany, N.Y., State University of New York Press, 1982, pp. 143–145.

10. Memo from Jack Watson to President Jimmy Carter dated May 17, 1980.

11. *New York Times,* May 16, 1980, p. 1.

12. Gibbs, pp. 148–151.

13. Notes taken at meeting of May 20, 1980, chaired by Eugene Eidenberg.

14. Notes taken at meeting of May 20, 1980, at which Hansen, Eidenberg, and Watson helped Blum, Macy, and Wilcox prepare for press conference.

15. Gibbs, pp. 159–160.

RONALD REAGAN
AND TAX EXEMPTIONS FOR
DISCRIMINATORY SCHOOLS

by David Whitman

Prelude to the Storm

IN LATE JANUARY 1982, Attorney General William French Smith appeared before a Senate Judiciary subcommittee to present the Reagan administration's views on renewing the 1965 Voting Rights Act. Despite the divisive nature of the subject he was testifying on, Smith's presentation was received with surprising placidity until Senator Edward Kennedy (D.-Mass.) interrupted to assail Smith about the administration's civil rights record. Kennedy's most damaging accusation was that "the administration has attempted to give encouragement to those who are committed to the concept of segregated schools by providing tax exemptions to them." Smith, his sangfroid shaken and "his voice rising with emotion,"[1] shot back that "the President does not have a discriminatory bone in his body. He has never taken an action in his entire life—"[2]

Smith never completed his sentence for the hearing room erupted with howls of laughter and jeers of derision. After much banging of his gavel and threatening to clear the room, subcommittee chairman Senator Orrin Hatch (R-Utah) managed to restore silence, but only after imploring the listeners to refrain from "sneering or snide comments."[3]

The controversy that had ignited this cynicism and cast such doubt upon the Reagan administration's commitment to civil rights began on January 8, 1982, when administration officials announced they were reversing President Nixon's 1970 decision to revoke the tax exempt status of racially discriminatory private schools. Before 1970, Johnson and Nixon administration officials had taken the position that the Internal Revenue Service (IRS) did not have the statutory power,

---

This is a heavily abridged version of the case study written by David Whitman. The abridgement was done by Martin Linsky. Unless otherwise noted, all quotations come either from unpublished government documents or from interviews with the author.

granted by Congress, to deprive "segregation academies" of their tax exemptions, despite the fact that the discrimination practiced by the schools was repugnant. Pressure to take away tax exemptions, however, continued to build. By 1970, an estimated 400,000 children were in segregated academies—which were widely viewed as a back-door alternative for circumventing school desegregation. Without tax exempt status, the schools would have a much rougher time raising money since donors would no longer be able to write off their gifts to the school.

Under pressure from Congress, the IRS was empowered to deny the tax exemptions. Under the theory articulated by then-IRS Commissioner Randolph Thrower, organizations that had appeared to be separately enumerated in the Internal Revenue Code as tax exempt—such as churches, charities, and educational organizations—all had to be "charitable" to be eligible for a tax exemption. Educational organizations that did not conform with federal "public policy"—such as the national policy against discrimination—could not be considered "charitable" (in the common law sense) and hence could no longer be tax exempt. During the next ten years, this interpretation of the Internal Revenue Code was implicitly assented to by Congress and vigorously defended by the Nixon, Ford, and Carter administrations. By and large, the 1970 decision was also upheld in the lower courts and court of appeals.

Then, in 1978, a federal district court in South Carolina ruled that Bob Jones University (BJU) was entitled to its tax exemption. The Fourth Circuit Court of Appeals narrowly overturned the decision and in 1981 the Supreme Court agreed to hear the claims of BJU and another Christian fundamentalist school, the Goldsboro Christian School located in Goldsboro, North Carolina. Each school argued that the IRS had unfairly deprived them of their tax exempt status because of their discriminatory admission policies, policies they contended were firmly rooted in the Bible.*

The schools at the center of the tax exemption controversy were fundamentalist religious institutions that, in the eyes of their detractors, turned their students into intolerant zombies, and in the eyes of their supporters, churned out downright upright young men and women. Goldsboro Christian School, founded in 1963 during the advent of desegregation, states in its articles of incorporation that its mission includes "combating all atheistic, agnostic, pagan, and so-called scientific adulterations of the Gospel; unqualifiedly affirming and teaching the inspiration of the Bible . . . [including] the incarnation and virgin birth of our Lord and Saviour Jesus Christ; His identification as the Son of God; His vicarious atonement for the sins of mankind by the shedding of His blood on the Cross."[4] Bob Jones University (BJU), founded in 1927, has a similar charter but a more public presence in the community than Goldsboro, owing both to its size (approximately 6,000 students, kindergarten to graduate school) and its highly visible president, the evangelical pastor Bob Jones III. Describing itself as "the

---

*The unabridged version of this case study contains an extended discussion of the legal history of the exemption controversy.

255

world's most unusual university,'' BJU has a plethora of rules for regulating the behavior of its students and faculty. The district court described the school environment as follows:

> Every teacher, no matter what are his academic credentials, is required to be a "born again" Christian, who must testify to at least one saving experience with Jesus Christ, and who must consider his mission at [BJU] to be the training of Christian character. . . . The institution does not permit dancing, card playing, the use of tobacco, movie-going, and other such forms of indulgences in which worldly young people often engage; no students will release information of any kind to a local newspaper, radio station, or television station without first checking with the University Public Relations Director; students are expected to refrain from singing, playing, and, as far as possible, from "tuning-in" on the radio or playing on the record player, jazz, rock-and-roll, folk rock, or any other types of questionable music; and no young man may walk a girl on campus unless both of them have a legitimate reason for going in the same direction.[5]

Although BJU's disciplinary rules are unusual, it was its racial policies that provoked the revocation of its tax exemption. Until 1971, BJU did not admit any blacks, on the grounds that the Scriptures allegedly proscribed a separation of the races and expressly forbade interracial dating and marriage. Between 1971 and 1975 BJU admitted blacks who were married to members of their own race,* and in 1975 BJU began admitting unmarried blacks who agreed not to date or marry outside their own race (or encourage others to do so). For all intents and purposes, however, Bob Jones remained a lily-white institution; in 1975 there were only five black students enrolled and the situation was much the same in 1981. The Goldsboro Christian School also alleged there was a biblical charter for segregation and had forbade the admission of all blacks since its inception.

In the early 1970s, each school lost its tax exempt status owing to these admission policies, and each instituted suits against the IRS, alleging both that the revocation was not within the IRS's statutory power and that it contravened the free exercise of religion protected under the First Amendment. For both schools the sum of money involved was substantial: during the years it had contested its potential revocation BJU had accumulated $490,000 in back taxes (which it would lose if it lost its case) and Goldsboro had accumulated a $160,000 bill.

In 1978, after the IRS had moved to take away BJU and Goldsboro's exemptions, the political complexion of the tax exemption debate changed. The IRS proposed new and tougher regulations which, in effect, required private schools to meet race quotas or lose their tax exempt status—even for schools that certified they had non-discriminatory admission policies and had tried to recruit black students. The proposed regulations proved to be one of the most unpopular in IRS history, with the agency receiving 150,000 protest letters within half-a-year.

---

*The university was also willing to admit unmarried students from other ethnic or minority groups or unmarried blacks who had been staff members for at least four years.

Congress blocked IRS from implementing the new regulations, but the controversy over the proposed rules rang alarm bells among a variety of religious groups. As a result, a number of religious organizations—all of which flatly rejected BJU and Goldsboro's claim that a biblical charter existed for segregation—filed "friends of the court" briefs with the Supreme Court in 1982, on the side of BJU and Goldsboro. They were concerned that the public policy doctrine might be used to take away exemptions if they dissented from or practiced beliefs at odds with federal policy. Orthodox Jews, for example, were worried about a challenge to their practice of separating sexes in the synagogue; Catholic leaders were concerned about their refusal to ordain women as priests; and various religious organizations, which condemned abortion, and so forth, believed their religious freedom to be threatened by the IRS policy.

The tax exemptions had been a minor issue in the 1980 elections except among Christian fundamentalists, who were incensed by the aborted 1978 IRS regulations. Reflecting this concern, the 1980 Republican Party platform stated that "we will halt the unconstitutional regulatory vendetta launched by Mr. Carter's IRS commissioner against independent schools,"[6] and in a 1978 radio talk and in several campaign appearances, Reagan made similar pitches to religious groups. The closest thing to an explicit rejection of the 1970 policy was a line in · the Reagan–Bush position paper on education, which stated that Reagan "opposes the IRS's attempt to remove the tax exempt status of private schools by administrative fiat."[7]

The Christian fundamentalists were a new, powerful force in the South which had supported the president enthusiastically and played a critical role in his election. Their conservative philosophy and Southern origin made civil rights activists uneasy, particularly since some fundamentalists had close bonds with the all-white "Christian" academies, and Reagan did little during his campaign to assuage this uneasiness. In January 1980, for example, Reagan actually went to Bob Jones University to give a speech and appeal for support. During his forty-five-minute speech, interrupted by three standing ovations and frequent applause, Reagan referred to BJU as a "great institution," said that he was "delighted to be here," and described the "vast throng" of six thousand white students and faculty attending the address as a "most impressive audience."[8]

Reagan did not mention the tax exemption issue, but his comments at BJU and elsewhere during the campaign hardly were of comfort to civil rights leaders. At BJU, for example, Reagan stated that "You do not alter the evil character of racial quotas simply by changing the color of the beneficiary."[9] Soon after Reagan's election, the estrangement between Reagan and the black community grew, following a series of incidents during 1981 that included Reagan mistaking the only black member of his cabinet (HUD secretary Samuel Pierce), the appointment of a black with suspect qualifications to head the Equal Employment Opportunity Commission, and a stall by the administration on extending several portions of the Voting Rights Act.

The last, and perhaps the most important, factor complicating the Bob Jones controversy, was that not only were the political stakes high, but the principled implications of the case seemed great, no matter which side one came out on. On the side of the religious organizations and conservative Republicans, there were legitimate concerns about the effect of the court of appeals ruling on religious freedom and separation of powers. The 1970 policy change was taken without any explicit request or legislation from Congress. This might have been inconsequential were it not for the fact that the IRS's statutory authority was not readily apparent and the policy had far-reaching potential ramifications for organizations, both liberal and conservative ones, that depended on tax exempt status for their survival. There was no easily discerned limitation to the public policy doctrine. Churches that counseled draft resisters, sheltered El Salvadoran refugees, supported the nuclear freeze, considered homosexuality sinful, or boycotted firms doing business in South Africa, all could lose their tax exemptions for pursuing activities at odds with federal "public policy." Similarly, hospitals that either did or did not permit abortions, universities that admitted only women, and nonprofit organizations that opposed provisions of the Clean Air Act, all, conceivably, could also lose their tax exemptions without explicit authority in the area first having been turned over to IRS bureaucrats by Congress.

On the other hand, while limitations on the public policy doctrine were not clear, many civil rights leaders believed that the judiciary would come up with plausible limitations, under which the antiracial discrimination policy would be recognized as uniquely important, both because of its historical significance and its explicit imbedding in the Constitution. More important, civil rights leaders, as well as many representatives of the tax bar, considered the argument against the public policy doctrine to be a prescription for immobility, both within the executive branch and Congress. Their view was that executive agencies routinely set social policy without explicit statutory support from Congress, and that if all those social policy determinations had to receive congressional endorsement, the operation of the government would be seriously impeded. Most strides in the civil rights arena had been taken by the executive branch or judiciary long before Congress passed legislation endorsing them. They pointed out that the IRS frequently made suspect determinations of social policy; i.e., was a church a "real" church, was a certain treatment "medical" treatment, was a training program "educational," all of which was not, and could not, be reviewed or authorized by Congress. Finally, insofar as exemptions constituted, at minimum, a form of indirect support, it seemed morally reprehensible to accord tax benefits to racist institutions. No one had any problem, civil rights advocates argued, in acknowledging that certain violations of "public policy" committed by tax exempt institutions—such as setting up Fagin's school for pickpockets or a school to train guerrilla fighters—were grounds for removing tax exempt status, without prior congressional approval. Practicing and preaching the virtues of racial separation, in their eyes, seemed to be just one of those gross "public policy" violations which should not be afforded exempt status under any circumstances. As events demonstrated in 1982, the vast majority of the media and public agreed with them.

The Administration's Review

The administration's review of the vexing constitutional, statutory, and philosophical issues raised by the *Bob Jones / Goldsboro* cases began routinely in September 1981. There was a solid consensus among the mid-level officials directly involved with the cases at both Treasury and Justice that the government ought to defend the position it had taken in the district court and court of appeals. Accordingly, the Justice Department filed a brief in September that acquiesced to the request for certiorari and defended the existing policy. In October the Court granted certiorari, and during the next two months the Tax Division at the Justice Department began drafting a brief consistent with the previous policy in anticipation of a mid-December filing.

In early December, when the draft brief was routinely circulated to the assistant attorney generals, it came to the attention of several senior Justice Department officials, who were troubled by the implications of the public policy doctrine and alerted Edward Schmults, the deputy attorney general, of their concern. Heading the pack were William Bradford Reynolds, the assistant attorney general for civil rights, and Bruce Fein, an associate deputy attorney general in Schmults's office. Reynolds recalled:

> I remember distinctly standing in Ed Schmults's doorway and saying, "Ed, I just read the brief the SG [Solicitor General] wants to file in *Bob Jones*. I think there's a lot of mischief in it, it's very unpersuasive, and I would like the opportunity to at least sit down and talk with you, from a legal standpoint, about the problems I see. Do we really want to file this, given all our pronouncements about federal intrusiveness and separation of powers?" Schmults looked at me like "What do you mean? We brought this to the Court, it's been argued forever, and we've got to file in a week!" But he said if I felt that strongly about it, I should prepare my legal response to the brief for his review and the Solicitor General's office.

While Reynolds began researching and articulating the counterargument to the SG's brief, Bruce Fein sent Schmults a memo on December 7 laying out in fuller detail the history of the controversy and arguments on each side. Fein, like Reynolds, clearly believed the Fourth Circuit decision in *Bob Jones* had nettlesome implications and reeked of the judicial activism that Attorney General William French had inveighed against.

After talking with Fein, Reynolds, and several other officials, Schmults was sufficiently disturbed that he decided to call Timothy McNamar, the deputy secretary of the Treasury Department, on December 8. Schmults felt the position ought to be reviewed because "first, the court ruling seemed contrary to the statutory language,* and second, the president was on record as being opposed

---

*Section 501(c)(3) of the Internal Revenue Code stated that organizations could be exempt if they "operated exclusively for religious, charitable, scientific, testing for public safety, literary or educational purposes." After Nixon reversed his stand on granting the tax exemptions, the IRS commissioner asserted that educational organizations had to be both educational *and* charitable; a reading at odds with the plain language of the statute. The commissioner cited common law as his basis for combining the requirements.

to IRS intrusion in schools except where clearly warranted.''

Over the next three weeks, senior officials in Justice and Treasury began an exhaustive review of the cases. In a series of meetings held primarily at the Treasury Department, Schmults, Reynolds, Fein, McNamar, and Treasury General Counsel Peter Wallison thrashed out the issues and began registering growing doubts about upholding the existing policy. Based on extensive discussions with the participants, it is difficult to overstate the degree to which these discussions were dominated by debate over the legal merits. Fein says that ''when we were debating what our position should be, the discussion was pure legal analysis—there was a lot of discussion of whether post-1970 legislative acquiescence somehow ratified the 1970 decision—but I don't remember a single thought being expressed as to how this would be received in the media.'' Wallison recalls ''a kind of ivory tower quality about it all. It was a lot of lawyers, people who understood the principle at stake and were articulating the pros and cons, but articulating them as you would before a court, instead of thinking about how you would articulate it to the public.'' Schmults strongly defended the ivory tower quality of the discussions, maintaining: ''We were the government's lawyers and were there to give legal advice. The responsibility for assessing the political or public impact of that advice lay with the White House, which is why we raised the case for them.''

It was the threat of the ''public policy'' doctrine that seemed the primary animus for the lawyers' reservations. Schmults stated:

> I remember saying, ''I read this brief and there is a strong public policy and set of laws against discrimination on the basis of sex. My wife went to Wellesley. Why couldn't the IRS commissioner take away the tax exemptions of Wellesley, Smith, Bryn Mawr, and other single-sex schools, if we support this?'' No one could answer that question for me, and it looked pretty clear that, under the argument put forth in the draft brief, that could be done.

As the discomfort of McNamar, Schmults, and Wallison grew over the position in the draft brief, officials began to search for ways to limit the scope of the brief. ''The effort right through the end of December,'' Schmults recalled, ''was to see if the brief could be narrowed, to see if a principled position could be established in the court to . . . have the IRS be authorized to deny tax exemptions to schools that discriminated on the basis of race, but not at the same time endorse or obtain a broader principle that would give the IRS authority to invoke its views of public policies on a whole variety of issues and deny tax exemptions.''[1] Some fleeting discussion did take place of whether the administration might minimize the perception that it endorsed racial discrimination, in the event the decision was made to drop the government's opposition to the court of appeals ruling, by filing legislation to establish the legal basis for the IRS policy. The idea was ''lost,'' in Wallison's words, under the pressure to meet the court deadlines for filing the brief.

Although Justice and Treasury officials did not give much thought to how to limit public disapproval of the reversal they were contemplating, they did register on the political antagonism a reversal could ignite. Earlier in the year, Congressman Trent Lott (R-Mass.), the powerful minority whip, began pressuring the president, secretary of Treasury, attorney general, solicitor general, and IRS commissioner to oppose the court of appeals ruling. Lott was joined in his opposition by several conservative senators, notably Strom Thurmond (R-S.C.), a trustee of Bob Jones University and chairman of the Senate Judiciary Committee. As it became increasingly clear that the administration might reverse itself and that it was stepping into a cauldron of controversy, Wallison wrote Regan on December 17 that "further discussions . . . within Treasury suggest that the issues in the *Bob Jones* case . . . are significant enough to raise at the White House level."[2]

Going to the White House: Strike One

Unbeknownst to Treasury and Justice officials, the president and several key members of the White House staff had already been alerted to the existence of the *Bob Jones / Goldsboro* litigation. In early December a letter from Congressman Lott to President Reagan had been summarized in Reagan's log of congressional mail as follows: "[Lott] writes regarding pending cases concerning the tax exempt status of church schools. Indicates that the Supreme Court has now agreed to review the case of *Bob Jones University v. United States,* and urges you to intervene in this particular case." In response, in the margin of his log, Reagan wrote, "I think we should." In the normal course of events, following a handwritten notation from the president, White House staff would have discussed and staffed out a response to Lott; for some reason, however, the notation fell back unnoticed in the files of the White House legislative liaison office until copies of the president's notation were made and sent anonymously to two individuals: T. Kenneth Cribb, Jr., and Trent Lott.

Cribb was a devout conservative who worked for Craig Fuller, the assistant to the President for cabinet affairs, and through Fuller reported to Edwin Meese, the senior aide responsible for legal issues that involved broad policy considerations. Meese, Chief of Staff James Baker, and Deputy Chief of Staff Michael Deaver constituted the powerful troika that, collectively, ran the White House for the president. In a three-page December 18 memo to Meese, Cribb gave an inaccurate pocket size review of the legal history of the litigation,* raised warning flags about the implications of the case, and sought to use the president's log notation as a vehicle for getting Meese to intervene, so that the court case might be short-circuited.

Cribb suggested to Meese that it would be unproductive to intervene in the

---

* Cribb's memo asserted incorrectly both that the lower court had upheld the denial of BJU's tax exemption and that a Carter administration regulation (rather than a Nixon administration regulation) was at issue in *Bob Jones*. He also implied, incorrectly, that only policies against interracial dating were at stake. That was technically true for BJU, but Goldsboro, as noted previously, had not altered its admission policies and did not admit blacks.

case at Justice because "the Solicitor General may be reluctant to revise his tentative position. Further, it would be a delicate matter for the White House to approach DOJ [Department of Justice] on policy grounds when that policy is so intimately tied to ongoing litigation." Noting, however, that the president's log notation indicated that it was appropriate to somehow intervene, Cribb pointed out that "The Secretary of Treasury could moot the *Bob Jones* case (and the consolidated *Goldsboro Christian Schools* case) by granting tax exempt status to these schools."

Following the Cribb–Meese memo, Meese apparently conferred with the president and shortly afterwards the president himself briefly mentioned the case to Treasury Secretary Regan. "Thinking of it as a procedural matter," the president recalled, "I just simply told the Secretary of the Treasury what was going on, and called his attention to it."[3] Regan, however, who played an inconsequential and passive role in the policy reversal, never mentioned his brief conversation with Reagan to any of the principals. No Treasury or Justice officials knew that members of the White House staff had recommended the cases be mooted.

Although the initial White House intervention seems to have had little, if any, impact on the policy debate in the departments, the dispatch of the notation from the presidential log—to Trent Lott—ensured that just the opposite conclusion would subsequently be reached in the media. Lott, not surprisingly, was delighted to receive the log page, and quickly fired off letters to Schmults and Regan, enclosing copies of the log and citing it as evidence that a "brief should [not] be filed which undercuts [the president's] position until he has had an opportunity to review it."[4] Lott's letters arrived December 22, about a week after Schmults had responded to Lott's initial letter on *Bob Jones,* by writing that "the department has been unable to conclude that abandonment of the legal position of the [IRS] Commissioner's regulations in *Bob Jones* and *Goldsboro* would be expedient."[5] When a copy of Lott's letter with the log notation was much later leaked to CBS News, the explanation for Schmults's sudden change of heart seemed disarmingly simple: the policy shift was a political sellout, a result of direct pressure applied by the president. Schmults, the only senior departmental official who both knew about the log notation and was active in the policy reversal, recalled ruefully:

> I remember the first time I saw Lott's letter with the log notation and I expressed some shock—"How the hell did he get this out of the White House?" Beyond that, though, I didn't pay any attention to it, send it around, or mention it to anyone. I already felt the president's position was pretty clearly staked out from the campaign so it didn't surprise me. I think I can say unequivocally, and be prepared to swear, that political influence—Trent Lott or anybody else—had zero influence on our legal advice. On the contrary, the administration decided to reverse policy despite recognition that it would be politically unpopular. But that's not, of course, how it came out in the media.

The administration, in short, ended up with the worst of both worlds: an unsuccessful presidential intervention which subsequently appeared to have generated a political sop to conservative congressmen. At the same time, the initial flagging of the issue had failed to alert the president or his key advisers to the racial sensitivity of the case. The president later claimed that when he spoke to Regan he "didn't know there were any [schools that still practiced segregation], and maybe I should have but I didn't. . . . I was getting complaints even before I got here as President . . . that some of the Internal Revenue agents were harassing some schools, even though they were desegregated. I didn't think that this was the place of Treasury agents to be doing this. So I told the Secretary of Treasury that . . . I didn't know that there were a couple of legal cases pending and all I wanted was that these tax collectors stop threatening schools that were obeying the law."[6] Craig Fuller, who the Cribb–Meese memo went through, commented:

> In the president's mind, at this initial stage, this was an issue that dealt with federal interference in a private institution, not racial discrimination. It was not clear from the log notation or Ken's memo that the federal interference, whether it was warranted or not, was done because the schools practiced racial discrimination. There was a line in Ken's memo about [BJU] forbidding interracial dating but the fact that this was a sensitive civil rights issue was not really appreciated until later. At this point I thought this was a case of religious institutions against the IRS and that the only potential source of controversy would come from the religious organizations.

The Departments Come to the White House: Strike Two

Although members of the White House staff initially whiffed on the racial sensitivity of the *Bob Jones* case, they did make some contact once departmental officials brought the issue to the attention of Fred Fielding, the White House counsel. Proceeding in blissful ignorance of Cribb's and Meese's interest in mooting the case, Deputy Treasury Secretary McNamar and General Counsel Peter Wallison met in Fielding's office on December 22 to discuss *Bob Jones*. Immediately prior to the meeting, Wallison sent Fielding, Regan, and McNamar a three-page briefing memo in which he argued that the administration should *not* change position. He argued that if the Court did find for the IRS, it would narrow the scope of the decision to the "unusual facts" of Bob Jones University. Wallison also raised the political risks:

> One must consider the politics of a change in the Administration's policy with respect to *Bob Jones* at this point. The case was commenced during a Republican administration in 1970 and carried through a successful appeal to the Fourth Circuit Court of Appeals. This suggests that the Service's position is neither frivolous nor the implementation of the social policies of the IRS bureaucracy. If the administration were now to take the position that the case should not be pursued before the Supreme Court, that view

would be read as a statement by the administration that overtly discriminatory practices are not objectionable, and as a significant retreat from the past policies in this area of both Republican and Democratic administrations. The explanation of the administration's position—that the tax laws are not the proper vehicle for pursuing racial discrimination—would be lost in the ensuing outcry.

At the conclusion of the meeting, "Fielding," Wallison recalled, "asked a few legal questions but he didn't have any reaction on the politics of the issue or the way it would be treated in the press." Fielding did ask to be kept informed of the progress of the case because, as he claimed, "from day one we all sensed a potential political problem here, even though we collectively may have miscalculated how a reversal would be perceived or portrayed."

Events within the departments began moving rapidly when the second draft of the solicitor general's brief was completed the following day, December 23. Schmults, Reynolds, and McNamar reviewed it immediately and found that it still did not resolve their problems with the public policy doctrine. McNamar, who read the brief over his kitchen table the night of the twenty-third, remembers "trying to be persuaded" but coming to the conclusion that the refurbished arguments still "didn't hang together."[7] Schmults and Reynolds reached the same conclusion, and, sometimes during the next few days Schmults and McNamar agreed over the phone that they were going to press for a reversal, although they would give the SG's office one final shot at narrowing the brief.

On December 28, McNamar briefed Regan and advocated that the administration reverse itself. Regan approved the policy change but told McNamar that Meese wanted to be apprised of the case and to check any change out with him first. Later that afternoon McNamar called Meese and told him that he was just about to recommend reversal, although he would await the final brief from the solicitor general's office before making a final recommendation. He also told Meese that though he felt the law argued for reversal, the policy change would be "politically very unpopular"[8] and that everyone "recognized the political sensitivity of taking a legal position that might be construed as contrary to the administration's policy against racial discrimination."[9] Meese's only response, according to McNamar, was "Are you sure you're comfortable with the law?"[10] The next day Schmults and McNamar got final drafts of the brief, and, after agreeing the brief was still uncompelling, McNamar called Ken Cribb, gave him a full briefing on the cases, and told him that he and Schmults were prepared to recommend reversal and to pass that news on to Meese.

At this point McNamar was convinced that the White House had been adequately informed about the potential policy change; Schmults, however, was not. He recalled that, "I heard the Treasury had 'cleared this with the White House' and I was nervous about that because I wanted to be sure the White House really understood what this change would entail. I wanted to hear for myself, and be able to say to myself, that they knew this was going to be highly controversial and were prepared for it. So I asked for another meeting." On December 30,

Schmults, Reynolds, and McNamar went over to Fielding's office for a second meeting to discuss the case. Reynolds recalled:

> that meeting was dominated by a rather sophisticated legal discussion about which side we should come down on. Fred probed about the government's possible change in position and he was very much leaning toward seeing whether we could successfully narrow the Solicitor General's brief. Most of us were sympathetic to that position, but we found there were no hard grounds on which to narrow it (much as the Court did later). There was recognition at that meeting that a change would not be well received in many quarters; I don't recall any discussion of the possibility of proposing legislation to assuage that. The focus was really on what does the law compel in terms of the position we want to take before the Court. Fielding never once said anything about the politics, pro or con.

Shortly after the meeting with Schmults et al. Fielding went in to discuss the case with Meese. Fielding "distinctly" recalled their discussion, explaining:

> This was between Christmas and New Year's Eve, and Jim Baker was in Texas. It was obvious to me by this point that Meese had assumed the policy action on this. I went in and said something like, "let me bring you up to date on *Bob Jones*"; that was when I found out that he had already been briefed with memoranda and had had discussions on the case. We talked about the legal side of it and the potential political impact; Meese knew it would be politically controversial but he thought it was the right thing to do. I don't think we discussed ways in which we might reduce public misunderstanding of what we were going to do. I should say that Richard Allen [the national security advisor] was then departing the White House and that was absorbing a lot of Ed's attention.

In addition to warning Fielding, Schmults triple-checked the White House support for the policy change when he briefly discussed the reversal with both Meese and Baker. He recalled:

> I had a brief conversation with Meese following a meeting on another issue and asked him whether he was aware of the *Bob Jones* case and that we were planning to change position. He said he was aware of the case and indicated that he knew it might produce controversy. I also mentioned the decision to Jim Baker. I'd have to say though that while Baker was aware of the decision there are different levels of awareness. It's probably fair to say that Jim Baker really didn't have his antennae up on this, although he was certainly aware this could be something controversial. Neither he nor Meese gave us advice on how to handle or present this.

The determination of Schmults and McNamar to fully inform administration officials, some of whom were away for the holidays—including the attorney general and the assistant secretary of tax policy at Treasury—led Schmults to request an extension on the December 31 filing date with the court. The department succeeded in getting an extension to January 11; in the interim, however, new internal dissent within Treasury and the Justice Department surfaced, and the White House staff received one last chance to review the controversial and fateful policy change.

Dissent at Justice and Treasury

The first signs of internal dissent surfaced within the Treasury Department. Several IRS officials who back in September had supported bringing the case before the Court and defending the court of appeals ruling met on January 4 with John "Buck" Chapoton, the assistant secretary for tax policy. Chapoton had been away in Houston during the Christmas holidays and had not played an important role, as he customarily would in the review of a tax case. Chapoton was alarmed by what he heard:

> My initial reaction to the new legal arguments was that they were not sound. But my disagreement wasn't so much over the legal side; I just thought it made no sense to take the case away from the court. If the law was uncertain, the worst thing we could do is take away the case from the court, because we needed their direction even if you thought the law was the other way.

Shortly after the meeting, Chapoton spoke to Secretary Regan telling him that he "disagreed strongly with the policy change, that it was much more of a disaster than people realized, and that it had not been focused on at a high enough level." Regan, whom Chapoton stated was "not a lawyer and considered this a legal issue," told Chapoton to call Schmults at Justice to go over his problems. Schmults told Chapoton that "Brad Reynolds feels very strongly that he is correct on the law and I support him." Chapoton then asked whether the White House was really aware of the significance of the case, to which Chapoton said Schmults replied: "The White House and Meese are totally aware of it," ending the conversation.

The second, more significant intervention occurred within the Justice Department. Attorney General William French Smith had been away during the holidays and had not been fully briefed on the case. To give the Attorney General the opportunity for a full review, a major meeting was scheduled in his conference room for January 6. The meeting turned into a two-and-one-half-hour debate. It began with Acting Solicitor General Larry Wallace, who had made the September filing and was supposed to argue the case before the court, laying out for almost twenty minutes why he felt the government ought to maintain its position. He was followed by Reynolds, who summarized why he believed the position ought be be changed. Then the meeting was opened for discussion. Wallace was surprised:

> I had heard rumors that we might change our position but frankly I had not given them much credence because we had already told the Supreme Court what we were going to do [in September] following pretty high level consultation. I had the responsibility to represent the United States in the Supreme

Court; it was my case. I can't remember another occasion during my four-teen years in office when we've changed position in a case after taking a position with the Supreme Court. I didn't consider it a close call whether the government should change position and I didn't think anyone else would either, frankly.

As the debate continued over the fine points of the law and the larger issue of what position to take before the court, there was little attention paid to the public ramifications of the decisions. There was no discussion of the possibility of proposing legislation and only a brief mention of how the public would per-ceive a reversal.

Immediately after the meeting, Attorney General Smith decided that he con-curred with Schmults and Reynolds on reversing the department's legal position. Some department officials, particularly those who lost out, were concerned right up to the last minute about the review process the department had followed. Subsequently, the review would be criticized by other officials because it had essentially by-passed the two hundred staff lawyers in the Civil Rights Division. (The appellate section of the division had reviewed the solicitor general's brief and supported it. Because Reynolds knew they supported it, he later claimed it was not necessary to inform the staff of the pending change of position.) Simi-larly, not a single black in the administration was aware of or reviewed the policy change; none of the senior officials in the White House, Justice, or Treasury were black, nor did officials seek any reactions from black officials elsewhere in the Administration.

In contrast to the view that the policy reversal constituted yet one more example of insensitivity and insularity from well-to-do Republican ideologues, there was also the view—popular among supporters of the reversal—that the departmental review was in many ways exemplary. Charles Cooper, Reynolds's special assistant, recalled that "in the three years I've been here, there was never a case that I know of that was deliberated on and considered more closely at the highest levels than this case was." Reynolds himself was very much of this view, commenting:

> If you were to sit down and write how you would like the government to work—how it ought to operate in addressing issues and arriving at deci-sions—you could not script anything more perfect than the way this was done. Whether you agree or disagree with the decision, it was the right way for the process to work. The attorney general made his decision after read-ing a lot of material, and getting a full articulation for three hours with the best legal minds around on the pros and cons. The Treasury Department had full input on the most minute details, especially in terms of the pro-grammatic impact of the policy. You couldn't ask for a more thorough, appropriate approach to the problem.

The White House: Strike Three

Within a few hours of making his decision, Attorney General Smith called James Baker, White House chief of staff, to inform him of it. Baker, who knew little about the matter, went to see Meese following the phone call and asked what was going on. After Meese briefly outlined the issue, Baker said he wanted the case discussed at the senior staff meeting the following morning, January 7.

What happened during the senior staff meeting, attended by a couple of dozen staff members, is not exactly clear. Fielding and Meese, who did the briefing, were later accused by some officials of blindsiding the White House staff. More than one official present at the briefing said that Meese left the impression that the administration had lost the appellate cases, and Michael Deaver claimed that Meese also mistakenly presented the reversal as a change to Carter's, instead of Nixon's, policies. Martin Anderson, one of the president's chief domestic policy advisors, who had not heard a word about the *Bob Jones* case until the meeting, remembered that "the matter was put out as a very brief announcement—as one of a dozen topics that we ran through in twenty-five minutes—and it was put forth in rather technical terms."

Other officials present argued that while there was not extensive discussion of the case, no one was blindsided. One official present said, "everyone agreed there was a political downside,"[11] and Fielding distinctly remembers warning about the explosiveness of the decision:

> The analogy I used was that if Bob Jones could get a tax exemption, under the same theory the American Nazi party might also be entitled to one, and that we would be accused of being sympathetic to such groups. At that, heads around the table snapped up; [David] Gergen [Director of Communications], I believe, asked for clarification as to why the American Nazi party could come under the same theory. The discussion then centered on whether we were legally sound in the opinion of Justice and Treasury, and either I or Ed assured people that we were.

Everybody does seem to agree though that while the public implications of the reversal may have been acknowledged, they were not seriously evaluated. One official present at the briefing stated that "we all sat there . . . and we agreed that, yes, there might be political repercussions, but that the decision was right. Nobody focused on the marketing of it."[12] Meese similarly recalled that the idea of simultaneously proposing legislation with the announcement on the case was not touched on. "It never came up in the context," he stated. "It came up as not allowing bureaucrats to make social policy. That's all."[13] Of course, we didn't focus much on the marketing aspects," Gergen explained with some exasperation. "Neither I, Jim Baker, or Mike Deaver appreciated how explosive this was and it was presented as a fait accompli. At that point the only marketing aspect was, 'Hey, here's one that's a little hot, we've got a deadline, so let's slip it out the door late in the day.' "

Shortly after the staff meeting broke up, Meese and Baker went in to talk to the president and told him about the policy reversal. According to Meese, Baker presented the matter to the president and neither he nor Meese stressed the reversal had weighty political implications. "The president was advised as an information matter," Meese later recalled.

Managing the News—Unsuccessfully

In anticipation of the policy reversal, Deputy Treasury Secretary McNamar called Anne McLaughlin, the assistant secretary for public affairs, on January 4 to warn her that a reversal was imminent, and that it "would be a major news item and would she figure out the right thing to do." Having just learned of the decision, McLaughlin realized that "it would be controversial, but so were many of the issues we dealt with. This was presented as a fait accompli which my superiors at Treasury, Justice, and the White House all agreed on."

On January 5 McLaughlin sent a memorandum back to McNamar and Regan, recommending a strategy for announcing the decision: At 4:00 P.M., Friday afternoon, the court motions would be filed; at the same time a press release under McNamar's name (which would include a chronology of the legal history of the cases and selected press clippings) would be released, supplemented by a background briefing for "legal reporters of key national publications."[1] McLaughlin elaborated on the advantages of the plan:

> At 4:00 P.M. release of documents allows time for wire service stories to meet A.M. newspaper deadlines and make 6:00 P.M. evening television broadcasts. Release of your statement at 4:00 P.M. insures that the first wire stories out—and thus the most widely used, especially by the broadcast media—will contain our rationale. An earlier release would give the media more time to conduct interviews with interest groups and thus politicize the story. A later release—one too late for the evening TV news—might cause the networks to hold the story until the next day, which would result in the same kind of expanded political story. The initial press release would stimulate wire service stories under the most controlled situation. The background briefing would allow us to flesh out the stories in the best light possible.[2]

There was no press conference in part because of the Justice Department's reluctance to argue a case in public and in part to keep a low profile. On January 8, the Treasury secretary, the attorney general, and other senior officials meticulously put the finishing touches on the press release at a session in Secretary Regan's office. They agreed it was important not to delay the announcement from Friday until Monday because the Justice Department was, coincidentally, announcing the settlement of the two largest antitrust settlements in history (AT&T and IBM) on Friday. "There was discussion about the fact," Reynolds acknowledged, "that there would be less attention focused on *Bob Jones* because there were other significant news items being released earlier that same day, and that it made sense therefore to do it Friday." This, and the administration's other carefully crafted efforts to "manage" the news, were subsequently considered by the officials to be of limited value, partly because there was a hint of sanguineness about the public reception that marked the internal discussions. Schmults commented:

> I don't think anyone thought the *Bob Jones* case was really going to get lost in the reaction to the AT&T and IBM settlements. I know I didn't. The

flavor of discussion was more that while there was going to be great controversy—it was going to be a civil rights issue—some people felt there would also be some support for our reservations about the regulations; that is, there would be discussion of whether the IRS commissioner should determine the consensus of the general public or whether Congress should write such provisions into the tax law. And that after the controversy initially broke, some people would appreciate that we had legitimate concerns that weren't racially motivated.

White House aides subsequently spoke with some derision about the press strategy. Martin Anderson summed up the sentiment by observing: "I don't think anyone on the White House staff thought the press would pay any attention to the administration's legal theory and reservations, and the idea that you could constrain the media coverage by putting it out late Friday afternoon—well, that was like letting an elephant lose in Central Park and hoping nobody would notice."

The Background Briefing

The three officials picked to do the briefing were Wallison from Treasury, and Bruce Fein and Carolyn Kuhl (special assistant to the attorney general) from Justice. As Kuhl recalled: "The only prepping we got was that our purpose was to explain the legal issues, and highlight the statutory interpretation and inherent dangers of granting unbridled authority to the IRS. We wanted to make it clear that this was a tax question, not a civil rights issue, and that we hadn't taken this position because we wanted to give tax exemptions to discriminatory schools."

The briefers got a taste of what lay in store when Wallison was handed an AP dispatch on the way into the briefing room that led with, "The Internal Revenue Service plans to allow tax exempt status to private schools that discriminate against blacks. . . . The announcement of the shift in government policy begun more than a decade ago came in a two-page statement filed with the Court by the Justice Department. There was no accompanying explanation." "I remember reading that," Wallison recalled, "and thinking, we're in a hole already and we'll have to dig our way out." Wallison, who did most of the talking during the forty-five minute briefing, wearily reconstructed the banter of the background session:

> I think I made all the arguments I wanted to make and I don't think that we got caught in contradictions of any kind. None of our arguments got through, though; I don't think the reporters wanted them to get through and they regarded all this discussion as silly lawyers talk. You could see then that we were in trouble because the questions kept coming back: "Well, did the White House direct you to do this?" "No." "Are you saying here that the administration favors racial discrimination in private schools?" "No, that isn't the point—" "But isn't that the effect of this?" "Well, that is the effect, but—" And it went on and on.
>
> We were really talking past one another. The real story to them was: Is the administration reversing ten years of policy against racial discrimination

in favor of racial discrimination? I was trotting out some principle that they weren't the least bit interested in, and they were talking about how great it was to catch the administration with its pants down.

Two of Wallison's comments at the briefing proved particularly damaging when the furor over the policy change broke several days later. The first was that Wallison—who had no knowledge of Reagan's log notation on the Lott letter—stated that "categorically, the White House gave no indication of what its position was until the Treasury made the decision," and that if the White House had such thoughts they "were not communicated"[3] to Treasury or Justice. The second, more consequential comment was Wallison's acknowledgement that the administration had not "yet made a decision"[4] on whether to propose legislation to deprive discriminatory schools of tax exemptions. Wallison's comments helped lay the ground for charges that the administration was not only callously insensitive, but disingenuous to boot about its purported opposition to racism.

The Story Breaks (January 8–12)

Much as the administration had hoped, there was little adverse commentary on the *Bob Jones* decision in the evening news* or in the wire reports on January 8. Both the wire service stories and news reports played below the AT&T and IBM stories, and in two instances (CBS's report and the AP wire stories) the stories were based simply on the filing of the statement of mootness at the Court.

The problem with the news stories was that no explanation was given for what the administration had done, and when one was given, it was incomplete if not incoherent.** Like much of the television coverage, the *Philadelphia Inquirer* story simply gave no explanation for the policy change.[5] The *New York Daily News* reported that "the official explanation for the move, given in a little-publicized late afternoon briefing . . . was that the federal tax code should not be used to foster 'social aims' and that Congress should write specific legislation instead."[6] The *Boston Globe* and *Baltimore Sun* articles*** elaborated a bit further, explaining vaguely that the policy switch "was a result of a new study within the government concluding that Congress has not said anything on the subject of tax exempt status for institutions that are violating national policy. . . . The official said the reinterpretation was based on the specific words Congress used in the law on tax-exempt status, and on the debates on the issue in Congress dating back at least to 1913."[7]

Even, however, when the news reporter did try during the weekend to spe-

---

* ABC and NBC did get to Benjamin Hooks in time to get some critical reaction. (NBC also got to John Jacobs of the National Urban League and Representative Charles Rangell [D-N.Y.].)

** The most common error was citing the overturned IRS regulation either as a Carter regulation or pre-Nixon regulation. Several reports, particularly subsequent editorials, also erroneously reported that the authority cited by the IRS for the 1970 policy change was Title VI of the Civil Rights Act. Title VI forbids "federal financial assistance" for race discrimination; the IRS, however, never made the argument that tax exemptions constituted federal financial assistance.

*** The *Boston Globe* carried Lyle Denniston's article from the *Baltimore Sun*.

cifically grapple with the issue of statutory interpretation—as did the prestigious *New York Times, Washington Post,* and *Los Angeles Times*—the administration's argument was either misunderstood or reduced to a quibble. Paul Houston of the *Los Angeles Times* implied, for example, that the administration's legal position was that it was undoing the IRS ruling because the IRS commissioner could not know, without being told by Congress, whether it was national policy to oppose race discrimination. Similarly, Fred Barbash of the *Washington Post* and Stuart Taylor of the *New York Times* reported that the administration's objection to the IRS position stemmed from its belief that Congress had not given the IRS authority to require charitable organizations to comply with fundamental public policies. (Barbash, for example, put it this way: "The non-discrimination policy [officials said] gives the IRS excessive power to define legitimate charitable tax-exempt activity. Only Congress, they said, should be allowed to draw those distinctions.")[8] This analysis missed, of course, the crucial nexus of whether educational institutions had to be both educational and charitable to be tax exempt, and effectively narrowed the administration's objections to whining over the fact that the IRS, instead of Congress, had proposed that charitable organizations ought to serve the public good to be exempt. The view that the administration was essentially sticking by a procedural quibble (if anything), was further exacerbated by the fact that only one news story on the announcement reported that the "public policy" doctrine potentially had broad policy ramifications and might, in fact, be used to deprive other groups of their exemptions in the future. The one story that did cite some of the troublesome applications Wallison had warned about in the briefing (Taylor's *New York Times* account) mentioned them in the next-to-last paragraph of the article, buried on page ten.

On Monday and Tuesday the op-ed and editorial writers returned to their desks to fill the void of understanding that had been left by the reporters over the weekend as to why the administration had taken this regressive action. Although there had been a dearth of reporting on the legal issues raised by *Bob Jones,* there was no shortage, already, of reaction from various interest groups. The reaction to the announcement from the left of the political spectrum was quite severe. Benjamin Hooks, president of the NAACP, stated that the policy reversal "panders and appeals to the worst instinct of racism in America,"[9] adding that "I have not yet had occasion to call the Reagan administration racist. But this latest series of retreats on discrimination puts them mighty close."[10] Charles T. Manatt, Democratic party chairman, claimed that the Reagan administration "has effectively made every American taxpayer a forced contributor to segregationist schools,"[11] and Americans for Democratic Action released a statement saying that "this obscene federal action reverses twelve years of civil rights progress by granting avowedly segregationist schools a license to discriminate."[12] Several senators also released critical statements, and Senator Daniel P. Moynihan (D-N.Y.), who had a hand in the original 1970 policy reversal, warned apocalyptically that "a quarter century's achievement [in race relations] could unravel in months."[13]

Conservatives and the religious right, on the other hand, were almost dancing in the streets. Connaught Marshner, chairman of the National Pro-Family Coalition, exulted "this is a real victory. This is the issue that made the religious right more than any other."[14] Senator Strom Thurmond (R-S.C.) cheered the decision, saying that "freedom of religion will no longer have to take a back seat to bureaucratic determinations of public policies. President Reagan has kept another campaign promise."[15] Bob Jones III confessed that he was "numb from what has happened, but we rejoice that God in His own way has allowed this to happen and He gets all the glory for it."[16]

Against this background, it was the political, rather than the legal significance of *Bob Jones* that was graphically highlighted in the straight news coverage, and with the issue framed this way, the overwhelming majority of editorial and op-ed writers decided that the side they wanted to line up with was the civil rights groups and Democrats, rather than than the religious right. Much as Benjamin Hooks and Charles Manatt had decried this subsidization of racism, one paper after another began analogizing tax exemptions with federal subsidies and sanction. The headlines above the editorials and op-eds that appeared on Monday and Tuesday ("DUBIOUS AID FOR SEGREGATED SCHOOLS" "RONALD CROW," "THE REWARDING OF BIAS," "ADMINISTRATION OKAYS ANTI-BLACK SCHOOLS," "REAGAN'S REVERSAL ON RACISM," "HYPOCRITICAL TAX CHANGE MEANS RACISM WILL PAY," "SUBSIDIZING DISCRIMINATION," and "TAX EXEMPT HATE")— in papers as diverse as the *Christian Science Monitor, Washington Post, Los Angeles Times, Baltimore Afro-American, Baltimore Sun, Tallahassee Democrat, Boston Globe,* and *New York Times*—convey some sense of the degree to which exemptions (which were held by many of the administration's most bitter critics), were equated with a government subsidy.

In addition to being portrayed as indifferent or sympathetic to racism, the administration's legal arguments received short shrift in the editorials, which dribbled out on Monday and poured in beginning Tuesday. It was not so much that the administration's legal arguments were rejected as wrong, it was more that the arguments were dismissed as being without merit. Of sixteen major newspapers that published editorials by Tuesday, one (the *Atlanta Journal*) supported the decision, and two others *(Dallas Times Herald, Christian Science Monitor)* acknowledged that the administration's position was not "wholly without merit."[17] The rest of the editorials reported the matter as though there had never been any legal controversy until the Reagan administration decided to reverse policy. Not one paper, for example, reported that the Johnson administration had also decided that the IRS was without authority to deny the exemptions, that the lower court in *Bob Jones* had seen it the same way, and that there was inconclusive precedent from the Court. Similarly, the administration's reservations about using the tax code to regulate social behavior were widely ridiculed, and starkly contrasted with the numerous reforms in the tax code the administration had proudly pushed through Congress in 1981.[18]

Insofar as an explanation was offered for why the administration had taken this repugnant step, two reasons were most prominently cited. The first, as has already been suggested, was that Administration officials were racist or insensitive to the problem of racism. The second was that Administration officials were paying off a political debt by oiling the palm of the religious right.

The White House Steps In

The media influence within the White House, and subsequently in Congress, in the days following the January 8 announcement was profound. On Saturday, January 9, David Gergen—after being quizzed by an incredulous reporter—began to worry that he would have "real problems of conscience staying in an administration that sanctioned this" and determined to raise the issue at the 8 A.M. senior staff meeting Monday morning. Michael Deaver and Jim Baker were surprised and annoyed to learn from the weekend newspapers that the IRS regulation being overturned was a Nixon regulation (instead of a Carter regulation) and that the schools being given exemptions were blatantly racially discriminatory. Deaver, who was a trustee of Howard University and had taken it as something of a personal mission to dispel the notion that the president was insensitive or prejudiced, was especially disturbed and decided to raise the issue before the Monday morning senior staff meeting, at the 7:30 breakfast of the troika.

At the Monday morning breakfast Deaver confronted Meese saying, "My God, what is this thing?" According to Deaver, Meese responded; "We do not want IRS bureaucrats setting social policy," to which Deaver replied: "We could have gone about this in a better way."[19] When the three recessed to the 8:00 A.M. senior staff meeting, Gergen broached the issue and found, much to his relief, that "there was a general sentiment at the meeting—Deaver, Fielding, and [Deputy to the Chief of Staff, Richard] Darman in particular—that we'd have to deal with this and somehow get the understanding of this turned around. Deaver felt the press coverage was horrible, that Reagan is not a racist, and that we were not going to be accused of that." The initial approach settled on at the senior staff meeting was to throw the issue back on Congress while a statement was prepared to clarify the president's position. Notes of the meeting indicate that the press guidance "re: proposed legislation . . . is that the matter should be up to Congress; bureaucrats should not be making policy; White House does not oppose the idea of legislation but would prefer to wait and see a specific bill."

After the meeting Gergen returned to his office to draft a brief statement for the president. The draft (see Appendix C) stated that the president was "unalterably opposed to racial discrimination in any form" and that "the action taken by the Treasury Department last Friday does not suggest otherwise. Rather, the decision announced by the Treasury reflects the fact that Congress has not authorized the [IRS] to determine and apply social policies independently . . . no matter how well intentioned." Later that afternoon Gergen reviewed the statement with Baker, and subsequently with the president. The president, Gergen recalled, was pleased that the statement emphasized "his opposition to racial discrimination and that he was viewing the issue in a legal rather than a racial context.'' ''All I wanted to do,'' Gergen summarized, ''was get something out quickly because we had a firestorm brewing.'' Deaver recalled that more dramatic action to rebut ''the misperceptions''—such as having the president comment on television or delivering an address on civil rights—was not in the cards. ''My own feeling was that you had a twenty-four or forty-eight-hour story,'' Deaver commented. ''Watch it and see what happens: if it boils then maybe you do that, eventually, but if you do it in the heat of the controversy, nobody is going to hear what you're saying.'

By Tuesday, three developments had put the White House at full boil. First, several Democratic senators, threatening to seize the initiative, had announced that they would propose legislation that would deprive discriminatory schools of tax exemptions. Second, a number of Reagan's black appointees were considering resigning and Reagan's only black cabinet member, HUD Secretary Samuel Pierce, was extremely upset by the decision. Finally, the media caught fire, decrying the administration's ''subsidization'' of racism. On the morning of January 12 the *Washington Post, New York Times,* and *Daily News, Los Angeles Times, Baltimore Afro-American* and *Sun, Tallahassee Democrat, Fort Lauderdale News, Dallas Times herald, Seattle Post Intelligencer* and *Times, Detroit Free Press, Boston Globe,* and *Newsday* all carried editorials lashing the administration for promoting what the *New York Times* icily labeled ''tax exempt hate.''

By the time the senior staff met that morning, their political antennae were ''quivering'';[20] notes of the 8:00 A.M. staff meeting indicate that it was agreed that a ''fact sheet [was] desirable to clarify misunderstandings'' and that interested senior staff were invited to attend an 8:45 A.M. meeting on *Bob Jones,* with Attorney General Smith and Treasury Secretary Regan in Meese's office. The meeting was extremely well attended. Fielding and Reynolds brought the participants up to speed on the legal issues, but most of the meeting centered on how the White House should best counter the growing perception that the *Bob Jones* decision had made the president appear racist and indifferent to bigotry. Several White House aides, reportedly Gergen, Fuller, and Darman toyed with the idea of simply reversing sides in the court case, or at least putting the case back before the court, but Meese, Fielding, and Smith were adamant that their legal position was correct. It was acknowledged at the meeting, while reviewing Gergen's draft statement for the president, that if legislation was forthcoming, it would be preferable for the administration to have its own legislation ready—a position which Senate majority leader Howard Baker (R-Tenn.) was also then pushing. Nevertheless, while there was a consensus that something needed to be done to calm the ''media firestorm,'' there was not yet a consensus on how the administration ought best attack the problem of how the president was perceived. Several of those attending, including Meese and Peter Wallison, felt that the administration ought to concentrate on doing more to explain what led it to moot the case, while others, led by Deaver and Gergen, argued that it was imperative for the president to propose legislation immediately to dispel the notion that he tolerated racial discrimination. Deaver summarized the debate as follows:

Some of us were concerned with perceptions, with the public view of how our actions were seen; it's not how they were necessarily. And there were others on the White House staff who felt very strongly about philosophical commitments; in their terms, you should do what is right, regardless of what the perceptions were—"this was right, and right therefore is on our side." I didn't believe this was the time to debate the issue on the merits; we had to get the president perceived in a better light—he is a caring man. On the other hand, the policy people, led by Ed, took just the opposite view. Their argument was that we came here to chart new legal policy and you just don't give up selling your case because the *Washington Post* and a bunch of liberals in the NAACP take you on.

At the conclusion of the meeting it was agreed that a marked up version of Gergen's statement for the president would be released later that day to the Cabinet and the media, and that it would be a good idea for the president to hear first hand of the reactions in the black community from two black White House aides, Mel Bradley and Thaddeus Garrett. Immediately after the meeting ended, Deaver and Meese accompanied Bradley and Garrett into the Oval Office, where "The president," Bradley recalled, "was visibly hurt by what he had read in the newspapers, because he had never supported segregated academies and had fought all his life on the opposite side of the fence. He stressed to us that he had done this because he didn't feel the IRS should go into private schools without legislative authority. He wanted to know if there were any people he personally should call to reassure, and he was ready to do it right then." After Reagan explained his position to Garrett and Bradley, he listened to their tales about the black community's reception of his decision; that exchange is succinctly summarized in Laurence Barrett's *Gambling with History:*

> Garrett described a black church service he had attended on Sunday. He recounted the minister's use of the parable of the serpent. A woman finds an injured snake, nurses it back to health only to be bitten by the ungrateful reptile. Garrett took on a preacher's intonation as he built to the climax: "Reagan is that snake!" The entire black congregation, Garrett concluded sadly, erupted in a chorus of amens. "The president was astounded," Deaver recalled later. Until that moment he didn't fully realize how this was being viewed. He was absolutely silent for a moment or two and then he turned to me and said, 'We can't let this stand. We have to do something.[21]' "

"If we hadn't gotten some blacks in there," Deaver stated, "I'm not sure we'd have been able to prevail, to turn the president around. They were the first people who discussed the issue with him from something other than a legal standpoint and he was very moved by their accounts." Within a few minutes of the meeting in the Oval Office, Reagan seems to have directed that legislation be drawn up and his statement changed to incorporate the fact that he would propose legislation. Senator Robert Dole (R-Ks.), chairman of the Senate Finance Committee, volunteered to sponsor the bill. Reagan's decision to propose legislation, belatedly, posed several obvious problems. The *effect* of the January 12 announcement was to reinstate the IRS policy that existed prior to January 8, since the administration did not plan to grant any more exemptions to discriminatory schools while the legislation was pending in Congress. That made it hard to explain why the administration ever bothered to wipe out the existing IRS policy. There was also, however, one key difference between IRS policy on January 8 and January 12 that was sure to draw criticism; since the administration had already taken the position before the court that the case was moot, it could not easily deprive BJU and Goldsboro of their exemptions and still claim mootness. Thus those two racially discriminatory schools would be eligible for exemptions, at least until the legislation passed.

The administration began the tricky task of selling its new position when Gergen appeared before the White House press corps on the afternoon of the twelfth to read the President's statement and give a fifty-minute backgrounder, devoted almost entirely to *Bob Jones*. Gergen's overriding purpose throughout the briefing was to establish that the president was not a racist. On eight occasions during the briefing Gergen stated that the president had concurred in the January 8 announcement only because he believed the IRS had not been granted the authority by Congress to take away the exemptions; six times he stated that the president was firmly opposed to racial discrimination; and five times he acknowledged that the January 8 announcement had been misinterpreted. Much the same points were made in a series of one-on-one backgrounders given by Deaver, Baker, Meese, and Gergen to *Time, Newsweek, N. Y. Times, Washington Post, Baltimore Sun*, AP, UPI, and the networks, between the January 12 announcement that legislation would be submitted, and the January 18 submission of the legislation.

The proposal for legislation did not appear to dampen the fire of Reagan's liberal critics in the least; Benjamin Hooks announced on *Good Morning America* on the thirteenth that Reagan was "playing into the hands of the segregationists, the Ku Klux Klanners, those who want to see the clock turned back."[22] That same day Senator Kennedy (D-Ma.) denounced the administration as being "the most anti-civil rights administration in the modern history of this country."[23] The following day Speaker "Tip" O'Neill declared Reagan's proposal for legislation "outrageous," stating that "what this country needs is not more legislation, but the clear and unmistakable commitment of the president . . . to enforce the law."[24]

More consequential, however, than the criticism from Reagan's traditional critics, was the ongoing condemnation of the administration that appeared throughout the nation's press. Quite a number (and variety) of papers between January 13 and January 18 (the following Monday) did welcome Reagan's proposal for legislation,* but the general tone of the welcome was one where the

---

*Among the papers that welcomed the proposal were the *Wall Street Journal, Los Angeles Times, Christian Science Monitor, Chicago Tribune, Tampa Tribune, Seattle Post-Intelligencer, Charlotte News, Raleigh Times, Detroit News, New York Post, Newsday, The State* (Columbia, S.C.), and the *American Statesman* and *Eagle* (Tx.). Fred Graham, CBS legal correspondent, also did a commentary on *Morning* on January 13, welcoming the legislation, but saying that its belated appearance "has made the Reagan Administration appear foolish and at best socially insensitive."[25]

new arrival was greeted as an amend, a presence made necessary only by the deplorable insensitivity of the administration. With the exception of a couple of conservative columnists (and Edwin Yoder), no op-ed writer supported the administration's mooting of the case, and the lack of editorial support was similar; out of the forty editorials compiled by the IRS that appeared between January 12 and 18, five expressed support for the administration's January 8 decision, with the *Wall Street Journal* being the only newspaper with a national reputation to side with the administration.

There was also a sizable selection of editorial opinion between January 12 and January 18 that did *not* welcome the introduction of legislation. The view of papers such as the *New York Times* and *Daily News, Providence Journal, Philadelphia Inquirer, Cleveland Plain Dealer, Albuquerque Tribune, Palm Beach Journal,* and *Washington Post,* was that the IRS had more than enough authority to continue its twelve-year-old policy of denying the exemptions. The alternative to legislation advocated by these papers was to rescind BJU's and Goldsboro's exemptions, reinstating the old IRS policy. It was not a big step from this viewpoint for various editorialists to conclude that the Reagan administration was not genuinely opposed to bigotry ''in any form'' since it was continuing BJU's and Goldsboro's exemptions.

Underlying the view that Reagan had acted out of political expediency (and the milder view that the legislation was belated restitution), was the perception that Reagan had ''reversed'' course. It is difficult to overstate the frequency with which TV and news reporters, cartoonists,* and op-ed and editorial writers described the January 12 announcement as a ''reversal'' or ''flip-flop.'' The flip-flop notion drove home the point that Reagan was ''acknowledging'' he had done something racist or, at best, shown an indifference to minorities from which he was now retreating. Rather, in short, than clearing up the misunderstanding of the administration's position, the offer of legislation seems only to have made the administration look extremely mixed-up.

Was the Media at Fault?

Senior officials who dealt with the media during the controversy suggest that the coverage came out the way it did both because of the press's own prejudices and because of the conflicting strategies with which federal officials approached the press. Several reasons were given for the media's unwillingness to believe that the administration had acted out of fairly narrow legal and philosophical considerations. Gergen, who may have done as much backgrounding on the subject as anyone following the January 8 announcement, stressed that the administration ran aground on long-standing suspicions that reporters shared about the administration:

> The press suspects that this administration is tinged with bigotry, and if there is one subject that the press corps is united about, and feels deeply

---

* A sampling of some of the editorial cartoons is contained in Appendix D.

about at a personal level, it's that the administration has set back the cause of civil rights. That's partly because they feel nobody in the administration follows civil rights with real care and partly because they see there are no blacks in a position of real authority. The other disposition they had was that they generally respected the administration as being competent. Their attitude was "You guys have this vaunted organizational efficiency, so how could you blow this unless you really didn't care?"

Peter Wallison, who was the point man for the press at Treasury during the controversy, differed a bit from Gergen in his assessment of the media's distrust of the administration. In Wallison's view the problem was not so much ingrained suspicion as a kind of self-inflicted "pack journalism:"

I was overwhelmed by reporters; they were coming in through the windows and doors, over the phone, and through the transom. I was terribly frustrated throughout this whole period because I said the same thing to every reporter who called; that we had done this out of concern over granting power to administrative authorities that didn't have a legislative basis. Not once could I get a reporter to focus on that, and there was barely ever anything in their stories that reflected Treasury's viewpoint, because they did not think our concern was responsive to what they felt the story was . . . the press themselves became entangled by their own framing of the issue. They were so directed at the one question of racial discrimination that they would have had to change the whole focus of their stories in order to admit any of our arguments—not to admit the correctness of them but just to acknowledge they were more than an aside.

A somewhat less charitable view of the media's motives was expressed by Brad Reynolds, who took press inquiries at the Justice Department. Reynolds suggested, essentially, that the press had been cowed by pressure from its liberal peers:

Once the press saw the hue and cry, saw this had gone down as anti-civil rights, none of them were willing to stick their heads above the bunker to get shot at. They had to be at the forefront of the "grand liberal press," and they were not going to take on the civil rights people, or print anything that might be perceived as anti-civil rights.

The media treatment of the administration's motives also, however, had its defenders. "It's unrealistic to think that if you really blow one," Gergen explained, "that you're going to be able to turn around the press coverage." Gergen's view was articulately echoed by Thaddeus Garrett: "If you go up to a man in the street and sock him in the eye, you're going to have a pretty tough time convincing that man and the public that saw you do it that all you meant to do was straighten out his hat, even if that really is what you meant to do."

Was the Administration at Fault?

White House officials did not, by and large, attempt to defend the position the administration had taken before the Court on January 8. Information that might have been available routinely on less controversial matters, such as fact sheets outlining the legal history of the case or quotations from the opposing *Bob Jones* opinions in the district and appeals court decisions, was not released quickly by the White House or the departments. No formal background briefings were given at the departments by their legal experts in the week after the announcement. Secretary Regan and Attorney General Smith did not speak out during the furor in a single interview or speech and avoided background press briefings on the subject. For ten days after the January 8 announcement not one administration official discussed *Bob Jones* in a televised interview over the news or on the Sunday talk shows. And no campaign whatsoever was mounted to convince the media and public that there were alarming implications to the "public policy" doctrine.

What accounts for the fact that the administration did not mount a serious educational effort in response to coverage that officials found personally offensive, misleading, and politically expensive? One answer lies out in the departments, which had pushed for the January 8 announcement and might have been expected to defend it. At the Treasury, Assistant Secretary for Public Affairs Anne McLaughlin recalled that the *Bob Jones* controversy escalated rapidly off her agenda to the White House. She received "no push whatsoever" from Regan or McNamar to mount an educational effort and simply delegated all press inquiries to Peter Wallison. Wallison, in turn, acknowledged that "we were retreating so fast we never had an opportunity to marshal our forces and set up a line of defense."

If the Treasury Department was conspicuous for its reactive and uncoordinated response, the Justice Department was conspicuous for its silence. Thomas DeCair, director of public affairs, felt it would be preferable to have Treasury comment on the issue both because he wanted to portray the case as a tax question rather than a civil rights issue, and because the Justice Department doesn't traditionally comment on litigation, at least not with the latitude that might be afforded the White House or Treasury. William French Smith's first (and only) comment during January to the Justice Department's press corps about *Bob Jones* came on January 28, and summed up well the position the department took while the furor was at its peak: "I can't really comment about the case," Smith stated, "because it is pending before the Supreme Court, other than to say that I think perhaps what the administration could certainly have done much better would have been to more effectively explain their position."[26]

Smith, of course, could have commented about the case. Reynolds did talk to several reporters, and Justice department officials had already participated in the press backgrounder on January 8. But Justice department representatives acknowledged that they were also worried about being bloodied by the press. Ed Schmults, the deputy attorney general, commented:

> What happened is that the press framed the issue as race and we were bathed in the heat. The *New York Times* called it "tax exempt hate," that was part of the white hot fury that just melted the administration. No one here, and

I include myself and the attorney general, was willing to stick their head above the trenches . . . everyone dove to the bottom of the foxhole; no one wanted to be personally identified with this disaster and no one wanted to say, "Hey, wait a minute," because they were afraid they'd be called racist.

Finally, Justice department officials also stayed quiet because they were, in effect, told to by the White House. "When a controversy like this erupts," Martin Anderson, the president's assistant for policy development stated, "most people who have been in Washington understand that you cannot begin to 'educate' the press and public in a manner of days—it can't be done—campaigns like that take time." And key members of the White House staff were in no mood to make the effort; as Gergen pointed out: "You have to face the fact that within the White House itself there were divisions as to what the policy should have been. There were many staff members, who, had they been consulted early on, would have opposed the [January 8] decision. And when there's not much enthusiasm in people's hearts, it's hard to muster a united educational campaign."

Did the White House Blow It?

Some officials contended the White House's intervention after the January 8 announcement only made matters worse. "We would have been attacked in any event for being insensitive," said Tom DeCair, "but the proposal to send up legislation, in effect, made us look expedient, like we were admitting that we had done the wrong thing when we asked the Court to moot the case. We really hadn't; we just weren't winning the battle in public." White House aides, however, vigorously defended the rapid announcement of legislation. "Sure," Deaver allowed, "there were some who argued that proposing legislation might make us look insincere, but most of us felt that to do something was better than to just sit there and take it. You had to show positive action, an interest in the subject, and a willingness to take a step. The coverage would have gotten even more ferocious if we hadn't announced the legislation." Above all the White House's sense of urgency seems to have been sparked by a deep personal sensitivity, shared among senior White House aides, that an indictment of racism, however unmerited, was intolerable both for them and the president. "I've seen the president up close for seventeen years now," Deaver stated, "and this particular issue he feels very strongly about. The one thing above all else that can get him excited, and to some degree defensive, is the accusation that he is prejudiced." Gergen stressed that the framing of the issue in racial terms was instrumental in elevating the issue out of the Justice and Treasury departments and into the White House:

Some people may claim that we never should have touched this; that we should have kept the president away from the issue and let Justice and Treasury fend for themselves. I think they're wrong. First, the White House and the president were too smeared with it to keep it out of the White House; we certainly had signed off on it. But, more important, it was a question of moral leadership and the president cannot abdicate that. We had to avoid the charge that we were bigoted. Insensitivity is lesser indictment—if your administration is perceived as racist, you can't exist, you can't govern in that situation.

What concerned Justice and Treasury officials, however, was that they felt the White House made little effort to explain why the legislation was consistent, and to some degree a logical outgrowth, of the January 8 filing. Peter Wallison suggested that while White House aides might well have saved the administration from a public relations fiasco if they had been more involved earlier, their acute political sensitivities did not make them the best spokesmen for the administration once the controversy had erupted:

> What happened is that we let the media determine what the issue was. It's funny because a precept for all lawyers is that if you want to win an argument, you never let your opponent state the question. And in this case, the media stated the question: "Was the administration in favor of racial discrimination?" If that's the question, then the January 8 filing shows, "Yes, they are in favor of it" and the January 12 announcement demonstrates, "No, they are not in favor of it," and is suppose to be a policy reversal. Of course the two were, in fact, perfectly consistent, but the White House spokesmen were not well equipped to make this point because as soon as the questions started coming, they retreated back to the politics of it.

Senior White House aides, including Deaver, Gergen, and Martin Anderson, found the department's concerns about defending the legal merits and philosophical significance of the January 8 position naive, and somewhat exasperating. Deaver stated:

> There were merits from the legal standpoint, but once the story got fuzzed up in the press and public's mind, you really had to go at it in a different way. I recounted to the reporters I talked to about the blacks getting in to see the president, how horrified he was by the reaction, and that he would never have condoned anything that smacked of a hint of racism. I also explained that the president had only talked to lawyers about this, and that the human and perceptual side of this was not considered and wouldn't be by the lawyers; I think the press found that credible and resonant with their own experience.

Baker, Deaver, and Gergen did not go out of their way in their backgrounders to stress that the president was not "reversing" or "retreating" by proposing legislation. The three of them shared a notable lack of enthusiasm for the January 8 decision and they focused their efforts instead on rebutting the notion that the president was racist. Once undercutting the impression of racism became predominant, there was actually some advantage to having the legislation be perceived as a reversal, since the White House could then claim that the president had undertook action that "demonstrated" he was not racist. One revealing aspect of the White House's preoccupation with the media's accusations of racism is that while there was nothing released during the week after the announcement to defend the legal merits of the administration's position, the White House did engage in a series of well-publicized meetings with black leaders, designed to show, presumably, that the White House was not out of touch with or hostile to the black community. On January 12, for example, a group of black White House aides who ate breakfast together periodically were invited unexpectedly to share their breakfast with Vice President Bush, whose activities were being filmed that day by NBC. On January 15, a visit from soul singer James Brown to Vice President Bush—which had previously been arranged as part of a celebration of Martin Luther King's birthday—was filmed, and a clip was shown on ABC's *Nightline* of Bush greeting Brown, saying, "I'm delighted to see you here, because we also know that we've got some perceptual problems. People are jumping on our president as not caring, and I'll tell you it's just not true."[27] Brown was then ushered in for a brief, private meeting with the president, which was immediately disclosed to the press. Three days later, John Jacob, the new head of the National Urban League, was at a meeting at the White House with Elizabeth Dole, when he too unexpectedly got brought into the Oval Office. The president had a brief conversation with Jacob, explaining that he had acted out of concern over IRS harrassment of private schools, that he had a minimal involvement in the decision, acknowledging that it was a mistake not to couple legislation with the original announcement. Jacob reported his conversation with the President that night on PBS's *MacNeil / Lehrer Report* and the next day on ABC's *Good Morning America*.

Although the White House's meetings with blacks may not have made much difference, the campaign to dispel the notion that the president was prejudiced was beginning to show some dividends by week's end, with fewer papers also accusing the president of being expedient and insincere. But the White House countercampaign was raising new problems for the president, and, more particularly, for his senior aides. As Gergen said, "We were able to erase some of the perceptions of bigotry, but then, ultimately, we took a round for being insensitive and incompetent—but that was the price you had to pay." The ultimate logic of the White House's defense of the administration's actions was perhaps best summed up in a column written by Tom Wicker on January 18:

> All right, Ronald Reagan is not a racist. The White House tells us that, instead, he's an uninformed and uninvolved President who on an important question of domestic policy didn't know what he was doing.
> Neither did his senior staff. Ed Meese, the key man, didn't understand either the social or the political meaning of his decision to grant tax exemptions to segregated private schools—thus reversing an 11-year-old policy begun by President Nixon. Michael Deaver and James Baker, the other members of the Reagan "triumvirate," didn't even know the decision was being made until it was too late to change it; then they inexplicably failed to appreciate its importance. Mr. Baker and Mr. Deaver didn't even know the Administration was reversing a *Nixon* policy—not a Jimmy Carter regulation—until they read it in the newspapers. As for Mr. Reagan himself,

he knew nothing whatever of the matter until it was settled; and when told, he said nothing, apparently recognizing no more than his staff had that an important decision had been made in his name.

That's not a critical outsider's account of what happened. That's the version told to the press by Mr. Meese and Mr. Deaver and other White House sources, in an effort to dispel the notion that the Administration, with Mr. Reagan's concurrence, had deliberately sought to assist racially segregated private schools. It's unlikely that this White House version is the full story. . . . But even taken at face value, the White House story makes all concerned look incompetent or uninformed or both.[28]

Unburying the Hatchet

The media interest in who bore responsibility for the January 8 filing was a logical outgrowth of the White House confession that an enormous mistake had occurred. Conceivably, however, the administration could have reduced the duration of the "whodunit" stories by having the president, or the senior staff collectively, assume responsibility for what had happened; instead, however, a number of White House aides anonymously pointed the finger of blame at Ed Meese, sowing some rancor and considerable distrust among the Big Three.

Slipping the Noose on Meese

Criticism that the president was disengaged, isolated from key policy decisions by his aggressive, competent staff had begun in August 1981 when Meese, to Baker's and Deaver's dismay, had let the president sleep for five hours instead of waking him up to inform him that American pilots had downed two Libyan jet fighters. The handling of *Bob Jones* offered fertile ground for renewing this charge, since White House aides could not claim the president was unaware of the racial implications of the *Bob Jones* filing without, at the same time, acknowledging that he had signed off on a critical civil rights decision while lacking even the crudest appreciation for its significance. As the following cartoon from *Doonesbury* illustrates, the defense of the president mounted by Deaver, Meese et al. clearly opened the president up to this kind of criticism:

DOONESBURY　　　　　　　　　　　　　　　　　　　　**by Garry Trudeau**

Insofar as White House aides anticipated such criticism, they initially sought to blunt it by minimizing the president's role in the policy turnaround, crediting his staff and cabinet departments with responsibility for the fiasco. CBS News reported on January 12 that "senior White House aides are saying tonight that the president was blind-sided, that he was totally unaware of the potentially severe political backlash. Sources told CBS News that the proposal was forwarded to the White House by the Treasury Department and passed quickly through a senior staff meeting as the elimination of an old piece of Carter administration policy."[1]

The effort to protect the president from assuming responsibility for the January 8 decision worked for a while, but the diversion of attention came largely at Meese's expense once reporters began probing who blindsided the president. On Friday, January 15, an anonymous White House official told Jack Nelson of the *Los Angeles Times* that Deaver and Baker were extremely upset with Meese for not having informed them earlier and more fully about *Bob Jones*. At the same time, Martin Schram of the *Washington Post* received a similar tip, and, like Nelson, put a call in to Meese to get his comments on the allegations. Meese summarily denied there was a problem. He explained to Schram, "I had some knowledge of what was going on but I didn't have anything major to do with it at all. . . . It was a departmental thing."[2] In a similar vein, he told Nelson, "At no time did I participate in the decision or in the deliberations." He also informed Nelson that he had spoken with Baker and Deaver "and they are not upset at me."[3] Schram was unable that day to get through to Deaver or Baker for comment (at least on the record), but Nelson did manage to get through to Deaver, who declined to blame Meese for what occurred, but acknowledged he was "upset from the very beginning at the way this matter was handled—none of the blacks in the administration were asked their opinion, and if that had happened the president would have been better advised."[4] Baker refused to comment to Nelson just as he had with Schram.

Despite Meese's denials, and the absence of direct corroboration from either Deaver or Baker, Nelson led his front-page article with the anonymous White House allegations that Baker and Deaver were "furious" and "livid" with Meese, and the same charges were highlighted in the second paragraph of Schram's story. (The *Post* played Schram's story on page 14 of its Saturday edition.) The next day the anti-Meese campaign reached a peak when the *New York Times* and *Washington Post* each ran stories on page one of their Sunday papers on the staff infighting.

On Sunday Meese decided to strike back. At a press conference that day in Nashville, Meese called Nelson's *Los Angeles Times* story "very incorrect,"[5] said "nobody is blaming anybody,"[6] explained that the moving force behind the policy shift was Treasury and Justice, and pointed out that Fielding, who reported to Baker, was the chief White House contact for the discussions on the case. Meese acknowledged that he had been present when the case was discussed with Reagan, but stated that he "was not responsible for the decision. It's a much more complex issue than we have time to go into here, but I didn't have any recommendation for the President. Actually Jim Baker took it to the president."[7] Meese also went on television, denying his direct responsibility in an interview with Mike von Fremd for ABC *World News Tonight.*

The impact of the "get Ed Meese leaks" was felt in at least two ways at the White House. The first purported effect was that once Meese got fingered in the media for being incompetent and insensitive, he reportedly dropped his support for several provisions in the draft legislation that he and the religious right favored. That particular thesis was most vividly expressed in the conservative weekly *Human Events,* which featured a long, anonymous article on the drafting of the legislation replete with precise quotations from White House meetings at which the legislation was shaped.[8] However, while various officials from the White House and Justice and Treasury Department did acknowledge that the media "firestorm" influenced the legislative drafting process, no one concluded that Meese made a sudden about turn on the bill because of the media beating he endured.

The second effect, which is not in dispute, was the suspicion and bitterness the stories stirred among key White House staffers. As Dave Gergen summed up:

> Meese was very upset about this . . . He feels, with some justification, that some aides were out to get him, to drag him down, or at least belittle him. I think he was, in part, victimized and there were some moments when people really tried to bloody Ed. To his credit, he didn't try to give much of that back, although some of his people would spread allegations in the conservative press about Baker, Darman, and me; that we were a pinko influence in the White House.

Containing the Infighting (January 19–24)

The first tactic to stop the infighting was to have White House aides blame the staff collectively for what occurred, rather than singling out Meese and Fielding. To some degree, this was attempted by a few officials. Deaver, as noted previously, publicly adopted this position by making on-the-record comments like, "all of those involved failed to see the sensitivity of the issue. It's a shame [the president's] reputation has to be tarnished by faulty staff work."[9] Similarly, Gergen told the AP on Tuesday, January 19, that, "if there's blame, all of us share responsibility for it, including myself,"[10] and the following night he allowed on PBS's *MacNeil / Lehrer Report* that, "I count myself among those who share the responsibility for the way it was handled."[11]

The problem with the collective defense was that it was not particularly heartfelt or convincing. Some of the people who took the position were the same aides that had informed the media the previous week, on background, that the president and senior staff had been blindsided by Meese's and Fielding's legalistic presentation of the issues. Furthermore, some of the anti-Meese stories had resulted not so much from a deliberate effort to get Meese, as from the desire of Baker, Deaver, and Gergen to personally disassociate themselves from the handling of a "racist" decision they had little advance appreciation of. As Martin Schram of the *Post* summed up: "They might have been willing to taint their reputation to protect the president, but they weren't willing to do it to save Ed Meese."

The second tactic used to contain the staff infighting was to lie to the press about the strained relations among the staff. Laurence Barrett, *Time*'s White House correspondent, obtained interviews with all three members of the trium-virate (later reported in *Gambling with History)*; and he concluded from the interviews both that *Bob Jones* "shattered what mutual trust remained within the troika after the first year,"[12] and, more specifically, regarding Baker, that he "and Deaver yearned for a realignment of responsibility [following *Bob Jones*] that would take Meese out of operations altogether. Baker even came to believe that all concerned would be better served if either he or Meese left the White House altogether, so that there could be one chief of staff with clear author-ity."[13] Baker, however, assumed quite a different posture in public when he finally commented on the controversy in an interview with Chris Wallace on NBC's *Today* show on January 20:

WALLACE: Why do we get these succession of stories about how unhappy you are, Mrs. Reagan is, Mike Deaver is with Ed Meese? What happened to that one big happy family over there?
BAKER: Well, the family is still one big happy family, Chris, and I don't know why we get these things. You'll notice that both Mike and I have said that there's nothing, no substance to those reports that we were upset with Ed. The fact of the matter is, this threeway, this troika, if you want to use that term, of running the White House has worked very well for the presi-dent in 1981, it's going to work very well to serve the president in 1982. We get along extremely well. That's not to say that there are not tensions, because there are going to be in any kind of relationship like that. But reports such as you have mentioned are just absolutely not true.[14]

The "one big happy family" story had almost no positive impact on the media coverage; reporters who were skeptical of Gergen's and Deaver's contentions that the staff collectively bore responsibility for the fiasco, were not about to believe that the staff not only accepted responsibility for what happened but also got along "extremely well" while doing so.

The effort to quiet the staff infighting did not succeed until the president himself took the blame for the fiasco. Underlying the president's acceptance of responsibility was the awareness that his log notation on Trent Lott's letter was about to leak to the media. On January 18, National Public Radio aired a news report that Reagan had suggested the administration intervene in *Bob Jones* after seeing a summary of a letter from Trent Lott.[15] At the morning press briefing, White House Deputy Press Secretary Larry Speakes told reporters that "National Public Radio knows far more than I because I do not know the facts of the Lott letter,"[16] but the issue would not go away so easily. Later that day the White House sent its legislation up to the Hill and held a background session for the press corps. The reporters were obsessed throughout the briefing with why Bob

Jones and Goldsboro were retaining the exemptions pending the passage of legislation and were convinced, as Gergen put it in his press guidance the next day for the president, that this "was done as a favor to Strom Thurmond and Trent Lott." (See Appendix D)

The issue of the president's responsibility for the January 8 decision came to a head the following day at the press conference when Sam Donaldson of ABC News asked, "[The January 8 decision] clearly gave aid and comfort to racial discrimination. Then in subsequent days you began a series of steps to sort of go back from that. My question is, what happened? Are you responsible for the original decision, or did your staff put something over on you?" Reagan, relying heavily on the Gergen / Baroody guidance, responded:

> Sam, no one put anything over on me. No, Sam, the buck stops at my desk. I'm the originator of the whole thing and I'm not going to deny that it wasn't handled as well as it could be. But I think that what we actually saw was confusion, and it was rather widespread and encouraged, about what—we had not anticipated the reaction because we were dealing with a procedural matter. And it was interpreted by many of you as a policy matter, reflecting a change in policy. And then therefore, when we went forward, you said well then this was another change back in policy.
>
> What we were trying to correct was a procedure that we thought had no basis in law, that the Internal Revenue Service had actually formed a social law and was enforcing that social law. And we think that that's a bad precedent and it's a bad thing to do. And so we—there was no basis in the law for what they were doing. So what we set out to do was to stop—to change that procedure and stop the Internal Revenue from doing this and then to have Congress implement with law the proper procedures. . . .
>
> [I] didn't anticipate that it was going to be as misinterpreted as it was. And we since—what we have accomplished . . . [is] we've prevented the IRS from determining national social policy all by itself. It'll now be by elected officials, the Congress. We'll continue to prohibit tax exemptions for schools that discriminate and for the first time that will be the law of the land. And we helped to preserve the rights and liberties of religious schools as long as they don't discriminate. . . . Maybe we didn't act as swiftly as we could have—and, as I say, I'm not defending that we proceeded on a course that was as well planned as it might have been. . . . But don't judge us by our mistakes—I'm probably going to make more of them. But judge us how well we recover and solve the situation.[17]

The president's comments at the press conference brought the media coverage and a public relations nightmare for the White House full circle. Two of the president's observations were linked by the media to considerable effect. First, the remark that "there was no basis in law for what [the IRS was] doing" was ridiculed by editorial writers and commentators. The political sop explanation for the *Bob Jones* filing was revitalized by Reagan's statement that he was "the originator of the whole thing," which appeared not to be an exaggeration once the president's log notation on Lott's letter was flashed across the television screen January 19 on the CBS Evening News. The president's concession that he had made a mistake did save his staff some public grief, but it came largely at his own expense, with another spate of articles appearing that questioned Reagan's depth of involvement and sensitivity to minorities.

The Aftermath of Bob Jones

Senior officials believe the *Bob Jones* controversy, and the media coverage of it, had a substantial impact in three areas: on the outcome of *Bob Jones* itself, on the administration's political ties (particularly with the black community), and on the process the departments and White House used in the future to reach decisions.

The effect of the media coverage on the disposition of *Bob Jones* was frequently cited by Justice Department officials, even though the attention devoted by the media to the case faded noticeably after the president's press conference and submission of legislation. The media coverage continued to frame the terms of debate, particularly in Congress. As the controversy moved into its third week, legal scholars finally began commenting on the controversy and rejected wholesale the administration's legal arguments. The general theme struck by the legal commentators was that the administration was not only wrong, but ought to return the case to the court instead of proposing legislation. Bernard Wolfman, a professor at Harvard Law School and chairman of an ABA Committee on Taxation, wrote, for example, on the *New York Times* op-ed page that, "If it is not the racist, lawless Government it appears to be, the Reagan Administration should proceed with the cases now in the Supreme Court and restore the policy of non-discrimination that has been acknowledged law since 1970."[1]

The position of legal scholars lent legitimacy to the position of liberal congressmen who were confident the legislation could be held up as a whipping boy on which to score points against the administration, forcing the administration eventually to go back into court. That is, after the administration sent up its legislation, the religious right renounced it, raising the threat of a battle to get it passed; within a few days, a number of liberal Democrats—including ones who had said that legislation was urgently needed before the President proposed it— now decided to *oppose* the legislation, purportedly on the grounds that the law was already so clear that no legislation was needed. Instead they decided to sponsor a concurrent resolution that would affirm "that current federal law clearly authorizes and requires the Internal Revenue Service to deny tax exempt status . . . to private schools that practice racial discrimination."[2] With congressional moderates the only supporters of the legislation—and most of them looking eagerly to the court to intervene—the administration faced an uphill battle to sell the bill by the time Congress returned from its recess in late January.

The first opportunity the administration received to sell its legislation was on February 1, when McNamar, Schmults, Reynolds, and Wallison testified before the Senate Finance Committee. The chairman of the committee, Senator Dole, had agreed to sponsor the administration's legislation, but allowed at the hearing that "I appreciate the White House sending [the legislation] up here with its best wishes, but I am not certain—we may want to send it back. I know we can't suggest that the court go ahead and make that decision, but hopefully they read the papers."[3] The hearing also marked the first time the administration was able to present its legal arguments in real detail, but, like the legislation, the moment for the administration seems to have been lost. As Dole told the witnesses:

> It just seems to me that everything you say may be absolutely correct, but there has been such an avalanche of feeling about racial discrimination. You are not going to get any votes in this committee for racial discrimination. But, I think, legislation is going to be very difficult until there is a full understanding. I don't know if what you said has reached the public yet, and it may never reach the public.[4]

The tepid support administration witnesses received from the Republican-controlled Finance Committee was more than offset by the scalding criticism dished out by the Democrat-controlled House Ways and Means Committee three days later. The hearings began with a well-choreographed parade of law professors, including Laurence Tribe from Harvard Law School, who accused the administration of "cynical disregard for truth, calculated defiance of law," and said its legal case was "pathetic."[5] The law professors were followed by a "bipartisan" panel composed of the IRS commissioners who had supported the 1971 IRS ruling and were similarly quite critical of the administration.

Whatever merit members of the committee might have seen in the administration's arguments withered rapidly under this attack, and when Schmults, McNamar, Reynolds, and Wallison arrived to testify that afternoon, the committee lit into them like hounds circling a cornered prey. "You have against you," Congressman Rangel (D-N.Y.) stated, "only the Constitution, the legal scholars, the American Bar Association, those of us in Congress and former [IRS] administrators. The other side is what I am concerned about. It is obviously more powerful than anything that I have mentioned, which are the political considerations."[6] Congressman Brodhead (D-Mich.) was even more to the point, telling administration witnesses that their testimony was "the shabbiest, most unbelievable bunch of crap I've heard since I've been here."[7] By the end of the hearing the legislation was stillborn, with Chairman Rostenkowski (D-Ill.) stating that he saw no need for it and had no plans for mark-up.

The media's response to the January 8 filing had contributed to the administration decision to propose legislation. Now the media was blamed by some officials for the Congressional rejection. As Theodore Olson of the Justice Department summed up:

> If you take the media out of the picture, it is hard to understand why congressmen ever opposed the legislation. The legislation codified two very simple propositions; first, that Congress, rather than unelected bureaucrats, should set the basic policy parameters for when exemptions should be denied, and second, that racially discriminatory institutions should not be tax exempt because we want to make it harder instead of easier for people to discrimi-

nate. A majority of American people would support those propositions, and I believe Congress would have as well were it not for the media coverage.

What the media coverage did was give congressmen an out for opposing the legislation. The consensus promoted in the media was that we had done a dastardly thing motivated by malice, hate and other ignoble qualities, and that our actions were "unprincipled" because law already existed on the subject. The coverage made the environment totally different, and in that environment it was easy for a congressman to say, "It won't benefit me to vote on this because I may alienate some conservatives and why stick my neck out if I can say the law already exists?"

Just as it appeared that the administration might be forced to endorse a concurrent resolution instead of the legislation, the administration was rescued, in a fashion, by the court of appeals for the District of Columbia circuit. The D.C. circuit court was handling the *Wright* v. *Regan* case* and on February 18, at the request of the Lawyer's Committee for Civil Rights, issued an order enjoining the secretary of Treasury and IRS commissioner from granting or restoring tax-exempt status to racially discriminatory schools. Banned, in effect, from implementing the January 8 decision—since the administration could no longer claim mootness if Bob Jones's and Goldsboro's exemptions were withheld—the administration agreed to return the case to the Court and ask for a ruling.** This step was widely hailed as another "reversal" and "flip-flop," one perhaps not without consequence for the administration. As Deputy Attorney General Schmults stated:

> We could not have taken an issue to the Supreme Court under more unfortunate circumstances. They saw the race issue framed in the press, saw the administration characterized as flip-flopping and jumping around, and Congress saying "it's already the law." There couldn't have been worse circumstances under which to get a clear, dispassionate review of the Internal Revenue Code and what sec. 501(c)(3) really meant. I'm not suggesting for a minute that the result would have been different, or that each Justice didn't do the best they could to be absolutely fair, but I think it defies human nature, in subtle and other ways, for all this outcry not to have had some impact on the Court.

In May 1983, the Supreme Court roundly rejected the administration's legal arguments, ruling 8–1 (with Justice William Rehnquist dissenting), that "the actions of Congress since 1970 leave no doubt that the IRS reached the correct conclusion in exercising its authority." In the wide-ranging opinion written for the majority, Chief Justice Warren Burger stated that tax exempt organizations must "demonstrably serve and be in harmony with the public interest."[8]

---

* *Wright* v. *Regan* was a case which parents of black school children in several states had opened to force the IRS to apply more aggressive tests of nondiscrimination for schools seeking exemptions.

** The administration also argued, as it had all along, that the revocation of the exemptions would not have violated the First Amendment rights of BJU and Goldsboro. Appointment of a special counsel gave the court the opportunity to hear oral arguments in support of the IRS policy.

The impact of the media coverage on the Court was a subject of some speculation. William Bradford Reynolds, who argued the losing side before the Court, contended that:

> the media coverage had a tremendous influence on the court. The court is fully sensitive to and aware of public perceptions, and although that is not how they call their decisions, it is also not lost on them.

The Court's decision, ironically coincided with a rash of news commentary expressing trepidation about the implications of the public policy doctrine. Signals of the shift emerged in October 1982 when Stuart Taylor of the *New York Times* and Nick King of the *Boston Globe* wrote the first news analyses—outside the conservative press—that contained any discussion of the troublesome implications of the public policy doctrine for tax exempt organizations. The *New York Times* and *Boston Globe* articles appeared right after the oral argument before the court, and they were followed, when the court rendered its opinion a number of months later, by similar articles in the *Washington Post, Washington Times, USA Today,* and the *National Law Journal*[9] (although a clear majority of the coverage hailed the Court's decision). Perhaps the most dramatic demonstration of the media's newfound willingness to examine the potentially nettlesome implications of *Bob Jones* was a piece by syndicated columnist Ellen Goodman, which ran under the head: "A Judgment Against Women's Colleges?" Goodman, a perennial critic of the Reagan administration, observed uneasily:

> If a private school that discriminates against blacks can lose its tax-exempt status, what about a school that accepts only one sex? . . . At the moment, there is no case pending against a women's college, but this is a tricky philosophical issue for women's rights supporters. Most of these women's colleges have been in the forefront of the right for equality and integration. Yet they are now vulnerable to charges of discrimination.[10]

The Political and Institutional Aftermath of Bob Jones

The impact of the media coverage of *Bob Jones,* in the eyes of senior officials, extended well beyond the outcome of the court case. The political fallout of the coverage was particularly damaging to the administration's relations with the black community. The administration's relations with civil rights leaders and the black community had been poor, of course, long before *Bob Jones.* But the *Bob Jones* controversy, as Attorney General Smith summed up in August 1982, "threw the whole focus of our civil rights efforts off."[11]

Reynolds also viewed the fallout of *Bob Jones* with chagrin, emphasizing that the aftermath of the controversy had extended beyond the administration's relations with civil rights leaders:

> *Bob Jones* was and will remain an albatross for us, particularly out in the black community. When the press blatantly labelled our actions as racist, the large majority of the black community—which don't have the kind of education that would permit them to sort through the legal issues—came

away with the attitude, "Gee, they must have people in there that really are racist!" That's just a fact. It would be silly for us to harbor any misperceptions that somehow this didn't have a lasting impact or a significant impact. The civil rights intelligentsia, of course, appreciated what was going on and played it for all it was worth; I'm talking about the effect on the largest proportion of people who really are reached by civil rights questions and should be reached by them. They, as a result of *Bob Jones*, carry around a degree of distrust and suspicion about everything we do. The rest of our civil rights record is quite positive; this was the only action we've taken that could be misconstrued as condoning bigotry.

The *Bob Jones* fiasco altered not only the administration's relationship with the civil rights community, but its public relations tactics on civil rights questions as well. After *Bob Jones,* Smith and Reynolds sought to assume the offensive, writing op-ed pieces, meeting periodically with editorial boards, appearing on television, delivering addresses on civil rights, and blasting the media for "irresponsible journalism" based only on "what the critics say."[12] On the political side, Michael Deaver claimed in March 1984 that "In the long run, I don't think it hurt the president politically." Gergen disagreed with Deaver's assessment: "Sure the president was always weak in the black community, but there's a difference between blacks being indifferent or negative and being antagonized and outraged. *Bob Jones* gave legitimacy, more legitimacy than we could stand, to the claim that the administration was insensitive if not bigoted." "Perhaps the most relevant question," Brad Reynolds concluded, "is whether the president would have been in a better position to pick up a larger percentage of the black vote in 1984 absent *Bob Jones*. My guess is the answer is yes."

The Institutional Aftermath of Bob Jones

Finally, the Bob Jones furor also had a institutional impact, an impact, that is, on the people and internal processes followed by the administration to reach decisions. The institutional impact, like the political impact, was sometimes ill-defined, but nonetheless was frequently cited by senior administration officials.

The most obvious institutional aftermath of *Bob Jones* was that it strained relations within the departments, between the departments and the White House, and within the White House itself. At the Treasury Department, for example, Anne McLaughlin "blew her stack" at McNamar for the incomplete and belated warning he gave her about the case. At Justice, Brad Reynolds faced more serious problems, after he received a letter from two hundred employees of the Civil Rights division (signed by over half his division's attorneys) which stated that "news reports that [Reynolds] was responsible for the legal research underlying the change in IRS policy . . . cast serious doubt upon the division's commitment to enforce vigorously the nation's civil rights laws."[13] Another set of relationships strained by *Bob Jones* were the departments' dealings with the White House, particularly those of the Justice Department. Finally, within the White House itself the fiasco diminished Meese's reputation for political acuity and facilitated, in the eyes of some observers, Deaver's tendency to side increasingly with Baker.

Despite, however, widespread unhappiness over the way the case had been handled, the controversy was not of serious personal consequence for any official. No one got fired, transferred, or disciplined because of *Bob Jones;* indeed a number of officials who played leading roles in the drama were promoted. At the White House, Mel Bradley, the black aide who had alerted the president to the dismay blacks felt about *Bob Jones,* was promoted to Special Assistant to the President, and given responsibility for reviewing sensitive recommendations affecting minorities. Edwin Meese, who took the lead at the White House in backing a policy reversal—and then allegedly blindsided the president and key aides about the significance of that reversal—was subsequently confirmed as attorney general. At the Treasury Department, Anne McLaughlin and her deputy, Marlin Fitzwater, the public relations experts who were either belatedly misinformed or underestimated the public sensitivity of the case, were both promoted. Fitzwater became assistant press secretary at the White House, and McLaughlin was appointed undersecretary of Interior. And at the Justice Department, Bruce Fein, Charles Cooper, and Carolyn Kuhl, who researched the legal position the court so thoroughly rejected, were also all promoted. Attorney General Meese's attempt to elevate Brad Reynolds to associate attorney general in 1985 was defeated in the Senate Judiciary Committee, but *Bob Jones* seems to have played little role in the committee vote. Reynolds remained on as head of the civil rights division. In short, while media commentators may have given Reagan administration officials low marks for competence and sensitivity, their stern job appraisals seem to have been shrugged off when it came time for assessing job performance.

The impact of the controversy on decision-making procedure also seems to have been modest. Mel Bradley's promotion, in his words, was "a direct outgrowth of *Bob Jones* because it pointed up the need to have input from someone, for lack of a better term, who had a special sensitivity for the 'black experience.' " Bradley's appointment added another White House checkpoint on civil rights issues, as did the establishment of a Cabinet Council on Legal Policy—which had been planned before *Bob Jones* but whose formation was speeded by the controversy. But the procedural changes seem less significant really than some of the subtly altered sensitivities with which some officials now approach decision making. Officials pointed, in particular, to two sore spots that developed from *Bob Jones* and remained raw long thereafter. The first was the suspicion and distrust nurtured within the White House by the attacks in the media made on Meese. And the second was a heightened awareness of the need to be more thorough and sensitive. Before the Reagan White House seeks to do battle there is, every now and then, a new murmur of caution heard deep within the strategy room. As Michael Deaver summed up: "On several occasions we reassessed decisions when some staffer has pointed out—'Look out, we've got another Bob Jones coming here!' "

APPENDIX A

Cast of Characters

The White House
- President Ronald Reagan
- Edwin Meese III, Counselor to the President
- James Baker III, Chief of Staff
- Michael Deaver, Deputy Chief of Staff
- Richard Darman, Deputy to the Chief of Staff
- David Gergen, Assistant to the President for Communications
- Fred Fielding, Counsel to the President
- Craig Fuller, Assistant to the President for Cabinet Affairs
- T. Kenneth Cribb, Assistant Counselor (under Fuller)
- Martin Anderson, Assistant to the President for Policy Development
- William Gribbin, junior aide, legislative liaison office
- Peter Rusthoven, Fielding's associate counsel
- Melvin Bradley, senior policy adviser (Anderson's office)
- Thaddeus Garrett, Jr., domestic policy advisor to Vice President Bush
- Larry Speakes, principal Deputy Press Secretary
- Elizabeth Dole, Assistant to the President for Public Liaison

The Justice Department
- William French Smith, Attorney General
- Edward Schmults, Deputy Attorney General
- William Bradford Reynolds, Assistant Attorney General for Civil Rights
- Bruce Fein, Associate Deputy Attorney General (in Schmults's office)
- Tom DeCair, Director of Public Affairs
- Theodore Olson, Assistant Attorney General, Legal Counsel
- Lawrence Wallace, Acting Solicitor General
- John Murray, Acting Assistant Attorney General, Tax Division
- Kenneth Starr, Counselor to the Attorney General
- Charles Cooper, Special Assistant (to Reynolds)
- Carolyn Kuhl, Special Assistant (to the Attorney General)

The Treasury Department
- Donald Regan, Secretary of Treasury
- Timothy McNamar, Deputy Secretary
- Peter Wallison, General Counsel
- John "Buck" Chapoton, Assistant Secretary for Tax Policy
- Anne McLaughlin, Assistant Secretary for Public Affairs
- Marlin Fitzwater, McLaughlin's deputy
- Roscoe Egger, Commissioner of the Internal Revenue Service
- Kenneth Gideon, Chief Counsel, IRS

APPENDIX B

TREASURY NEWS

Department of the Treasury Washington, D.C. Telephone 566-2041

FOR IMMEDIATE RELEASE   Contact: Marlin Fitzwater
Friday, January 8, 1982   (202) 566–5252

TREASURY ESTABLISHES NEW TAX-EXEMPT POLICY

The Treasury Department announced today that without further guidance from Congress, the Internal Revenue Service will no longer revoke or deny tax-exempt status for religious, charitable, educational or scientific organizations on the grounds that they don't conform with certain fundamental public policies.

"In the past," said Deputy Treasury Secretary R. T. McNamar, "the IRS has revoked the tax exemptions of organizations which did not adhere to certain fundamental national policies, such as those forbidding discrimination on the basis of race, even though this requirement is not explicitly stated in the Internal Revenue Code except in the case of social clubs."

"Whether or not the Treasury Department or this Administration agrees with the position of the IRS in particular cases is not the issue," McNamar stated. "The question is whether the IRS is required under the Code as enacted by Congress to decide—as a condition to granting or continuing tax-exempt status—whether private organizations conform with fundamental national policies. The Treasury Department has concluded that this kind of judgment—which may mean life or death for certain organizations—is fundamentally a question for Congress; and if the authority to make this judgment is given by Congress to an administrative agency it should be done in explicit terms and subjec to specific guidelines."

As a consequence of this decision, the IRS will restore the tax exemption of certain organizations which had previously been revoked. In particular, the appeal of Bob Jones University, and the Goldsboro Schools, which are currently before the Supreme Court will be rendered moot.

"In taking this action," McNamar stated, "we are attempting to protect the independence of all private tax-exempt organizations—many of which may follow practices and adhere to principles with which we disagree. But before the government gets into the business of deciding which organizations are worthy of tax exemption and which are not, we want Congress to fully consider the implications of such a course."

The Treasury Department decision reflects the advice of the Department of Justice that the authority which the IRS previously had been asserting as its basis for revoking the tax exemptions in question is not supported by the language of the Internal Revenue

Code or its legislative history. The Internal Revenue Code provides tax exemptions for "Corporations (or other organizations) organized and operated exclusively for religious, charitable, scientific . . . or educational . . . purposes. . . ." IRC Section 501(c)(3), 26 U.S.C. Section 501(c)(3). The Justice Department has advised that both the language of Section 501(c)(3) and the statute's legislative history provide no support for the statutory interpretation adopted by the Commissioner in 1970. Thus the IRS is without legislative authority to deny tax-exempt status to otherwise eligible organizations on the grounds that their policies or practices do not conform to notions of national public policy.

This new policy is reflected in a motion filed with the Supreme Court today by the Justice Department to vacate a case in which the Internal Revenue Service revoked the tax-exempt status of Bob Jones University and Goldsboro Christian Schools. IRS revoked the Bob Jones University tax exemption in 1970 on the grounds that the school's racial policies violated Federal policies on racial discrimination. This decision was nullified by the U.S. District Court in South Carolina on June 30, 1971. However, the lower court's decision was reversed by the 4th Circuit Court of Appeals on December 30, 1980.

Similarly in 1974 the IRS determined that Goldsboro Christian Schools Inc. did not qualify for an exemption on the grounds that it maintained a racially discriminatory admissions policy. On May 7, 1980 the District Court for the Eastern district of North Carolina upheld the IRS decision. On February 24, 1981 the Court of Appeals for the 4th Circuit affirmed this judgment period.

Both schools appealed the Circuit Court decision to the Supreme Court which accepted their petitions for certiorari on October 13, 1981.

APPENDIX C

President Reagan's Statement

Draft Statement

The issue of whether to deny tax exemptions to non-profit, private, educational institutions raises difficult questions.

As my record and that of my administration demonstrate, I am unalterably opposed to racial discrimination in any form. The action taken by the Treasury Department last Friday does not suggest otherwise.

Rather, the decision announced by the Treasury reflects the fact that Congress has not authorized the Internal Revenue Service to determine and apply social policies independently in deciding which educational institutions should be granted tax exemptions under the Internal Revenue Code.

Administrative agencies, no matter how well intentioned, should not take it upon themselves to decide what is national policy without the explicit guidance of Congress. This should be the case regardless of the social purpose involved and even if private, tax exempt institutions engage in practices with which many—including this administration—disagree.

In coming months, this administration will work with the Congress to determine what steps should be taken to prohibit racial discrimination by private organizations, including tax exempt organizations.

Statement Released by President Reagan on 1 / 12 / 82

THE WHITE HOUSE

Office of the Press Secretary

For Immediate Release   January 12, 1982

STATEMENT BY THE PRESIDENT

This issue of whether to deny tax exemptions to non-profit, private, educational institutions raises important questions and sensitive policy considerations.

My administration is committed to certain fundamental views which must be considered in addressing this matter:

• I am unalterably opposed to racial discrimination in any form. I would not knowingly contribute to any organization that supports racial discrimination. My record and the record of this administration are clear on this point.

• I am also opposed to administrative agencies exercising powers that the Constitution assigns to the Congress. Such agencies, no matter how well intentioned, cannot be allowed to govern by administrative fiat. That was the sole basis of the decision announced

298

by the Treasury Department last Friday. I regret that there has been a misunderstanding of the purpose of the decision.

I believe the right thing to do on this issue is to enact legislation which will prohibit tax exemptions for organizations that discriminate on the basis of race.

Therefore, I will submit legislation and will work with the Congress to accomplish this purpose.

APPENDIX D

Guidance for President Reagan's January 19 Press Conference

DOMESTIC MATERIALS

Tax Exempt Decisions

> *Here's what the administration has done in a nutshell:*

• RR has submitted legislation which would bar tax exemptions for schools that discriminate on the basis of race. (Other types of discrimination such as sex discrimination are not covered.)

• Don Regan has directed the IRS not to grant any more exemptions for schools that discriminate until the Congress acts on the legislation. This is in keeping with traditional IRS practice when the administration sends up legislation.

• The only two schools that will receive exemptions are Bob Jones and the Goldsboro Schools. *And* if your legislation is enacted, their past practices would mean that their exemptions would be lifted—retroactively. In other words, Bob Jones and Goldsboro won't receive any real benefit from this.

(Note: the press corps was hostile on Monday to this notion of Bob Jones and Goldsboro receiving exemptions. They think it is favoritism and might have been done as a favor to Strom Thurmond and Trent Lott. In reality, we are going forward with their exemptions because that is exactly what the Justice Department told the Supreme Court some 10 days ago that we would do—this fulfills our pledge and is consistent with our position that the IRS lacked legal authority *not* to grant those exemptions.)

The net positive effect of what RR has achieved, then, is this:

• The government is continuing its practice of denying exemptions to schools that racially discriminate.

• Once legislation is passed, the actions by the IRS will be on much more solid foundations—the law of the land.

• Furthermore, IRS will no longer have unfettered power to make national social policy all by itself.

At the same time, there is no escaping the fact that this could have been handled more smoothly by us. As you said earlier today, the best solution would have been to send up the legislation at the time the first announcement was made—or to enact the legislation first and then change the way the IRS operates.

Here are some questions that may arise:

Can you explain how such a major—and politically sensitive—decision could be announced by the Administration apparently without any extensive White House review?

• We never understood the decision as a *policy* change; Treasury and Justice were proposing a *procedural* change in tune with my own thinking and the Republican platform.

• policy is *unchanged;* we oppose school segregation; we oppose tax exempt status

300

for schools that do segregate; and we are asking Congress to pass legislation to deny them exemptions.

• but *also oppose letting bureaucrats make social policy.* That's why the change in *IRS procedures* was approved in the first place.

But shouldn't someone have seen the danger that it would be perceived as a policy change? Didn't anyone anticipate the political reaction? How come Blacks on your staff (Bradley and Garrett) weren't even consulted 'till after the announcement?

• with 20–20 hindsight, the answer is yes. Suppose we should have foreseen the reaction.

• the meaning of the decision was misperceived and we moved quickly to correct that misunderstanding.

• didn't promise we won't be misunderstood—or make mistakes—from time to time. Ask to be judged not on basis that we'll never make mistakes but how we act to correct them when they arise.

• trust our opposition to school desegregation is clearly understood. Should be no mistake about that—among minorities in this country or among those who seek to discriminate against them.

• input from Bradley, Thad Garrett, Secretary Pierce and others was instrumental to clearing up the misperception.

Deaver and Baker are reportedly "furious" at Meese over this. Has the "Troika" finally fallen apart?

• there are still people who believe it can't work. It does work, remarkably well in fact, and that's because of the good will and mutual respect that they have for each other.

NOTES

Prelude to the Storm

1. Ellen Hume, "Charges Fly in Turbulent Session on Voting Rights Act," *Los Angeles Times,* January 28, 1982, p. 19.

2. Senate Judiciary Committee, Subcommittee on the Judiciary, *Voting Rights Act,* p. 78.

3. Ibid., p. 79.

4. *Goldsboro Christian Schools* v. *U.S.,* 436 F. Supp. 1314 (1977), p. 1316.

5. *Bob Jones University* v. *U.S.,* 468 F. Supp. 890 (1978), p. 894.

6. Cited, among others places, in Dr. Bob Gray, "Use of Tax Power to Shape Religious Thought Repugnant," *Florida Times Union,* May 15, 1982, op-ed page.

7. The position paper is reprinted in Senate Finance Committee, *Legislation to Deny Tax Exemption to Racially Discriminatory Private Schools,* p. 63.

8. Transcript made from tape of Reagan's January 30, 1980, address at Bob Jones University.

9. *Ibid.*

The Administration's Review

1. House Committee on Ways and Means, *Administration's Change in Federal Policy Regarding the Tax Status of Racially Discriminating Private Schools,* hearing, 97th Cong., 2nd sess., Feb. 4, 1982, p. 204.

2. *Ibid.,* p. 443.

3. Transcript of interview with Reagan on PBS's *Tony Brown Journal,* February 18, 1982.

4. House Committee on Ways and Means, *Administration's Change in Federal Policy . . . p. 447.*

5. *Ibid.,* p. 426.

6. *Ronald Reagan: Public Papers of the Presidents of the United States, 1982,* Vol. I (Washington, D.C.: U.S. Government Printing Office, 1983), p. 604.

7. *Ibid.,* pp. 298, 191.

8. Martin Schram and Charles Babcock, "Reagan Advisers Missed School Case Sensitivity," *Washington Post,* January 17, 1982, p. 9.

9. House Committee on Ways and Means, *Administration's Change in Federal Policy. . . .,* p. 80.

10. Martin Schram and Charles Babcock, "Reagan Advisers Missed School Case Sensitivity," *Washington Post,* January 17, 1982, p. 9.

11. Martin Schram, "Meese Involved in Tax-Exemptions Shift," *Washington Post,* January 16, 1982, p. 14.

12. Martin Schram and Charles Babcock,

"Reagan Advisers Missed School Case Sensitivity," *Washington Post,* January 17, 1982, p. 9.

13. *Ibid.*

Managing the News—Unsuccessfully

1. *Ibid.,* p. 589.

2. *Ibid.,* pp. 589, 590.

3. Lyle Denniston, "Segregated Schools Get IRS Tax Break," *Baltimore Sun,* January 9, 1982, p. 1.

4. *Ibid.*

5. Kevin Costelloe, "U.S. Abandons Tax Penalty for School Bias," *Philadelphia Inquirer,* January 9, 1982, p. 1.

6. "Allow Exemptions for Biased Schools," *New York Daily News,* January 9, 1982.

7. Lyle Denniston, "Segregated Schools Get IRS Break," *Baltimore Sun,* January 9, 1982, p. 1. Denniston's article, on the same date, also ran on page one of the *Boston Globe.*

8. Fred Barbash, "Tax Penalty on School Bias Ended," *Washington Post,* January 9, 1982, pp. 1, 10.

9. Quoted in "Tax-Exempt Schools," *Dallas Times Herald,* January 12, 1982, editorial page.

10. Glenn Fowler, "Private Schools Assail Tax Shift," *New York Times,* January 10, 1982, p. 1.

11. Stuart Taylor, "School Tax Ruling Faces Test," *New York Times,* January 10, 1982, p. 18.

12. "Groups Decry Government Move in Bob Jones case," *Greenville (S.C.) News,* January 10, 1982, p. 1.

13. "Pat: Feds Immoral on School Tax," *New York Daily News,* January 10, 1982.

14. Stephen Wermiel, "Race Bias Won't Bar Tax-Exempt Status for Private, Religious Schools, U.S. Says," *Wall Street Journal,* January 11, 1982, p. 12.

15. "Exemption from IRS Restored," *Atlanta Journal / Constitution,* January 9, 1982, p. 1.

16. "NAACP Blasts Private School Tax Ruling Reversal," *Muskegon (Mich.) Chronicle,* January 9, 1982, p. 1.

17. See, "Tax Exempt Schools," *Dallas Times Herald,* January 12, 1982, editorial page.

18. See, for example, "Hypocritical Tax Change Means Racism Will Pay," *Tallahassee Democrat,* January 12, 1982, editorial page; "Subsidizing Discrimination," *Boston Globe,* January 12, 1982, editorial page; "An Appaling Move," *New York Daily News,* January 12, 1982, editorial page; and Richard Cohen, "Ronald Crow," *Washington Post,* January 12, 1982, p. C-1.

"Reagan Advisers Missed School Case Sensitivity," *Washington Post,* January 17, 1982, p. 9.

13. *Ibid.*

19. Quoted in Martin Schram and Charles Babcock, "Reagan Advisers Missed School Case Sensitivity," *Washington Post*, January 17, 1982, p. 9.

20. Laurence I. Barrett, *Gambling with History* (New York: Doubleday, 1983), p. 416.

21. *Ibid.*

22. Transcript of ABC's *Good Morning America*, January 13, 1982.

23. Greg McDonald, "Kennedy Blasts Reagan Policies as Pro-Wealthy, 'Anti-Civil Rights,' " *Atlanta Journal*, January 14, 1982.

24. "O'Neill Assails Reagan's Action on School Bias," *Washington Post*, January 15, 1982, p. 4.

25. Transcript of CBS's *Morning* with Charles Kuralt and Diane Sawyer, January 13, 1982, p. 16.

26. Justice Department transcript of Attorney General Smith meeting with the press on the Voting Rights Act, January 28, 1982, p. 13. Smith also stated that *Bob Jones* "represents not the slightest retreat from [the president's] position with respect to the overall question of racial discrimination. . . . In that case, the question was not racial discrimination. It was whether or not an unelected administration official should have the authority to determine tax exempt status on the basis of his idea of public policy."

27. Transcript of ABC's *Nightline*, January 15, 1982.

28. Tom Wicker, "Where the Buck Stops," *New York Times*, January 19, 1982, p. 27.

Unburying the Hatchet

1. Transcript of CBS Evening News with Dan Rather, January 12, 1982, p. 6.

2. Martin Schram, "Meese Involved in Tax Exemptions Shift," *Washington Post*, January 16, 1982, p. 14.

3. Jack Nelson, "Baker and Deaver Reportedly 'Livid' Over Meese Action," *Los Angeles Times*, January 16, 1982, p. 10.

4. *Ibid.*

5. Robert Sherborne, "Meese Says Baker Handled School Issue," *Tennessean (Nashville Tenn.)*, January 18, 1982.

6. Mike Pigott, "Meese: No White House Squabble," *Banner* (Nashville, Tenn.), January 18, 1982.

7. Robert Sherborne, "Meese Says Baker Handled School Issue, *Tennessean*, January 18, 1982.

8. See, "How White House Blew Religious School Issue," *Human Events*, February 13, 1982, pp. 4–6.

9. Martin Schram and Charles Babcock, "Reagan Advisers Missed School Case Sensi-

tivity," *Washington Post*, January 17, 1982, p. 9.

10. AP Dispatch by Michael Putzel, January 19, 1982.

11. Transcript of PBS's *MacNeil / Lehrer Report*, January 20, 1982.

12. Laurence I. Barrett, *Gambling With History* (New York: Doubleday, 1983), pp. 416.

13. *Ibid.*, p. 99.

14. Transcript of NBC's *Today*, January 20, 1982.

15. Cited in White House transcript of press briefing by Larry Speakes, January 18, 1982, p. 10.

16. *Ibid.*

17. Transcript of President Reagan's press conference reprinted in *New York Times*, January 20, 1982, p. 20.

The Aftermath of Bob Jones

1. Bernard Wolfman, "Law, Cut on a Bias," *New York Times*, January 19, 1982, p. 27. Wolfman was chairman of the Committee on Taxation of the ABA's Section of Individual Rights and Responsibilities.

2. Reproduced in Senate Finance Committee, *Legislation to Deny Tax Exemption to Racially Discriminatory Private Schools*, hearing, 97th Cong., 2nd sess., February 1, 1982, pp. 6–7.

3. *Ibid.*, p. 235.

4. *Ibid.*, pp. 254–255.

5. The "pathetic" label is cited in Stuart Taylor, "Exemptions Bill Assailed at Hearing," *New York Times*, February 5, 1982, p. 12. The other quote is in House Committee Ways and Means, *Administration's Change in Federal Policy . . .* , p. 11.

6. *Ibid.*, p. 188.

7. *Ibid.*, p. 217 and quoted a bit more literally in Nadine Cohodas, "Congress Cool to Legislation On Tax Breaks for Schools that Discriminate Racially," *Congressional Quarterly*, February 6, 1982, p. 209.

8. *Bob Jones University* v. *United States*, 103 S. Ct. 2017 (1983), pp. 2029, 2032.

9. See Fred Barbash, "Burger's Activists," *Washington Post*, May 29, 1983, p. C5; Majorie Hyer, "Many Church Leaders Are Torn by Supreme Court's Tax Ruling," *Washington Post*, May 28, 1983, p. C14; Smith Hempstone, "Bob Jones and the Consequences Beyond," *Washington Times*, June 1, 1983, p. C1; Tony Mauro, "Tax-Exempt Ruling Upsets Religious Groups," *USA Today*, May 25, 1982, p. 8; and Kathleen Sylvester, "Does the Bob Jones Case Have Wide Ramifications," *National Law Journal*, June 6, 1983, p. 3.

10. Ellen Goodman, "A Judgment Against Women's Colleges?" *Washington Post,* May 31, 1983, p. 21.

11. Interview with William French Smith in *Legal Times,* August 2, 1982, p. 1.

12. Justice Department text of William French Smith's address before the Conference Board, July 27, 1983, p. 12. Also see Storer Rowley, "President Defends Right Role," *Boston Globe,* August 2, 1983, p. 1.

13. The letter is reprinted in the *New York Times,* February 3, 1982, p. 21.

TELEVISION
AND THE 1981–84 REVIEW
OF THE DISABILITY ROLLS

by David Whitman

E ARLY IN HIS administration, Ronald Reagan sought to establish that domestic spending could be slashed without hurting those who really were in need:
"Those who through no fault of their own must depend on the rest of us, the
poverty stricken, the disabled, the elderly, all those with true need, can rest
assured that the social safety net of programs they depend on are exempt from
any cuts."[1]

In subsequent years, whether or not Reagan had in fact shredded the safety
net was a matter of great debate, but no charge within that debate was more
damning than the allegation that Reagan presided over a "witchhunt" that
"purged" tens of thousands of genuinely disabled recipients from the Social
Security rolls. The review of the disability rolls—referred to as the CDI (Continuing Disability Investigation) process—had been mandated by Congress in 1980
following reports that the Social Security Administration (SSA) had been lax in
reviewing the rolls (which had expanded dramatically under Presidents Nixon
and Ford). Congress directed the CDI review process to begin no later than
January 1982, and allotted three years for the massive number of reviews; then
in February 1981, at the behest of the Office of Management and Budget and the
General Accounting Office, Reagan appointees accelerated the implementation
of the reviews, more than doubling the number of CDIs scheduled for 1981.

SSDI Program

The Social Security Disability Insurance (DI) program had been plagued
with problems since the early 1970s. The DI program is a relatively recent addi-

---

*This is a heavily abridged version of the case study written by David
Whitman. The abridgement was done by Martin Linsky. Unless otherwise
noted, all quotations come either from unpublished government memoranda or from interviews with the author.*

tion to Social Security—it was created in 1956—and has always been distinguished by an extremely rigid test of disability. The chartering legislation language stated that a DI recipient has to be "unable to engage in any substantial gainful activity by reason of any medically determinable physical or mental impairment . . . expected to result in death or be of long-continued or indefinite duration." In 1965, Congress specified the period of "long-continued or indefinite duration" had to last for a minimum of twelve continuous months.

The DI review process itself was also ill appreciated and quite complex; over the years elaborate procedural safeguards had been installed that enhanced due process for the applicant but weakened SSA's control over the program. In a nutshell, the system worked as follows: 1) The claimant went to a federal Social Security office where he / she was interviewed and sources for medical evidence recorded. 2) The case was then sent to a state vocational rehabilitation agency, which, acting as SSA's agent, made the initial determination of eligibility using SSA guidelines. (This state review was mandated by Congress to encourage potential applicants to link up with local vocational rehabilitation efforts.) A small sample of the initial determinations then received a "quality assurance" review from SSA field offices. 3) If the claimant was rejected, he had 60 days to request reconsideration. The reconsideration was also done by state disability examiners, using personnel other than those who made the initial determination. 4) If the claimant was rejected again, he had 60 days to request a face-to-face hearing before an Administrative Law Judge (ALJ).The ALJs, like the personnel doing the reconsideration, performed a de novo review (i.e., not being limited to examining evidence previously introduced). 5) If the ALJ affirmed the denial, the applicant had 60 days to appeal to a 13-member "Appeals Council." 6) And finally, if the Appeals Council was also negative, the applicant had 60 days to bring suit in District Court. The entire process, with the exception of the initial application at SSA, was essentially the same for an enrollee that was appealing a discharge from the rolls.

There were a couple of noteworthy aspects to this process besides its complexity. The first is that it was very time consuming, which placed a heavy burden both on the system's personnel and on borderline applicants (who might go through several levels of appeal before receiving their benefits). The second noteworthy aspect of the process were the multiple levels of appeal, which had produced remarkable discrepancies of treatment, particularly between the state examiners and the ALJs. In 1980, state personnel handling reconsiderations upheld initial denials 85 percent of the time; the ALJs, however, overturned 59 percent of their denials.[2] The ALJs' more liberal allowance rate seems to have resulted chiefly from the opportunity to see new evidence (such as deterioration of a condition, additional medical evidence, and the face-to-face interview), as well as the different review rules the ALJs followed. Unlike the disability examiners, who were required to follow SSA's internal "Program Operation Manual Systems" (POMS) guidelines when making a disability determination, the ALJs were bound by the law as interpreted by the Federal courts, statutes, regulations, and SSA's public "Social Security Rulings."

The debate over what was causing these patently inconsistent disability rulings was complicated, finally, by the inherently subjective nature of the disability determination itself. It is not difficult, at either extreme, to determine whether an individual is physically capable of holding a job, but the gray area in the middle is considerable, and leaves room for independent judgment despite SSA's voluminous POMS. If, for example, a sixty-year-old man had had two major heart attacks he might be ruled disabled—but what about the fifty-seven-year-old man who had had one major heart attack, was overweight, and had dangerously high blood pressure? How much chronic back pain did a claimant have to suffer before they were "disabled?" What was conclusive evidence that a claimant was too mentally disturbed to hold a job? The list goes on. The inconsistency problem thus was not limited to differences between the ALJs and state examiners. SSA studies found, for example, that there was a 15 percent probability that two randomly chosen states would disagree in their decisions about the same case and there was a 12 percent probability that two examiners in the same state would disagree. Similarly, average state allowance rates varied from about 24 percent in Arkansas to around 47 percent in South Carolina; a gap that could not be attributed to demographic differences.[3]

In short, even if the ALJs and examiners had used identical guidelines, it is likely that their interpretations of the "substantial gainful activity" test would have differed and resulted in periodic errors. And this leeway for subjectivity was important because it opened the possibility for substantial changes occurring in the program that resulted more from subtle alterations in the economic, political, or managerial climate than from legislative, judicial, or regulatory program additions. This is precisely what occurred between 1969 and 1977, when the number of recipients on the DI rolls doubled (to 2.84 million) and the program's cost more than quadrupled (to $11.5 billion), while only modest legislative or regulatory changes occurred.

During the Carter administration, management of the DI program was substantially tightened and the allowance rates dropped sharply so that by 1981 they were at their lowest levels since 1964. Nevertheless, there remained concern that the rolls had swelled too precipitously in the early 1970s, and that some action needed to be taken to make disability status less attractive by capping DI benefits, tightening program administration, and adding incentives for disabled recipients to reenter the labor force. In 1979, Health and Human Service (HHS) officials, led by Secretary Joseph Califano and Undersecretary Hale Champion, produced a legislative initiative along these lines, which passed Congress in 1980 (despite the lack of enthusiasm exhibited for it by Patricia Harris, who succeeded Califano in mid-1979). Parts of the legislation, particularly the cap on disability benefits, were bitterly contested by advocacy groups; however, the portion of the legislation that called for all "non-permanently" disabled DI receipients to be reviewed by January 1985 was noncontroversial. Indeed, every witness who commented on the CDIs during the hearings on the legislation—including Wilbur Cohen, the former HEW secretary who led the opposition to the bill—lauded the notion of periodic reviews of the rolls.

Following Ronald Reagan's election in November 1980, SSA completed a random review of 3,000 Social Security DI cases which indicated that as much as 20% of the DI caseload might be ineligible, representing about a $2 billion loss annually to the Social Security trust fund. This information made its way into the hands of the General Accounting Office (GAO), which heralded the finding in a report to Congress, the draft of which was given to Reagan's SSA transition team and budget examiners in the Office of Management and Budget. Although both the SSA and GAO reports warned that the $2 billion was not fully recoverable (because numerous cessations would be overturned on appeal), there were now clearly big bucks at stake. With this unexpected payoff looming on the horizon, the GAO explicitly urged that SSA accelerate the CDI start-up. OMB recommended that the target for completed reviews be doubled to 275,000, and the recommendation was accepted. There seems to have been little thought given at the time to the overload the acceleration might produce. There is nothing in the record, even after the administration announced it was accelerating the reviews, that would indicate serious reservations about the CDI process. What was missed by all parties to this debate was the depth of problems with the existing review process and the unprecedented nature of the CDI reviews. As it turned out, the existing process, which had been marginally appropriate for the small number of DI recipients with impairments most prone to recovery, was entirely inappropriate for the massive numbers of "nonpermanently" disabled recipients. Unlike previous review cases, who were told at the time of their admission they would be subsequently reviewed, the overwhelming majority of recipients targeted for the expanded CDIs were assured they were on disability insurance for life. The conditions of the "expanded CDI" population, moveover were not so easily discerned by the paper process through which CDI's were conducted. Obtaining current evidence for, say, whether a bone was still fractured, was altogether distinct from ascertaining whether a recipient still was mentally ill, a heart condition had improved, and so forth. What happened, in short, was a kind of multiplier effect; all of the inadequacies that had existed within the DI system for years, most without attracting any attention from the media, were suddenly writ large by the seemingly innocuous expansion of the reviews.

Between 1981 and 1984 hundreds of horror stories appeared in newspapers around the country recounting the suffering of thousands of individuals who were cut off the Social Security disability rolls. As over 490,000 recipients lost or were threatened with the loss of their Disability Insurance, editorial after editorial appeared in the nation's leading newspapers urging the Reagan administration to slow or stop the review process. While the adverse print coverage troubled HHS officials, the stories drew little attention in the Reagan White House, rarely provoking a response unless one special factor was involved: television coverage. As David Gergen, President Reagan's assistant for communications acknowledged, "The disability cutoffs had a much more profound impact on television than in print because you could see that these people were clearly disabled. They were very powerful stories and, apart from the human toll, the political price of the stories was very high: they enabled our critics to say, with some truth, that our cuts were really hurting poor, disabled people, and we didn't have much of a defense for that.''

In addition to having a distinctive power when viewed instead of read, the disability horror stories raised the "fairness issue" in a singularly gripping fashion. Television stories on the cutoffs provoked questions about the administration's compassion and fairness for two reasons. First, as HHS spokesperson Claire Del Real summed up, "It was almost impossible to rebut the charge of mean-spiritedness when it came to the disability stories because we were talking about the most vulnerable part of the population; the TV stories showed we were 'picking on' obviously disabled people.'' Second, unlike cuts the administration instituted in other welfare / social insurance programs—cuts, say, like the lowering of the earned income disregard in AFDC—axing recipients off the disability rolls was easily conveyed visually. It was the difference between having a welfare recipient up on the screen saying how the Reagan administration hurt her because she could only make $40 a week on the side instead of $50, and a mentally retarded person, or a man in a hospital bed with cerebral palsy who had just lost their chief or sole source of support.

This case explores how the Reagan administration responded to this adverse television coverage, recounting three vignettes in which the White House chose to intercede. In vignettes 1 and 2, the White House chose to rebut television stories about the Continuing Disability Investigation (CDI) cutoffs. In the first case they alleged that the DI recipient portrayed was a fraud, and in the second they claimed that CBS correspondent Bill Moyers had done a hatchet job on the administration. In vignette 3, involving the cutoff of Medal of Honor winner Roy Benavidez, the White House was on the defensive with some of those involved arguing that embarrassment over Benavidez's case helped spur major reforms of the CDI process.

Overview: Local and National Television Coverage

The sensitivity of the White House and SSA officials to network coverage of the CDIs was all the more remarkable considering how little of it there was. According to Vanderbilt University's *TV News Index Abstracts,* from June 1981 to June 1983, ABC did not cover the disability horror stories on the evening news at all. NBC ran one report on the nightly news in May 1983, recounting the Benavidez story. CBS was alone in devoting substantial coverage to the subject, running two "horror story" segments apiece on the morning and evening news, and several short updates on the progress of reform legislation.*

Although there was very modest network coverage of the CDIs—particularly when compared to the enormous coverage devoted to the reviews by the

---

*In June 1983, after HHS announced new reforms to the CDI process, PBS's *Frontline* devoted a show to the disability cutoffs. The *Frontline* documentary hosted by Jessica Savitch, is discussed below. PBS also ran a segment on the cutoffs in the February 14, 1983 newscast of the *MacNeil / Lehrer Report.*

nation's leading newspapers—the CBS stories provoked frustration and heightened concern among White House officials. This was not just because of the visual power of the stories or owing to the greater audience the stories reached; it also reflected the fact that the stories were virtually impossible to rebut or put in perspective. In the four horror-story segments run by CBS, SSA spokesmen were given brief opportunities to present "their side" of what was transpiring; but the points they were trying to make were obscured and their highlighted comments made them look like icy bureaucrats.

These points can perhaps best be illustrated by looking at the first horror story segment, which appeared on CBS's *Morning* program on December 21, 1981. The segment opened with Charles Kuralt observing that SSA "started" reviewing the DI rolls in March 1981 with "the idea that many of them are no longer disabled. But, as Jane Wallace tells us now, many of those who have since been dropped from the rolls contend they are disabled." (See Appendix A for transcript.) Wallace then interviewed a thirty-five-year-old woman with cerebral palsy who had been cut off the rolls; the recipient's mother; a Vietnam Vet with a plastic leg (his other leg filled with schrapnel); and a thirty-four-year-old woman with borderline intellect, emotional problems, and a serious lung disorder. Wallace concluded the interviews with the cutoff recipients by observing: "Faustine and Karen and Bill are all files here at the Social Security headquarters in Baltimore, where they've decided there are too many files on people on disability benefits. A GAO report estimated that 20 percent of the 2.8 million on disability were really ineligible. So far 113,000 have been dumped from the disability rolls and next year, 200,000 more are slated for termination." Kuralt's statement, that SSA "started" performing CDIs in March 1981 was simply incorrect, and while Wallace's statement about the GAO report was accurate, it missed, like Kuralt's introduction, the fact that CDIs had gone on for many years on a modest scale, were being dramatically expanded at the direct order of the Congress, and had been accelerated, in part, at the suggestion of the GAO. The clear implication of the segment so far was that these bloodless reviews not only began under the administration but were initiated by them.

Next the camera shifted to Sandy Crank, an SSA associate commissioner, who was shown explaining why SSA was trying to reduce the number of recipient files in Baltimore. "We believe we've got a real responsibility to the American tax-paying public," Crank said, "as well as to the people who are dependent upon the Social Security system for benefits under the law." No explanation of the law governing DI eligibility was given, no mention of the explosive growth of the rolls in 1970 was made, no evidence was cited as to what happened to the majority of recipients cut off by CDIs, nor was there any discussion of whether the recipients previously shown on camera were capable of holding a job. Here the implication was that SSA's rationale for hurting defenseless people is "we follow a textbook approach to the law"—with the viewer left to guess whatever that may be.

Most of the misimpressions conveyed by the *Morning* segment also appeared in the print coverage. What distinguished the television coverage was the absence of virtually any material that could qualify potential misunderstandings. Roger Woodworth, an aide who played a key role in managing HHS Secretary Margaret Heckler's press relations,* put it this way:

> When you only have thirty to sixty seconds to do a story, you're looking for something dramatic and simple. No matter how skillful we are at public relations and no matter how well-intentioned the media is, it is just not the nature of the beast that TV looks at the second and third level of a complicated issue. "The unfair Reagan administration is going after defenseless people" is a simple, dramatic story. "These reviews were mandated by Congress because the rolls expanded, it's very hard to get on disability, there are a lot of problems not attributable to the administration that have to do with this paper 'process' and so on," is not a simple story. Television wanted to show the dramatic injustice of what was occurring and they did; the problem was that they didn't do a very good job explaining why the injustice was occurring or that reforms were on the way. With say, Robert Pear of the *New York Times,* you might at least get a few extra paragraphs in a story that would give an extra dimension, some explanatory material. . . . Essentially every problem we faced in responding to the newspaper horror stories was magnified when it came to television.

Although brevity and omission were one means by which television reinforced the impression that the trauma from the CDIs was caused by Reagan bureaucrats, the second technique reinforcing this impression was the "when did you stop beating your wife" question, used in nearly all of the CBS segments. In two of the four CBS segments, reporters asked SSA officials how they felt about recipients who committed suicide or died from their disability after being terminated from the DI rolls. For example, in the CBS *Morning* segment previously referred to, the only other comment Sandy Crank got an opportunity to make (his first being the mention of SSA's efforts to comply with the law), is when he was asked how he feels about a cutoff recipient who killed herself, leaving a note behind saying "Social Security [is] playing God." "What do you want me to say about that?" Crank replied feebly. "We're not playing God, no more than we play God when we allow people disability benefits." Similarly, a subsequent CBS *Evening News* "horror story" segment concluded with CBS correspondent Ed Rabel pointing out that recipients were dying from the same disabilities SSA had previously determined were not serious enough to keep them on the rolls. The camera then turned to SSA Deputy Commissioner Paul Simmons, who said, "We are not out to kill people, we are not out to have a—we're not out to support a system that—that is harsh, cruel, or otherwise unfair to people."**[4] Simmons says that Rabel asked the question, "Are you trying to kill people?" but the question was edited out leaving only his answer and the impression either that he was indifferent to the horror stories or that he agreed

---

*Heckler succeeded HHS Secretary Richard Schweiker in January 1983.

**Rabel then adds: "For those whose benefits have stopped, there is little left. And if they lose their benefits for good, they say life is impossible for them."[5]

with the criticism of the reviews. In either case, the viewer would have no reason to see any positive results from the reviews—such as discharged reentering employment. Television thus tended to have a doubly powerful impact. It not only graphically confirmed the horror stories, but also graphically conveyed the sense that administration officials were cold-hearted bureaucrats because they could not provide shortened answers to emotionally charged questions which required a lot of time to respond.

The administration whipping-boy motif on television was completed by coverage at congressional hearings. Congress did not pass any legislation to reform the CDI process in 1982, and passed temporary legislation of modest scope in 1983 (when more far-reaching reforms got bottled up in committee in the Senate). Despite the virtual absence of congressional action, there were over a dozen hearings during 1982 and 1983 on the CDIs and a lot of finger pointing. Between the voluminous constituent complaints and local news stories, it is not hard to fathom why congressmen got involved. In addition to being concerned over the tragic results of the reviews, congressmen knew that getting involved was good politics. As one of Senator Sasser's (D-Tenn.) aides put it in a December 21, 1982, memo to Sasser: "Disability is a good political issue. Few dispute the need for a program which purports to care for those who cannot care for themselves due to a disabling condition . . . the political risks are minimal." Television increased the incentive for congressmen to turn the hearings into a kind of theater, where they paraded obviously disabled recipients to the witness stand or excoriated administration officials by bringing up one horror story after another. For example, before a Senate Budget Committee hearing at which the HHS secretary was testifying, the same aide to Senator Sasser wrote him on March 15, 1982:

> A television crew from *Sixty Minutes* is supposed to cover this hearing. . . . There is a good chance if you ask Mr. Schweiker about the problems of the new accelerated disability review procedures you may get some good press. Especially since I have been talking with someone from CBS in New York on this matter who is doing a documentary in April for Bill Moyers' *Journal*.
>
> There have been numerous reports outlining problems with removing eligible people from the Disability rolls according to a quota system. CBS was interested in a letter that our office received which was unsigned but went to the very heart of the callous indifference and cruelty of the system of disability reviews. You could read this letter to the Secretary as it would be an interesting human interest piece.*

A variation on the finger-shaking routine was putting obviously disabled people up on the witness stand at congressional hearings. There were half a dozen "road shows" of this sort held on a regional level that attracted local TV

---

*As recommended, Sasser did read the anonymous letter to Schweiker and inquired whether SSA was using a quota system. Schweiker replied that SSA was not using a quota system, but the exchange was never broadcast.[6]

coverage and employed an identical format: a handful of congressmen on hand for the hearing would open by denouncing the reviews, followed by a parade of cutoff recipients, attorneys representing recipients, beleaguered administrative law judges, and state officials, all of whom also stiffly criticized the reviews. The administration did not testify at the regional hearings and typically submitted a statement for the record. In some instances, the road show was brought to Washington. In one notable case, Senator Heinz (R-Pa.), chairman of the Senate Select Committee on Aging, convened a hearing where several mentally ill recipients who had been cut off attempted to testify. Profiles on two of these individuals were already being worked up for incorporation in a *Frontline* show hosted by Jessica Savitch (which appeared after the hearing on PBS). The *Frontline* piece used the same format, in an extended version, that the CBS horror story segments employed: it began with interviews and pathetic shots of obviously disabled recipients who had lost their benefits, proceeded to scenes where disaffected examiners, ALJs, and doctors criticized the CDIs, which were contrasted with brief, defensive comments from SSA officials. The *Frontline* documentary included shots of the mentally ill ex-recipients testifying before Heinz's committee, contrasting them with an excerpt from Simmons at the hearing (deleted, for some reason, from the show's transcript) occur when he turns to an aide and mumbles: "This is a set up." Simmons, whom one viewer of the show described as coming across like "a goddamn thug," ruefully recalled that when he showed up to testify Senator Heinz was the only senator in attendance and the hearing room was filled with disabled people. No stations were covering the hearings except for PBS and Heinz's own PR firm. It was then that Simmons turned to an aide and made his infamous "this is a set up" comment. Savitch read it to show how much "antagonism" there was between the administration and Congress but failed, Simmons recalled, to use a single line of the half-hour interview he gave *Frontline*.

The kangaroo court proceedings fostered by television were essentially limited to the House and Senate Aging Committees, the leadership of which were desperately seeking to halt or slow the CDIs. Hearings before the House and Senate Finance Committees—which had legislative jurisdiction over the CDIs— were not characterized by these parades of CDI victims between 1981 and 1984.* Indeed, several key committee members, aware of the potential influence of the television coverage, went out of their way to criticize network coverage of the reviews. For example, on December 8, 1982, a couple of days after CBS ran that horror story segment reported by Ed Rabel, Jake Pickle (D-Tx.), chairman of the House Ways and Means subcommittee on Social Security, assured Simmons at a subcommittee hearing:

---

*It is interesting to note that in 1984, the Ways and Means subcommittee on Social Security began to indulge the road show approach when its Chairman, Jake Pickle (D-Tx.), got fed up with the administration's blanket opposition to legislative reforms of the system. Ways and Means staffer Pat Dilley contends that Pickle resorted to field hearings "when the administration announced its opposition [in January 1984] to any legislation, and the theme of the hearings was that we needed a bill to fix the problems."

Your testimony this afternoon indicates to me that you have made a lot of changes, and that you are making improvements to the procedure, and that a lot of good has been done and that we are hearing less of the horror stories, and I am pleased, I know a network ran one of the horror stories, one of those series. I haven't had a chance to see it so it is difficult for me to comment on it, but the people who have heard it up here associated with this think it was an exaggeration, extreme in some instances. Perhaps to confine the issue at—it was dramatic and graphic, but the question of a disability case is far more than a drama as such. . . . Some of the things you have done in the last year and a half have been horror stories. I am sorry that they have picked out some of those horror stories and not given credit for the 95 percent of the good things that we do, but that is part of it, our program.*[7]

Local television coverage

There was also television coverage at the local level. And while local coverage only drew the attention of the White House once, it is clear that local television, like the national coverage, had an impact that far exceeded that of local newspapers. A dramatic example of this occurred in Massachusetts, where television coverage rocked the state legislature, while news coverage by the *Boston Globe* and other papers raised barely a flutter. Leading the television coverage in Massachusetts was WBZ-TV, an NBC affiliate. WBZ-TV ran segments on August 25 and 26, 1982, its "I-Team" (Investigative Team) which focused on CDI problems in Massachusetts, using the same format as the CBS segment: shots of several devastating horror stories were followed by criticism of the disability reviews from disaffected workers, administrative law judges, and incredulous doctors. This was then contrasted by a brief comment from a state official, who came across sounding pedantic and callous.** (See Appendix B for a copy of the transcript.) In the next year, WBZ aired ten editorials about the need to reform the CDIs, five of them coming within six weeks. WBZ called upon Governor King to form a ninety-day task force to conduct hearings on the CDIs and recommend changes. Governor King didn't immediately act on the recommendation but within ten days the Committee on Human Services had held hearings. The committee put together legislation to form an investigative commission; WBZ then editorialized in favor of that legislation three times: once when it was announced, a second time when it threatened to stall in the House Ways and Means Committee, and a third time when it was awaiting Governor King's signature. On each occasion, WBZ's recommendations were followed.

---

*Simmons joked with Pickle that "after last night's hatchet job, I am now parting my hair in the middle."[8] While CBS did not cover Simmons's criticism of Rabel's segment, it was the only network that covered the hearing, briefly taking note of several reforms the administration had implemented to improve the CDIs.

**In its first broadcast, the extent of the commentary by Disability Service Director Lorraine Cronin was as follows. Joe Bergantino, WBZ reporter asks Cronin: "Do you think there is anything wrong with your program? Yes or no?" Cronin responds: "In terms of my program here? No, I don't." Bergantino: "Nothing at all?" Cronin: "No."

After Michael Dukakis succeeded King as governor in January 1983, WBZ urged Dukakis to join a suit against SSA, brought by disabled residents to restore a "medical improvement" test for recipients subject to periodic review.* Dukakis agreed to join the suit, leading, in the process, a rebellion of state governors against SSA's procedures that spread like wildfire throughout 1983. Esther Pina, chairperson of the Ad Hoc Committee on SSDI, summed up WBZ's impact by stating: "Months previous to the WBZ reports I went to the Boston *Phoenix* and other newspapers with the information about what was happening but their stories didn't make a dent. WBZ coverage really created the Special Commission and the public support for a lot of what happened."**

Vignette 1: The Man from South Succotash

The first time the White House responded to a story about a disability cut-off, the story actually was a local evening news story, aired on WRC-TV, an NBC affiliate. WRC-TV is in Washington, D.C., and the president happened to see the segment when it was rebroadcast the following morning as part of the local news on the *Today* show. "The President was disturbed by the broadcast and thought we ought to knock it right from the beginning," Dave Gergen stated. "But we went after it essentially because he had seen the story, not because of its national prominence."

The WRC segment aired November 15, 1981, and depicted the financial and emotional toll losing disability benefits had wrought upon Stuart Kindrick and his family. Kindrick, a gaunt, white, thirty-six-year-old, lived with his wife and three young children in Fredricksburg, Virginia. In October 1973, Kindrick was working as a sheet metal mechanic when he smacked his head accidentally on a low-hanging steel beam. Kindrick suffered brain damage, including a blood clot in his brain, and had several transparent impairments; besides being subject to seizures, Kindrick's left side was partially paralyzed, making his left arm useless and forcing him to drag his steel-braced left leg behind him when he walked. During the next two years, Kindrick tried working on a state-funded rehabilitation project and as a one-armed welder on the side. He contends he quit in 1975 and that his welding tools were stolen in 1977 when he was in the hospital for brain surgery. In 1977, Kindrick was put on DI and in August 1981 received a letter from the DDS stating that his seizures did "not occur at the frequency required by the Social Security regulations."[9] Two months later Kindrick's benefits were cutoff, and the following month, while his family was being evicted from their home, Kindrick's wife began calling Washington area newspapers and TV stations to attract coverage of their plight. "You see things like this on TV all the time," she explained, "and I wanted to get some help, so

---

*The Special Commission created by the legislation also supported this recommendation. A medical improvement test had been used by SSA from 1969 to 1976.

**The WBZ I-Team reports actually achieved some national notoriety. Large parts of the reports were used to introduce the February 14, 1983, *MacNeil / Lehrer Report* segment, "Cutting Disability—Is it Fair?"

I called everyone and [WRC-TV] was interested. . . . I wanted the public to see, with the Reagan budget cuts, this is the way it is."[10]

The WRC segment was short and to the point. It was introduced by a reporter who stated that the "Kindrick family . . . has seen some hard times before, but they say this time they just don't know how they're going to survive." The reporter, with shots of Kindrick as a backdrop, then recounted that Kindrick had been kicked off the DI rolls, even though the state rehabilitation agency he previously worked for said he was too severely disabled to be helped by them. After the reporter noted that Kindrick and his family were being evicted, the segment closed with Mrs. Kindrick sobbing, "So, I don't know what we're going to do." In the rewrite for the *Today* show, one critical change was added to the introduction which had the announcer saying: "Many Americans are finding it difficult to cope, especially those hit by administration budget cuts. Stuart Kindrick and his family are hurt because their Social Security benefits are being cut off."

When President Reagan saw the story he claimed to have gone "storming into the office [and] said, 'Look, this guy is disabled. What are we doing?' "[11] Deputy Chief of Staff Michael Deaver then called HHS Secretary Schweiker and Paul Simmons was called as well. Schweiker assured Deaver the story was inaccurate because the CDIs were not a "budget cut" but were rather part of a congressional mandate enacted under the Carter administration. And Simmons gave the White House even stronger assurances, stating that the evidence in Kindrick's file showed he had had a sufficient medical recovery from his injuries by June 1981, and alerted them to the existence of a newspaper story that indicated Kindrick might have worked while drawing DI benefits.[12] (The November 5, 1981, story in the *Reston Times* (N-Va.) said that Kindrick had sup‚orted his family as a one-armed welder by "being willing to work 24 hours a day, and by being willing to do dangerous jobs that no one else was willing to do." According to the story, Kindrick stopped working in 1977; it is not clear from the story whether he stopped before or after he started to draw DI benefits.)

Fortified with this information, Deaver called WRC-TV News Director David Nuell the following day, November 17. According to Nuell, Deaver said that he

> had found the story "quite moving, especially the part where the wife cried on camera." He recounted calling Schweiker to ask him "Are we doing this to people?" Deaver said that Schweiker, after checking into the case, called him back and told him that the administration "was not doing this to recipients" and that Kindrick had been removed under a congressional mandate enacted under Carter. Deaver offered to have Schweiker call me, complained of gross errors in the story, and asserted the Administration was being hammered; I told him it was our policy to correct any errors. The next day [Paul Simmons] called and told me in confidence that "We had a bad story because Mr. Kindrick really was holding a full time job."

As Nuell and reporter Jack Cloherty rechecked the story, they discovered that Kindrick had been part of the CDIs that the Reagan administration had accelerated, but that because of the 1980 mandate, Kindrick was not literally a victim of Reagan's "budget cuts." On November 27, WRC aired another story noting that Deaver had "called to say that the fund cut off was not the fault of any Reagan administration policy," followed by more heartrending footage of interviews with Kindrick and his wife. In mid-December, Nuell sent Deaver a transcript of the second story, suggesting that the confusion over the "acceleration" vs. "budget cuts" distinction pointed up the need for local television to have greater access to administration officials, and asked for a series of briefings from top administration officials plus an interview with the president. In a January 28 reply to Nuell, Deaver ignored Nuell's request for an interview, noted that the Kindrick case was being appealed, and thanked him for sharing the transcript.

The story might have died there except for its becoming fixed in the president's mind as an example of how television misrepresented his policies. On March 7, 1982, columnist George Will recounted on ABC's *This Week with David Brinkley* how the president had told him of a Washington TV station that reported a man had been cut off Social Security benefits, yet the president's investigation into the matter revealed the man was cut off "in 1980 when Mr. Carter was president and he was cut off because he had a full-time job."[13] During the ten days following Will's comment, there was a steady crescendo of criticism of television news coverage from administration officials. "We were getting attacked by this time on the fairness issues," Dave Gergen acknowledged, "and were sensitive. We were looking for opportunities to rebut the case— something that would show it wasn't as bad as was being painted—and the Kindrick case seemed like a grievous example of where they hadn't caught all the facts. I thought it was ripe for attack and urged that we do so." On March 16, Edwin Meese, counselor to the president, asserted in a speech that the Reagan administration had generally received fair press treatment, but that TV news had been unnecessarily negative on Reagan's economic program, reporting a number of examples of suffering from reduced government spending that hadn't panned out when traced by the White House. The following day the president himself jumped into the fray in an interview with the *Daily Oklahoman* stating:

> You can't turn on the evening news without seeing that they're going to interview someone else who has lost their job—or they're outside the factory that has laid off workers and so forth. The constant downbeat can contribute psychologically to slowing down the recovery. I wonder sometimes if it isn't the battle of the ratings, the Neilsen ratings, and if they aren't more concerned with entertainment than they are with delivering news. Is it news that some fellow out in South Succotash someplace has just been laid off, that he should be interviewed nationwide? . . . One station put a family on television some months ago, a man obviously disabled somewhat because he was limping, had been dropped from Social Security disability payments. And his wife was crying and didn't know what they were going to do and the children were all disconsolate and so forth. I saw that on television. I went storming into the office in the morning. I said, "Look, this guy is disabled. What are we doing?" We hadn't taken him off! He had been taken off disability in 1980 because it was found then that he was holding a job for three years while he was drawing disability payments. And yet they ran it as if it was something we had just done.[14]

Reagan's remarks created a minor sensation, with both CBS and NBC News devoting the second story of the evening newscasts to what CBS's Lesley Stahl described as Reagan's "harsh attack" on television news. Stahl reported that "the presidents of CBS, NBC, and ABC all had no comment," adding that "this is not the first White House to go after the media once the president's political honeymoon is over. In fact, it's become almost a ritual."[15] NBC devoted two minutes and ten seconds to the story, including showing the original WRC segment and asking Nuell for comment. The NBC segment concluded with then White House correspondent Judy Woodruff observing: "David Gergen insisted today that there is no campaign underway against the news media. But he conceded that the president's irritation level has built up as the economic recovery he predicted continues to be delayed. After blaming the Congress, Wall Street, and the Federal Reserve Board at various times, Mr. Reagan has now decided to lash out at television news."[16]

As reporters began looking into Reagan's criticism, it soon developed that Reagan and Gergen had sucker-punched themselves by selecting the WRC story for attack. First, Reagan had the fundamental facts wrong: Kindrick was cutoff in 1981 during the Reagan administration's tenure; he was removed from the rolls because of an alleged medical recovery, not because of a return to work; and there did not appear to be a shred of evidence to indicate Kindrick had worked full time for three years while drawing disability payments.* Moreover, Kindrick had been reinstated by an ALJ in early March and received a check for $2,324 in backpayments covering the benefits that had been cutoff while awaiting the outcome of his appeal. After George Will mentioned the president's recollection of the Kindrick case on the Brinkley show, Nuell had become concerned that Kindrick might become the subject of a misleading "welfare chiseler" anecdote from Reagan himself. On March 11 and 12—almost a week before Reagan, in fact, cited the Kindrick case—Nuell repeatedly called the White House press office to warn Deaver that Kindrick had been reinstated.** On the evening of March 12th, Nuell received a phone call from the press office saying that "Mr. Deaver wants you to know he is fully aware of the situation." The president, in short, was not only wrong on the facts, but his advisers had explicitly been warned that he was misstating the case. To drive this point home, Nuell commented on it in his interview in the March 17 NBC Nightly News, as well as alerting Helen Thomas of UPI and Lou Cannon of the *Washington Post* to it,

---

*The *Reston Times* article indicated that Kindrick might have worked for part of 1977 when he drew disability benefits; an interpretation that Kindrick and his lawyer hotly disputed. There is no evidence, at least in the public record, that Kindrick worked full time from 1977 to 1980. (The *Reston Times* reported that Kindrick said "if he had his tools he could work on the days he felt fairly good." "I'm not asking for a handout," Kindrick is quoted as saying, "I'm just asking to be able to work.") According to news accounts, the *Reston Times* story was the only evidence SSA officials had that Kindrick might have worked in 1977.[17]

**Nuell also sought to clarify matters with Will, who dropped by WRC on March 10 to discuss Nuell's concerns about the anecdote. According to Nuell, Will acknowledged the president had the facts wrong but didn't offer to correct what he had said on ABC. "Presidents sometimes pull these things out of thin air," Will allegedly said as he left the studio.

both of whom wrote stories that appeared the morning of the eighteenth detailing Reagan's inaccuracies.

That afternoon Gergen's press briefing erupted when WRC reporter Stan Bernard arrived with a series of documents which indicated that Reagan had mangled the facts about Stuart Kindrick and his staff had known better. The White House press corps quickly lit into Gergen, who acknowledged that some of the president's facts might have been wrong but that his essential point was correct; i.e., that TV was unfairly painting Reagan as a "Scrooge" when, in fact, it was state workers who had removed Kindrick from the roll operating under a 1980 congressional mandate. That didn't satisfy the press corps, who saw the Kindrick case—as Howell Raines of the *New York Times* put it—raising questions about "the quality of the president's mind and the quality of his caring for unfortunate people."[18] By the end of the briefing—with reporters demanding to know "why the president felt free to hold up to ridicule a one-armed man with seizures . . . [erroneously] making it appear that the man was a fraudulent person"[19]—questions about the "fairness" of Ronald Reagan were raised anew.

As Reagan's anecdote began collapsing, the White House beat a hasty retreat. Departing from his prepared text in a March 18 speech to the National Association of Manufacturers, Reagan stated, "Presidents, even Thomas Jefferson, have their moods just like everyone else, including members of the press. Some of the things we say and do regarding each other may cause a little momentary frustration or misunderstanding, but that's all it is. So, I hope I didn't touch a nerve with any of the press because I think that most of the time the overwhelming majority of them are doing a fine job."[20] Reagan's apology received substantial coverage on all three networks—ABC used it as the basis for a four-minute segment on Reagan's relationship with the media—and seemed, for the moment, to calm the waters. "White House officials," Lesley Stahl summed up on the March 19 CBS Evening News, "have urged the President to temper the harshness of his attacks. They say the best thing he has going for him is that he's perceived as a nice guy whom everyone likes. The aides say the last thing the President needs now is a hostile press corps and a public that no longer finds him likable."[21] Asked the following day if Reagan had anything more to say about the media, White House spokesman Larry Speakes mumbled, "We're off that kick."*[22]

Vignette 2: "People Like Us"

The White House was "off that kick," but not for long. When it returned a month later to boot Bill Moyer's CBS documentary "People Like Us," it came far better prepared than it had on the Kindrick case.

By mid-April 1982, the adverse coverage Reagan and the White House were receiving on the "fairness" issue had turned into a deluge. Especially not-

---

*There is an ironic footnote to the story. In 1983, felony charges were brought against Kindrick and his wife for defrauding Spotsylvania County, Va., of $652.12 in welfare benefits.

able was *Newsweek*'s April 5, 1982 story, "Reagan's America: And the Poor Get Poorer." The cover showed a dirty-faced little white girl with her arms crossed and the kind of glassy look that one associates with malnourished children in underdeveloped countries. The *Newsweek* story used hard-hitting language,* recounted several hardship cases, and that Reagan's policies were hurting the working poor, not just welfare chiselers. Not only had the coverage become more adverse, so too had the polls. "The charge of unfairness had become a significant political concern by this point," Dave Gergen recalled, "because the polls showed that charge was really sticking. We were looking for a chance to counterattack on the fairness questions and 'People Like Us' provided a special opportunity; it became the mountain top in terms of our efforts to counteract the coverage."

Concurrent with the *Newsweek* story, the administration was being overwhelmed with print stories focusing on the anguish of recipients who had been cut off, most of whom were mistakenly terminated. SSA Commissioner John Svahn and his deputy Paul Simmons began to take steps to control the damage. They decided to try to prevent the stories by catching them before they could happen, and to defend the program head-on against its critics. First, they exempted 125,000 recipients slated for review by moving them into the permanently disabled categroy. Then they sent out a program circular to the regional offices to assist them in explaining the CDI process to the local press. They met with national reporters who were following the story, and had a session with the editorial board of the *New York Times*. None of this seemed to help much.

In early April, Gergen learned of the CBS documentary from HHS field reports which indicated that it was "tough." Several days before the April 21 broadcast of the documentary, Gergen discovered the program was going to display three case histories of recipients who had suffered from Reagan's budget cuts, and through a former associate of Deaver's, managed to get hold of the names of the recipients from a CBS mole. When advance reviews of the documentary appeared the morning of April 21, Gergen hastily directed HHS to begin working up profiles on the three recipients.

The advance reviews of the show, from the White Houses's viewpoint, were nothing short of devastating. The *New York Times* review, for example, lauded Moyers's work and revealed that Moyers concluded his documentary with a strong indictment of the administration. The *Times* critic observed:

> Bill D. Moyers . . . virtually alone among network correspondents is allowed to bring a personal vision and voice to his reports. . . . Mr. Moyers does what he does best—talking directly to the people. He sits with distraught families, he strolls with a gently optimistic youth, he probes the feelings of

*Among other things, *Newsweek*'s article, subtitled "Reagan's Polarized America," asserted: "Three is little question that the needy have borne the brunt of Reagan's budget cuts. . . . Ultimately, the issue is political morality—whether it is right, in the end, to increase the burden on the poor and near poor even temporarily so that the nation can regain its economic momentum. . . . The question is no longer whether the Federal government should slow its fiscal policies in favor of the poor or even remain neutral. It is whether the government should favor the affluent."[23]

those forced to take charity. The camerawork . . . captures fleeting expressions that tell more than volumes of statistics. Mr. Moyers is fair to all sides, but he refuses to come down in the middle of the nowhere sometimes called "balance." In his concluding remarks he says:

"There is no question but that the Federal programs which help the poor are riddled with waste and fraud. So are programs that help the middle class. So are subsidies to corporations. So are the billions being spent on the military-industrial complex. But the President and the Congress have chosen not to offend the rich, the powerful and the organized. It is easier to take on the poor. They have been asked to sacrifice because the economy is in trouble and because some people are cheating the system. But for all the fraud and waste, for all their inefficiencies, these programs are a life-support system for the poor. For many, we are pulling the plug."[24]

As strong as Moyers's conclusions were, the potential power of the prime-time documentary was best summed up by Tom Shales, the *Washington Post*'s TV critic. Shales's column, "Through the Safety Net," stated:

"People Like Us," could mark a turning point in American public opinion toward the Reagan Administration and its cavalier treatment of the poor. This could be the most influential network documentary since "Teddy," the 1979 Roger Mudd interview that effectively killed Sen. Edward M. Kennedy's chances for the Democratic presidential nomination. . . . It is difficult to watch the program's stories of hardship and destitution and not invoke the visual memory of the president romping in the surf outside Claudette Colbert's house in Barbados, and the distressing symbolism that goes with it: The president splashes about in the lap of luxury while Americans go hungry. . . .

"These are people who have slipped through the safety net and are falling away," says correspondent Bill Moyers in his introduction. "In the great outcry about spending, some helpless people are getting hurt. No one knows how many." But the number of people isn't the issue. What is happening to those profiled shouldn't be happening to anybody, anywhere, and most of all, not here. This program is a killer. Perhaps some of official Washington will be able to tear itself away from its white wine long enough to watch it. . . .

Where [Moyers] shines most is probably in the interviews with the victims, whom he never patronizes. Moyers has his detractors, and even his fallibilities, but *damn*, he's good. He may be The Best. . . . This documentation of a shameful moment for America constitutes another proud hour for CBS News.[25]

As the impact of "People Like Us" was ballyhooed, the White House began situating itself for a possible counterattack on the documentary. On the morning of April 21, Gergen called one of the producers of the show and asked that the administration be allowed to both screen the documentary in advance and be given time, at the conclusion of the documentary, to have an administration spokesman respond to the documentary. When his request was turned down, Gergen asked for the names of the recipients and a transcript of the show, which was also turned down. That afternoon Gergen sent a telegram to Van Gordon Sauter, president of CBS News, formalizing the White House requests. CBS News quickly issued a statement saying that it rejected the White House requests "based on long-standing CBS News policy," pointing out that "the administration's budgetary, economic and social policies have been the subject of intensive and detailed coverage [on CBS News] for more than a year. . . . 'People Like Us' is a relevant and newsworthy part of our continuing coverage . . . CBS News has and will continue to provide extensive opportunities to the administration for the presentation of its views."[26] "What we were trying to do," Gergen summarized, "was build up a case that we had been stomped on by intentionally seeking entry at every point. CBS did the show without interviewing a single administration official, wouldn't let us have a transcript or advance screening— even though they were showing it to reviewers ahead of time—and then wouldn't let us respond at the end of the broadcast. To make sure, however, that we didn't build up an audience for the show, we waited until the last day to begin raising a fuss."

When the CBS special aired that evening, Reagan watched from his private quarters at the White House, Gergen watched from his White House office, and Gergen's deputy director of public affairs, Michael Baroody, watched in the Old Executive Office Building, along with a "SWAT" team of White House and HHS officials who had been assigned to critique the broadcast. As promised, the documentary opened with Moyers contrasting Reagan's pledge to protect the truly needy with Moyers's contention that "some helpless people are getting hurt. No one knows exactly how many. This broadcast concerns only a few. Except for matters of chance, they are people like us." Three hardship portraits plus an interview with a priest (who provided free meals at his church) followed, out of which Moyers deducted that the administration's budget cuts were "pulling the plug" on "many" poor people. However loose Moyers's reasoning may have been, the footage was powerful and compelling, particularly the first hardship case, which showed Larry Ham, a CDI victim who suffered from cerebral palsy, struggling to deal with his loss of DI benefits. As Tom Shales wrote, Ham "almost weeps as he vows to Moyers that he will not give up his home in spite of the new crisis. In one heart-wrenching sequence, the camera captures the humiliation and degradation in the faces of the man and his wife as they sit quietly while a welfare worker phones a local charity in an effort to get them some hand-out food."[27] However, Moyers—who wrote as well as narrated the show—did not note that CDIs had gone on for years, that they were being expanded under a 1980 law, or that the appeals process had been a protracted, painful mess for almost a decade. (For a script of the Ham segment and Moyers's concluding remarks on the broadcast, see Appendix C.)

The morning after the broadcast, Reagan told a meeting of his senior staff, "I think there's a lot in there we can come back on."[28] Gergen felt strongly that the administration should deliberately attack the documentary, and was supported by a less-vehement Chief of Staff James Baker and Counselor Edwin Meese. The view among the senior staff, however, was by no means unanimous.

Noting that the show had come in third in the ratings—attracting only a 17 percent share of the audience—Deputy Chief of Staff Michael Deaver argued that an attack against the CBS show might only heighten the public's awareness of the administration's "fairness" problem. Richard Darman, deputy to the chief of staff, agreed with Deaver, suggesting that the administration counterattack on the fairness issue without making reference to CBS or the Moyers documentary. Darman reportedly likened attacking the documentary to Virginia Senator William Scott's strategy when he "called a press conference to rebut a magazine report that declared him the least intelligent member of the Senate."[29]

Asked to explain why he disagreed with Darman's analogy, Gergen replied tersely:

> Darman has many strengths, but this is not one of them. . . . The notion that you should let people bang you over the head when you're in the White House is one of the stupidest ideas that anyone can entertain; if you're not willing to speak out when you're being wronged, you're going to get taken to the cleaners politically. People who make these kind of arguments really don't know much about communications; they may have an personal axes to grind or just have an interest in not taking on an issue. It gets down to your philosophy of communications, and while I never sought to get in a war with the press across-the-board, you can't be afraid to put a shot across the bow of a network sometimes; otherwise they'll run all over you.
>
> The networks think about whether they're going to get a White House reaction and don't particularly like to get publicity raising questions about their broadcasts. CBS did not want to be in a position where it was singled out in people's minds as the "anti-administration" network, and although it's not so much true now, they were starting to lean in that direction then. We didn't realistically expect a retraction from CBS, but we did think that the next time we'd make them think twice and get a fairer show.

Gergen was similarly well stocked with arguments for why "People Like Us"—unlike many of the "fairness" stories, including the *Newsweek* cover story— merited a counterassault. Elaborating on the conditions under which he felt the White House should take on adverse coverage, Gergen stated:

> There were a number of factors that distinguished the Moyers show. First, we felt it was unfair to take a few cases, attribute all their problems to the Reagan administration, and generalize from there about our attitudes toward the poor. Second, the show was inaccurate; some of the facts were on our side, even in the cases they did look at. Finally, this was an hour-long show in prime time, and it was a devastating piece of journalism. You would think from watching this show that we were the most hard-hearted administration—that we were just kicking poor people in the teeth.
>
> You couldn't allow that kind of charge to lay out there unanswered. . . . The political stakes were very high when you're dealing with fairness issues and Reagan's attitude toward the poor. Those issues matter with the swing constituency—the moderates—who like Reagan worry about the effects of some of his policies. No single show like that will lose you a lot of moderate votes, but if you allow those perceptions to harden over time, it's very

difficult to turn them around. I also knew there would be a lot of support from the conservatives; *Human Events,* Pat Buchanan, John Lofton, and people like that, felt we were being hammered by the networks, and that we ought to strike back. And CBS was not only the hardest hitting network, it also could be the most arrogant, particularly in terms of our relationship with New York.* So, no, I had very few reservations about taking them on, knowing that it was going to be a story and knowing it would highlight the show.

Gergen's position, with the backing of Baker and Meese, carried the day, and the White House immediately launched a very visible counterattack on CBS and "People Like Us." At a breakfast with reporters that morning, Reagan's domestic policy adviser, Edwin Harper, criticized the accuracy of "People Like Us": "The producers of this show are going to have some credibility problems. It would be totally without justification, totally unreasonable to characterize this administration's policies as a war on the disabled. There are people who are cheating the taxpayer out of $2 billion a year. How do you root out the $2 billion cheaters?"[30] Later that morning, Gergen sent Sauter a second telegram, taking the unprecedented tack of requesting thirty minutes of network time to respond to the documentary. (Gergen proposed a thirty-minute film, financed through private sources, be shown in rebuttal.) A little after noon, Gergen appeared in the White House briefing room, handed out copies of the two telegrams to Sauter, and took questions from the press corps for about thirty minutes. Gergen derided the program as hitting "below the belt"[31] and throughout the briefing sought to establish that CBS had been unfair, particularly in its insistence on denying the administration an opportunity to review or comment on the allegations contained in the show. Gergen also objected to Moyers's method—without ever mentioning Moyers's background as LBJ's press secretary—by arguing that "what we have problems dealing with is a story which lays all the problems of [the poor and hungry] . . . that have been with this country for a long time . . . on Ronald Reagan's doorstep."[32] A number of reporters expressed alarm that the administration's request for an advance transcript and rebuttal time might have a "chilling effect" on First Amendment rights, but Gergen was largely able to defuse that issue by arguing that the administration was not questioning CBS's right to broadcast or the even-handedness of most of the coverage the administration received; it was only challenging whether the CBS documentary had been "balanced."

Following the White House press briefing, a number of reporters went to HHS, where their colleagues in the press corps received a briefing from Dr. Robert Rubin, the HHS assistant secretary for planning and evaluation. At the White House briefing, Gergen had challenged CBS's fairness and methods but deferred questions about the accuracy of Moyers's profile to HHS. Accordingly, the HHS briefing opened with Rubin reading a statement critiquing the three

*For criticism from the conservatives, see, for example, Fred Barnes, "TV News: The Shock Horror Welfare Cut Show," *Policy Review,* Spring 1983, pp. 57–73.

hardship cases presented in "People Like Us," followed by forty minutes of questions. (See Appendix D for the text of Rubin's criticisms of the Ham profile.) Like the White House briefing, the HHS briefing was contentious, with much of the questioning devoted to the administration's role in the review of the disability rolls.

While the administration was knocking the CBS documentary, CBS News was not sitting on its hands. During the administration briefings, Van Gordon Sauter released a telegram to Gergen that reiterated the points CBS News had made in its statement the previous day, and rejected the request for an Administration rebuttal broadcast.[33] That night CBS News was the only network that covered the administration's attack on the documentary, giving an accurate summary of the administration's general objections to the newscast (although not noting specific factual criticisms.)* The following day, CBS News issued another statement, this time one that addressed the specifics of the three hardship cases and was designed as a rebuttal to the HHS rebuttal. The statement (see Appendix D for the section dealing with Larry Ham) asserted that the "spokesmen for the Reagan administration yesterday, criticizing the accuracy of our broadcast, are incorrect. . . . CBS News continues to believe that the facts in each of the cases presented . . . are accurate, and were portrayed correctly. We stand by our broadcast." Moyers and Sauter also jumped into the fray, both to protest their innocence. "I didn't believe that this was going to be interpreted as an attack on the administration," Moyers told a *New York Times* reporter. "We leaned over backward not to juxtapose Presidential statements with people's circumstances" he added (dismissing the fact that the show opened with such a juxtaposition). "I don't believe for a moment that the administration set out deliberately to hurt helpless people. But at the same time, I don't believe the administration recognizes that some truly needy people are being hurt."**[34] Sauter adopted a gee-whiz tone too, commenting: "I didn't see the program as having a political agenda or expressing an advocate point of view. . . . It never was our intent to hit a nerve, to hit a target."[36]

Who won the battle of the rebuttals? It's not clear. The administration did succeed in drawing print coverage, with papers like the *Wall Street Journal* and *Chicago Tribune* reporting Gergen's objections to the show, and others, like the *Baltimore Sun, New York Daily News, Philadelphia Inquirer, Washington Post, Los Angeles Times,* and UPI, highlighting Rubin's specific objections to the profiles. On the other hand, a majority of the handful of editorial and op-ed writers

---

*In the Eastern editions of the newscast, CBS anchor Dan Rather also noted that Van Gordon Sauter had "respectfully" rejected the White House's request for rebuttal time. CBS News did not try to whitewash Moyers's suspect background. In fact, they used a shot of Congressman John Rousselot (R-Ca.) declaring on the floor of the House: "Having LBJ's press secretary reporting on the Reagan administration is like sending out Jack the Ripper to baby-sit for lonely girls."

**Moyers also dismissed his political history as irrelevant, stating: "The issue is not the political views I held when I was a young man. Since I left Washington I have not had any role in partisan politics and I have taken liberal Democrats to task as often as I've taken the administration to task. What's happening here is an attempt by partisan politicians to divert attention from people who would not be heard at all were they not being heard by journalists."[35]

who commented on the controversy sided with CBS, and news stories highlighting CBS's "counter fact sheet" appeared in the *Washington Post* and on the AP wire.*[37] The sentiment among most commentators was that Reagan had demonstrated some real chutzpah in criticizing Moyers for using an anecdotal approach to explain a public policy problem; those who live by the anecdote, the feeling was, die by it too.

Given that the battle for coverage was inconclusive, it's not surprising that senior officials still disagree about whether the administration should have taken on the CBS documentary. Simmons, for one, thinks that it was not worth the effort because neither the show nor the controversy about it was very important in the hinterlands. David Gergen, on the other hand, strongly defended the administration's rebuttal to "People Like Us," commenting:

> Looking back, I have no reservations whatsoever. Our counteroffensive put the media on notice that when something was unfair, we were willing to respond to it. Reporters, in subtle ways, were more thorough after that. I don't think it affected Moyers personally, but I feel it made some of the people at CBS think about what the White House response might be to future newscasts. In fact, the next time we had a problem with CBS News— on a food stamp story—they handled it very professionally, checked it out quickly, and ran a correction. The other way to look at the success of our efforts is to imagine what kind of coverage we might have received if we weren't willing to strike back at unfair coverage.

While the debate over the administration's public affairs strategy, like the debate over whether CBS had its facts right, ended inconclusively, there seems to be little doubt that "People Like Us" did subsequently have some impact on the administration's policy toward the disabled. Simmons and Gergen agree on this, but disagree on the roles of the White House and HHS in taking the initiative. For Simmons, the documentary forced the White House to pay attention to a problem that he and Jack Svahn had been trying to interest them in for over a year. Gergen saw the White House pushing a reluctant bureaucracy:

> After the [documentary] the White House started moving to get the [CDI] system cleaned up. Prior to the show, Mort Allen [then a specialist in foreign affairs in the press office] and Mike Baroody had suggested periodically to me that the [CDIs] might pose a problem, but the network coverage really raised the issue forcefully that some people were being treated in a crude way. Some of us on the communications side [of the White House] started calling HHS and OMB after this and saying "Can't we do something with this policy?"
>
> When I started to look into this I learned from Simmons and Pam [Bailey, the HHS assistant secretary for public affairs] that the disability cutoffs were accounting for 60 to 70 percent of the fairness stories we were getting around

---

*The same split was reflected in the news magazines. *Time* labeled the documentary "a devastating but unbalanced indictment of Reagan's social policies."[38] *Newsweek* wrote that Rubin's critique "was uneven."[39] In May, 1982, Ham won his appeal, which CBS reported on the *Evening News*.[40]

the country, and that really put me on the warpath to clean this thing up. We discussed the reviews at several senior staff meetings: Baker was sympathetic to reforming them, although he thought others could handle it; Meese was aware and got involved; and Duberstein [assistant to the president for legislative affairs] was quite concerned, because there was a lot of pressure building from moderate Republican senators, who understood the price we would pay in the big industrial states. Svahn eventually got into the spirit of trying to reform the program, but the HHS bureaucracy was very slow. Later [in 1983] it developed that OMB was vetoing further reforms because they felt they were too expensive.

One reform that Gergen pressed hard for was to have benefits for recipients who were terminated continued through the ALJ appeal. On March 16, 1982, in testimony before the House Ways and Means subcommittee on Social Security, Svahn had opposed continuation of benefits because "this approach might encourage frivolous appeals and add to our already large backlog."[41] Gergen and Baroody, however, felt it was very important to have the benefits continued because, as Gergen put it, "it was clear that mistakes were being made, which not only left [the recipients] in bad shape but also left us vulnerable politically. Continuing the benefits would not only help the cut off recipients, it would also help dampen and cut down the horror stories." Shortly after the "People Like Us" show, Gergen called HHS Secretary Schweiker several times to press him to continue payment of benefits during the appeals process. On April 28, 1982, seven days after the Moyers show aired, HHS issued a statement from Schweiker and Svahn announcing that they had reversed themselves, and would now support legislation providing for continuation of benefits. "The Reagan Administration," the press release explained, "wishes to be fair to those persons whose cases are being reviewed, and to prevent financial hardship for persons who appeal their removal."[42]

Vignette 3: Axing a Medal of Honor Winner

In the months following the April 1982 production of "People Like Us," SSA officials instituted several significant and meaningful reforms, all designed to slow the pace of the CDIs and curb abuses. The most important of these was instituting an initial face-to-face interview in order to catch some of the most egregious mistakes before they happened. These steps took place against a backdrop of voluminous print coverage (but little television coverage), which fueled a burgeoning congressional interest in doing something about the problem.

On January 12, 1983, Reagan appointed Margaret Heckler as HHS Secretary to replace Richard Schweiker (who had taken a job in private industry). A scrappy, veteran congresswoman from Massachusetts—who lost her seat in 1982 after she was thrown into a re-election fight resulting from redistricting—Heckler had made no secret while in Congress of her dismay over the disability reviews. On July 13, 1982, Heckler voiced her support for reform legislation on the floor of the House, observing that "The Administration, in March 1981, decided to accelerate the [CDIs]. This was done despite the lack of appropriate resources to handle the large increases in State agency caseloads. The lack of resources . . . is in large part the reason for unfair treatment of recipients and erroneous denials.''*[43] When she was appointed, Heckler was advised by Reagan that the CDI mess was "one of the first issues that he hoped I would tackle.''[44] During the spring of 1983, she sat through a series of briefings on the CDIs and had SSA continue work on a package of additional reforms.

One obstacle standing in the way of Heckler taking over the CDI reform process was Jack Svahn. Svahn, who had been promoted to HHS undersecretary when Heckler was appointed, had reportedly received White House assurances that he would be running the department, with Heckler acting largely as a figurehead. Heckler immediately sought to establish that she would be managing the department. Social Security issues were Svahn's and Simmons's forte (Simmons was then acting commissioner of SSA), and so while Heckler and her staff were involved with the 1983 reform package, Heckler let Svahn and Simmons control the process, preferring to do battle on other issues. Heckler and her staff felt they were in a real bind, trying to promote CDI reform without criticizing Svahn, Simmons, and Schweiker.

The ironic result of all this was that Heckler and her aides ended up adopting the same low-key public relations strategy toward the CDIs during their first few months that Svahn and Simmons had. As George Siguler, Heckler's chief of staff, summarized: "Our public affairs strategy, if you want to call it that, was to fix the program so that you stopped suffering. We weren't going to say much to the press until we had some new reforms, because they weren't going to buy it so long as there were legitimate problems in the program. Talking about how misunderstood the program was or the positive side of what had been done—like the billions of dollars the government had saved—wasn't going to play much in the *Post* or *Times,* or anywhere else by that time.''

The efforts to put together an administration package of reforms in the spring of 1983 were complicated, finally, by burgeoning sentiment in Congress to halt or radically overhaul the CDIs. In the House Ways and Means subcommittee, Chairman Jake Pickle (D-Tex.) was immersed in negotiations with SSA officials over a reform package, and members of the House Aging committee introduced a bill in February 1982 that reinstituted the "medical improvement" test (used before 1976), which would seriously diminish SSA's capacity to cut people from the rolls. That same month, Senators Levin (D-Mich.) and Cohen (R-Maine) introduced legislation that not only would reinstitute a medical improvement standard but also undercut SSA's policy of "nonacquiescence" with court decisions. (To maintain national standards in the DI program, SSA had applied court decisions only to the plaintiffs on whose behalf the complaint had been brought. The Levin/Cohen bill would require SSA to apply a circuit court decision—like, say, one reinstituting the use of a medical improvement test—to all recipients

---

*The day before Heckler voiced her support for the reform legislation, Congressman Barney Frank (D-Ma.)—Heckler's rival in the 1982 election—made a similar appeal on the Floor.

who lived in the region over which the court had jurisdiction, unless the HHS secretary appealed the case to the Supreme Court.) In April, more kindling was thrown on the reform movement fire when GAO testified that 91 percent of the mental impairment cases being appealed to the ALJs were getting reversed,* a statistic which the GAO largely attributed to the "hard-line" SSA was taking in interpreting its criteria.[45] By mid-May, legislation that would provide for a CDI moratorium on all mental cases was drawing substantial support in both houses. It was against this background that the White House learned in late May that the NBC show *Real People* was preparing a segment on Roy Benavidez, a Congressional Medal of Honor winner whose war wounds had been deemed insufficient to keep him on the DI rolls.

Master Sergeant Roy Benavidez's extraordinary exploits were well worth a segment on *Real People*. His story runs as follows.[46] In May 1968, the thirty-two-year-old Green Beret volunteered to help rescue a group of twelve soldiers who were pinned down in the Cambodian jungle in a North Vietnamese stronghold. After Benavidez was dropped by helicopter, he started to run the 75 yards to where the men were encircled but got shot in the leg and had schrapnel from a hand grenade tear into his face. Rolling over, he resumed running, making it to the eight American survivors. As the helicopter came down to pick the men up, Benavidez, seriously wounded, dragged two men into the copter. He then went back to get the body of the team leader and was shot in the back. As he lay on the ground, the helicopter pilot was shot and the hovering helicopter tipped over and crashed. Benavidez then went back to the helicopter and led the survivors back into the jungle, where they were again pinned down by enemy fire.

While the wounded men hunkered down awaiting another helicopter, Benavidez took a third bullet, this time in the thigh, while administering first aid. Nevertheless, when the helicopter arrived, Benavidez dragged two injured men aboard and went back for the rest of his comrades. As he bent down to pick up a wounded man, a North Vietnamese soldier struck him in the back of the head with a rifle butt. The North Vietnamese lunged at Benavidez with his bayonet, which Benavidez pulled aside by grabbing it, cutting his hand wide open. With his free hand, Benavidez pulled a knife out of his belt and stabbed the enemy soldier, killing him. He then continued carrying more wounded soldiers to the helicopter, dropping them to shoot two enemy soldiers who had sneaked up behind the door gunners. With all eight men finally on board, Benavidez went back into the jungle, making one last sweep for injured soldiers and classified material. He climbed aboard the helicopter, passed out, and came to when the helicopter landed at Loc Ninh, Vietnam, where a doctor peered down at Benavidez and pronounced "There's nothing I can do for him."[47] Unable to speak, Benavidez defiantly spat in the doctor's face.

There was more to the Benavidez story than just the man's stark heroism. Due to a delay in locating survivors of the Cambodian battle (who could corroborate what occurred), it took a special act by Congress in 1980 to extend the time

---

*SSA hotly disputed the 91% figure, claiming it was substantially lower.

limit for medals to grant Benavidez his Medal of Honor. The result was that the Vietnam vet received his award from the Reagan administration, and, more to the point, from the president himself. In an emotional, filmed ceremony at the Pentagon on February 24, 1981—with those in attendance including the secretaries of State and Defense, the Joint Chiefs of Staff, Nancy Reagan, and Benavidez's wife and children—Reagan read a citation lauding Benavidez's feats, hung the Medal of Honor around his neck, and the two embraced. "I wanted to salute my Commander in Chief," Benavidez recalled. "And then when he hugged me, and he embraced me, and our eyes started getting misty. . . . Now that was . . . American, the love of country and fellow man."[48]

Adding to the embarrassment the administration felt over Benavidez's removal was Benavidez's ethnic and political background. Benavidez was Mexican-American and something of a local hero in Texas, a key state in Reagan's election plans. A few weeks before the White House learned of Benavidez's cutoff, Reagan had cited Benavidez as an example of the administration's recognition of Hispanic citizens at a Hispanic rally in San Antonio, declaring that when soldiers "Place their lives on the line for us, we must make sure that they know we're behind them and appreciate what they're doing."[49] Finally, Benavidez had traveled all over Texas giving patriotic speeches, and in 1982 had served as Mexican-American coordinator for a Republic candidate who successfully sought the lieutenant governorship. At the time the White House learned of his cutoff, Benavidez was scheduled to speak within weeks to a National Conservative Political Action Committee (NCPAC) rally called "American Heroes for Reagan."[50] "An Hispanic war hero," Dave Gergen summarized, "who had been honored and then mistreated by the administration was one of the worst stories we could imagine from a communications standpoint."

Enter Real People

Real People learned of Benavidez's cutoff quite by accident. *Real People* had planned to do a segment on Benavidez for its Veterans' Day show (scheduled for November 1983) and was down in El Campo, Texas, Benavidez's home town, to shoot some footage of a parade in Benavidez's honor on May 14, 1983. (The local National Armory was being renamed that day in honor of Benavidez.) While in El Campo, *Real People* did an interview in Benavidez's house and in the midst of shooting it, a cameraman noticed a letter from the Social Security Administration on the desk and asked Benavidez what it was about. The letter, Benavidez explained—sent on George Washington's birthday—was his notice that he was being dropped from the DI rolls. At that point, *Real People* quickly shifted the angle of their story. Pam Bailey, who had just left HHS to join the White House staff (as Baroody's deputy in the Office of Public Affairs), recalled that "the story was no longer about an American hero; by the time they approached us it was about how America turns its back on its heroes."

The producer of the Benavidez segment, Bob Wynn, was genuinely upset over Benavidez's cutoff and sought help from the administration almost immediately. Wynn first went to see Dick Childress, a member of the National Security Council staff who had helped *Real People* with a previous segment on veterans missing-in-action. Childress was outraged by the Benavidez case and arranged several calls from Wynn to SSA officials; after several lower-level SSA bureaucrats proved uncooperative, Wynn finally got through to Paul Simmons. "I told him," Wynn recalled, "that this was a very ugly story—the man is a Medal of Honor winner—and I think you ought to deal with this. His reaction was, 'Let's stonewall it and let it go through due process.' " Simmons recalled that conversation a bit differently. Feeling that one couldn't take an individual case and give *Real People* a philosophical explanation of how the disability program works, Simmons declined to go on camera. Then, he claims, Wynn started screaming at him, suggesting that they were going to hold him up in front of 40 million Americans, that there was not an eligibility test for Benavidez to go into that clearing in Cambodia, and so on. Simmons, rapidly concluded that Benavidez was too hot a potato to handle and that the best course of action was not to give Benavidez's case any special treatment because such behavior would soon leak out.

With Simmons declining to intervene or be interviewed, Childress arranged calls from Wynn to Pam Bailey and Bailey's boss, Mike Baroody. Bailey had received an inkling of the Benavidez cutoff the week before (from a departing member of Ed Meese's staff) and had immediately sent a note to Gergen about it (although her knowledge was fuzzy at the time about when the segment was being shown and the particulars of the Benavidez case). Wynn recalls that Baroody's reaction to hearing of the Benavidez cutoff was simply: "Oh, my God, no. . ."

Baroody encouraged Wynn to come to his office to talk over the situation, but before Wynn arrived put calls in to George Siguler, Heckler's chief of staff, and several other HHS officials to get a rundown on the Benavidez case. Claire Del Real (then HHS acting assistant secretary for public affairs) summed up Baroody's inquiry be saying that he "was just about apoplectic." Siguler channelled Baroody's request to SSA officials, and the response that Baroody got back indicated that Benavidez's cutoff was by no means a clear-cut mistake. According to Benavidez, his war wounds had left him with two pieces of schrapnel lodged in his heart, bayonet wounds in both arms, severely impaired functions in his arms and legs, a punctured lung, restricted pulmonary function, and back pain that prevented him from sitting or standing for more than forty-five minutes at a time. However, several officials familiar with Benavidez's file contended his physical impairments were not severe enough to qualify him for DI. In 1976, eight years after receiving his wounds in Vietnam, Benavidez retired from the military with an 80 percent disability rating and opted for Social Security disability insurance as well. In the intervening years, Benavidez remained quite active; he attended junior college for two years, was involved in politics, and gave frequent speeches to local Texas high schools, veterans associations, and the like. Moreover, as letters from El Campo residents attested, Benavidez had made no secret of the fact that he lifted weights and jogged to stay in shape.[51] There was little doubt in the minds of some SSA officials that Benavidez did not meet the strict DI test for being physically disabled; he was not, they felt, "unable to engage in any substantial gainful activity" for at least a year due to his impairments. There was, however, one "out" in Benavidez's file that officials were enjoined against speaking about because of the confidentiality requirements of the Social Security Act. On May 16, Benavidez had had a hearing before an administrative law judge with a psychiatrist present. The psychiatrist had introduced a new element in the case, suggesting that Benavidez's war injuries had wrought such an emotional toll on the man that he was no longer capable of holding a job. The ALJ had directed Benavidez, much to the latter's dismay, to see another psychiatrist, with an examination scheduled for Benavidez in early June.

This information on Benavidez's case was communicated to Gergen and other White House officials, who received it with some skepticism. "There was a feeling," one White House aide commented, "that as a Medal of Honor winner, Benavidez did not deserve to have this happen to him, no matter what the facts were in his case, and certainly Dave [Gergen] felt that way. We had read the [April 1983] *Reader's Digest* story on Benavidez's heroism in Vietnam and he clearly was severely injured in battle. When we heard [SSA's] warnings, we weren't sure whether it was coming from someone way down the bureaucratic line or from someone way up the line who was trying to defend the reviews." Doubts among the White House public affairs specialists grew when Wynn met with Baroody and Pam Bailey in mid-May. Wynn had brought with him what Bailey described as "some very powerful footage that showed, among other things, that Benavidez limped."

The meeting between Baroody and Wynn went amicably, although Baroody was able to do little to help Wynn. "Bob explained to me," Baroody recalled, "some of Benavidez's objections not only to the cutoff but to the procedure that he was being made to follow by way of appeal; he had to go back for more physical exams and he felt he'd been through enough already. We were both sympathetic to Benavidez's plight, but the White House lacked the legal authority to intervene so long as the case was before the [ALJ]." Wynn asked if Benavidez could come into the White House the following weekend since *Real People* was bringing its crew to town, and would be taping by the Washington Monument on Memorial Day. Baroody said that would be fine, and told Wynn that the White House would like to help Benavidez find a job if he lost his appeal and was kicked off the rolls.

Right before Benavidez and *Real People* arrived in Washington, events started breaking quickly. On Thursday (May 26), Benavidez received two phone calls from a White House aide in the private sector liaison group, who was seeking to help Benavidez find a job. Benavidez turned down the offers because, as he summarized later, "I will never work anywhere unless I am in the military. I cannot do any other jobs because all I know is how to jump out of airplanes and run with a rifle and kill an enemy and have men follow me and give orders. By my standards, I don't think that I should ever have a job as a construction chief; I think my standards would be so high that even the president of a corporation would dismiss me three or four days later.''[52] At the same time that Benavidez rejected the White House's offer of assistance, news of Benavidez's cutoff started leaking out. Following a Thursday morning meeting of HHS public affairs personnel—at which SSA's press spokesperson Jim Brown had warned people about the Benavidez case—someone who had been at the meeting or heard about it tipped off Spencer Rich of the *Washington Post* about the war hero's cutoff. Rich immediately started calling HHS and White House officials for information and comment.

The following morning the *Post* ran Rich's story on page one, next to a photo that showed Reagan embracing Benavidez after he received the Medal of Honor. Rich's story led with ''A Vietnam war hero awarded the Medal of Honor by President Reagan at an emotional ceremony two years ago has been removed from the Social Security disability rolls on the grounds that he is capable of some type of work despite his injuries, sources said yesterday.''[53] The story went on in this vein, recounting Benavidez's heroism, Reagan's previous praise for the man, and the ''widespread protests'' against CDI cutoffs that had occurred around the nation. The story beautifully framed the irony of Benavidez's cutoff, but did not mention that Benavidez had retained his benefits—which were being continued pending his appeal under the 1983 legislation Reagan signed—nor did it assess the issue of whether his cutoff was appropriate because he might be able to hold some kind of job.

The *Post* story was briefly highlighted on the CBS Morning News and by noon, UPI, the *Dallas Times Herald,* the *Houston Post,* and NBC Nightly News were all preparing stories in Benavidez's cutoff. To complicate matters, Wynn asked Baroody whether Benavidez's meeting at the White House on Saturday could be filmed and had informed him that Benavidez would, in any event, be giving interviews at the Washington Monument. With the president and all of his senior aides at the economic summit in Williamsburg, Va., the decision on how to handle Benavidez's visit was left to Baroody and Pam Bailey.

Milk and Donuts for Everyone
The task of answering press inquiries about Benavidez fell largely to HHS. At HHS headquarters, Acting Assistant Secretary for Public Affairs Claire Del Real declined comment, citing privacy laws. ''The secretary's view of how to handle this,'' Del Real recalled, ''was to pray it would go away.'' Jim Brown took the same tack, and with Undersecretary Svahn in Geneva, the chore of responding to inquiries ended up delegated to Acting SSA Commissioner Simmons. Simmons was interviewed by D'Vera Cohn of UPI (who covered SSA for the wire service) and NBC Nightly News. In the interviews, he sought to shift the focus of the stories away from the question of whether the administration had deserted and exploited Benavidez, to the question of whether Benavidez met the requirements for DI benefits. In Cohn's UPI stories, Simmons acknowledged that ''Reagan is doing everything he can to make sure this man does not fall through the cracks,'' but the bulk of his comments tended to downplay the uniqueness of Benavidez's background. ''This program by law is fairly strict. It

says you have to be unable to do any job in the economy," Simmons was quoted as saying, "not just the job you used to do. . . . [The ALJ] is apparently unsatisfied with the medical evidence in [Benavidez's] file. . . . This program is painstakingly based on evidence of medical disability."[54] It had been determined, Simmons told Cohn, that Benavidez could do "greater than medium exertion," which, Cohn reported, meant that the war hero could lift up to 50 pounds.

Simmons's contribution to the NBC Nightly News segment was similar. The Benavidez story, which was the eleventh carried that night by NBC—like the *Post* and UPI articles—framed the story around the administration turning its back on a disabled war hero, implying that Benavidez had already lost his benefits. While there had been some cursory discussion in the *Post* and UPI pieces of how tough requirements for DI benefits were, there was none in the NBC piece. The heart of the 100-second segment used footage of Reagan awarding Benavidez the Medal of Honor as a backdrop, against which NBC correspondent Jamie Gangel contrasted Benavidez's war injuries with Simmons's attitude toward his loss of disability benefits. The transcript read:

> JAMIE GANGEL: Two years ago, Sgt. Roy Benavidez, a former Green Beret was honored by President Reagan for his heroism in Vietnam. Benavidez saved the lives of at least eight other Green Berets.
>
> PRESIDENT REAGAN: [Footage of Medal of Honor ceremony] For service above and beyond the call of duty, the Congressional Medal of Honor.
>
> GANGEL: During the rescue, Benavidez was wounded in almost every part of his body. He still suffers from schrapnel in his heart, a bad lung and back injuries. Since his return, he has not been able to work. But now Benavidez has been told he will no longer receive Social Security payments because under tighter regulations, he is now considered able to work.
>
> BENAVIDEZ: This is absolutely ridiculous. It's—it's salt in my open wounds.
>
> PAUL SIMMONS: I don't think it's an insult to anyone who is on the system to be asked to demonstrate their continued eligibility.
>
> BENAVIDEZ: I'd like to ask all my comrades and the public, to kneel down and say a prayer, and God save the Republic for (garbled) there's just no hope.

While Paul Simmons was attempting to defuse the notion that Benavidez merited special attention because of his war wounds and connection to the President, Mike Baroody had decided to recommend quite the opposite course of action for the White House. On Friday, Baroody called Gergen to suggest that they accept *Real People*'s invitation to film a meeting between him and Benavidez. Baroody rejected less drastic options, such as seeing whether the story died over the weekend, invoking privacy laws to withhold comment, or issuing a press statement. He explained his reasoning as follows:

> We were presented with a situation where *Real People* was going to do a show featuring a national hero who had run afoul of the disability review process, whether we liked it our not. We knew also that the president had

personally awarded Benavidez his medal and that they had footage of that in their segment. As far as I was concerned, no matter what we were told about Benavidez's file, the White House was already identified with the man; the story wasn't going to go away from our doorstep if we tried to ignore it, and with the case still being appealed, it wasn't going to die in the newspapers either.

Sure, what we did was unusual, but it's unusual that they already had fifteen minutes of a feature television show in the can and gave us the opportunity to respond. It didn't really matter that it wasn't CBS News or Bill Moyers; it's a show that millions of people watch and it was a remarkable story. We did not want to be or appear to be disinterested in this man and his problems, and for that reason it was better to go on camera. If we had put out a statement expressing the president's concern, the most we would have gotten on the show would have been somebody reading it on our behalf.

Gergen accepted Baroody's recommendation, concluding that any alternative course would make matters worse:

I felt strongly that Benavidez was entitled to the finest treatment, and that if he wanted to meet at the White House, we shouldn't lock the gates. If we had done that, I'm sure *Real People* would have literally put Benavidez outside the gates, filming him trying to get in. All that would have done is accentuate the insensitivity of the administration.

Although Gergen and Baroody were concerned and embarrassed by Benavidez's cutoff, they had some hope that bringing *Real People* into the White House might accelerate reform of the CDI system. "Ordinarily," Gergen stated, "I would have checked out what we did with *Real People* with other staff members, but everybody at Williamsburg was busy and there are times when you get frustrated enough to say 'to hell with it, let's just do it.' I didn't run this through the bureaucracy because I knew there would be people who would try to kill it. And sometimes when the White House gets involved, it sends a signal through the bureaucracy to make sure things run better." One signal sent by Gergen on Friday was communicated by White House spokesman Larry Speakes, who told D'Vera Cohn of UPI not only that "the president was personally concerned" when he read about Benavidez, but that he was also "sympathetic to the plight of . . . all other unfortunate victims of the squeeze created by the [1980] law. We recognize it as a problem that affects many Americans. The president has asked [HHS] to seek some way we can be helpful."[55] Cohn noted appropriately that Speakes's comments represented "a sharp break with those of other Administration officials who staunchly defend the reviews, although conceding some mistakes are made."[56]

An important consequence of the White House strategy was that they ducked altogether the issue of whether Benavidez was qualified for disability insurance. If, as SSA had communicated to the White House, Benavidez plainly did not meet the requirements for physical disability, the only way Benavidez would be restored to the rolls—and end the administration's embarrassment—was if the psychiatrist Benavidez was to see in June certified he had disabling emotional problems. If that didn't occur, it appeared Benavidez would lose his appeal, and the White House might get tarred with having sympathized with—as one official put it—"a guy who was jogging all the way to the bank." Gergen defended the fact that the White House, unlike Simmons, downplayed the toughness of DI regulations, commenting: "Yeah, there were some warning flags raised in the bureaucracy about what was in the private files and that we should be careful in handling this case. But we had reason to believe that we didn't run much of a risk in expressing concern about his case because we knew he had serious war wounds and could well carry on a conversation. The risk, as far as I was concerned, was all on the other side because we knew he felt hurt by the White House, and if we didn't talk to him, it was going to leave a very bitter man doing interviews all weekend. Anyway, the country owes more to a war hero, you can't just turn your back on them." Whether Gergen was right or wrong, it does seem clear that it was not only appropriate but savvy of officials to avoid intimating that Benavidez might have mental problems. "I would have given anything," Bob Wynn stated, "to have had them tell me that Benavidez had mental problems. I would have used it and strung them up by the highest yardarm. It's bullshit anyway; if Benavidez is a mental case so are you and so am I."

After receiving Gergen's go-ahead, Baroody called Wynn to tell him to bring the cameras in with Benavidez. "I have to say that Mike was fabulous," Wynn stated, "he didn't impose any conditions on the filming or suggest anything be off-the-record. Frankly, I was astonished he'd step up to this because it was very, very nasty, and very tough to see how it could redound to their credit." At 9:00 A.M., Saturday morning, Wynn, Benavidez (in full uniform), Benavidez's wife and three children, Executive Producer George Schlatter, and *Real People* reporters Mark Russell and Sarah Purcell arrived at the White House to meet with Baroody, who had reserved the Roosevelt Room for their meeting. The conference table in the Roosevelt Room, normally reserved for weighty policy discussions, had coffee, glasses of milk, and donuts at every place setting. "I felt sorry for Baroody," Mark Russell recalled with a laugh. "Here they had tried to make this homey setting and before we sit down Mike is exchanging pleasantries and says something like 'Well, it looks like it's going to cloud up out there,' and Benavidez responds: 'Yeah, I always feel a day like this in the schrapnel in my heart'—which kind of, you know, put a damper on things right away."

As the meeting proceeded, Baroody made all the points that he and Pam Bailey had gone over beforehand: the White House appreciated full well the hardship that losing benefits had resulted in for Benavidez and other veterans; the administration was looking at ways to improve the system; and by law Benavidez's appeal was out of the president's hands, but the president was personally concerned about his case and would make sure he found a job if he lost his appeal. Once *Real People* edited the film from the meeting the only point of Baroody's that remained intact was the last one. The transcript, with the lead-in, read like this:

MARK RUSSELL: [Standing on steps of Old Executive Office Building] Roy Benavidez is a fighter. He had to fight his way from the poverty of the barrio. He had to fight his way through a brilliant military career, and then, he fought for and finally gained the recognition he deserves. Today, Roy Benavidez is still fighting. Less than two years after receiving the Congressional Medal of Honor, Roy was informed that due to cutbacks his Social Security disability benefits were to be terminated. In spite of the fact that he has enough schrapnel in his head, body and heart to set off metal detectors in airports, he was informed by the Government that he was no longer to receive his benefits. To find out more about this, Real People set up a meeting for Roy, his wife and three children at the White House to discuss the problems of veteran benefits for Roy and other disabled servicemen.

MICHAEL BAROODY: [Shot of Roosevelt Room meeting] Well, even though President Reagan isn't here, he did want you to know that he hasn't forgotten what you did for your country, that he's determined you are not going to be left out in the cold. There are plenty of folks out there who can and will pitch in if any help is needed. And when your country needed your help, you gave it without a second thought, and almost gave your life. And now if you need any help, President Reagan is going to do all he can to make sure you get it.

RUSSELL: [Voice over, shots of meeting] Roy surprised everyone in the White House when he turned down the offer of help from the private sector.

BENAVIDEZ: I can't accept from him or the private sector. I just want what I am entitled to. [Shot of *Real People* reporter, Sarah Purcell, with tears welling up in her eyes.] Those same people that are denying these benefits of ours, they are living free at the expense of my buddies' lives, at the expense of our blood, of our limbs. Yet they're enjoying their freedom, but they are denying us our benefits.

BAROODY: Well, we're going to work with Congress if that's . . .

RUSSELL: [Another voice over] Roy continued to explain [Camera focuses on Benavidez's "Airbourne" patch] that his concern was not to get charity from the private sector for himself, but rather the reinstatement of benefits for the thousands of other disabled veterans who have also served their country. And Roy kept fighting.

The Benavidez Aftermath

There was no television coverage of Benavidez's cutoff in the week following the Benavidez–Baroody meeting, even though *Real People* made clips of the meeting available to the networks. There was, however, substantial print coverage, most of it framed by Benavidez instead of the White House. After Benavidez left the White House, he did a number of interviews at the Washington Monument, expressing his displeasure with the White House's intervention. Benavidez considered Baroody to be a White House underling with little authority, who "didn't know anything about my case, and [didn't] understand the social security system."[57] In stories in the *New York Times, Philadelphia Inquirer,* and *Washington Times,* Benavidez was quoted describing his cutoff as "an insult to my integrity, to the military and to all veterans" and constantly reiterated what we had told Baroody about fighting for the reinstatement of disability benefits for all veterans. Benavidez's comments only served to reinforce the deserted war hero slant to the story, which dominated subsequent coverage, as it had the Spencer Rich and *Real People* stories. With a handful of exceptions, no newspaper reported that Benavidez was still receiving his benefits* (a fact that so annoyed Simmons that he wrote to the *Los Angeles Times* to correct a mistaken editorial).[58] Similarly, the only stories that highlighted how tough the eligibility requirements were that Benavidez had to meet were Cohn's UPI stories, which quoted Simmons on the subject. Simmons's statements didn't earn him any kudos, with columnists like Richard Reeves restating Simmons's comments by writing "There was still something [Benavidez] could do, some light work, decided the new anti-bureaucracy bureaucrats, despite the hunks of schrapnel still in his heart, despite his damaged lungs and his almost useless arm."[59] Seeing how cold and cruel his comments about eligibility looked in print, Simmons soon decided to stop commenting altogether. By the end of the weekend, the White House had stopped commenting too.

Although the administration stopped commenting, the stories kept coming, with editorials appearing the following week in the *Washington Post, Los Angeles Times,* and *Philadelphia Inquirer,* all of which cited the Benavidez case as evidence of the need to reform the system. Benavidez rapidly emerged as a symbol of what was wrong with the reviews, fulfilling, in some sense, the White House's hope that his cutoff would build pressure for new reforms.

Inside the administration the stories were also having an effect, although just how much is in dispute. Before the Benavidez fracas erupted, Svahn and Simmons had already prepared a detailed package of additional reforms that included exempting 200,000 more recipients from the CDIs (resulting from moving more "nonpermanent" listings into the "permanent" category), a moratorium on the bulk of mental impairment cases (exempting another 135,000 recipients from review), and removing some biases in the system that raised the termination rate.** Heckler and her staff had completed their review of the package, approved it, and sent it over for processing by OMB staff (who had some reservations about it because of the estimated $200–300 million savings which would be lost) and the Cabinet, a meeting of which had been set up for June 1. Four days before the Cabinet meeting, the Benavidez story broke. While Benavidez's cutoff clearly did not prompt the reform package, his case did seem to grease the skids. After the NBC News and *Post* stories appeared, President Reagan, according to Heckler, "asked how we were doing and shared my concern that we must have a

---

*The *New York Times, Cuero Record* (Tx.), and the editorial page of the *Washington Post* noted that Benavidez retained his benefits, pending the outcome of his appeal.

**These biases showed up in two ways. First, SSA had profiled the CDI recipients, selecting ones for review who were most likely to be ineligible. Under Svahn's and Simmons's recommendations the reviews would be done randomly, which would lower the termination rate and ease the backlog of appeals. The second bias was that under the 1980 amendments SSA was required to review ⅔ of all allowances by the DDS; SSA had done some reviews of disallowances on its own but did not have resources to review more than a small number. The Svahn / Simmons package proposed the statute be changed to permit SSA to do a proportional sample of both allowances and denials.

compassionate review system. . . . The Medal of Honor winner, of course, was a case the President felt strongly about."[60] Nevertheless, Heckler stressed that Benavidez was "not the catalyst" for the reforms, a view which Simmons seconded.

The new SSA / HHS reforms may not have been inspired by the Benavidez case but that's not what came out in the press. Following the Cabinet meeting, SSA officials selectively leaked information that an announcement of new reform was pending within a few weeks, without specifying what the new reforms were.* However, when an early draft of the administration reform package was leaked to Robert Pear of the *New York Times,* administration officials felt they "had to announce"[62] the reforms as soon as possible. Pear's front page story—which appeared June 7, 1983, preceding Heckler's press conference by several hours— gave, among other reasons, the following explanation for the reforms: "The [reforms] . . . [were] described by one Health and Human Services official as a 'capitulation' to the critics . . . An Administration aide said White House officials had directed Mrs. Heckler to correct problems in the $18 billion disability program after reading reports that her department had stopped benefit payments for Roy P. Benavidez, a Vietnam War hero who had been awarded a Medal of Honor by President Reagan."[63] Heckler denied Pear's report twice—once at her press conference and once the following morning on CBS Morning News—but Pear's account of how the reforms came about became standard, with the *Dallas Morning News, Baltimore Sun, Los Angeles Times, Chicago Sun-Times* and others picking up the allegation that Benavidez had spurred the reforms.**

Although the June 7 reforms drew a lot of press—including coverage on the ABC, CBS, and NBC evening news—they didn't earn the administration much good will. Advocates for the disabled labelled the reforms a half-hearted step designed to preempt more serious reforms by Congress, and Congressman Pickle (D-Tx.) was infuriated. When the administration, in response to Pear's forthcoming story, jumped the gun on announcing the reforms, it failed to alert Pickle of what was coming. "We had been talking in this committee with the administration," Pickle later lectured Simmons at a hearing, "about changes we might make, should make. . . . We were close to introducing a bill, had a date set. And then lo and behold, we woke up one morning before coffee time and saw that the secretary had made broad, sweeping changes, and hadn't called us about the time of day."[65] Pickle's commitment to try to work with the administration (which was already wavering) rapidly eroded after the June 7 announcement, clearing the way for sweeping reforms to be passed by the House.

The Benavidez story, however, didn't quite die on June 7. In mid-July,

---

*Don Kirkman of Scripps-Howard News Service and Dwight Cunningham of the *Washington Times* both wrote stories along these lines. In the June 2 *Washington Times* story, Cunningham paraphrased SSA deputy spokesman John Trollinger as saying that "adverse media publicity and Congressional concern . . . has forced the agency to overhaul its entire review process."[61]

**A lengthy takeout on the issue of whether Benavidez prompted the June 7 reforms (by C. Fraser Smith of the *Baltimore Sun*) was more equivocal, concluding that "the Benavidez case seemed to have the effect of accelerating the Administration's 'reform'."[64]

Benavidez was restored to the rolls by the ALJ, prompting another round of articles. (Benavidez's lawyer claimed the ruling was "strictly physical,"[66] an interpretation that was privately rejected by government sources.) Internally, Heckler's people saw the Benavidez story as having been a turning point for her. As one aide commented:

> The Benavidez case was significant primarily because it was an almost grotesquely apt illustration of the system gone haywire; don't forget that when you talk about the impact of the story what context it came in. If there hadn't been a lot of previous horror stories, Benavidez's cutoff would have been treated as one of the strange ways that the federal government occasionally screws up. But with all the previous stories, the Benavidez wave became ten times taller and knocked everything down that had been left standing on the beach. The administration was left naked and indefensible, and everybody threw up their hands.
>
> For some valid reasons, the Benavidez case totally discredited what had gone on before Margaret [Heckler] and helped her completely move in and take over the department. People at the White House—and I don't mean the president but down the ladder—who felt that the nitty-gritty should be left to Svahn and that Margaret shouldn't get involved in administrative matters, had their reservations about Margaret swept aside by the Benavidez case. They were painfully, painfully embarrassed.

A footnote to the Benavidez and "People Like Us" stories was that the administration's earlier efforts to fight for more balanced TV coverage of the reviews was modestly reflected following the Benavidez cutoff. On June 20, three weeks after the Benavidez story broke, PBS aired its *Frontline* documentary on the CDIs, hosted by Jessica Savitch. The show, like Moyers's highlighted terminations of obviously disabled recipients and had generous footage of interviews with ALJs, doctors, and disability advocates that were critical of the reviews. However, unlike "People Like Us," Savitch's show did have some background on the CDIs and had some clips of administration officials defending what they had done. Savitch's show, unlike Moyers's, was panned in the advance reviews. *USA Today* TV critic Jack Curry wrote that "the show's emotional appeal might be lost on viewers looking for a more balanced presentation. . . . at times, the material does seem slanted [and] the tilted rhetoric used here cries out for some commentary by the accused."[67] Writing in the *Washington Post,* Spencer Rich described the show as "an angry, emotional documentary with lots of heart-tugging pictures" but concluded that the "PBS documentary makers appear one-sided."[68] Rich noted that the program completely missed the point that a recipient could fail to meet the stringent test for eligibility and still be so disabled as to be unable to work. Under pressure, the producers of the documentary agreed to give Secretary Heckler an opportunity to comment on their allegations at the close of the show (in an interview with Savitch)—granting, in effect, the chance for rebuttal that CBS had so definitively ruled out in the "People Like Us" episode. But the media's heightened awareness of the need for "balanced" presentation, like the June 7 Heckler reforms, came too little and too late for federal officials. The administration, it turned out, had won a skirmish but lost the war. During the year following Heckler's announcement, the beleaguered disability program fell apart.

Epilogue: The Administration Gets Routed

The collapse of the Social Security disability program resulted not so much from the presence of new horror stories, as from an all-out assault on the system by the nation's governors and courts starting in mid-1983. The governors were perturbed for a variety of reasons: some were running for re-election and saw disability as a failsafe issue; others faced increased general assistance costs, as disabled recipients who couldn't find jobs were added to state welfare rolls; and many of them, of course, were simply upset by the cutoffs of thousands of deserving recipients who complained to the governor's office following terminations by state agencies. By March 1984, the governors' resentment had spread into a real sagebrush rebellion, with fifteen of them instituting blanket moratoria on CDI terminations.

Simultaneously, SSA suffered one loss after another in the courts, particularly on the issue of medical improvement. By March 1984, fourteen states had been ordered, either by a district court or by the court of appeals, to reinstitute a medical improvement test and 100,000 beneficiaries had had their benefits reinstated retroactively, pending review under the standard. Besides losing every case it argued on the medical improvement question, SSA enraged the courts, which were swamped with CDI appeals. By early 1984, 43,000 disability cases were pending in district court, the backlog was growing at 2,000 cases per month, over 100 disability class actions were pending, and there had been several hundred motions or threats to hold Secretary Heckler in contempt. An internal SSA study bluntly acknowledged in mid-1984 that "there is a crisis in SSA's litigation process . . . [SSA's] credibility before the federal courts is at an all-time low. . . . A great deal of adverse publicity surrounds many Social Security litigation cases and court orders are written in increasingly critical terms."[69]

By early 1984, in short, it was clear that the disability program had fallen apart, with thirty-eight states operating under court-ordered or self-imposed moratoria (or having significantly altered the CDI process). Legislative steam was building up in Congress too. On the last day of the 1983 session, Senators Long (D-La.) and Dole (R.-Kan.) narrowly averted having the Cohen / Levin CDI reforms attached as an appropriations rider, but Cohen, Levin, and Heinz, as well as many senatorial allies, vowed to try again in 1984 when senators up for re-election would be particularly sensitive to distraught constituents. In the House, Congressman Pickle (D-Tx.) renewed his efforts early in the 1984 session to enact legislation that, like the Cohen and Levin bill, would reinstate the medical improvement test and force SSA to acquiesce to any circuit court decision the Supreme Court decided not to review.

In response to this rapidly growing pressure, the administration, over Heckler's objections, dug its feet in, reversing its previous position (at OMB's insistence) that further legislation was required to reform the CDIs. At a January 25, 1984, hearing before the Senate Finance Committee, the new Acting SSA Commissioner Martha McSteen* unveiled the administration position, stating that they "strongly oppose[d] enactment of disability legislation,"[70] while insisting that additional administrative steps could clean up the program. To drive home the administration's intent in proceeding with the reviews, McSteen announced that the administration would start the CDIs up again—which had been temporarily halted in December 1983 when the benefit protections enacted by Congress the previous year had expired. It soon became clear, however, that the administration had radically underestimated the level of bipartisan support for overhauling the CDI process. Pickle's bill whistled through Ways and Means in two months and was brought to a floor vote on March 27, 1984. Four days before the vote, White House and HHS officials leaked the information that HHS Secretary Heckler was prepared to announce an eighteen-month moratorium on the CDIs and might do so before the House vote.[71] Dangling the moratorium, however, did not in the least prove helpful to the administration, which was walloped when the House went ahead and approved Pickle's legislation 410–1.

Sensing the handwriting on the wall, Heckler announced on April 13, 1984, that she was suspending the CDIs until legislation could be enacted to restore "order and consensus in the disability program."[72] At the same time that the administration halted the reviews, they, with the help of Senators Levin and Cohen, won a commitment from Senator Long (D-La.) to let the Finance Committee mark up a bill and bring it to the floor without the threat of a filibuster. The bill fashioned by the Senate Finance Committee had Long's stamp on it, reversing two of the critical provisions in the House bill: nonacquiescence to circuit court decisions was permitted under the legislation, and the burden of proof in the medical improvement test fell upon the recipient, rather than SSA, requiring the recipient to show that his or her condition had *not* improved. On May 22 the Senate enthusiastically approved the Finance Committee bill 96–0.

During the next three months, the legislation was stalled in conference, and articles appeared in the *Congressional Quarterly* and elsewhere questioning whether the legislation was fated to be stillborn. "Part of our problem," Pat Dilley, a staffer on the Ways and Means subcommittee stated, "was that the moratorium stopped people from being kicked off the rolls and so you didn't have the constituent complaints or media stories that had previously pressured the Senate." Nevertheless, a number of Republican senators up for re-election were anxious to get legislation passed, and in mid-September the conference finally reached agreement. (In essence, the Senate acquiesced to the House on the medical improvement issue and the House agreed to drop the statutory provisions regarding nonacquiescence.) The conference agreement was approved 99–0 by the Senate and 402–0 by the House.

Under the new legislation, which SSA estimates to have a price tag of about

---

*In September 1983 Svahn left HHS to become the president's assistant for policy development. Simmons also left to join Svahn's staff at the White House.

$3.5 billion, the CDI process is dramatically liberalized: Recipients can only be removed if they show medical improvement or are able to engage in "substantial gainful activity";* the moratorium on patients with mental impairments was extended, pending consultation and publication of more realistic regulations; SSA was directed to pay more attention to the cumulative effect of multiple impairments (none of which individually might be severe enough to keep a recipient on DI); continuation of benefits through the ALJ hearing for cutoff recipients was authorized through 1988; and some 40,000 cases pending in federal courts are to be handled retroactively under the medical improvement standard. The legislation, in short, is designed to safeguard against the abuses that plagued thousands of disabled citizens during the preceding years, while allowing the reviews to continue under more liberal standards.

Despite these apparent improvements to the process, some administration officials question whether the new legislation represents an overreaction. In their view, the legislation ironically was enacted just at the point when some of the key shortcomings on the CDIs were being brought under control; face-to-face interviews at the initial level were catching some horror stories; the increase in DDS and ALJ staffing was finally complete; cases on which the DDS were most likely to make mistakes had been exempted or put under moratoria; and the CDI termination rate had fallen from a high of 47 percent in 1981 to 21 percent by 1984. Paul Simmons predicts that the current CDI reforms are cyclical and that five years from now the press will be back to writing stories about how recipients are getting disability while jogging or chopping wood in the backyard. The press, in his view, simply accelerates the swing of the cycle, by dramatizing extreme aspects of the DI program.

Whether to not the media one day tilts the pendulum back to heightened concern about "freeloaders" on disability, it seems indisputable that the media played a powerful role in framing debate over the CDIs, spurring congressional and White House involvement. In the end though it's not clear whether the media coverage had a profound impact on administration policy toward the disabled. Administration officials cite a handful of specific decisions—the continuation of benefits through the ALJ hearing, the timing of the June 7, 1983, reforms, and so on—that resulted from or were influenced by press coverage, particularly television coverage. But for the most part they refer to the press coverage as causing a procedural headache, alleging the media misrepresented their policies, their disposition toward the disabled, and sent them on endless missions to put out fires. On the other hand, the policy impact of the media—in the view of the administration's critics—can only be assessed by imagining what might have occurred if the administration had not received adverse coverage. Congressional critics, and the representatives of interest groups representing the disabled, contend that the administration would have been even more reluctant to slow or

---

*There are several specific exceptions where recipients may be terminated (if, for example, they are found to be working) but the medical improvement and SGA test are the primary criteria.

liberalize the CDI process had the cruelty of the reviews not been exposed by the media.

Much the same indeterminateness applies when examining the political, as opposed to policy, impact the coverage had. As Michael Baroody summed up:

> The disability stories were damaging every time they appeared in terms of the fairness issue. And because they involved such a vulnerable part of the population, I suspect they were particularly instrumental in building a framework in the back of people's minds, from which the Democrats hope to build their attack on the fairness issue. On the other hand, I watched very carefully the various ways they found to charge us with unfairness [at the 1984 Democratic National Convention] in San Francisco. The disability cutoffs weren't mentioned. It's a bit ironic that the [disability cutoffs] initially made for good drama on television, but are too complicated to open a good line of political attack when later recounted. "They cut food stamps" is easy to articulate on television; "They implemented reviews of the disability rolls in an unfair way" is not.

Within several weeks of Baroody's statement, Walter Mondale lambasted President Reagan during their first televised debate for the administration's callous treatment of the disabled. Citing the purge of the disability rolls twice as evidence that the administration had "singled out . . . the most vulnerable in American life," Mondale, in his closing remarks, offered this admonishment: "I would rather lose a campaign about decency than win a campaign about self-interest. . . . And when we sought to assault Social Security and Medicare, as the record shows we did, I think that was mean-spirited. When we terminated 400,000 desperate, hopeless, defenseless Americans who were on disability, confused and unable to defend themselves, and just laid them out on the street, as we did for four years, I don't think that's what America is all about."[73] Reagan's only rebuttal to Mondale's allegations came earlier in the debate when he started to comment, "I haven't got time to answer with regard to disability—." With Reagan's time expired, debate moderator Barbara Walters cut off the president. "Thank you, Mr. President. Mr. Mondale?"

APPENDIX A

The First CBS Horror Story Segment

Morning with Charles Kuralt and Diane Sawyer   12/21/81

KURALT: Back in March, the Social Security Administration started reviewing the cases of those who receive disability benefits. The idea was that many of them are no longer disabled. But, as Jane Wallace tells us now, many of those who have since been dropped from the rolls contend they still are disabled.

JANE WALLACE: Thirty-five-year old Karen Andrews is good at doing simple tasks, but she will never be a self-supporting adult. Karen has cerebral palsy, and her brain damage leaves her unable to handle normal stresses and strains. She used to get by on Social Security disability benefits, but now those have been cut off. Social Security has declared Karen no longer disabled.

KAREN ANDREWS: I feel like I've done something wrong. And I don't know what I did to cause anything like this to happen.

WALLACE: Social Security terminated Karen's benefits, despite a report from their own doctor that Karen's ability to hold a job is severely impaired. Karen's mother thinks the decision is ridiculous.

SHIRLEY ANDREWS: Cerebral palsy is a permanent condition. And the problems that she has are caused by this. So, therefore, I don't see how they can make a determination that it suddenly is better. It is not better. It is no different than it was five years ago or ten years ago.

WALLACE: Watching the unevenness of his gait, it's easy to see that thirty-three-year-old Bill Zeigler walks with difficulty. That's because he once walked over a mine in Vietnam. Bill went on disability after two years in an Army hospital. One of his legs is still full of schrapnel, the other a substitute of squeaky plastic. Still, Social Security also told him he's no longer disabled enough for benefits. They told him to find a job.

BILL ZEIGLER: There's 250,000 people out of work now, and they're perfect, you know, condition. And their—they don't have jobs, and I—I haven't worked for ten years and I'm handicapped. I have to go out and compete with them. Where am I going to find a job?

WALLACE: Thirty-four-year-old Faustine Williams is on as many as eighteen different medications. She suffers from a lung disorder that reduces her breathing capacity to 55 percent of normal. She also has a borderline intellect and emotional problems. Disability also told her no more benefits, not disabled enough.

FAUSTINE WILLIAMS: It means I can't get some medicine that I have to have sometimes.

WALLACE: Faustine and Karen and Bill are all files here at the Social Security headquarters in Baltimore, where they've decided there are too many files of people on disability benefits. A GAO report estimated that 20 percent of the 2.8 million on disability were really ineligible. So far this year, 113,000 have been dumped from the disability

347

rolls, and next year, 200,000 more are slated for termination. Sandy Crank is an associate commissioner of Social Security.

SANDY CRANK: We believe we've got a real responsibility to the American tax-paying public, as well as to people who are dependent upon the Social Security system for benefits, to be sure that people who are no longer eligible for benefits under the law do not get benefits under the law.

NANCY SHOR: It's just in this situation, seems that they're—the baby is thrown out with the bath water.

WALLACE: Nancy Shor directs the National Organization of Social Security Claimants Representatives.

SHOR: We would guesstimate about half—about half the terminations seem to be invalid. The difficulty is that many of them are being terminated without any consideration being paid to their current medical evidence.

WALLACE: Perhaps the most desperate case is that of forty-six-year-old Hubert Tuttle. When disability cut him off, he came here—to the local Lansing office—and shot himself. In his suicide note, Tuttle said that Social Security was playing God. Now his widow and children qualify for survivor benefits.

Reverend Earl Vansipe is the Tuttle family minister.

REVEREND EARL VANSIPE: There must have been a lot of anger and a lot of hostility that suddenly welled up within him against the Social Security department because the benefits had been cut off. And this was his way, I—I guess, of getting even.

CRANK: What do you want me to say about that? We're not playing God, no more than we play God when we allow people disability benefits.

WALLACE: For those persistent enough to question their terminations, each statistically has a 50 percent chance they'll get their benefits back on appeal. The decision usually takes five months. Hurbert Tuttle couldn't wait for his appeal to be decided. Faustine Williams is waiting out her appeal in the basement of her mother's home. The Zeiglers are holding out on Veterans' benefits, and Karen Andrews mother is afraid if she loses the only thing she can do is sell her house to keep her disabled daughter going.

SHIRLEY ANDREWS: Legally, I'm not responsible for her. Morally, I am. What else do I do? She's my daughter. (Pause) I don't mean to be emotional, but, you know, that's what it is.

(Announcements)

ANNOUNCER: Now four minutes before the hour.

APPENDIX B

Local Television Coverage

ANCHOR LEAD-IN: Tonight, the first of a special I-Team Report. The subject: The victims of drastic cutbacks in Federal Disability Benefits and the questionable practices used by the government agency that decides their fate. I-Team reporter Joe Bergantino unravels the details of this tragic story that affects thousands of disabled men and women.

JOE BERGANTINO (I-Team reporter): For Donald Cook these home movies are just fond memories; being up at bat at Beachmont Park in Revere; tossing pebbles into the Sacco River while on a trip to the White Mountains of New Hampshire. The year was 1966. But Don Cook's life changed drastically after an accident here on the job at Logan Airport in 1973. He was hauling luggage onto an airport bus when he ruptured two discs in his back. Today Cook spends much of his time in local hospitals. His back injury has resulted in serious nerve damage. He's lost most of the use of his back and has limited use of his legs. Both he and his doctor agree, he is totally disabled and unemployable.

DON COOK (Claimant): I can't lift. I can't bend. I can't sit too long or stand too long. I have pain all the time. Sometimes it's much more severe than others, when it gets too severe you require more medication.

JOE BERGANTINO: Is there any way you can work?

DON COOK: No.

BERGANTINO: Because?

COOK: Because there are days I can't even get out of bed. I don't know how I could go to work everyday.

BERGANTINO: Does that occur very often?

COOK: Yes it does. I don't know from one day to the next day whether I can get out of bed or I can't.

BERGANTINO: Since 1975, Cook and his wife and daughter have survived on a monthly check from the Social Security Disability Program. That's a program most of us contribute to through payroll deductions. Only those totally incapable of working because of an unexpected accident or crippling illness are eligible for benefits. The average is about $442.00 a month. Despite his ever worsening condition, Don Cook has been told he no longer qualifies and is capable of going back to work.

What's your most serious concern?

COOK: How do I survive?

BERGANTINO: If you don't get that money, what does that mean to you?

COOK: That means move out of wherever I am.

BERGANTINO: To where?

COOK: To any place I can find.

BERGANTINO: So you couldn't afford your rent?

COOK: No sir. No way.

BERGANTINO: Could you survive without this $550.00 a month?

COOK: No. No, I couldn't. I have no way to survive.

BERGANTINO: The people here at the State's Disability and Determination Service refused to tell us exactly why they cut Don Cook's benefits, but our month long I-Team investigation has found several serious problems in this agency; an agency that is cutting off benefits to hundreds of truly disabled here in Massachusetts.

One reason for the drastic cuts: Questionable practices here at the State's Disability Service. Workers are under orders from Washington to conduct a speedy review of every disability case on the books. The goal is to eliminate fraud in an estimated 20 percent of the cases. But in the process, almost 40 percent of those on disability in Massachusetts are being cut off the rolls.

ED KELLNER (Disability Worker): I've been with the Agency almost eight years now, and it's amazing to see cases that of people who have automatically allowed for disability before, are now just being denied left and right.

BERGANTINO: And these are people who are disabled?

KELLNER: Without a doubt. Without a doubt. Without a doubt. We are asking people to go back to work, who just can't work.

BERGANTINO: Ed Kellner is among a group of Disabled Service workers who risked their jobs to talk with us. From conversations with these workers, with federal judges, with several disability claimants, as well as a review of confidential internal government documents, the I-Team has uncovered some facts:

The fact that the government is paying out millions of dollars to consulting physicians, some of whom perform only brief and superficial examinations.

The fact the State ignores pain as an element in evaluating disability.

The fact that State workers feel pressured to process large numbers of cases and as a result often make inaccurate decisions. And most startling of all, the fact that State staff doctors often take as little as 15 minutes to decide if a person is seriously disabled and that decision is made without ever seeing the patient.

ADMINISTRATIVE LAW JUDGE CHESTER SCHATZ: The State agency doctor that does this work, he ignores the treating physicians' reports all the time or at least he doesn't comment on them in his write up and he ignores many times the impartial examining doctor that the State themselves sent the person out to be examined by and he ends up with a different conclusion and doesn't explain it away.

BERGANTINO: Federal Hearing Judge Chester Schatz has ruled on the appeal cases of several claimants cut off the disability rolls.

SCHATZ: The average time that a State agency doctor spends in reviewing a person's file, in Massachusetts, anyhow, is between fifteen and twenty minutes. Now some of those files are an inch thick.

BERGANTINO: Albert Locke's files are 6 volumes thick. Since 1972, he has spent a total of two years in a hospital for a number of serious stomach and intestinal problems. In fact, he was in the hospital when he got word he was being cut off the disability rolls because the State said he was fit to return to work.

What was your reaction when you first heard about this?

ALBERT LOCKE (Disability Claimant): Just shocked me. I couldn't believe it. I couldn't believe it.

JOSEPH WHELAN (Locke's Doctor): I cannot think of a single major company that he would be able to pass their pre-employment physical.

BERGANTINO: No question about it?

DR. WHELEN: No question.

BERGANTINO: Dr. Joseph Whelan of Waltham has been Locke's personal physician for 10 years.

DR. WHELAN: He has almost constant abdominal pain, recurrent bleeding of his ulcers, multiple hospitalization, his absentee record with any employer would discourage any employer and there is not hope of improving it because the condition is not going to get better, it's going to get worse.

BERGANTINO: How long do you think it would take for someone to look over Mr. Locke's medical history and make an accurate, objective, determination of whether he is disabled?

DR. WHELAN: An eight-hour working day.

BERGANTINO: Both Al Locke and Don Cook hope they can get a more accurate decision on their disability claims at an appeals hearing like this one. In recent months, 74% of the State's decisions that are appealed are overturned in these hearings.

ALJ SCHATZ: Just looking at them, you see how they walk and you know, reviewing that medical file, you scratch your head and wonder how the State agency ever came to the conclusion that that person was no longer disabled.

DON COOK: I worked all my life. I used to work 2 jobs. I worked overtime. I was like a workaholic.

BERGANTINO: So it was a real adjustment here.

DON COOK: Right, to go from 90 mph to zero, that's where I went.

ROSE COOK (Don's wife): I knew what he was like before and now he can't do anything. Oh, I'm not saying he can't breathe, have a cup of coffee, you know, exist. Yes, he can exist, but not in the fashion and the style we used to.

BERGANTINO: Do you think there is anything wrong with your program? Yes or no?

LORRAINE CRONIN (Disability Service Director): In terms of my program here? No, I don't.

BERGANTINO: Nothing at all?

CRONIN: No.

BERGANTINO: Tomorrow some answers from those in charge of the State's Disability Service about why so many disabled people in Massachusetts are being stripped of their only income. I'm Joe Bergantino for the Channel 4 I-Team.

Later in this newscast the Management of WBZ-TV will be calling for an immediate State investigation of the problems uncovered by our "I-Team."

WBZ "I-Team" Report, Part II   August 26, 1982

ANCHOR LEAD-IN: Tonight, more on the I-Team's continuing investigation of those drastic cuts in the Federal Disability rolls. I-Team reporter Joe Bergantino has learned that in some cases brief and superficial medical examinations are being used as a key element in deciding whether someone's disabled.

JOE BERGANTINO: From the candidate Ronald Reagan the promise in 1980 was a stern and popular one; to kick the cheaters off the welfare rolls, the food stamp lines and the disability rolls. Who could disagree?

But for some, that promise is now turning into a nightmare. In neighborhoods all across Massachusetts, hundreds of truly disabled are getting word they are being cut off the Social Security Disability rolls. It happened here in Revere, to a 48-year-old man with a wife and two children. A proud and self-reliant carpenter, till he was seriously injured on the job. A few months after he got word, he went down into his basement with a 45 revolver and shot himself in the head. His wife has told us he didn't want to go on living knowing he was unable to contribute anything to his family's income.

Judy Fittery of Tewksbury has thought about suicide. The government has stopped her benefits despite her ever worsening back injury. An injury doctors say prevents her from holding a job.

JUDY FITTERY (Disability Claimant): My spine feels like there's a hot rod up through my spinal column and burning constantly. I have pain radiating out from the middle of my back, outwards on both sides, both left and right from my waist down.

BERGANTINO: How will you survive without this money?

FITTERY: Emotionally with a lot of help from my friends and my family. Financially, I don't know.

BERGANTINO: Judy Fittery has no income to support herself or her 17-year-old daughter Cheryl. Her pain is so intense she is forced to spend most of her day on the floor of her parents livingroom. So why would the government cut her and others like her off the disability roll? The I-Team has found that much of the problem lies here, in the State agency that decides whether or not someone is disabled. Our month long investigation has found the State's Disability Determination Service has been using some highly questionable procedures in making its decisions.

One questionable procedure, the State's reliance on medical reports from consulting physicians. Those doctors are considered the chief objective source of information on whether a claimant is disabled. This year the government will pay out $2.4 million dollars to consulting doctors.

LORRAINE CRONIN (Disability Service Director): I feel they do an excellent job.

BERGANTINO: Lorraine Cronin runs the State's Disability Determination Service.

CRONIN: The consultants will spend as much time as it takes any other doctor to spend with a patient. None of our consultants rush through an exam.

BERGANTINO: But after spending a day recently outside the office of two consulting physicians, the I-Team found somewhat of a different story. Some of the patients sent here for an objective examination were not at all satisfied. Dean Kent says he suffers from a serious back injury.

DEAN KENT (Disability Claimant): She didn't even look at my back at all. She didn't have me bend over. She didn't look at my vertebrae. There were no tests really, on my spine. The kind of things she did was have me walk up and down the room.

BERGANTINO: Rolland Joley has a long history of heart disease.

ROLLAND JOLEY (Claimant): I saw the doctor for 10 minutes and the EKG was done prior to that by the woman and the machine it was done on had no censors to attach to my chest.

BERGANTINO: Marie Young is another claimant with a heart condition. She visited the consulting physicians office last March and soon after got word her benefits were being stopped.

MARIE YOUNG (Claimant): My height was measured, my blood pressure taken, after that, I was taken into a room where I was told I would have an EKG.

BERGANTINO: How long did that take?

YOUNG: I would say no more than 10 minutes, probably.

CRONIN: None of our claimants are seen for 10 or 15 minutes.

BERGANTINO: That's not true. We've talked to people who say they have. We talked to 3 people yesterday outside one doctor's office who said the most they were seen for was 10 minutes.

CRONIN: Well then I would like to know who these people are and we will be happy to investigate.

BERGANTINO: But some of the people who work for Cronin say that she's been well aware of various complaints against consulting physicians, yet little is done to correct the problem.

LINDA STACEY (Disability Worker): Claimants call us and tell us they have seen them for 10 minutes and they've made a determination on if they are disabled or not. I mean there is no way that that could happen and you get 5 or 6 claimants that tell you the same thing; it obviously seems like a real pattern of it.

BERGANTINO: These workers are also aware of complaints against a doctor who helped decide that this man, Don Cook, is able to go back to work. Cook suffers from a serious spinal nerve injury.

ED KELLNER (Disability Worker): What this doctor will do is physically take your head and go like this and push you down and then will write down in a report that you have full range and motion of the neck.

BERGANTINO: Another serious concern among workers at the State's Disability Agency: excessive pressure they say to rush through a review of every disability case on the books. This internal memo we obtained says the workers are expected to decide on the disability of 400 claimants a week.

STACY: We have so much pressure being brought to bear on you because you have so many cases, you just don't have the time to get all the medical evidence there. There's alot of basic medical stuff that isn't being looked at.

JOHN TEMPLETON (Local 509 President): There's been a bureaucratic decision made that these people are to be pushed off in large numbers and for all the government cares, the bureaucratic system, they can go away or should go away and die.

MARK COVEN (Legal Services): These statements that we are making about people and their ability to work aren't true statements.

CRONIN: We have a quality assurance department . . .

BERGANTINO: Quality assurance aside for a second, I'm talking about people who are making decisions. They're saying without a doubt in their minds, that they know they are denying disabled people who deserve to be getting benefits.

CRONIN: They are following the rules the Administration has set up by Social Security.

BERGANTINO: Is there something wrong with the rules then?

CRONIN: No.

BERGANTINO: Do you think there is anything at all wrong with this program?

CRONIN: In terms of my program here, no I don't.

BERGANTINO: Nothing at all?

CRONIN: No.

BERGANTINO: Boston Legal Services Attorney, Mark Coven strongly disagrees. He authored a highly critical report on Cronin's agency two years ago.

COVEN: There is a consistent pattern of inadequate jobs being performed by the State Examiner. When these cases are appealed, that over 50 percent of them are reversed by Administrative law judges. That means that in at least half the cases that they are deciding they are wrong and that is shocking.

WOMAN AT SENATE HEARINGS: What kind of system is this?

BERGANTINO: Coven has been among the witnesses at these Senate hearings in Washington where an investigation is underway to find out why so many truly disabled are being cut off the rolls nationwide.

Here in Massachusetts, 1,352 people have lost their disability benefits so far and the State's Disability Service wants to review 14,000 cases over the next year.

For those who lose their benefits, like Al Locke, like Judy Fittery, and like Don Cook, it could take as long as a year before their appeal is heard. A year with little or no income.

FITTERY: At this point, I would like to ask President Reagan to give me a job, that I can do. I challenge him, to find a company that I can possibly work for.

COOK: I never dreamed that anything like that was ever going to happen to me, because nobody is excluded from bad injury, no one.

BERGANTINO: I'm Joe Bergantino for Channel 4 I-Team.

Our I-Team reports on the Disability program have stirred emotions on both sides of the issue. We've been plagued with phone calls praising our work. We've also heard from the boss of the woman who runs the State Disability Service. State Rehabilitation Commissioner, Elmer Bartells, acknowledges there are problems in the State Disability Service program but says they are caused by bad Federal regulations. If you are among the disabled who received word your benefits are being stopped, we have two numbers you can call for information: Massachusetts Organization for Disabled Workers (272–0100) and at the Ombudsman office of the State Rehabilitation Commission (727–2170).

APPENDIX C

Excerpt from "People Like Us"

Broadcast April 21, 1982 on CBS

BILL MOYERS: I'm Bill Moyers. By the late 1970s there was widespread sentiment in America that government spending was out of control. Many voters were fed up with inflation and taxes and appalled by stories of waste and fraud in government programs for the poor. Their feelings helped to elect Ronald Reagan President. He said he would balance the budget, cut taxes, and get the economy moving again.

His first budget cut nearly in half the growth in federal spending for the next two years. But neither the President nor the Congress would tackle popular spending programs which have strong constituencies. So the least popular programs have been cut the most. These are the programs on which the poorest Americans depend for help, the truly needy, whom the President had said would not be hurt.

PRESIDENT RONALD REAGAN: We will continue to fulfill the obligations that spring from our national conscience, those who through no fault of their own must—must depend on the rest of us. The poverty-stricken, the disabled, the elderly—all those with true need can rest assured that the social safety net of programs they depend on are exempt from any cuts.

MOYERS: It has not worked out quite that way. Larry Ham, a victim of cerebral palsy, has just been cut off the Social Security disability rolls.

LARRY HAM: Because of this, we could lose everything, you know, and I—I don't know what we would do. You know, we worked hard to put our kids in a good school, good neighborhood and everything. To go and lose it all? You know, if I was able, believe me, I would go back out there. I would—I would go back out there and go to work.

MOYERS: Francis Dorta is trying to support three children at a low paying job. She has just been cut from the welfare rolls.

FRANCIS DORTA: Since I was cut off from welfare, I couldn't pay for the rent. I'm supposed to go Wednesday to see the judge and they'll tell me if I'm evicted or not.

MOYERS: Cathy Dixon's child is leaving home today because the government has changed some of the rules covering her home health care.

CATHY DIXON: If they tell me, "Mrs. Dixon, we will furnish you nurses," I'd bring her home in a minute. Why can't I keep her at home? I'm just throwing her away.

MOYERS: Twice as many people than a year ago are coming to this church basement for a free meal. Hunger in America is back.

ST. BENEDICT'S VOLUNTEER: You go home and think about that. When you sleep, you think of all about how people are hungry like this. You can't sleep at night for thinking about the people. They need help.

MOYERS: These are people who have slipped through the safety net and are falling away. In the great outcry about spending, some helpless people are getting hurt. No one knows exactly how many. This broadcast concerns only a few. Except for matters of chance, they are people like us.

(Signature music; titles shows on screen: CBS REPORTS: "People Like Us" With Bill Moyers.)

ANNOUNCER: This portion of CBS REPORTS is sponsored by . . .

(Announcements)

(Church music, congregants singing)

MOYERS: This is an ordinary Sunday for Larry and Loretta Ham and their four children. They are attending mass at their parish in Brooke Park, Ohio. But this is not an ordinary time in the life of the Ham family. Larry Ham, a victim of cerebral palsy, has just been cut off the Social Security disability rolls.

HAM: We get a lot of help from the Church. Thanksgiving, they sent a turkey. They sent canned food. Christmas, they sent two gift certificates for food. They've helped us a lot over the holidays.

CONGREGATION (in unison): We believe in one God . . . Heaven and earth . . . We believe in one lord, Jesus Christ, the only Son of God . . .

MOYERS: The government estimates that as much as two billion dollars may go every year to people who are no longer disabled. So the Social Security Administration is trying to remove from the rolls everyone but the truly needy. Larry Ham has been judged not to be truly needy.

HAM: In October, I received a letter stating that I was to go see a doctor and submit forms, medical forms to them, on my disability.

MOYERS: Was there any notice that you were going to receive this examination? Did—did you have any advance warning?

HAM: No, I didn't.

MOYERS: Did a doctor examine you to see if your condition had improved before you received this letter, before you were cut off?

HAM: No, no.

MOYERS: No one contacted you from the Social Security Administration?

HAM: Nobody.

MOYERS: The letter you received told you that you were supposed to work at a—at a desk job, a sedentary job. How did that strike you?

HAM: I—I really didn't understand. I—I took the letter and—and I was really upset, because I didn't know what I could do.

MOYERS: So what did you do then?

HAM: I—I called a lawyer.

JAMES BROWN: The people coming in with terminations usually receive a notice telling them they have seven to ten days to get proof that they're still disabled. In this seven to ten days, it's virtually impossible to obtain a medical report and get it to the Administration. I have more clients coming in with no resources.

MOYERS: Attorney Jim Brown agreed to take Larry Ham's case.

BROWN: And people receiving Social Security disability are working people. They've spent most of their life contributing to their government and supporting their government. The only place that they thought they could turn was to the United States government. And now the United States government has turned against them. My opinion is that there has to be some proof that the person's condition has improved if they're to be taken off of disability. The government right now is taking people off with no proof that it's improved and sometimes with proof that their condition is deteriorating. But to take a person like Larry, who's unskilled, severely disabled and unable to turn to help, and to cut him off the way they did is unconscionable.

MOYERS: Larry Ham, who today spends part of his time volunteering at the school his children attend, dropped out of school in the ninth grade.

HAM: I went to a crippled school. The kids were so good to me. They used to carry me, and then I found, you know, I had to work to live, really. I needed things. I had to work to get 'em.

(To child, at school): What are you making?

MOYERS: Last year, the Reagan Administration proposed to limit qualifications for disability benefits to medical factors alone. Education, job skills and age would not be taken into consideration. The legislation did not pass Congress.

HAM (to child): Let's see your design. Got some more with the crayon?

MOYERS: But the letter Larry Ham got, told him he should be able to get a job in a "sedentary occupation."

HAM: I just kept reading the letter. I didn't understand what sedent—you know, what they meant.

MOYERS: About what sedentary occupation is?

HAM: Right. Right, right. What—what, you know—what kind of desk job can I do, you know?

MOYERS: Have you tried to get a desk job?

HAM: No, because I don't have the ability—I—you know, I know this. I have trouble with things, you know.

MOYERS: Did you know just how ill Larry was when you met and married him, Loretta?

MRS. LORETTA HAM: I knew of his condition, physical condition, you know. I was quite aware of—of what his condition was.

MOYERS: You knew that it was difficult for him to work?

MRS. HAM: Right, right. But we could work together. You know, we've done it for eleven years, you know. And we worked together. We worked hard, you know. Larry worked hard at what he could do. You know, and—and I did my job on—you know, on my end.

MOYERS: What were you doing Larry, when you married?

HAM: I was working for a bakery. I worked there for about five or six years.

MOYERS: Doing what?

HAM: Uh—I started off in what they call the crumb room, with bread crumbs and, you know, you bake; the bread gets cut up and it comes down and you brown it, bake it, make croutons and make bread crumbs.

MOYERS: And what happened?

HAM: Well, after a while, it just got so it was more work put on than I could handle. And I just told them I had another job, you know, and that was it. I—I just couldn't handle it anymore.

MOYERS: Did you have another job?

HAM: No.

MOYERS: So, seven years ago, Loretta Ham had to go to work. How did you feel about Loretta working? Did you want your wife working?

HAM: I never wanted Loretta to work, 'cause when we first got married, we talked—you know, we talked about different things and that, and I always said, "Honey, you know, you—you take care of the kids, and I'll take, you know, I'll take care of us," because my mother, she did—she worked very hard for us, to raise us. And then, she worked cleaning schools, you know, and she worked too hard, and I never wanted Loretta to do this.

MOYERS: What did you say to him about that?

MRS. HAM: Well, you know, what can you say? You know, Lar has pride, you know, and—and he did his manly job, you know. If it meant working two jobs, this is what he felt he had to do, you know, to support his family. I was the first to go out there and be more than willing to help him work, you know, to carry the load.

MOYERS: Are you working now?

MRS. HAM: No. Things are cutting back at Ford. So, I'm unemployed. You know, it's kind of like we're just stripped of everything, you know, because it was boom, boom, one, two and that was it.

ATTORNEY BROWN: In the last couple of months, I've spent more and more nights thinking about people. You can go to sleep at night and you think about the person who may not have food tomorrow, whose kids don't have shoes for school, and you do worry about them.

One of the problems is the people who are the so-called "cheats" are the ones that are still getting it. They're the ones who know how the system works. They're the ones that know what the doctor's report should say and they can find a doctor to say it. And they're the ones that aren't going to get subjected to what the people like Larry Ham get. The difficult part is to have somebody sit in your office and tell you how they're suffering and how they're starving, and have to tell them that, well, we'll get you a hearing in ten months and we'll probably win because you're entitled. But you're going to have to survive until then.

MRS. HAM: We'd like to apply for food stamps.

SOCIAL WORKER: Okay, do you have a card?

MRS. HAM: Yes, I do.

MOYERS: Larry Ham was removed from the disability rolls without the chance to plead his case. He will have to live with no benefits until he can get a hearing before an Administrative Law Judge. But there is such a backlog of appeals that Larry Ham still has not been given the date for a hearing, although he lost his benefits four months ago. In the meantime, the problem for the family is food.

ELIGIBILITY WORKER (Mrs. Smith): Now, with your unemployment benefits, you'd be getting $115 a month for the months February through April.

MRS. HAM: That's not very much.

MRS. SMITH: I know it's not, but it's just enough to get you by, not to make things comfort—comfortable.

MRS. HAM: Yes.

MRS. SMITH: You can come in and pick that up or we can mail it out to you. You'll get it in a few days. What would you like to do?

MRS. HAM: I—I think we should come pick it up. The fewer days we have to wait, the better. (Laughing)

MRS. SMITH: Okay, fine.

MRS. HAM: But, like, this month, okay, I have not yet to receive an unemployment check, and these utilities are—you know, they desperately need to be paid. You know, what would I do, like, if somebody comes to the door to cut the utilities off? You know, do I tell them this form is in the mail? You know, it's in Columbus? Are we eligible to go down to welfare, you know, for assistance there? You know, you go down there and you wait a day and—and then you come back three days later, and in the meantime these people are knocking at your door. You know? And—and you've got four small kids, you know, and you're saying: "My papers are waiting—they're at welfare. They're waiting." These people don't want to hear this. You know, this is something we're faced with, and where do you go? This one says, "You just made enough money to qualify for food stamps,'' and welfare says, ''You're making way too much to qualify for welfare.'' You know, so what do you do in the middle?

MRS. SMITH: I don't—I don't have all the answers. The best thing I can do is to be honest with you. Did you have food in the house for the weekend?

MRS. HAM: We were basically running out, between my mother and my sister-in-law. That's how we've had food for the past four weeks.

MRS. SMITH: If you don't have food in the house for the weekend, I'm going to have to call to find the nearest hunger center—that's what we call them—near you.

(Dialing telephone): What it is, is that this is, like, private works of charity, okay? And the various churches and that, they only want to give to their little community, you know, their—

VOICE OF WOMAN (on phone): Hello.

MRS. SMITH: Hi, this is Mrs. Smith from County Welfare. I have a client and I was given your number to call.

WOMAN (on phone): Well, what seems to be the problem?

MRS. SMITH: The problem is that they need food for the weekend and they won't be able to pick up a food stamp card until Monday.

WOMAN (on phone): Well, who is this?

MRS. SMITH: Their name is Loretta and Larry Ham and four children.

WOMAN (on phone): Four children. Gosh! What are their ages?

MRS. SMITH: They're like, eight through twelve.

WOMAN (on phone): Yeah. They need food through the weekend?

MRS. SMITH: Right.

WOMAN (on phone): Well, I would say that it probably—I wonder if they have anything at all for supper tonight? The lady that called last week had a baby eight months old. I could hear it crying, and I said: ''What did you give him for supper?'' And she said her neighbor gave him a can of carrots and that satisfied him. But she didn't have one solitary thing in the house.

MRS. SMITH: Right. So, you will call them this evening and then someone will bring some food over? Thank you very much.

MOYERS: Is there a chance that—that you could lose this house?

HAM: There is a chance, but we're going to do everything we can to keep it. I mean anything possible we're going to do because we can't lose it. We can't start over again we got to do everything we can to try to get help somehow, make somebody understand that, you know, this is wrong.

MOYERS: You're not going to—you're not going to lose your home?

HAM: No. We're not going to lose our home. No matter what we have to do, we'll do it.

MOYERS: How is this affecting your children? What kind of holiday season did they have?

HAM: I'm very proud, very proud for the children. They, like, they went out caroling for Christmas. They had about seven dollars apiece and they took it and they bought each other gifts.

MOYERS: Hmm!

HAM: The boys went up to the corner and they carried groceries at the store and took the money and bought each other Christmas presents.

MOYERS: Are you angry at the government?

MRS. HAM: Angry at the government? You're supposed to put trust in the government. The President of the United States is—you know, if you can't trust, you know, the top man, so you have to kind of have confidence in what he's doing, that this is right, he's doing it for a reason, and this—this is a hard way—it—it definitely is a hard way to go.

(Church singing)

Sometimes things happen and you think, "Oh, gosh! Why did that happen to me, you know?" But that doesn't make you lose faith, you know, in God. So, the same things with the President; you kind of can't just lose trust in him. This is the man that runs our nation. This is the man that has, you know, got the whole nation in his hands.

CHURCH CONGREGANTS (singing): And lead us not into temptation, but deliver us . . .

MOYERS: In February, Loretta Ham went back to work for the Ford Motor Company.

CONGREGANTS (singing): Deliver us from all that is evil here on earth. . . .

MOYERS: It is true that in trying to make the American experience work federal programs which help the poor are riddled with waste and fraud. So are programs that help the middle class. So are subsidies to corporations. So are the billions being spent on the military-industrial complex. But the President and the Congress have chosen not to offend the rich, the powerful and the organized. It is easier to take on the weak. Social programs were cut almost $30 billion this year. The new budget proposes more cuts of 26 billion dollars. The burden falls most heavily on the poor, and some of the truly needy are truly hurting. They have been asked to sacrifice because the economy is in trouble and because some people are cheating the system. But for all the fraud and waste, for all their ineffi-ciencies, these programs are a life-support system for the poor. For many, we are pulling the plug.

I'm Bill Moyers, for CBS REPORTS.

APPENDIX D

Excerpts of Administration Critique of *"People Like Us"*
And CBS Response

From transcript of April 22, 1982 briefing by Dr. Robert Rubin, HHS Assistant Secretary for Planning and Evaluation.

DR. RUBIN: Last night, CBS broadcast a television documentary narrated by Bill Moyers entitled, "People Like Us." As you all know, the show depicted three individual cases involving our department's programs. Using these cases, the show implied that people such as those shown had fallen through the safety net President Reagan had promised to preserve for Americans who genuinely need help. We have been looking into the facts of these three cases since the broadcast. We do not believe they support the thesis that the safety net has been shredded by the Reagan Administration. I will get to the facts of the three cases in a moment.

First, let me point out a few broader facts that the documentary ignored. First, safety net spending under President Reagan is not going down, but it is going up, both in actual dollars and as a percentage of our federal budget. Spending on safety net programs was 37 percent of the total budget in 1981 and will climb to 39 percent in 1984. In our department alone, a proposed Fiscal 1983 budget contains an increase of some 20 billion dollars, or 8 percent; $253.9 billion to over $274 billion dollars. We are spending money at the rate of three quarters of a billion dollars a day. The proposed 1983 budget is, contrary to what you may have heard, higher than the defense department budget by some $56 billion. In the area of safety net programs the Federal Government is providing $5.5 billion for AFDC, $68 billion for Medicare and Medicaid and $55 billion in cash and in kind benefits for eight means tested federal programs.

I list these facts to put this matter into perspective. As evidenced, we are committed to preserving the social safety net. Our point is that by suggesting that Reagan Administration policies and actions have pulled the plug on disadvantaged Americans, misleading pressures were put on the American people by that broadcast. We hope to correct it by this conference.

To get to the specific cases, the first case is of the Social Security Disability program, and implies that the program was designed to deny aid to the truly needy. This is not true. Congress wrote the law to contend with economic need. It looks only at the severity of disability. The issue is, can a person perform any gainful work? If so, we have no choice but to find that person ineligible for disability benefits.

There is the feeling that the Reagan Administration is solely responsible for the current crackdown on the current ineligible disability insurance recipients. They mention the Congress only in an offhand way. In reality, Congress initiated the crackdown in 1980 ordering us to begin reviewing each ongoing case every three years, beginning in January 1982. [We] move[d] the starting date up nine months, [in] direct response to March, 1981 General Accounting Office recommendations that we redirect the existing resources in a crash effort to reduce the estimated 20 percent ineligibility rate that is costing the trust fund in excess of two billion dollars a year.

It is interesting to note that in the first 94,000 cases found ineligible during the first half of FY 82, only about 46,000 or half, chose to appeal the decision. This gives a general indication that the program is indeed targeting on ineligible cases.

In addition, it is alleged Mr. Ham had no recourse but to appeal to an administrative law judge or have to wait as long as four months for a hearing. This is incorrect. Every recipient has immediate appeal rights to reconsideration of his case, including any new evidence as to his medical disability. This would be appealed to the State Disability Determination Agency that initially found him ineligible. Recipients have 60 days to file and decisions are usually rendered well within the sixty day period.

In this particular case, Ohio could find no records that Mr. Ham chose to file for such reconsideration until April 5, some 112 days after the original decision. It is concluded that this family had fallen through the safety net. We disagree. Mr. Ham had no fewer than four field levels open to him; the State Agency, the SSA Administrative Law Judge, the SSA Appeals Council and finally, the federal courts.

The broadcast also failed to note that Ohio is one of 22 states that provide welfare benefits for intact families such as were described in the broadcast. In this case, the federal government reimburses the State at least 50 percent of their costs. If the Hams were eligible by lack of income there is no reason why they would not receive such help from this most basic of safety net programs.

Therefore, in conclusion, it is clear that no Reagan administration policy changes caused Mr. Ham's disability review or his ineligibility. . . .

Excerpt of April 23, 1982 Statement by CBS News

CBS News believes that the reporting on our CBS Reports documentary, "People Like Us," was accurate. The statements of spokesmen for the Reagan Administration yesterday, criticizing the accuracy of our broadcast, are incorrect.

Health and Human Services Assistant Secretary Robert Rubin stated in his briefing yesterday that Larry Ham, a cerebral palsy victim notified of his possible removal from Social Security Disability payments last November without prior medical exam, had not appealed that decision until early April. This, Mr. Rubin contended, showed that our documentary was in error, and that the fault lay not with the Social Security system, but with Mr. Ham.

In fact, beginning on November 9, Mr. Ham and his attorney, Jim Brown, tried repeatedly to apply for reconsideration of Mr. Ham's removal from Social Security Disability payments, through a series of phone calls and letters from Mr. Brown. These included calls on November 9, December 23, January 14 and January 15, and a letter on November 24 to the Bureau of Disability Determination.

Contrary to Social Security regulations, Mr. Brown was not sent a copy of the letter to Mr. Ham notifying him that benefits had been terminated. Mr. Ham assumed that his attorney had received such a letter, and therefore did not notify his attorney about the letter.

Nevertheless, in mid-January, Mr. Brown attempted to ascertain his client's status from the local Social Security office, and was told that they had no record of Larry Ham. Not until March 31 did the local Social Security office notify Mr. Brown that the mislaid records had been located. Mr. Brown promptly filed an appeal.

Mr. Brown has informed CBS News that the time period from the date on which a Social Security Disability beneficiary receives his last check to the date of reinstatement, should a successful appeal be waged, is now approximately one year in Northeast Ohio. In 1980, Mr. Brown notes, that time period was approximately two months. The acceleration of review of Social Security Disability recipients begun in March of 1981 has not been accompanied by staff increases necessary to process these cases.

Our documentary did not condemn the Administration's desire to remove cheats from the Social Security rolls; we did note, however, that innocent people were suffering as a result. Our review of the facts indicates that Mr. Ham's case illustrates this point well. . . .

We have contacted each of the individuals whom we profiled in "People Like Us." Each has indicated that our profile of his or her situation and case history was entirely accurate. CBS News continues to believe that the facts in each of the cases presented in "People Like Us" are accurate, and were portrayed correctly. We stand by our broadcast.

NOTES

1. "President Reagan's Economic Proposal Text," in *1981 Congressional Quarterly Almanac,* Vol. XXXVII (Washington, D.C.: Congressional Quarterly, Inc., 1982), 15–E.

2. Mordechai E. Lando, Alice V. Farley, and Mary A. Brown, "Recent Trends in Social Security Disability Insurance Program," *Social Security Bulletin,* August 1982, vol. 45, no. 8, p. 13.

3. Senate Special Committee on Aging, *Social Security Disability: Past, Present and Future,* Committee Print, 97th Cong., 2nd sess., March 1982, pp. 18–19.

4. Transcript of CBS Evening News, December 6, 1982, p. 12.

5. *Ibid.*

6. See the exchange in Senate Budget Committee, *First Concurrent Resolution on the Budget—Fiscal Year 1983,* Vol. III, hearings, 97th Cong., 2nd sess., 1982, pp. 180–181.

7. House Committee on Ways and Means (hereafter HWMC), Subcommittee on Social Security, *Continuing Disability Investigation Program,* Serial 97–90, hearing, 97th Cong., 2nd sess., Dec. 8, 1982, pp. 30, 31.

8. *Ibid.*

9. Quoted in Sandra Boodman, "Man Reagan Singled Out as a Cheat Denies Charge," *Washington Post,* March 2, 1982, p. 1.

10. *Ibid.*

11. Allan Cromley, "Television News Angers Reagan," *Daily Oklahoman,* March 17, 1982, p. 1.

12. Information that Simmons had alerted the White House about the *Reston Times* piece appeared in Sandra G. Boodman, "Man Reagan Singled Out as a Cheat Denies Charge," *Washington Post,* March 21, 1982, p. 2. The *Reston Times* article, "Comeback Becomes Battle for Survival for Reston Man," was written by Laura Dalton and appeared November 5, 1981 on p. 1.

13. Transcript of "This Week with David Brinkley," March 7, 1982.

14. Allan Cromley, "Television News Angers Reagan," *Daily Oklahoman,* March 17, 1982, p. 1, and Helen Thomas, "TV Executive Says Reagan Wrong About Crippled Man," UPI dispatch, March 17, 1982.

15. Transcript of CBS Evening News, March 17, 1982.

16. Transcript of NBC Nightly News, March 17, 1982, p. 4.

17. See Sandra G. Boodman, "Man Reagan Singled Out as a Cheat Denies Charge," *Washington Post,* March 21, 1982, p. 2.

18. Text of press briefing by David Gergen, White House Office of the Press Secretary, March 18, 1982., p. 21.

19. *Ibid.,* p. 19.

20. Transcript of CBS Evening News, March 18, 1982, p. 1.

21. *Ibid.,* p. 2.

22. Helen Thomas, "Anecdotes: He's Got a Million of 'Em," UPI dispatch, March 21, 1982.

23. "Reagan's Polarized America," *Newsweek,* April 5, 1982, pp. 17, 19.

24. "TV:," *New York Times,* April 21, 1982.

25. Tom Shales, "Through the Safety Net," *Washington Post,* April 21, 1982.

26. Statement issued by CBS News, April 21, 1982.

27. Tom Shales, "Through the Safety Net," *Washington Post,* April 21, 1982.

28. "CBS, Reagan, and the Poor," *Newsweek,* May 3, 1982, p. 22.

29. Lou Cannon, "Reagan & Co.," *Washington Post,* May 10, 1982.

30. Lars-Erik Nelson, "Politically, There's No Antidote for an Anecdote," *New York Daily News,* April 23, 1982.

31. Text of press briefing by David Gergen, White House, Office of the Press Secretary, April 22, 1982, p. 3.

32. *Ibid.,* p. 13.

33. Don Irwin, "CBS Rejects White House Request to Rebut Broadcast," *Los Angeles Times,* April 23, 1982.

34. Steven R. Weisman, "White House Assails CBS News, But a Bid for Reply Is Rejected," *New York Times,* April 23, 1982.

35. Tony Schwartz, "Protest on CBS Show: 'Fairness' Dispute Renews," *New York Times,* April 23, 1982.

36. "CBS, Reagan, and the Poor," *Newsweek,* May 3, 1982, p. 22.

37. See, for example, "CBS Backs Documentary's Accuracy," *Baltimore Sun,* April 24, 1982 and Herbert Denton, "CBS Rebuts Criticism From the White House on Program About Poor," *Washington Post,* April 24, 1982.

38. "The White House vs. CBS," *Time,* May 3, 1982, p. 24.

39. "CBS, Reagan, and the Poor," *Newsweek,* May 3, 1982, p. 22.

40. Transcript of CBS Evening News, May 2, 1982, p. 10.

41. HWMC, Subcommittee on Social Security Disability. *Disability Amendments of 1982,* Serial 97-54, 97th Cong., 2nd sess., March 16, 1982, p. 6.

42. Statement on Social Security Disability by HHS Secretary Schweiker and SSA Commissioner Svahn, *HHS News,* April 29, 1982, p. 1.

43. *Congressional Record,* July 13, 1982, p. H4043.

44. Transcript of Press Conference by Margaret Heckler, HHS, June 7, 1983, p. 20.

45. Senate Special Committee on Aging, *Social*

Security Reviews of the Mentally Disabled, S. Hrg. 98–170, hearings, 98th Cong., 1st sess., April 7, 1983, p. 8.

46. This recount is based largely on William A. Lowther, "A Medal for Roy Benavidez," *Reader's Digest,* April 1983, pp. 121–125.

47. *Ibid.,* p. 124.

48. Transcript of "Real People," November 9, 1983.

49. Spencer Rich, "Vietnam-Era Hero Falls Victim to Cuts in Social Security," *Washington Post,* May 27, 1983, p. 1.

50. Andrew M. Williams, "Hero Angered by Strake," *Port Lavaca Wave* (Tx.), June 3, 1983.

51. See "Benavidez Complaint Criticized," *Victoria Advocate* (Tx.), June 7, 1983.

52. House Select Committee on Aging, *Social Security Disability Reviews: A Federally Created State Problem,* Comm. Pub. 98–395, hearing, 98th Cong., 1st sess., June 20, 1983., p. 55.

53. Spencer Rich, "Vietnam-Era Hero Falls Victim to Cuts in Social Security," *Washington Post,* May 27, 83, p. 1.

54. D'Vera Cohn, "White House: We're Sympathetic," UPI dispatch, May 27, 1983.

55. *Ibid.*

56. *Ibid.*

57. House Select Committee on Aging, *Social Security Disability Reviews: A Federally Created State Problem,* Comm. Pub. 98–395, hearing, 98th Cong., 1st sess., June 20, 1983, p. 41.

58. Paul Simmons, "Plight of the Disabled," *Los Angeles Times,* June 22, 1983, editorial page.

59. Richard Reeves, "You Can Keep Your Blessed Handouts, Mr. President," *Detroit Free Press,* June 6, 1983.

60. Heckler's comment is a composite taken from the transcript of her June 7, 1983 HHS press conference, p. 23, and a transcript of the CBS Morning News, June 8, 1982, p. 9.

61. See Dwight Cunningham, "Social Security To Effect a 'More Humane' Image," *Washington Times,* June 2, 1983, and Don Kirkman, "Hero's Ordeal over Disability Benefits Brings Changes," *Pittsburgh Press,* June 6, 1983.

62. Simmons told Congressman Pickle at a June 30, 1983 hearing that "our initiatives would not have been announced on [June 7, 1983] had they not leaked out of the Department and made it to the front page of the newspaper. So, we had to announce them." See HWMC, Subcommittee on Social Security, *Social Security Disability Insurance,* Serial 98–25, hearing, 98th Cong., 1st sess., June 30, 1983, p. 41.

63. Robert Pear, "U.S. Plans to Ease Disability Criteria in Social Security," *New York Times,* June 7, 1983, p. 1.

64. C. Fraser Smith, "What Drives Public Policy?" *Baltimore Sun,* June 12, 1983.

65. HWMC, Subcommittee on Social Security, *Social Security Disability Insurance,* Serial 98–25, hearing, 98th Cong., 1st sess., June 30, 1983, p. 41.

66. D'Vera Cohn, "Vietnam Medal of Honor Winner Regains Disability Pay," *Philadelphia Inquirer,* July 13, 1983.

67. Jack Curry, "Show on Disability Benefits Needs More Balanced View," *USA Today,* June 20, 1983, p. 5D.

68. Spencer Rich, "Plight of the Disabled," *Washington Post,* June 20, 1983.

69. Quoted on p. 1 of SSA's "Litigation Management Project Statement," forwarded by Deputy SSA Commissioner Louis Enoff to all SSA Executive Staff on August 27, 1984.

70. Senate Finance Committee, *Social Security Disability Insurance Program,* S. Hrg. 98–674, hearing, 98th Cong., 2nd sess., January 25, 1984, p. 111.

71. See Patrick Owens, "Social Security Plans 18-Month Halt to Disability Aid Cutoffs," *Newsday,* March 24, 1984; Robert Pear, "Reagan Reported Prepared to Stop Cuts in Disability," *New York Times,* March 24, 1984; and Spencer Rich, "HHS Plans Delay in Disability-Aid Cutoffs," *Washington Post,* March 24, 1984.

72. HHS News release, April 13, 1984, p. 2.

73. "Transcript of Louisville Debate Between Reagan and Mondale," *New York Times,* October 9, 1984, pp. 28, 29.

INDEX